TRANSFORMATION AND CONTINUITY IN REVOLUTIONARY ETHIOPIA

AFRICAN STUDIES SERIES   61

GENERAL EDITOR
J. M. Lonsdale, *Lecturer in History and Fellow of Trinity College, Cambridge*

ADVISORY EDITORS
J. D. Y. Peel, *Charles Booth Professor of Sociology, University of Liverpool*
John Sender, *Faculty of Economics and Fellow of Wolfson College, Cambridge*

PUBLISHED IN COLLABORATION WITH
THE AFRICAN STUDIES CENTRE, CAMBRIDGE

OTHER BOOKS IN THE SERIES

 6 *Labour in the South African Gold Mines, 1911–1969*   Francis Wilson
11 *Islam and Tribal Art in West Africa*   René A. Bravmann
14 *Culture, Tradition and Society in the West African Novel*   Emmanuel Obiechina
18 *Muslim Brotherhoods in Nineteenth-century Africa*   B. G. Martin
23 *West African States: Failure and Promise: A Study in Comparative Politics*
   edited by John Dunn
25 *A Modern History of Tanganyika*   John Iliffe
26 *A History of African Christianity 1950–1975*   Adrian Hastings
28 *The Hidden Hippopotamus: Reappraisal in African History: The Early Colonial Experience
   in Western Zambia*   Gwyn Prins
29 *Families Divided: The Impact of Migrant Labour in Lesotho*   Colin Murray
30 *Slavery, Colonialism and Economic Growth in Dahomey, 1740–1960*   Patrick Manning
31 *Kings, Commoners and Concessionaires: The Evolution and Dissolution of the Nineteenth-
   Century Swazi State*   Philip Bonner
32 *Oral Poetry and Somali Nationalism: The Case of Sayyid Mohammad 'Abdille Hasan*
   Said S. Samatar
33 *The Political Economy of Pondoland 1860–1930: Production, Labour, Migrancy and Chiefs
   in Rural South Africa*   William Beinart
34 *Volkskapitalisme: Class, Capital and Ideology in the Development of Afrikaner Nationalism
   1934–1948*   Dan O'Meara
35 *The Settler Economies: Studies in the Economic History of Kenya and Rhodesia 1900–
   1963*   Paul Mosley
36 *Transformations in Slavery: A History of Slavery in Africa*   Paul E. Lovejoy
37 *Amilcar Cabral: Revolutionary Leadership and People's War*   Patrick Chabal
38 *Essays on the Political Economy of Rural Africa*   Robert H. Bates
39 *Ijeshas and Nigerians: The Incorporation of a Yoruba Kingdom, 1890s–1970s*   J. D. Y. Peel
40 *Black People and the South African War 1899–1902*   Peter Warwick
41 *A History of Niger 1850–1960*   Finn Fuglestad
42 *Industrialisation and Trade Union Organisation in South Africa 1924–55*   Jon Lewis
43 *The Rising of the Red Shawls: A Revolt in Madagascar 1895–1899*   Stephen Ellis
44 *Slavery in Dutch South Africa*   Nigel Worden
45 *Law, Custom and Social Order: The Colonial Experience in Malawi and Zambia*
   Martin Chanock
46 *Salt of the Desert Sun: A History of Salt Production and Trade in the Central Sudan*
   Paul E. Lovejoy
47 *Marrying Well: Marriage, Status and Social Change among the Educated Elite in Colonial
   Lagos*   Kristin Mann
48 *Language and Colonial Power: The Appropriation of Swahili in the Former Belgian Congo,
   1880–1938*   Johannes Fabian
49 *The Shell Money of the Slave Trade*   Jan Hogendorn and Marion Johnson
50 *Political Domination in Africa: Reflections on the Limits of Power*   edited by Patrick Chabal
51 *The Southern Marches of Imperial Ethiopia: Essays in History and Social Anthropology*
   edited by Donald Donham and Wendy James
52 *Islam and Urban Labor in Northern Nigeria: The Making of a Muslim Working Class*
   Paul M. Lubeck
53 *Horn and Crescent: Cultural Change and Traditional Islam on the East African Coast,
   500–1900*   Randall L. Pouwels
54 *Capital and Labour on the Kimberley Diamond Fields 1871–1890*   Robert Vicat Turrell
55 *National and Class Conflict in the Horn of Africa*   John Markakis
56 *Democracy and Prebendal Politics in Nigeria: The Rise and Fall of the Second Republic*
   Richard A. Joseph
57 *Entrepreneurs and Parasites: The Struggle for Indigenous Capitalism in Zaire*
   Janet MacGaffey
58 *The African Poor: A History*   John Iliffe
59 *Palm Oil and Protest: An Economic History of the Ngwa Region, South-eastern Nigeria
   1800–1980*   Susan M. Martin
60 *French Policy towards Islam in West Africa, 1860–1960*   Christopher Harrison

TRANSFORMATION AND CONTINUITY IN REVOLUTIONARY ETHIOPIA

CHRISTOPHER CLAPHAM

Senior Lecturer in Politics, University of Lancaster

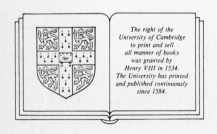

The right of the
University of Cambridge
to print and sell
all manner of books
was granted by
Henry VIII in 1534.
The University has printed
and published continuously
since 1584.

CAMBRIDGE UNIVERSITY PRESS

CAMBRIDGE

NEW YORK   NEW ROCHELLE   MELBOURNE   SYDNEY

Published by the Press Syndicate of the University of Cambridge
The Pitt Building, Trumpington Street, Cambridge CB2 1RP
32 East 57th Street, New York, NY 10022, USA
10 Stamford Road, Oakleigh, Melbourne 3166, Australia

© Cambridge University Press 1988

First published 1988

Printed in Great Britain at Redwood Burn Ltd, Trowbridge, Wiltshire

British Library cataloguing in publication data

Clapham, Christopher
Transformation and continuity in
revolutionary Ethiopia. – (African
studies series; 61).
1. Ethiopia. Political events, 1974–1987
I. Title II. Series
963°.062

Library of Congress cataloguing in publication data

Clapham, Christopher S.
Transformation and continuity in revolutionary Ethiopia /
     p.   cm. – (African studies series: 61)
Bibliography.
Includes index.
ISBN 0 521 33441 1
1. Ethiopia – Politics and government – 1974– I. Title.
II. Series.
JQ3752.C55 1988
963.07 – dc 19   88–2622

ISBN 0 521 33441 1

WD

In memory of
Tibebu Deribe
1961–1987

Contents

List of tables	*page*	x
Preface and acknowledgements		xi
List of acronyms		xiv
Glossary of Amharic words		xvi
Map of administrative regions of Ethiopia		xviii

1 Revolutions — 1
The conditions for revolution — 2
The construction of a revolutionary political order — 6
The analysis of revolution — 12

2 Monarchical modernisation and the origins of revolution — 19
The bases of state and nation — 20
The rise of a modernising autocracy — 26
The origins of revolution — 32
The debacle — 38

3 The mobilisation phase, 1974–1978 — 41
The revolutionary option, February–November 1974 — 41
The great reforms, December 1974–July 1975 — 45
The control of the towns, 1975–1978 — 51
The conflict for the periphery, 1975–1978 — 57

4 The formation of the party, 1978–1987 — 65
The origins of party formation — 65
COPWE — 70
The Workers' Party of Ethiopia — 77
The People's Democratic Republic of Ethiopia — 92

Contents

5   **The Ethiopian state: structures of extraction and control**   101
The old regime   101
The impact of revolution   105
The structures of control   108
The structure of production   114
The external economy   119
Surplus extraction and government spending   123
The structures of distribution   125

6   **The control of the towns**   129
The kebelle   130
The mass organisations   136
Housing and the control of residence   141
Socialist distribution   145
Industry, employment and the urban economy   148
Education and literacy   150
The reaction from control   153

7   **Rural transformation and the crisis of agricultural production**   157
The peasants' associations   157
Land reform: its implementation and effects   161
Agricultural marketing   168
Agricultural producers' cooperatives   171
Villagisation   174
The state farms   179
The export sector: coffee, sesame and chat   182
The origins of famine   186
The domestic politics of famine relief   189

8   **The national question**   195
Ethnicity and revolution   195
Representation and control in regional administration   201
Regional opposition: the north   204
Regional opposition: the south   214

9   **The external politics of revolution**   220
The structure of foreign relations   220
Revolution and the reversal of alliances   223
The foreign policy of proletarian internationalism   228
The Western response   236

10   **Conclusion**   241

Contents

Notes	244
Bibliography	262
Index	276

Tables

1   Composition of the Central Committee of the WPE   *page* 85
2   WPE militants attending the Founding Congress   88

Preface and acknowledgements

This book was conceived during a visit to Addis Ababa in November and December 1984, to participate in the Eighth International Conference of Ethiopian Studies. I was then struck both by the enormous changes which had taken place in Ethiopia since the revolution, and by the framework of continuity within which many of these changes seemed to me to have occurred. The main fieldwork was carried out during a seven-month stay in Ethiopia, from September 1985 to April 1986, when I served as Visiting Professor at Addis Ababa University. While I am most grateful to the University for allowing me this opportunity, and to the University of Lancaster for giving me paid leave to enable me to take it up, I must make it more than usually clear that neither university, nor any section or individual within it, bears the slightest responsibility for the views that I have expressed. Following completion of the initial draft early in 1987, I revisited Ethiopia for four weeks in May 1987 to check and update it, and completed the final text in September 1987 – a date which conveniently coincided with the formal declaration of the People's Democratic Republic of Ethiopia.

Anyone who has undertaken research in Ethiopia will be aware of its peculiar rewards and difficulties, and especially of the secrecy which surrounds even the most apparently innocuous information, the multiple and contradictory accounts of any political event, and the extraordinary persistence even of myths which can clearly be shown to be fictitious. To take just one example, it is often claimed that at the beginning of this century, some 40% of Ethiopia was forested, a percentage reduced in recent times to less than a tenth of that amount. This figure is confidently asserted even in such authoritative documents as the UNDP/World Bank energy assessment report,[1] while a map published by the Ethiopian government shows almost all land over 1,500 metres as having been forested in the recent past.[2] Since the northern highlands have been under plough agriculture for about a thousand years, this seems unlikely, and early nineteenth-century prints show the highland areas of present-day Tigray and Eritrea as carrying only occasional scattered trees – though certainly more than now remain.[3] There is, indeed, convincing biological evidence that most of the Ethiopian highlands have never been forested. They contain, for example, no fewer than twenty-one endemic species of montane non-forest birds, found nowhere else in the world, which can only have evolved over many millennia; Ethiopia is by contrast exceptionally poor in montane forest birds.[4] Deforestation may of course make an important contribution to erosion, environmental degradation, and agricultural decline in some parts of Ethiopia; but the very convenience of the deforestation argument has served to perpetuate myths which examination of the evidence shows to be unfounded.

Only the most foolhardy scholar would assert that his own work was free from similar misconceptions. The most I can claim is that I have examined the available (and often fragmentary) evidence as dispassionately as possible, and have tried to be both accurate and fair. This has inevitably meant using figures which may (especially under revolutionary conditions) be subject both to deliberate bias and to an understandable temptation to dream up a number where none exists. I can only say that I have done what I can, and that I apologise for any faults that remain. I should add that so far as I can judge, most Ethiopian official statistics on a wide range of topics seem to me to be generally honest and accurate.

When I first started to study Ethiopian politics, a quarter of a century ago, I could feel that I was venturing into almost untrodden territory. That is true no longer, and my most important academic debt is to those social scientists, a very high proportion of whom are Ethiopians, who have continued to work in revolutionary Ethiopia, often under very difficult conditions, and who have done by far the greater part of the research on which this volume rests. Individual sources are acknowledged in the notes and bibliography; but no work of this scope could possibly have been completed without the availability of a great deal of basic research, and at some points I am all too aware that I have done little more than take other people's findings, and apply them to my own concerns. I have cited sources wherever possible, even when these may not be readily accessible, but must emphasise that none of these authors bears any responsibility for the use which I have made of their work. I have also relied on information given me by a wide range of informants in Ethiopia, who must perforce remain anonymous, and am particularly grateful to those who have read all or part of this book in draft, and corrected some of my mistakes. I have not always accepted their advice, however, and responsibility for a final text which has often had to rely heavily on personal judgement remains mine alone.

I am grateful to the Nuffield Foundation of London, for meeting the costs of travel, subsistence and research materials, and hope that they will feel, at a time when pressure on research funding is intense, that the result repays their confidence. I wish to make it clear that this research was not funded by any government body (whether British, Ethiopian or other), or by any international organisation.

My greatest debt, finally, is to two families – one in Lancaster who allowed me to abandon them for eight months, and one in Addis Ababa who looked after me when I got there. It is such that any further comment would be inadequate.

Tibebu Deribe, to whose memory this book is dedicated, was a third-year student in statistics at Addis Ababa University, who died of rheumatoid arthritis in May 1987.

Lancaster, September 1987   CHRISTOPHER CLAPHAM

Acronyms

AEPA	All Ethiopia Peasants' Association
AETU	All Ethiopia Trade Union
AMC	Agricultural Marketing Corporation
ANLM	Afar National Liberation Movement
CELU	Confederation of Ethiopian Labour Unions
COPWE	Commission for Organising the Party of the Working People of Ethiopia
CPSC	Central Planning Supreme Council
CPSU	Communist Party of the Soviet Union
DPRK	Democratic and Popular Republic of Korea (North Korea)
EDDC	Ethiopian Domestic Distribution Corporation
EDU	Ethiopian Democratic Union
EH	The Ethiopian Herald
ELF	Eritrean Liberation Front
EPA	Ethiopia Peasants' Association (formerly AEPA)
EPDM	Ethiopia People's Democratic Movement
EPLF	Eritrean People's Liberation Front
EPRP	Ethiopian People's Revolutionary Party
ETU	Ethiopia Trade Union (formerly AETU)
GDR	German Democratic Republic
NG	Negarit Gazeta (Ethiopian government official gazette)
NRDC	National Revolutionary Development Campaign
OLF	Oromo Liberation Front
ONCCP	Office of the National Council for Central Planning
PADEP	Peasant Agricultural Development Extension Programme
PDRE	People's Democratic Republic of Ethiopia
PDRY	People's Democratic Republic of Yemen (Aden)
PMAC	Provisional Military Administrative Council
PMGSE	Provisional Military Government of Socialist Ethiopia
PNDR	Programme of the National Democratic Revolution
POMOA	Provisional Office of Mass Organizational Affairs
REWA	Revolutionary Ethiopia Women's Association

REYA	Revolutionary Ethiopia Youth Association
RRC	Relief and Rehabilitation Commission
SIDA	Swedish International Development Authority
TPLF	Tigray People's Liberation Front
UDA	Urban Dwellers' Association
WPE	Workers' Party of Ethiopia
WSLF	Western Somali Liberation Front

Glossary of Amharic words

Abyotawit Seded	*see* Seded
awraja	province; the second level of local administration
birr	Ethiopian monetary unit ($1 = 2.07 birr)
chat	a narcotic leaf, widely chewed in the Red Sea region
chika shum	village headman under the imperial regime
Derg	the military committee formed in June 1974
Echaat	Ethiopia Oppressed Masses Unity Struggle, 1975–78
Emaledih	Union of Ethiopian Marxist Leninist Organisations, 1977–79
Emalered	Ethiopian Marxist–Leninist Revolutionary Organisation, 1976–78
enset	false banana; a plant which provides the staple food of parts of southern Ethiopia
idir	a cooperative association in Ethiopian towns
Ityopya tikdem	'Ethiopia first', the revolutionary motto
kebelle	local urban dwellers' association
keftenya	higher urban dwellers' association
kifle hager	region; the highest level of local administration
malba	simplest form of agricultural producers' cooperative
Meison	All Ethiopia Socialist Movement, 1975–78
neftenya	northern settler in southern Ethiopia
rist	system of land inheritance in highland Ethiopia before 1975
Seded	Revolutionary Flame, 1975–79
shengo	parliament or soviet, 1987
teff	a food grain widely grown in highland Ethiopia
Wazleague	Labour League, 1975–79
weland	highest form of agricultural producers' cooperative
welba	intermediate form of agricultural producers' cooperative

woreda	district; the lowest level of local administration
zemecha	campaign; especially, the National Development Campaign, 1974–75

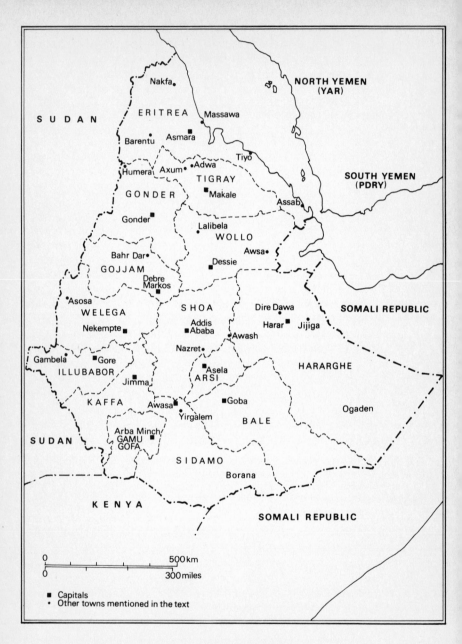

Administrative regions of Ethiopia, 1974–1987

xviii

1

Revolutions

This book seeks to explore the effects of the Ethiopian revolution on Ethiopia's people. It is thus, centrally, a book about revolution; and though one of its lessons is that revolutions and revolutionary regimes – like any other form of government – depend on the particular circumstances and societies in which they occur, some idea of what revolutions are, how they come about, and how they should be studied, must necessarily underlie it. That is what this chapter attempts to provide.[1]

A revolution marks a fundamental and irreversible change in the organisation of a society; the destruction, often rapid and violent, of a previous form of social and political organisation, together with the myths which sustained it and the ruling groups which it sustained, and their replacement by a new institutional order, sustained by new myths and sustaining new rulers. Such a change has taken place in Ethiopia: a change indeed in many ways comparable to those experienced during the 'classic' revolutions of France and Russia. Since this change is the subject of this book, it will be detailed at many points in the pages that follow, but it may be helpful to indicate, right at the start, some of the features that mark Ethiopia's experience as unquestionably revolutionary: the overthrow of an ancient and well-established monarchy; the execution, exile or imprisonment of virtually all those who held high office under it; a period of intense and violent conflict for control of the new regime; the nationalisation of all major means of production, urban and rural; the abolition of private land ownership, and the organisation of rural production into peasants' associations and cooperatives, and state farms; the transformation of urban government, through the creation of urban dwellers' associations, and the nationalisation of urban land and rented housing; the expansion of the armed forces, including national military service and a militia several hundred thousand strong; the creation of a new and government controlled system of agricultural marketing and of food distribution in towns; the establishment of a Marxist–Leninist political party and associated mass organisations, allied to intensive efforts at ideological reorientation; the creation of a new constitutional system on Marxist–Leninist lines; the resettlement of some 600,000 peasants

from the north and east of the country in the south and west; the organisation of several million scattered peasant homesteads into centrally located
villages, as a prelude to the collectivisation of agriculture; and a reversal of
diplomatic and military alliances from the USA to the USSR. In Africa,
rhetoric has often filled the broad gap between leaders' aspirations and their
very limited capacity to organise, control or change the societies which they
govern, and pretensions to revolution are often greeted in consequence with
well-deserved scepticism. This one is real. It thus takes its place, not only
with France and Russia, but with that small group of third-world states
which have likewise gone through an unquestioned revolutionary experience since 1945: China, North Korea, Cuba, Kampuchea, Vietnam. There
are others – Iran, Mozambique, Bolivia, Nicaragua – whose status is still
uncertain or debatable.

For such a revolution to be achieved, two basic conditions must be met.
First, a set of circumstances must be present which prompt the collapse of
the existing institutional order, and which amount in sum to a 'revolutionary
situation'. Secondly, measures must be implemented to construct a new
institutional order. The first condition has understandably attracted greater
attention from political scientists and activists in non-revolutionary states,
concerned with the question of whether a revolution is likely (or can be promoted) in their own societies; the second is correspondingly of greater
interest to the rulers, and analysts, of revolutionary states themselves. The
central part of this chapter will look at each in turn.

THE CONDITIONS FOR REVOLUTION

Revolutions are rare events. No state has experienced more than a single
revolution in the sense defined above, and most have never experienced one
at all. The conditions which promote them must therefore be exceptional.
At the same time, there are sufficient similarities between those major
revolutions which have taken place to encourage the belief that common
causal factors are involved, even though these must obviously be subject to
variations in local historical experience. In looking for such factors, this
study parts company entirely with the classic Marxian theory of revolution –
by far the dominant tradition in the field – which sees it as deriving from
inherent class conflict, and especially the conflict between an industrial
bourgeoisie and an exploited proletariat. Its reason for doing so is simply
that this theory does not work. Whether it is of any value in explaining those
few revolutions which have taken place in industrial states is arguable,
though I would discount it. When it comes to third-world revolutions, it is of
no value whatever.

Nor, more generally, does there appear to be any necessary connection
between revolution and any particular form of economic structure. Some
modern theorists have sought a link between revolution and the incorporation of third-world societies into a global structure of production and

exchange dominated by capitalist industrial metropoles.[2] There is no need to deny that such a structure exists, that it is often highly exploitative of third-world peoples, and that – should a revolution occur – the conditions of incorporation and the reactions of workers caught up in the global economy will strongly influence the form which it takes. The problem is that such incorporation does not seem to be of any significant value in explaining why or whether a revolution should occur in the first place. Cuba, for example, had been incorporated into the global economy under the intensely exploitative conditions of plantation slavery, and subsequent landlordism, for over four centuries before the revolution in 1959. This evidently does much to explain the nature of the Cuban revolution, notably its hostility to the United States, and the willingness of the revolutionary regime to aid fellow revolutionaries whose situation they view as similar to their own. The Nicaraguan experience is in many ways analogous. Yet many of the other plantation economies in the Caribbean have shown little sign of revolutionary upheaval, and even if one allows for the effects of American support for anti-revolutionary regimes, do not appear to be likely candidates for revolution. Equally, while Scott and others have identified some of the bases for revolution in South-East Asia in the exploitative conditions of the rice-exporting economy,[3] these economies are both very different from the Caribbean ones, and are matched by equivalents in non-revolutionary states. When one comes to states such as Ethiopia, one of the least intensively incorporated of African or indeed of third-world states, the role of the international economy is little more than incidental. Revolutionary change in Ethiopia has indeed been eased by the very paucity of the country's external economic links.

This rejection of class, economic structure and international economic connections as necessary causal factors in the explanation of revolution does not, of course, mean that they are to be dismissed as irrelevant. Classes, like other social groups, will be caught up in the revolutionary process, and relations between classes will inevitably be affected by the general restructuring of social and political relationships that revolution entails. Particularly important in this respect are the relationships between urban and rural classes, and within the rural economy. Many of the more important recent theorists of revolution have identified the critical role of rural society and its relations with the political centre.[4] The worldwide spread of markets, ideas and organisational techniques likewise provides an important part of the context within which all twentieth-century revolutions have taken place. The point is simply that these universalist categories provide no adequate criteria for distinguishing those states in which revolutions have occurred, from those in which they have not.

When one turns from the economic to the political sphere, however, the similarities between revolutionary states leap to the attention. Revolutions overwhelmingly take place in states where the existing regime has failed either to provide political opportunities for the urban intelligentsia, or to establish effective links with the countryside. It is political ineffectiveness, rather than economic exploitation, which leads to revolution. Skocpol is right to emphasise that revolution emerges from specifically political crises centred in the structures and situations of the old regime states,[5] and her findings for France, Russia and China are in this respect entirely supported by the Ethiopian case. The two classic types of political system whose inherent weaknesses are liable to prompt revolutionary upheaval are first, a decaying traditional monarchy, and secondly, a colonial regime which refuses to decolonise; but equivalent situations may occur under a land-owning oligarchy or some types of military regime. In each case, a revolutionary modernising elite is able to gain access to a source of rural support which both sustains it (when the revolution is achieved through guerrilla warfare) during the struggle to overthrow the old regime, and also helps to ensure, once the takeover has been achieved, that the new regime does not simply degenerate into a restricted urban coalition.

The astonishingly high proportion of successful revolutions which have taken place in traditional monarchical states is much too great to be dismissed as coincidence. The revolution does not always, as in Ethiopia or France, overthrow the monarchy itself. It may, as in Russia or China, overthrow a regime which has directly succeeded the monarchy, but has been unable to organise for itself an adequate political base. The basic reasons for the success of revolution nonetheless lie in the legacy of traditional monarchy: its weakness as a source of political mobilisation, but also its strength (when appropriately transformed) as a source of centralised national government. The process of modernisation normally involves the centralisation of power in a monarch, who heads an administrative apparatus which in many ways resembles the state structure established elsewhere by colonial regimes. One of the ways in which this apparatus resembles the colonial structure is in its failure to make provision for political representation, except through traditionalist mechanisms which find their equivalent in the colonial use of indirect rule. Even these mechanisms may be suspect; in Ethiopia, as in France during the Versailles period, the monarch sought to consolidate his power by reducing the autonomy of local notables who had previously provided some kind of connection between the central government and political authority in the countryside, and in so doing undercut the basis for his own position. But whereas the new educated nationalist group in colonial territories can usually achieve its goals by mobilising support against a colonial regime which is ultimately prepared to relinquish power and depart, the same outlet is not available in states which are already independent. While it is always possible for the urban elite simply to oust the monarch and take over the central government, the new regime will then inherit the political weakness of its predecessor – further enfeebled by the destruction of what remained of monarchical legitimacy – and will either have to mobilise a broader base of political support, or like the Kerensky regime in Russia or the Kuomintang in China, fall to someone else who does.

Unlike other third-world revolutions, those directed against traditional monarchies often do not require any recourse to rural guerilla warfare. The revolution may, as in Iran or Ethiopia, follow what Huntington terms the 'western' pattern (in contrast to the 'eastern' or Chinese model), where the revolutionaries first seize power at the centre, and only afterwards go out to organise the countryside.[6] This is simply because the regime is feeble enough, in terms of its inability to control its own cities, to be overthrown by a radical *coup d'état* or even by the urban mob. Where, as in China, the monarchy has already been replaced by a fairly effective urban government, the retreat to the countryside becomes the only possibility, and the mobilisation of the peasantry gains a critical importance.

This rural revolutionary strategy is commonly used against recalcitrant colonial regimes, as in Angola, Mozambique and North Vietnam, and against externally supported governments with a limited urban base, such as the Somoza dynasty in Nicaragua, the Batista dictatorship in Cuba, and the post-colonial regimes of Kampuchea and South Vietnam. In the distinctive circumstances of the Horn of Africa, it is important as the means by which alternative revolutionary elites, with regional bases especially in Eritrea and Tigray, have sought with considerable success to mobilise the countryside against the central government. Northern Ethiopia is indeed a battleground between rival revolutions based on opposed (but equally revolutionary) principles and techniques: a centralising and nationalist revolution originating in the towns, which has spread out to organise the countryside, and a decentralising and regionalist revolution organised in the countryside, seeking to surround and capture the towns. A further revolutionary technique, that of urban guerilla warfare, was also attempted in Ethiopia by urban elites opposed to the military regime. As in other areas of the third world, it was entirely unsuccessful.

Even where the revolutionary regime first seizes power in the capital, however, the extension of its organisation and support into the countryside is essential if it is not to become an essentially reformist government, dependent on established groups whose interests it dare not offend. Where, as in parts of Ethiopia, a high proportion of rural land is controlled by landlords, and especially where these are ethnically or culturally distinct from their peasants, land reform provides the essential means by which this extension of support can be achieved. To a large extent, though not entirely, the reaction of different rural regions of Ethiopia to the new regime in Addis Ababa can be related to the differential impact of land reform on the varying pre-revolutionary systems of land tenure. Where land reform succeeds, it can give the peasantry a vested interest in the revolution which no rival political programme can outbid. Where, on the other hand, it is seen as a threat to control by peasant proprietors over their own means of production, it can have the opposite effect. But land tenure, like other aspects of economic structure, influences the form which revolution takes, rather than whether it takes place at all. Both the exploited peasantry of southern

5

Ethiopia, and the 'free' peasantry of the north, have been mobilised into revolutionary movements – but in one case, usually in support of the government, in the other, often against it.

THE CONSTRUCTION OF A REVOLUTIONARY POLITICAL ORDER

The initial phases of a revolution are violent, spectacular, and destructive. If the revolution breaks out in the towns, it is likely to start with some act of mass popular insurrection – such as the storming of the Bastille, or the huge demonstrations against the Shah in Iran – which decisively undermines the authority of the old regime, and sets in train the sequence of events which lead to its collapse. This may well be followed by an equally dramatic, and in many cases still more violent, conflict for control among the heirs of the revolution itself. It is during this phase, indeed, that the terror is often at its worst; the overthrow of an old regime which everyone saw as discredited and ineffective may be achieved with very little difficulty, and without much need for bloodshed save in gratuitous acts of revenge. The conflict between rival leaders, organisations and ideologies, all of which see themselves as representing the future or the true revolutionary path, is one in which no quarter can be given, and which ends only once a Stalin or a Mengistu Haile-Mariam has established uncontested control. In the case of rural revolutions, leadership rivalries are not usually so salient, and much of the action takes place in the distant fastnesses of Yenan or the Sierra Maestra. But the 'heroic' phase of establishing the base areas, the often long civil war against the entrenched urban regime which follows, and the final triumphal entry of the guerrilla forces into Havana, Phnom Penh, Saigon or Managua exercise a fascination every bit as great as that of the heroic days on the streets of Paris or Petrograd.

Once the inevitable dictator has established control, or the forces of the old regime have decisively been ousted, the revolution seems to be over. In fact, it has scarcely begun. What makes a revolution is not the destruction of the old order, but the construction of the new one. This is unspectacular, even boring. Its violence, when it takes place (as it often does), is a matter of bullying helpless peasants rather than fighting the privileged and corrupt. But a revolution has no claim to the name unless the organisation of the new society is substantially different from that of the old; and such organisation can only be achieved by deliberate effort over a long period. Much of this process will inevitably be concerned with the management of the economy. In an age in which revolution is almost invariably associated with Marxism (quite regardless of the inadequacy of Marxist precepts in explaining its occurrence), the nationalisation of the principal means of production is normally one of the new regime's first actions; and the problem of how to manage the economy which it has taken over provides it with one of its first and most important lessons in government, and in the salutary differences between running a civil war or an urban insurrection on the one hand, and

6

running a bureaucratic machine on the other. But even more basic is the establishment of a new *political* order. The primacy of the political, which is as I have argued central to the understanding of why revolutions occur in the first place, is equally central to the process of post-revolutionary institutionalisation. It is organised political power, in the hands of the new rulers of the state, that has to be used in order to bring about a deliberate transformation of economy and society which could not take place on its own.

Far from leading to mass participation, equality or any of the other ideals propounded in the pre-revolutionary years, the most important outcome of revolution is thus the creation of a powerful state, which is then used by its leaders as an instrument for national integration and economic trans-formation. The destruction of the old class structure, and especially of those classes which control land and people in the countryside, is essential not in order to liberate classes which were previously exploited, but in order to enable the state to gain direct control over people and resources which were previously insulated from it by an intermediary layer of local notables who controlled them in their own interests. An initial upsurge of participation, fuelled by measures such as land reform, may be useful and perhaps essen-tial in transferring peasant allegiances from their previous local-level attach-ments to a new attachment to the central government; but to allow this to lead to the creation of an autonomous peasantry controlling their own land would defeat the very purpose of the revolution – a fact which accounts for the reaction against 'kulaks', and the characteristic emphasis of revolution-ary regimes on cooperatives, collectives or state farms, through which agricultural production can be brought under central control. In this way, the vast mass of the rural population can be organised for state purposes, not only as producers but also in other ways, and notably for military recruit-ment. Revolutionary leadership, in all the cases examined by Skocpol and likewise in Ethiopia, is drawn from educated marginal elites oriented to state employment.[7] So far from seeking to promote the interests of broad social and economic classes such as proletariat, peasantry or bourgeoisie, their objective is to establish a centralised state machinery, autonomous of any social class save that of the state employees who run it.

It is in the creation of this new political order that those revolutionary states which are heirs to long-established monarchies often demonstrate their superiority over those which derive from collapsed colonial regimes. A large part of this order, after all, is there already. A territory which has been under common rule for a considerable period will almost certainly have acquired some form of state organisation, however weakly articulated or ineffectively managed this may have been. A complex of popular habits and ideas relating to the exercise and acceptance of authority will already be in place, and can be adapted to the rhetoric and ideology of the new regime. The nationalism which most revolutionary regimes assert in an intensified form is no mere negative anti-colonialism, but can draw on a historical

7

tradition and sense of identity. Even colonised monarchies like Vietnam and Kampuchea can draw on pre-colonial identities which are lacking in states such as Angola and Mozambique. In Ethiopia, as in other multiethnic imperial monarchies such as Russia and China, the ultimately successful revolutionary leaderships have also been associated, much more than their rivals in the post-revolutionary struggle for power, with the ethnic and regional bases of the old imperial order.[8] They could thus present themselves as the heirs of the core tradition of the state. So far from marking a totally fresh start, revolutionary regimes may find it much easier to succeed if they can draw on a substantial legacy from the past.

Part of the new political order is likely to consist in an expansion in the numbers, powers, and organisational complexity of the state bureaucracy. The bureaucracy is the first and most important instrument which rulers have at their disposal, and institutionalisation in many ways means bureaucratisation. Initially, there may be problems due to the mutually antagonistic perceptions of bureaucrats and revolutionaries. Revolutionaries who have come to power through rural guerilla warfare are particularly likely to see the established state machinery as representing all that they have been fighting against. In the extreme and limiting case of Kampuchea, they carried this hostility to the length of destroying the bureaucracy altogether, and physically liquidating a great many of its members; but this destruction in turn does much to account for the Khmer Rouge state's failure to survive, in the face of its own organisational inadequacy and the domestic and international revulsion which paved the way for the Vietnamese invasion and the establishment of the more 'orthodox' and bureaucratised Heng Samrin regime. Often, too, leaders who have proved effective at guerilla warfare (or the vicious infighting that may accompany an urban revolution) are quite unable to cope with the very different requirements of running a large organisation, and a period of friction with the bureaucracy follows, before they are purged or moved out to some honorific position. Even leaders like Castro, or most of all Mao Tsetung, who have adeptly managed the transition from revolutionary fighter to established government leader, may hanker for the simple glories of spontaneous action, in Mao's case going so far as to dismantle, in the Cultural Revolution, much of the system which he had created. Revolutionaries who, as in Ethiopia, were themselves mostly drawn from the state bureaucracy (in the form of the armed forces), are likely to share much of its elitist attitude and centralised organisation; though even here, strains occur as the revolutionaries seek to root out 'reactionary' elements, and reluctantly come to grips with the limitations of what can be achieved by issuing orders down the hierarchy. The constant attacks on 'bureaucratic capitalism' during the early years of the Ethiopian revolution reflected, not so much the hostility of the bureaucracy towards the revolutionary regime, as its sheer incapacity to carry out the multitude of tasks suddenly thrust on it. As the immediate aftermath of revolutionary takeover fades into the past, however, the role of the bureaucracy is bound to increase, and the most important danger which a revolution faces is not, as often appears to be the case in its early years, that of relapsing into anarchy, but that of degenerating into the sclerosis of bureaucratic privilege and torpor.

The bureaucracy, nonetheless, is by no means enough. One of the weaknesses of regimes overthrown by revolutions is often indeed that they have become little more than administrative states, run from the top by bureaucracies increasingly divorced from the societies which they govern. The revolution itself likewise involves an enormous upsurge in popular political mobilisation, which needs to be channelled and restricted in the post-revolutionary period, but which cannot be totally obliterated. The mechanism commonly chosen to achieve the central task of relating institutionalisation on the one hand to some form of popular participation on the other is of course the vanguard single party. While discounting entirely the Marxist conception of the causes of revolution, I would not in the least discount the Leninist conception of its organisation. Any revolution which is to succeed in establishing a new and lasting political order will need to create a party as the foundation of that order. The question mark against the revolutionary status of such states as Angola, Mozambique and Guinea-Bissau is due not so much to the upheavals which they went through during the period of the regime's establishment, as to the apparent inadequacy of their revolutionary parties once in power. In some cases, including both Cuba and Ethiopia, the revolution itself takes place without any guiding Leninist party, and this organisation has then to be created – a process, in the Ethiopian case, accompanied by numerous conflicts and traumas. Even when, as in Russia, the party itself existed prior to the revolution, its conversion from an instrument of agitation into one of government, involved radical changes in organisation, ethos and personnel. The process of party formation or adaptation is thus the most critical feature of revolutionary institutionalisation, and inevitably receives a good deal of attention in the chapters that follow.

The Leninist principle of democratic centralism appears to provide an extraordinarily effective mechanism for combining tightly centralised elite control with the co-optation of the able and ambitious, and at least a token level of mass participation and democratic accountability. The second major task associated with the party, the propagation of a new official ideology, is much harder to assess. Revolutions invariably involve a change not just in political organisation, but also in the official mythology through which government authority is legitimated. The main function of this mythology or ideology is then to justify the actions of the revolutionary regime, and especially its unrestricted use of state power.[9] For a limited number of individuals in the thick of revolutionary activity, ideology can come to be a matter of extraordinary importance, exciting bitter conflict over issues which to the outsider may seem trivial. Even for revolutionaries, however, ideology is generally (as Marx quite correctly identified it) a mere rationalisation of the interests of its proponents, and issues which seem trivial in purely ideological terms can generally be explained by the real differences which they imply in power political ones. For the mass of the population, and even for many of those who take leading positions in the revolutionary regime, ideology is usually little more than prudential adaptation to a new rhetorical style. It may be that the role of ideology is limited in Ethiopia by the profound scepticism of the indigenous political culture; and the application of the Marxist theory of revolution to a society at Ethiopia's level of socio-economic development must raise severe incongruities. In any event, despite the impressive amount of effort that has been dedicated in the Ethiopian case to political education, I remain unpersuaded of the centrality of ideology to revolutionary reconstruction.

Along with the party come a set of auxiliary institutions linking it to the population at the most basic level. One of the features of a Leninist party, and one of its greatest sources of strength, is that it is not a mass organisation, but consists only of a carefully selected and organised elite. The principles on which it is constructed are quite different from those of the nationalist parties which, in many third-world states, managed the transition from colonial status to independence. There, party membership was entirely indiscriminate, and was expected from (and at times even enforced on) the population at large. In states where the party does not have this universalist character, other organisations are needed that do. The two most important kinds of auxiliary institutions are first those that organise the countryside and the process of agricultural production, and secondly those that organise the towns. In Ethiopia, this urban–rural distinction is formalised through the roles of peasants' associations on the one hand, and urban dwellers' associations on the other. These institutions, created since the revolution, provide the base level of local administration – in principle, self-administration – in countryside and town respectively. Trade unions have a secondary role as urban mass organisations, such importance as they possess being due mostly to their symbolic representation of the proletariat, which is smaller in Ethiopia even than in the great majority of non-industrialised third-world states. Finally, the women's and youth associations organise their own special sections of the population, with the effect – especially in the case of the women – of emphasising their separateness from the core institutions through which actual power is exercised.

A further set of revolutionary institutions also requires attention: the apparatus of physical control and especially the armed forces. From one viewpoint, the enormous expansion in the Ethiopian armed forces since the revolution provides the most impressive evidence of the increase in organisational capacity which the revolutionary regime has achieved by comparison with its predecessor. From another, it likewise indicates the increase in coercion which the establishment of the revolutionary order requires. These again are normal features of revolutionary regimes, going back to the original French example and the mass levies of 1792. Revolutions characteristically induce a high level of conflict and insecurity, both domestically and internationally. Domestically they often have to impose their rule by force, not only against 'white' or reactionary groups or interests seeking to maintain or restore the old regime, but equally against groups which have been caught up in the process of mass political mobilisation which the revolution brings with it, but which have in the event been mobilised against the new regime rather than in its support. Internationally, any revolution is likely to be seen, justifiably enough, as a challenge to the existing order, since revolutions are usually founded on some universalist principle, which is implicitly or explicitly applicable to neighbouring states. The French, Soviet, Chinese, Cuban and Vietnamese revolutions all provide examples, though Ethiopia is something of an exception. Further, the period of chaos which accompanies the initial stage of almost any revolution provides a tempting opportunity for intervention or invasion – successfully in the case of the Vietnamese invasion of Kampuçhea, disastrously for the Somali invasion of Ethiopia and the Iraqi invasion of Iran.

It is thus very likely that any revolutionary regime will soon be compelled to defend itself, and that its survival will depend on its capacity to do so. One of the great advantages that a revolution built on the ruins of an ancient monarchy is then likely to possess is that it can draw on an existing capacity for military organisation and sense of national identity, and turn the threat ultimately to its own advantage by using it to associate the new revolutionary system with the inherited tradition of the state. The value of the wars of intervention and the 'great patriotic war' in entrenching the Soviet state in Russia is the classic example. Furthermore, the regime will emerge from the crisis, assuming that it survives it, with a greatly enhanced repressive apparatus which it can use both to maintain itself at home, and to extend its control or support its allies abroad. France, the Soviet Union, Cuba and Vietnam are all again cases in point. Here, as so often, Ethiopia falls into the mainstream of revolutionary political change.

Finally, any revolution, and especially one taking place within the global economy and the bipolar security system which have characterised the second half of the twentieth century, is also likely to involve the transformation of the connections between the state and the external world. In Ethiopia's case, this transformation has been no more than partial. It has been sharpest in the realm of superpower alliance and strategic dependence, marked by a dramatic shift from the United States to the Soviet Union, and in the ideological and organisational linkages constructed with the Communist parties of the Soviet Union and Eastern Europe. There has however been little corresponding transformation of international trading connections, which remain heavily oriented towards the Western capitalist economies; a state so weakly incorporated into the global economy as Ethiopia has been able to combine domestic revolution with the maintenance of existing trading links, in a way that would scarcely be possible, for example, for the highly penetrated economies of the Caribbean.

11

THE ANALYSIS OF REVOLUTION

Ethiopia has attracted a fair amount of the attention which any revolution almost automatically evokes; but this attention has tended, in my view at least, to exhibit a number of characteristic weaknesses in the Western – and especially perhaps the Western Marxist – analysis of revolutions, which this study seeks to correct.

The first of these weaknesses has been a tendency to concentrate on the early, violent and dramatic phase of the revolution, to the neglect of the period of institutionalisation which follows. In part, this merely reflects the uncontentious fact that the early phase happens first, and is therefore available for record at a time when later developments are uncertain. In part, too, it reflects the occurrence of events sufficiently newsworthy (synonymous, in this context, with violent) to come to the attention of the Western media. Thus, a generation of books on the overthrow of Haile-Selassie[10] has been followed by a generation of books on the events culminating in the terror and the Somali war of 1977–78,[11] and in turn, after a gap of a few years, by a generation of books on the famine.[12] The absence of violent events is reflected, with startling directness, in the absence of literature. Yet at the time of writing in 1987, it is nine years since the Ethiopian victories against the Somalis in March 1978, and the establishment of firm central control through the red terror and the supremacy of Mengistu Haile-Mariam, brought the 'heroic' phase of the revolution to a close. The absence of any extended analysis of the institutionalisation phase of the revolution reflects partly the difficulties of fieldwork – and any attempt to follow developments from a distance must almost necessarily suffer from enormous problems of both information and perspective – but partly also from a straightforward tendency to ignore that aspect of revolution which I would regard as most important. Precisely because it consists not in violent events, but in the steady implementation of bureaucratic routine, the institutionalisation phase loses in dramatic impact but gains in long-term importance. If, in particular, we want to answer the questions of *how* a 'revolutionary' system of government and economic management can be implemented in one of the least developed of third-world states, and of *what difference* such a system makes to the people who live under it, then this is the period which we should be looking at.

A second weakness in the study of revolution, and certainly of the Ethiopian revolution, is almost the converse of the first: a neglect, not only of what follows the first and heroic phase, but of what precedes it. This is, in a sense, surprising. One of the key positive contributions which the Marxist approach to the study of revolution has made has been to emphasise that revolution can only be understood as an event within a continuous historical process. In practice, though, other elements in the Marxist approach have often deprived it of the advantages that the appreciation of this basic truth

12

should have given it. The most important in conceptual terms has been the resolute universalism of Marxist explanation: its attempt to analyse events in terms of categories – especially, of course, class categories – applicable to all societies, and its outright rejection of cultural variables as having any explanatory power independent of the economic relationships which are deemed to have brought them into existence in the first place. This awkward interaction between the peculiar experiences of particular societies and the universal principles which are held to account for them raises issues in Marxist historiography which lie well beyond the scope of this book. Its importance in the context of the Ethiopian revolution is to downplay the specific characteristics of the Ethiopian political tradition – which I would regard, in keeping with the political analysis of the conditions for revolution already outlined, as central to the understanding of the forces at work – in favour of generalised categories (such as 'feudalism') which are only of very limited value. The effect is to reduce the past from a dynamic series of complex interactions into a two-dimensional backcloth from which appropriate figures – feudalism, imperialism, exploitation – can be cut out and propped up to serve as pointers to revolutionary developments. What is lost in the process is not simply an understanding of the past in itself, but equally a conception of history as something that continues with undiminished force into the present. For the Marxist, the revolution falls like a sharp concussionary shock between the present and the past. (Like a concussion victim, indeed, the Ethiopian revolutionary regime is able to recognise distant events, continuing for example to celebrate Menilek's victory over the Italians in 1896, while displaying an extraordinary amnesia towards more recent history.) Inherited attitudes or institutions which have managed to struggle across the chasm between past and present are readily treated as 'residues' which are doomed to disappear once the new revolutionary system is fully established. Since such attitudes are no more than the product of the socio–economic system which spawned them, they resemble, in Marx's famous analogy, the hair which continues to grow on a corpse.

A further reason for the neglect of history in much that has been written about revolutionary Ethiopia is a simple and practical one: that revolutions, understandably enough, attract the attention of writers who are interested in revolution, and who often have little previous knowledge of the society in which a given revolution has taken place.[13] It is then all too easy to ascribe any particular manifestation of post-revolutionary attitudes or practices to the effects of revolution in itself, whether these be regarded as good or bad, while failing entirely to recognise the extent to which they duplicate pre-revolutionary equivalents. In studying revolutionary Ethiopia, I have been constantly grateful for my experience of the imperial regime. This experience has not led me to the converse illusion that 'plus ça change, plus c'est la même chose'. There *has* been a revolution. Much has changed. But a sense of *what* has changed, and how, is to be gained only through an appreciation of continuity.

My sympathies thus lie with an alternative tradition of revolutionary historiography contemporary with Marx – that of Alexis de Toqueville, whose analysis of the relationships between the *ancien régime* and revolutionary France remains to my knowledge unrivalled.[14] No revolution – not France, nor Ethiopia, nor certainly the Soviet Union – can wipe the slate clean and start again. For a foreigner, returning like Rip Van Winkle to an Ethiopia changed by a decade of revolution, it is the sheer physical familiarity that is overwhelming. The hills still stand where they did, the same round thatched houses dot the landscape;[15] the little knots of people and animals trailing along country paths are distinctively Ethiopian. These impressions are not trivial. They are central. A revolutionary regime, like any other new government, inherits a physical endowment which establishes the context for many of its actions, and which it can change only slowly, if at all. The land and most of the people stay the same. This rather obvious fact is worth mentioning, because revolution acquires in the minds of many of its adherents almost magical powers of transformation. These do not include the power to change either Ethiopia's spectacular topography, or its tragically fickle climate. Nor, except partially and very slowly, do they include the power to change the ways in which Ethiopians think, or do things. Time and again, measures imposed centrally and from the top are affected in their implementation, for better or worse, by well-established attitudes and practices at the bottom. Indeed, it is one of the central conclusions of this book that the Ethiopian revolution has 'succeeded' – in so far as it can be said to have done so – not despite but because of its inheritance from imperial Ethiopia.

It must equally be recognised that there is much that a revolution does not *try* to change: that its goals are, in many respects, the same as those of past regimes; and that many of its differences from them lie simply in a determination to achieve these more effectively. In Ethiopia, as in many revolutionary states, this continuity of goals is most obvious in the determination to maintain the national territory, and in the opportunity which this gives the new regime to establish its legitimacy as the successor to a national political tradition. But this is no more than one aspect of a much more basic continuity, the continuity of the state. The central goal of revolutionary leaders, like that of the leaders of nationalist movements against colonial rule, is to take over the state structure established by their predecessors and to use it, suitably adapted, as an agency for economic development, national integration, and the consolidation of their own power. Pre-revolutionary leaders, generally speaking, were not trying to do anything very different, even though their own position within the existing structure often led them to choose a different rhetoric, and restricted the means which they could employ. The revolutionary regime in Ethiopia, as the next chapter will seek to show, may in many respects be seen as lying in the direct line of succession to a series of centralising and state-strengthening emperors going back to the accession of Tewodros in 1855. 'Nation-building' measures, including the expansion of communications, the spread of the Amharic language, the strengthening of the hierarchy linking regional administration to the central government in Addis Ababa, and especially the increase in the size of the centrally controlled armed forces, are all ones which Ethiopia's emperors attempted to achieve in their own time. This likewise helps to explain the opposition to those measures by peripheral peoples such as the Somalis and many of the Eritreans who likewise resisted them in imperial days.

These evident continuities, and perhaps especially the critical role played by the armed forces in the Ethiopian revolution, have proved awkward and perhaps even embarrassing to those who have approached it from a Marxian perspective. John Markakis, to take one example, has coined the phrase 'garrison socialism', which he has applied to the Siyad regime in Somalia and to the Nimairi one in Sudan, as well as to Ethiopia, to describe military governments which espouse socialism as a means of imposing and defending a centralised state apparatus.[16] This is indeed precisely what the Ethiopian regime (like its fellows) has done; nor does Markakis overlook the differences between the transformation which has taken place in Ethiopia, and the far less deep-seated changes in its two neighbours. The problem lies in an implicit Marxian conception, which sees revolution as being directed against the structures of the state. If the intensely state-centralising ethos of the Ethiopian revolutionary regime is seen as falling within the mainstream of the revolutionary (or Jacobin, or Leninist) tradition, rather than as marking a deviation from it, the apparent anomaly of a revolution launched by the state's own servants ceases to be one at all.

Halliday and Molyneux approach the same problem by attempting to adapt Ellen Kay Trimberger's concept of revolution from above.[17] As originally devised to fit the cases of Turkey and Japan, this is a process in which the economic and political base of the aristocracy is destroyed, with little violence, mass participation, or appeal to radical ideology, by the high military and sometimes civilian bureaucrats of the old regime. Halliday and Molyneux suggest that in Ethiopia, 'this most radical of revolutions from above' could be accompanied by mass movements and uprisings from below. Their analysis suffers, however, from the basic difficulty that none of Trimberger's criteria apply to Ethiopia. The Ethiopian revolution was not led by high military or civilian bureaucrats, who almost without exception were exiled, imprisoned, or shot; it involved a high level of mass participation, both in the original uprisings in the towns, and in the implementation of land reform in the countryside, with a corresponding level of violence, and it has been accompanied by continuous appeals to radical ideology. Once again, an inadequate concept has been brought in to account for a revolution led by members of the state apparatus, and directed towards maintaining and strengthening the state, rather than overthrowing and displacing it.

Within the conceptualisation of revolution proposed by Theda Skocpol, however, these apparent anomalies become the norm. Skocpol's approach is appropriate to the Ethiopian situation in several critical respects. First,

15

her three cases – France, Russia and China – while differing from Ethiopia as they do from one another, place revolution within the context of rapidly changing, but predominantly agrarian, countries with absolutist monarchical state structures and peasant-based social orders. They are thus comparable with Ethiopia, in a way that revolutions in states such as Cuba and Vietnam are not. Secondly, her case-study approach also ensures, in contrast to more abstract treatments of revolution, that the critical importance of specific historical circumstances is not overlooked. Indeed, just as Skocpol carried out detailed historical examinations of her three revolutions before looking at the theoretical literature, my own concern for Ethiopia long predates my acquaintance with revolutionary theory, and the first draft of this book was completed without any reference to the work of Skocpol herself. Its appropriateness to Ethiopia thus derives from a genuine coincidence of theory and data, not from the mere application of a 'model' to circumstances different from those for which it was devised. Thirdly and most important, the emphasis in Skocpol's approach on the centrality of the contest for state power in the early phase of revolution, and of state building in the later phase, precisely corresponds with the Ethiopian experience. Nor does Skocpol overlook the fact, likewise confirmed by the Ethiopian case, that revolution does not take place solely at the level of political organisation, but must also involve the transformation of productive relationships, especially in the countryside. It is this transformation which distinguishes the Ethiopian revolution from Markakis' other two cases of 'garrison socialism', and marks it as a qualitatively different kind of event. While no theory, least of all one which places as heavy an emphasis as Skocpol's on specific historical experiences, can be mechanically applied to inevitably varying cases, her approach does seem to me to provide far greater insight than any of the others currently available to understanding the Ethiopian revolution.

Finally, there is one further weakness in much of the analysis, especially Marxist analysis, of revolutions, and one which applies in the sharpest form to Ethiopia: a very high level of political and emotional commitment, much of which in turn invokes a teleological conception of revolution which I would hold to be misguided. With much of this commitment I sympathise, even though I do not share it. For many Ethiopians, and also for some foreigners, the revolution has been a traumatic experience, in which many thousands of people, including their friends and members of their families, have been killed, imprisoned, or driven abroad. For many people, the actions and attitudes which they took at key points of the revolution have been matters, literally, of life or death; and for the survivors, the defence of those actions or attitudes has become central to the maintenance of their own self-respect. I sympathise; but in opposition to supporters of the Marxian doctrine of 'praxis', who hold commitment and participation in revolutionary politics to be essential qualifications for analysing it, I cling rather to a belief in the value – so far as it can be achieved – of dispassionate observation. This is not the same as a 'value-free' social science, a goal which I believe to be unattainable, but it does involve a conscious attempt to avoid moral judgements or identification with one or another group of political actors.

Commitment in a personal sense is often also associated with a teleological viewpoint which assesses revolution in terms of the ends to which it is assumed to lead. This again is characteristic of the Marxian approach, which readily assumes both that revolution is necessary in order to achieve the basic goals of human existence – freedom, democracy, health, prosperity, equality, justice, peace – and that these goals will in fact be achieved once the revolution has occurred. Once accepted, these assumptions lead to either of two logical corollaries. If on the one hand, it is granted that the event concerned *is* a revolution, then the appropriate consequences must be seen to be following: an approach which leads in its extreme form to 'Webbism', so called from the experience of two aged British socialists who visited the Soviet Union at the height of the Stalinist purges, and came back with the conviction that they had seen the future and it worked.[18] Conversely, if it is accepted that the benefits to be provided by revolution have not been achieved, then it follows equally ineluctably that the event concerned cannot have been a 'real' revolution at all. These attitudes may well seem too absurdly simple-minded to be worth consideration, even as 'Aunt Sallies' for instant demolition. A reading of much of the literature on the Ethiopian revolution has however convinced me that, while rarely articulated in so crude a form, these teleological assumptions are powerful contributors to the way in which it is assessed.

Oddly, although the immediate response of much of the Western left is usually to take a Webbist approach to third-world revolutions, in the Ethiopian case the opposite reaction has been dominant. The revolution, certainly, has its supporters,[19] but I think it would be fair to say that Western leftist comment has generally been hostile, sometimes virulently so. This is partly the result of the fact that quite a number of Ethiopian Marxist intellectuals took up the cause of the EPRP, which was from the start violently opposed to the ruling military council (the Derg), and after its shattering defeat in the red terror many of the survivors took refuge in the West. References to 'the revolution betrayed', or to the burial by the Derg of 'true socialism', clearly reveal the teleological assumptions to which I have referred.[20] Another strand was the development of links between the Western left and the separatist Marxist guerilla movements fighting the Ethiopian central government, notably the EPLF in Eritrea, which similarly led Western Marxist commentators to downplay the revolutionary credentials of the Ethiopian central government.[21] Nor did Soviet support for Ethiopia any longer carry with it the automatic Western Marxist approval for the Ethiopian regime which it would once have provided. Finally, perhaps, and despite the achievements which the regime can claim, famine and endless warfare may simply make it too implausible to present Ethiopia as a model of what revolutionary development in the third world may be expected to achieve; it may be easier just to write it off as not being 'really' revolutionary at all.

These are not disputes on which I wish to take sides. My disagreement is not with the supporters of the Ethiopian government, nor with its opponents, but with a conception of revolution which must seriously hamper our efforts to understand it. I regard the view that Ethiopia has undergone an experience which must – by the normal usage of the word, and by comparison with the cases to which it has previously been applied – be treated as revolutionary, as having been incontestably established. My task is then to look at this experience, and to assess its results as best I can.

2

Monarchical modernisation and the origins of revolution

The rulers of revolutionary Ethiopia display an instructive ambiguity towards their country's impressive historical record. On the one hand, the two millennia or so prior to 1974 are dismissed as a period of unenlightened and exploitative feudalism, further marred in the twentieth century by capitalistic elements. A pamphlet produced for the tenth anniversary of the revolution in 1984, for example, contrasts the 'serfdom' of the pre-revolutionary centuries with the 'total freedom' attained in the preceding decade.[1] On the other hand, they constantly look back to this same past for sources of national pride and identity, especially in combatting foreign foes. The battle of Adwa in 1896, the resistance to the Italian occupation of 1936–41, and the liberation of 1941, are annually celebrated with official ceremonies and articles in the press. The problem of the relationship between the identity of the nation, and the imperial system of government which was central to the existence of an Ethiopian state and such sense of nationality as it attained, is solved in practice by recognising previous emperors up to Haile-Selassie's immediate predecessor, while totally castigating Haile-Selassie himself. Thus, the Menilek II School retains its name, while places and institutions named after Haile-Selassie and his immediate family (of which there were an inordinate number) have all been rechristened. This neat solution enables the regime to place itself in the line of national continuity, while dissociating itself from the immediate past; but the actual relationships between national continuity and revolutionary transformation are not so easily established. This chapter will therefore seek to describe the basis of the imperial political system, and to show how it changed in the last century or so of its existence, and in so doing laid itself open to revolutionary overthrow. This will in turn help to indicate the extent to which the revolutionary regime can be seen as part of a continuous process of Ethiopian political change, as against the ways in which it should be seen as wrenching Ethiopia out of that continuity.

THE BASES OF STATE AND NATION

A familiar distinction can be made between the state, as an organised hierarchy exercising effective control over a territory and people, and the nation, as a community of people possessing common values which, ideally, serve to identify them with the political arrangements through which they are governed, and, in a nation-state, with the state authorities. In Ethiopia, the concepts both of state and of nation have indigenous points of reference. They are not merely, as is often the case elsewhere in Africa, alien ideas imported and imposed by an external colonialism. But the forms which they take, and the ways in which they relate to one another, raise issues which are central to the structure of the Ethiopian political system under both imperial and revolutionary regimes.

A tradition of the state is evident from the way in which highland Ethiopia has maintained, over many centuries, a level of continuous large-scale political organisation found in few if any other parts of sub-Saharan Africa. Such a state, with its own coinage and impressive monuments, existed with its capital at Axum at about the time of the birth of Christ, and controlled both the Red Sea coastline around Massawa and a considerable part of the highland agricultural areas of present-day Tigray and Eritrea. The combination of highland agriculture on the one hand, and long-distance trade between the African interior and the Red Sea on the other, has provided the economic basis for the Ethiopian state from the earliest times until the present day.[2] Early in the fifth century, the Axumite monarchy was converted to Christianity, which spread through the northern Ethiopian plateau, and, with the conquest of much of the surrounding area by Islam from the seventh century onwards, helped to create and maintain a distinctive insular Ethiopian sense of political and religious identity. By the ninth century, the centre of government had moved to Lalibela in present-day Wollo, where the rock-hewn churches are not only amazing creations in their own right, but also monuments to the authority and extractive capability of the state which could build them.

The displacement of the Zagwe emperors of Lalibela by the 'Solomonic' dynasty in the mid thirteenth century led to the articulation of much of the official state mythology (such as the legendary descent of the dynasty from Solomon and the Queen of Sheba), which survived in attenuated form through to the Haile-Selassie era, and to a further southward and westward expansion of the imperial territory. This medieval empire reached its apogee in the fifteenth century, when it maintained control – in a rugged mountainous region presenting enormous difficulties of communication – over a territory extending about 600 miles from north to south, and 300 from east to west. From the sixteenth century onwards, both resurgent Islam in the east, and the spread of the Oromo peoples from the south, reduced its access to international trade, and hemmed its territory into the highland area, where the authority of the emperors was increasingly challenged by regional lords. For about a hundred years from the mid eighteenth century, effective central government collapsed.

Despite its need for strong central leadership and its emphasis on the dynasty as a source of political authority, this state was not a personal nor even a dynastic one. It was firmly rooted in the structure of indigenous society, both through its economic base and through a distinctive set of values, myths and attitudes. Economically, the state was maintained primarily by the surplus extracted from ox–plough agriculture, secondarily by long-distance trade and the conquest of tributary peoples to the south and west of the central highland core. The emperors travelled continuously over the central plateau, in a tented capital which enabled them both to live off the land and to maintain control over regional rulers who, as mini-emperors in their own homelands, provided a constant threat to imperial authority. Culturally, the highland area was primarily inhabited by Amharic and Tigrinya speaking peoples – Tigrinya in present-day Tigray and Eritrea regions, Amharic in Gonder, Gojjam, western Wollo and northern Shoa. Although Ethiopia has continuously formed a multiethnic political system, participation in national political life normally required assimilation to the cultural values of the Amharic core: the Amharic language, Orthodox Christianity, and a capacity to operate within the structures and assumptions of a court administration.

There is always a problem in assessing the extent to which political arrangements can be explained by reference to cultural factors, but in the case of highland Ethiopia some such reference is inescapable. At its most basic, a political structure capable of surviving over such an astonishing period of time must have drawn on, and in turn helped to strengthen, attitudes towards political authority which may be expected to continue even after the imperial system of government has been destroyed. These attitudes briefly comprise both a general belief in hierarchy, and a set of specific relationships between superiors and inferiors. A quotation from Donald Levine will make the point[3]

> The complex of beliefs, symbols and values regarding authority constitute a key component of Amhara political culture. Throughout Amhara culture appears the motif that authority as such is good: indispensable for the well-being of society and worthy of unremitting deference, obeisance, and praise. Every aspect of Amhara social life is anchored in some sort of relationship to authority figures, and the absence of such a relationship evokes feelings of incompleteness and *malaise*.

This *malaise* appeared in its most extreme form in battle, where Ethiopian units characteristically disintegrated on the death of their leader;[4] and in the succession to the throne, when prolonged periods of anomic behaviour and factional violence could occur until a successful leader gained acceptance and recreated the pattern of authority and deference about himself. At one level, the violent period of the Ethiopian revolution, from 1974 until

Mengistu Haile-Mariam established his personal dominance in 1977–78, could be seen as mirroring the upheavals which had marked Haile-Selassie's rise to power some sixty years earlier. This authority, moreover, was in principle open to anyone. Though the system could in some respects be described as 'feudal' – in that it constituted a hierarchy of relationships ultimately resting on the control of arable land and peasant labour – it did not produce any hereditary ruling class or caste. Titles were not hereditary, and rights in land were derived from complex combinations of inheritance, political office, and personal assertion.[5] Aptly characterised as a 'tough man' system, it allowed anyone (and most obviously successful soldiers), to rise to positions of authority by demonstrating a capacity for leadership. Anyone who reached high office could acquire a title and perhaps marry into an established family, and if he had the personal capacity he could attain a position almost indistinguishable from that of a nobleman born and bred. Though the system was highly inegalitarian, in the sense that it depended almost exclusively on hierarchical relations of authority, it carried no 'premise of inequality'. Dajazmatch Balcha, a castrated Gurage prisoner of the Emperor Menilek, had by the 1920s established such a powerful position in his governate of Sidamo that he was able to defy all the central government's attempts to displace him, and fell only when he overreached himself by marching on Addis Ababa. At times of exceptional upheaval, as in the nineteenth century, a regional warlord such as Kassa of Kwara (later the Emperor Tewodros) could even claim the throne. The revolutionary regime, while changing both individual leaders and the formal ideology on which political power rests, has thus been able to draw on an acceptance of authority inherited from the previous system of government.

It was an authority, nonetheless, which at least under the pre-revolutionary system, was inherently limited. To start with, there were the insuperable practical difficulties of exercising the formally absolute powers of the throne in a large and mountainous country with minimal communications. Secondly, the acceptance of hierarchy which underlay the power of the Emperor could likewise serve to sustain provincial rulers who might assert their own independent power. At any level, a veneer of deference might hide a disaffection which awaited only the right opportunity for rebellion. Most important of all, power was respected only so long as it was effective. A leader capable of holding power, and thereby assuring the welfare of his subjects and supporters, was looked up to with unbounded reverence. Once he failed, he was abandoned. Political loyalties were ultimately instrumental – designed to achieve something, not valued in themselves. It was not unusual, in the days of constant warfare between rival provincial lords, for the soldiers of a clearly outnumbered army to desert it on the eve of battle, reappearing the following morning on the winning side. When Haile-Selassie was driven off to imprisonment in September 1974, the deference which he had attracted during nearly sixty years in power collapsed like a pricked balloon.

A system in which authority depended on the personal capacity of the leader, and in which even the apparently most trustworthy subordinate was never entirely to be relied on, helped to foster two further features of Ethiopian political culture and administration which are still relevant to a revolutionary regime. One was a pronounced lack of inter-personal trust. Ethiopian suspicion is proverbial, and brings with it a secretiveness, a reserve and a tendency to intrigue no less suited to a communist than to a court administration. Along with this went a considerable difficulty in building institutions, in the sense of regularised ways of doing things which were in large part independent of the personal loyalties and inclinations of the individuals involved in them, and which would therefore allow a dispersal and delegation of power. The leader was required to be both omnipresent and omnicompetent, capable of intervening at will in the smallest details of any aspect of administration, and his personal involvement was normally essential where any innovation was involved. To take decisions independently of the emperor would conversely be regarded as a slight on, even a challenge to, his authority.

It should not be assumed that these traits simply carry through unchanged into the post-imperial era. We are not dealing merely with a replication of imperial authority in Marxist–Leninist colours. But the pre-revolutionary system nonetheless forms an important point of departure for the post-revolutionary regime.

While the legacy of the Ethiopian state was relatively straightforward, that of the 'nation' was more complex. Ethiopia is not, and as far back as its long historical record reaches, has never been, an ethnic political community. It has consistently comprised peoples of different ethnic groups, speaking different languages, and practising different religions. It constituted an empire, not simply in the formal sense that it was ruled by an emperor, but equally in that it embodied a claim to universal domination, and sought to govern any people whom it was able to bring under its control. It was, though, a system with a cultural and in some degree ethnic core, formed by the Amhara people of the central highlands. Amharic was the language of government; Orthodox Christianity, which the Amhara share with several other Ethiopian peoples, notably the Tigreans to the north, was the religion of rule – not for the most part enforced on other people, but expected of those who sought any important part in political affairs; and, less tangibly, an Amhara culture formed the basis of the Ethiopian system of government. While it is conceivable that Oromos or Tigreans, Gurages, Kaffas, Sidamas, Kambattas or any other of Ethiopia's numerous peoples might secede from Ethiopia, it was no more conceivable for the Amhara to do so than for the English to secede from the United Kingdom. Had they done so, there would have been no Ethiopia left.

The Amhara are capable of forming the core element of a multiethnic state, however, only because – again like the English – their own ethnicity is so weakly defined. Unlike the great majority of African peoples, they do not constitute a 'tribe' – a group, that is to say, defined by a mythology of common descent from a single ancestor. Unlike, say, the Somalis, for whom descent through the paternal line is critical in determining clan membership and hence social identity, Amharas draw almost impartially on any relationship through either the male or female line, and any sense of genealogical identity swiftly becomes blurred. Haile-Selassie, for example, derived his claim to the throne (such as it was) through his father's mother. Genealogical vagueness in turn greatly aids the process of cultural and political assimilation, which is likewise assisted by the spread of Amharic personal names throughout much of Ethiopia, and by a system of nomenclature which blurs an individual's ethnic origins. Ethiopians are normally identified by their own personal name, followed by their father's personal name. Mengistu Haile-Mariam, for example, is Mengistu, the son of Haile-Mariam. There are no family names, though occasionally the paternal grandfather's name is added to avoid confusions: there is a Special Court judge called Mengistu Haile-Mariam Lencho, the last being a grandpaternal name added on to distinguish him from the head of state. This means that after a couple of generations, many Kaffas, Kambattas or Oromos are simply indistinguishable by name from Amharas. And provided that they speak Amharic, and do not explicitly identify themselves with their areas of origin, they will be taken for Amharas – or more accurately, perhaps, will simply be members of a composite Ethiopian nationality. Haile-Selassie, again, was in terms of his parentage more Oromo than Amhara, and also had a Gurage grandmother. He married an Oromo, but politically speaking, these ethnic connections were virtually irrelevant. Mengistu Haile-Mariam's father is often referred to as a Wollamo, from Sidamo region in the south; but while this may help to give him some local prestige, it scarcely matters for purposes of national politics. The contrast with Somali government, where the leader's clan membership is vital in determining patterns of support and opposition, is very marked.

It is essential to emphasise the plasticity of Amhara – and hence, in a sense, of Ethiopian – identity, in order to correct the very misleading impression that can be given by associating it with the descent-based ethnic identities characteristic of many other African societies. Being Amhara is much more a matter of how one behaves than of who one's parents were; and without this capacity for assimilating other peoples into a core culture which can be regarded as national, and not the exclusive property of a particular group of people, the Ethiopian state would probably have been unable to sustain itself in the first place. At the same time, it is precisely because Ethiopia has this core identity, associated with one people but also claiming a special national status, that it suffers from much more intense problems of national identity and integration than other African states, in which ethnicity is the result of the almost haphazard process by which different peoples were tossed by colonialism into a common political unit. Assimilation to the core identity, while it offers on the one hand the chance of participating in the national political system, involves on the other hand the subordination of one's own original affiliation. This is much more of a problem for some groups than for others, but at its worst it has fostered a level of resistance which few other African states have had to face; and under the guise of the 'nationalities' question, has presented the revolutionary regime with its single most intractable problem.

Historically, much of the opposition between the expansionist highland core and its periphery was expressed in terms of a clash between Orthodox Christianity and Islam. Highland Ethiopia has long possessed a distinctive sense of self-identity as a Christian island in a Moslem sea – accounting, for example, for a strong sense of popular sympathy for the Israelis. One of its abiding folk memories is of the catastrophic Moslem invasions led by Ahmed Gragn (Ahmed the left-handed) in the 1530s, from which Ethiopia was eventually rescued with Portuguese assistance. In practice, the boot has usually been on the other foot; the highland peoples, with their comparatively dense population and effective political organisation, have been much better equipped to dominate the scattered Moslems of the lowlands than vice versa. Both literally and metaphorically, they have looked down on the people around them. Nomadism has in itself aroused the contempt of a settled agricultural population for people of no fixed abode. Excluded from the central political system by religion, lifestyle, and simple physical distance, it is not surprising that several of the lowland Moslem peoples have turned against it – especially when, as in the case of the Somalis, they could look across the artificial frontier to another state which was governed by their own kind. But even so, the religious difference should not be elevated into a rigid line of demarcation between incompatible peoples. Moslem noblemen, especially from Wollo, have been involved in high positions in imperial government at least since the mid eighteenth century. Some other Moslem groups, like the Adere from the city of Harar, with a high level of education and no independent political ambitions, have readily gravitated to central government posts. The Moslem–Christian distinction itself implies a very different relationship in Wollo, where Christians and Moslems have long lived side by side in reasonable amity and without much assumption of relative superiority, from the position in highland Hararghe and Arsi where Christianity has been associated with an imposed official and landowning elite, Islam with the subject indigenous population. Even among the Somalis or in western Eritrea, the central government has been able to use local rivalries in order to gain tactical allies among peoples generally hostile to it. And under the revolutionary regime, determined – though, as we shall see, in some ways counterproductive – efforts have been made to bring all Ethiopians together into a common secular nationalism.

Religion, moreover, by no means coincides with ethnicity. Some peoples, such as the Somali or the Afar, are exclusively Moslem; others, such as the Amhara and Tigreans, almost entirely Christian. The largest and in many ways most important of Ethiopian ethnic groups, the Oromo (who until a decade or so ago were generally referred to as Galla), are however divided between religions in ways which mirror the ambivalences of Ethiopia itself. The Oromo are the single most important ethnic group in Shoa, Hararghe, Arsi, Bale, Welega, and Illubabor; they also have substantial populations in Kaffa and Sidamo in the south and Wollo in the north, and are represented in all of Ethiopia's fourteen regions except for Eritrea and Gonder. In recent years, and especially since the revolution, efforts have been made – and will be examined in a later chapter – to foster a sense of Oromo political identity; but these have foundered, and seem likely always to founder, on the near impossibility of defining any conception of 'being Oromo' which can be made to serve a coherent political purpose. The Oromo have in this respect paradoxically differed from the Tigreans, historically Christian and associated with the Ethiopian state since its formation at Axum in Tigray some 2,000 years ago, who have nonetheless formed an effective resistance movement, the Tigray People's Liberation Front (TPLF), directed against the present government in Addis Ababa. Tigrean nationalism, too, is a complex of differing and potentially contradictory elements; Eritrean nationalism still more so, since it has neither an ethnic nor a religious base, and despite its extraordinary capacity for military and social organisation, has constantly been riven by factional disputes.

Nationality is thus an issue of great complexity, which has been both illuminated and intensified by the experience of revolution: revolution has exploded the easy assumption of Ethiopian student Marxists in the 1960s, that ethnic and regional separatisms were no more than expressions of local resentment at the economic exploitation and political autocracy imposed by the imperial regime. Land reform, mass mobilisation, and the abolition of such symbols of core domination as the special status of the Orthodox Church, have failed to end local separatisms and have in some ways exacerbated them. At the same time, the resilience of the centralising nationalism of the core has convincingly demonstrated that Ethiopia is neither a 'Habsburg' state, dependent on its dynasty to hold together a congeries of disparate peoples, nor an ethnic empire depending on the domination of one of its peoples over the others. It is a multiethnic nation riven by conflicts not only with those who deny the basis of Ethiopian nationalism, but even with many of those who accept it.

THE RISE OF A MODERNISING AUTOCRACY

Like other ancient empires – Iran, Thailand, Japan – Ethiopia responded to the challenge of European encroachment through the conversion of its monarchy into a modernising autocracy. This drew both on an existing national identity and conception of monarchical authority, and on a greatly increased level of social, economic and military contact with the outside world. It led to the creation of a state modelled on European lines, the ultimate achievement of which was to secure recognition by European states as a sovereign jurisdiction existing on terms of formal equality with themselves. Ethiopia, like Iran and Thailand, acquired in the process many of the attributes of the colonial administrations simultaneously under construction in other parts of Africa and Asia, but with the critical difference that the state was controlled not by colonial rulers, but by an indigenous elite led by the monarch.

This process is coterminous with the reigns of the great centralising emperors from 1855 onwards: Tewodros (1855–68), Yohannes (1872–89), Menilek (1889–1913), Haile-Selassie (1916/1930–74). Tewodros was in many ways the most remarkable of them all; originating at best from the minor local nobility, in an Ethiopia in which central government had for the past century collapsed, he was driven by a vision which encompassed the restoration of a powerful Ethiopian state, its use of Western technology and recognition by Western powers, and a programme of conquest ultimately culminating in the liberation of Jerusalem. It was a vision the inevitable failure of which took him close to madness, and led to his suicide in the face of a British expeditionary force sent to rescue imprisoned Europeans; even his defeat of the major regional warlords was no more than temporary. He succeeded however in re-establishing a conception of Ethiopia as a single state led by a powerful emperor – a vision which his successors sustained, and which was ultimately responsible for Ethiopia's survival as the sole independent indigenous African state.[6] His successor, the Tigrean Yohannes, claimed the throne after defeating his rival regional rulers, and successfully defended Ethiopia against Egyptian invasions in 1875 and 1876, the first Italian incursions from the coast, and the Sudanese Mahdists, fighting whom he was killed in 1889.[7]

Menilek of Shoa, who then took over, had the best claim of all the three great nineteenth-century emperors to be considered as the founder of the modern Ethiopian state.[8] His decisive defeat of the invading Italians at Adwa in 1896 secured Ethiopia's independence, and his conquests in the south and west established its present boundaries (save for Eritrea, which despite Adwa came under Italian rule) and vastly increased its territory. The foundation of Addis Ababa set up a permanent capital, linked to the outside world through the railway to Djibouti, in which the first Western educational and administrative structures were created. Thereafter, succession to national political power was determined by control of Addis Ababa rather than by conflict between rival regional lords. Following the deposition of Menilek's grandson Iyasu in 1916, Haile-Selassie became Regent and heir to the throne (with the title and name of Ras Tafari), with Menilek's daughter Zawditu as titular empress.[9] Haile-Selassie became emperor on Zawditu's death in 1930, and (save for the five-year hiatus caused by Italian invasion and occupation from 1936 to 1941) reigned until 1974.

During this 120-year period, the structure of the state was decisively altered. The first thing to change was the means of access to high office. During the period of the Solomonic dynasty, for some five centuries from

1268, succession to the throne was governed by descent, or at least was restricted to a small group of princes. After 1855, it was governed almost solely by the control of force. Tewodros, Yohannes and Menilek were in no way related to one another, and had no relevant connection with the old imperial dynasty, while even Haile-Selassie was only one, and by no means the senior, of a group of noblemen related to the Shoan ruling house. Having seized power he, like his predecessors, called himself emperor, and claimed the threadbare cloak of legitimacy provided by an imperial mythology of descent from King Solomon and the Queen of Sheba. We are thus dealing, not with a 'traditional' monarchy, but with a military autocracy, the power base of which changed with the centralisation of military force.[10]

Secondly, this centralising monarchy subjected regional lords to a progressively increasing level of imperial control – a process ultimately completed only by Haile-Selassie, following the decisive reduction of regional autonomy during the Italian occupation. This in turn required a shift in military power, from a system which ultimately depended on the control of personal retainers and local levies, which a regional governor could raise for his own use as well as that of the crown, to one which depended on imported firearms and ultimately a professional military organisation, both controlled by a monarch with access to external aid. Both Yohannes and Menilek used imported firearms to establish themselves in power and defeat foreign invasion, but a professional standing army was not created until the reign of Haile-Selassie. Started in the early 1930s but aborted by the Italian invasion, it was consolidated from the 1940s onwards with aid first from the United Kingdom, and then from the United States. By 1960, Ethiopia had the largest armed forces in black Africa, with a four division army and imperial bodyguard, a brigade of tanks, an air force flying jet fighters, and a small coastal defence navy, amounting in all to some 45,000 men.[11] These forces reduced the military autonomy of regional governors to vanishing point, and their political autonomy with it; only in Tigray did Haile-Selassie feel the need to appoint his regional governors from members of the old ruling house, and elsewhere they were drawn overwhelmingly from his own central region of Shoa. Over the same period, however, both the military functions and the social and political base of the armed forces changed. The external threat came not from European imperial powers but from African neighbours, notably the Somali Republic, which after independence in 1960 reached a military agreement with the Soviet Union, in order to build the armed forces needed to wrest the Somali-inhabited south-eastern part of the country from Ethiopian control. The domestic threat came not from local noblemen but from guerilla movements, especially after 1962 in Eritrea. And the new armed forces, though they shared the centralising ethos of the Ethiopian state, had no particular commitment (save in the case of senior officers drawn from the court aristocracy) to the maintenance of an increasingly anachronistic monarchy.

Thirdly, the central Ethiopian government could only maintain itself through an increasing level of external contact in all fields – diplomatic, military, economic, administrative, educational. The need for external allies to provide armaments was only the most obvious of these connections. The difference between Menilek's defeat of the Italians in 1895–96, and Haile Selassie's defeat by them forty years later, resulted partly from the increasing sophistication of European weapons and partly from Menilek's ability to acquire weapons which were denied to his successor. Along with the new army came all the rest of the imported paraphernalia of the modern state: the creation of an educated elite, at first by sending young men abroad for education, subsequently by establishing the necessary institutions at home; the creation and progressive expansion of the central government bureaucracy, radiating out from the court to ministries in Addis Ababa and ultimately into regional government as well; and most important of all, the creation of a foreign exchange economy through which to pay for imported goods and provide a tax base for the imperial government. The key to this economy was coffee, a plant growing wild in Ethiopia which had been exported to the Middle East since the earliest times. Coffee production for export, already established under Menilek, was further expanded during the 1920s, and by the time of the Italian invasion in 1935 had created a viable base for economic and administrative expansion.[12] It has consistently accounted for well over half of published Ethiopian exports up to the present day.

But coffee mattered, not only as a source of foreign exchange and central government revenue, but also because of its geographical location within Ethiopia. It was not grown in the central highlands of 'traditional' Ethiopia, which were too high and too cold, but in the conquered territories of the south and west, which had been incorporated into the empire only in the later nineteenth century. The primary area of production was in the south-western region of Kaffa (from which the crop is said to take its name), with the neighbouring regions of Illubabor, Welega and Sidamo; it was also grown in the highlands of Hararghe in the south-east, where production was smaller, but the beans were of high quality and conveniently placed for export. The coffee economy thus entirely by-passed the core areas of the grain-growing highlands which had previously provided the economic basis for political power in Ethiopia. Control of the economy now required control of the south-west, together with the new lines of communication which led to Addis Ababa, and thence along the line of rail (completed in 1916) through Hararghe to the port of Djibouti in the French Somali Coast. The centrality of Shoa, the region around Addis Ababa, to the new economic basis of the Ethiopian state prompted an internal shift in power which has been intensified over the years with the progressive peripheralisation of the highland subsistence economy – a process recently culminating in its destruction by drought and erosion, and in large-scale shifts in population to the south and west. Other zones of cash agriculture were likewise sited outside the Amhara–Tigrean highlands, not only for ecological reasons, but

29

also because the tenacity of highland social structure – especially over the control of land – prevented its exploitation for commercial purposes with the conversion of subsistence agriculture to cash crops. The other major locations for commercial agriculture were the Awash valley, south and east of Addis Ababa, where foreign multinationals established irrigated plantations for sugar, fruit and cotton from the 1950s onwards, and the Arsi region, again south of Addis Ababa, where a massive expansion of commercial grain cultivation took place from the 1960s. The lowlands around Humera, on the Sudanese border in Gonder region in the north-west, were another area of rapidly expanding commercial agriculture in the 1960s, especially for sesame seed.

This new commercial economy produced in turn a new social and political superstructure. Menilek rewarded his soldiers with grants of land in the south and west, a practice which continued throughout Haile-Selassie's reign, thus establishing a local class of military colonists whose allegiance was to the central government. Generals, noblemen and court officials, who like the soldiers came very largely from Shoa, received larger tracts of land and were appointed as governors of the newly incorporated regions. These could often in turn use their administrative powers to acquire additional estates, coffee land being specially sought after. The local inhabitants were converted into a subject labour force, and sometimes, as in parts of Arsi in the 1960s, cleared off the land altogether in order to permit the more efficient management of commercial agriculture.[13] The ways in which this system worked varied widely from place to place. Sometimes the would-be settlers found their allotted area too low, hot and inhospitable, sold their land grants to the local inhabitants and went back to the north. Some areas, like the Chercher highlands in western Hararghe, fostered smallholder agriculture. Others, as in much of Kaffa, had large estates owned by absentee landlords. On the whole, as in neighbouring Kenya, the commercialisation of agriculture was associated with the imposition of an alien settler class associated with the new centrally imposed government – the key difference being that in one case this class came from Europe, in the other from an indigenous African ruling group. All of these settlers were apt to be regarded by the local population as Amhara, despite the fact that many if not most of them were ethnically Oromo, like many of those among whom they settled; speaking Amharic, coming in the train of a central Ethiopian army, they had 'become' Amhara, both in their own perceptions and in those of the people among whom they settled. For the eventual revolutionary government, this association of central administration (which as nationalists they upheld) with an imposed system of economic exploitation (which as socialists they rejected) was to pose a major dilemma, and one which in some respects remains unsolved.

This system provided not only the economic basis for central government, but also many of its personnel. Haile-Selassie was one of its products. The son of Menilek's governor of Harar, the key south-eastern region astride the

trade route to Djibouti, he eventually became governor there himself, maintained close connections with it during the troubled period of the Regency,
and brought many of his followers there to positions in Addis Ababa. The
army too was closely associated with government in the south, through the
grants of land to old soldiers, and the characteristic tendency of settler populations (as in Ulster, for example) to have an intensified sense of loyalty to
their parent regime and a high propensity to go into the military; these connections have been reflected in the military regime. If, as is generally
supposed, Mengistu Haile-Mariam is part-Amhara, part-Wollamo, he
would embody the effects of the expansion to the south no less than his
predecessor.

All in all, then, the new Ethiopian state as it emerged from the time of
Tewodros, and especially as it evolved under Menilek and Haile-Selassie,
constituted a 'system' of interlocking and complementary parts. At its apex,
the emperor had achieved a position of precarious dominance, wielding a
power both over central administration and over regional government which
none of his predecessors had been able to achieve. At the centre, the new
bureaucracy provided him with an administrative staff, whose routine functions were progressively devolved from the palace, but whose members had
no political base of their own. A host of other 'modern' institutions helped
to sustain the increased power and scope of the state. At the periphery,
imperial control was maintained by centrally appointed officials, and
enforced if need be by a centrally controlled army. This army was armed,
and the political structure as a whole supported, by the United States, for
which Ethiopia was – along with Saudi Arabia and Iran – one of a ring of
client states around the Middle East. This diplomatic support was most
explicitly expressed when the UN General Assembly voted in 1951, with
American encouragement, for the federation with Ethiopia of the former
Italian colony of Eritrea, and Ethiopia in turn granted the United States use
of a telecommunications base near Asmara in the Eritrean highlands. The
whole structure was in turn maintained by a system of commercial agriculture, by-passing the subsistence economy of the highlands, which was itself
sustained by centralised political and military power, and which created an
explosive combination of economic exploitation with ethnic differentiation.

In many respects, this system was not very different from that found in
many other African states; the exploitation of a cash-crop producing
peasantry in order to maintain a state structure which is run for the benefit
of urban educated elites and supported by external alliances is part of the
common experience of post-colonial Africa. The differences lay partly in a
peculiarly Ethiopian pattern of land alienation to an indigenous elite, but as
much or more in the inadequacy of the political formula, autocratic
monarchy, available to hold the different strands of the system together.

THE ORIGINS OF REVOLUTION

The political inadequacies which led to the collapse of the imperial system of government in Ethiopia were structural and not merely personal. It fell, not because it was badly managed, but because it was by its nature incapable of handling the increasing demands which were placed on it. Haile-Selassie operated, like his predecessors, within the setting defined by the imperial court. This was an essentially household system of government, in which the emphasis on personal leadership in Ethiopian political culture was brought to its peak, providing a skilled emperor with limitless opportunities for the manipulation of the personal relationships through which political power was exercised. This was an activity at which Haile-Selassie was unsurpassed, as his presence at the centre of power for nearly sixty years, and his forty-four year tenure of the throne, help to indicate. Far from autocratic in the actual exercise of power, he was a cautious ruler whose skill lay in the management of factions and individuals in a manner which promoted their dependence on himself, while maintaining his own freedom of action. It was a skill which was not simply ascribable to his position as emperor, and his courtiers' dependence on him for rewards. As his diplomatic successes showed, notably the management of the factions, groupings and often touchy leaders of independent African states which led to the formation of the Organisation of African Unity, it could be exercised even over individuals beyond his direct control. Within the context of domestic Ethiopian politics, its effect was to suck decision-making into the court. Decisions of the most trivial kind had to come to the emperor for formal approval, and patronage especially attracted his personal attention. Most important of all, it became impossible for any politician to build up any personal political base, or indeed any personal reputation, beyond that provided by the emperor. To some extent, powers might be delegated, or the imperial confidence used, in such a way as to give special status to some particular politician. The most powerful minister of Haile-Selassie's reign, Wolde-Giorgis Wolde-Yohannes, held from 1941 until 1955 the post of *tsahafe tezaz*, or Minister of the Pen, an office whose powers consisted essentially in writing down and issuing the emperor's verbal orders. But, as this example graphically illustrates, power could not be exercised independently of the emperor; it could only be exercised as something which descended directly from him. One of the ground rules of the system was that any commendable development had to be presented as the result of the emperor's personal wisdom and benevolence; while at the same time, Haile-Selassie remained extremely adept at avoiding responsibility for anything that went amiss.[14]

In its way, this system worked extremely well. The manipulation of different factions, for example, helped to maintain a variety of viewpoints in the advice given to the emperor, and to give a stake in the system to individuals who were at daggers drawn with one another. An attempted *coup d'état* led by the trusted commander of the imperial bodyguard in December 1960 helped to demonstrate the strength of the system, since the bodyguard commander was defeated by rival military leaders who mounted a rescue operation in the emperor's defence. It was equally characteristic that in the wake of the *coup*'s failure, Haile-Selassie did not engage in any widespread repression, but sought instead to undercut the bases of opposition by bringing a new generation of younger and more liberal ministers into government. There were nonetheless severe limitations in what a system of this kind could do. It was eminently adapted to manipulating individuals, once these could be identified. Potential opponents could be flattered with the award of titles, rewarded by grants of land or political office (ambassadorships were a common form of comfortable exile), while reminded with an occasional touch of the whip that these benefits were conditional on good behaviour. It was on the other hand entirely incapable of dealing with any social movement or grouping which went beyond the scale of a small court faction; and in reducing politics to the level of the court, the regime cut itself off from a wider and ultimately much more important set of political constituencies which were developing in the country at large.

The most obvious of these constituencies were the products of imperial modernisation itself. There were few features of 'modern' Ethiopia on which Haile-Selassie so publicly prided himself as the educational system. He long retained a titular tenure of the Ministry of Education, and much play was made of the fact that he had donated his own palace to be the centre of the new Haile Sellassie I University. (There were, fortunately, two others that he could use instead.) He sedulously fostered the symbolic links between himself and the educational system, and formally received students going abroad for education on their departure and return. Despite all this activity, the alienation of tertiary and increasingly even secondary level students from the regime grew progressively greater. The first major crack in the façade appeared in December 1960, when university students demonstrated in favour of the momentarily successful military *coup*. The years from then until the revolution were punctuated by student strikes and demonstrations, the occasional closure of the university or police invasion of the campus, and other indications of dissent. Abroad, Ethiopian students took enthusiastically to Marxism, and formed the factions which were to emerge after the revolution as the starting points for a series of would-be civilian Marxist–Leninist parties. These students expressed more a general sense of alienation from the regime than any very specific grievances. The issues which prompted student dissent were often purely symbolic. Students were drawn on the whole from the more privileged sectors of urban society, and could expect to be appointed to reasonably well-paid government posts on graduation. Though they demonstrated in favour of 'Land to the Tiller', they generally had little conception of conditions in the countryside. Yet for these very reasons, their detestation of imperial government was all the more significant, indicating its failure to attract the loyalty of those who would gain from it and on whom it would directly rely.[15]

Less public but still more threatening indications of alienation came from the armed forces. Here again, the 1960 bodyguard *coup* provided the first overt indication of the regime's incapacity to control the forces which it had created. In the immediate aftermath of the *coup*, the loyalist forces which had suppressed it used their enhanced political muscle to press for an increase in pay. Further semi-covert pressure led to further increases in 1964 and later years. Many of the junior officers shared the students' disgust with what struck them as the unprogressive inadequacy of imperial government, apparently dedicated to little more than the gross adulation of an aging puppet. Their contempt extended to the small group of senior officers, often with aristocratic connections, who were admitted to the charmed circle of the court and rewarded with land grants and other favours. Contacts between students and junior officers were closer than might be expected. In contrast to most armies, where the officers are normally volunteers even though the other ranks may be conscripts, Ethiopia had volunteer other ranks with a partly conscripted officer corps. During the period of the army's rapid expansion in the 1950s and early 1960s, the best secondary-school students were often compelled to join the army, and nursed a lasting resentment against a government which sent them to serve in distant and inhospitable areas like Eritrea and the Ogaden, while their contemporaries gained professional or civil-service jobs in Addis Ababa. Army officers in the capital frequently attended evening classes at the university, and were affected by the prevailing climate of ideas; quite a number of these officers, indeed, later held high office in the revolutionary regime. Though the armed forces imbibed the nationalist and centralising traditions of Ethiopian government, they thus had no reason to associate these with the maintenance of an anachronistic imperial regime.

A third element in the modern urban structure of Ethiopian government, the bureaucracy, was less evidently alienated than either students or armed forces. Though foreign-educated Ethiopians, especially, often had considerable difficulties in reintegrating themselves into local society, for the most part they accepted the comforts of a government job, and the limitations on political action which this implied.[16] Much of this may well have been the protective colouration at which Ethiopians (and indeed bureaucrats) have long been adept, and the progressive radicalisation of all sectors of Ethiopian urban society from the mid 1960s onwards must certainly have affected government officials. But at all events, the bureaucracy seems to have made little positive contribution to the upheavals that followed.

Finally, among the urban groups, there were the great unrepresented: urban workers, petty traders, the innumerable hangers-on in one kind of semi-employment or another, down to the lumpenproletariat with which Addis Ababa was as well provided as any other major African city. Trade unions were recognised following the issuing of a Labour Relations Decree in 1962, and by the early 1970s the Confederation of Ethiopian Labour Unions (CELU) had a membership of about 55,000, heavily concentrated in Addis Ababa and satellite towns along the line of rail to the coast.[17] The right to strike was formally recognised though severely limited in practice. The trade unions were to take an active role in the upheavals which followed from 1974 onwards, and the conflict for control of them was often violent. Since union membership was small and workplace-based, the unions were however far less significant than the local neighbourhood associations, known as idir, which as in many African cities helped to provide the local social services which were beyond the scope of government. The idir, rather than the unions, were to form the basis for the mass involvement of urban dwellers in the revolution.

The imperial regime thus had on its doorstep large numbers of people whom it could not control, and who became progressively more alienated from it, ranging from students and young army officers at one end of the spectrum to the poorest of the poor at the other. These were in themselves quite sufficient to overthrow it. The revolution was, in its early phase, an urban event, owing nothing at all to rural opposition. Even the impact of the famine in Wollo made itself felt through its effect on urban groups, not through any action by the famine victims themselves. But a revolution that was solely the result of urban alienation might have been expected to give rise simply to an urban modernising regime, which would sweep away the monarchy, replace it by some more radical form of government appealing to disfranchised urban groups, and leave the countryside undisturbed. It might even be possible to envisage a conflict between the 'modernisers' entrenched in the new regime in Addis Ababa, and the 'conservatives' or 'traditionalists' who gained their support from the countryside.

In fact, no such scenario was realised because the assumptions on which it was based were, largely at least, illusory. There was no traditional countryside waiting to be mobilised on behalf of the imperial regime, because that regime had cut itself off from the countryside even more effectively than it had done from the towns. The effects of monarchical centralisation in reducing the capacity of the regional nobility to act as intermediaries between central government and the countryside have already been discussed. Almost nothing was put in their place, save for a hierarchical administrative structure, often manned by central appointees from Shoa rather than by natives of the region itself, and largely directed to the basic functions of security and public order. The one partial exception was the House of Representatives, the lower house of the Parliament (balanced by an imperially appointed Senate) which, under the Revised Constitution of 1955, was from 1957 elected at four-yearly intervals by adult suffrage. To some extent – for example in debates over a proposed agricultural income tax – this assembly did indeed articulate rural interests.[18] It was nonetheless far too weakly organised at both central and local levels to bridge the gulf between the two. At the centre, it had some legislative responsibilities, but was totally divorced from the executive role of government, and had no connections with the court circles through which government was carried on. The Senate had such connections, but only in the sense that it served as a parking lot for semi-retired or out of favour notables; it was derisively known as the 'garage'. At the local level, the absence of any kind of party system prevented representatives from organising any political base which extended beyond their own constituencies and personalities. It served as a means by which local gentry or petty officials (especially, as so often in Africa, schoolteachers) could project themselves onto the fringes of Addis Ababa political life, but their inability either to create a local organisation or to meet their electoral promises to their constituents led to a high turnover at elections.[19] In southern regions, elections were sometimes flagrantly rigged to favour central settlers and officials over the indigenous population.[20] The whole institution died without a whimper in 1974.

The imperial regime's inability to construct linkages with regional political interests was most sharply demonstrated in Eritrea. This region, an Italian colony from 1890 to 1941, then came under British administration until 1952, when it was federated with Ethiopia by decision of the United Nations General Assembly, as part of the post-war disposal of the colonies of the defeated powers. Ethiopia pressed strongly for 'reunification' with Eritrea, much of which had indeed formed part of Ethiopia before 1890. The Unionist Party, though financed and heavily backed by the Ethiopian government, also had an effective level of local organisation, especially through the Orthodox Church in Christian areas of Eritrea, and won nearly half the seats in the first elections to the Eritrean Assembly.[21] Yet the imperial government's incapacity to capitalise on this favourable position was such that, long before its demise, it faced an effective guerilla insurgency not only in the western lowlands (where the bulk of the population was in any event hostile) but in much of the highlands as well. Central governments throughout Africa have generally been entirely unwilling to accept federal arrangements (or indeed any limitation on their powers) negotiated as part of the decolonisation settlement, and in this respect the Ethipian regime was no different from any other. The Eritrean government was from the start regarded as a threat and its freedom of action whittled away, until in 1962 the Eritrean Assembly was induced, under heavy central pressure, to vote for its own abolition and the full incorporation of Eritrea as an ordinary region into the Ethiopian empire. The party system which had developed under the British administration had already been abolished, and the means used to maintain support for the central government within the region amounted to little more than personal palliatives like the awarding of titles to local notables and an ambassadorship to the ousted head of the former Eritrean government. In the political vacuum that resulted, the Eritrean Liberation Front and its successors had an open field in which to organise guerilla opposition.[22]

The same inadequacy was however present even in regions where its effects were not so obvious or so disastrous. In some areas, like the Somali-inhabited territory in the south-east, the central government tried to win local clients by personal favours (with titles again to the fore) and the manipulation of rivalries between different Somali clans; but this was largely because the Somalis, with their access to the Somali government across the frontier in Mogadishu, had external links and presented a major security threat. Other peoples were either ignored (like the Afar of the Red Sea lowlands) or subjected to an insensitive and often exploitative central domination. Sometimes this gave rise to revolt; the Wako Guto rebellion in Bale in the late 1960s and early 1970s provides one example.[23] More often, it merely fostered a resentment with no evident political outlet.

Exactly the same was true of the 'core' Amhara areas. Even though these were not subjected to settlement by outsiders, land alienation, or the creation of a cash-crop economy for expropriation by central elites, the political mechanisms connecting them with central government were as weak (or non-existent) as in the conquered territories to the south. The most striking example of this weakness was provided by an uprising in Gojjam in 1968.[24] The culmination of a long period of Gojjami resentment against Shoan governors appointed from Addis Ababa, armed opposition broke out following promulgation of an Agricultural Income Tax Proclamation, which was interpreted by the peasantry as threatening their ancestral rights in land. The measurement of land required by the proclamation was forcibly resisted, and peace was only restored after the removal of the regional governor-general and a number of subordinate provincial governors. Ultimately, the issue was resolved without extensive bloodshed, but it dramatically illustrated the absence of any 'normal' channels through which political demands even in the Amhara highlands could be brought to the attention of central government. A similar lesson can be drawn from the 1973–74 famine in Wollo, a notoriously ill-governed region under the titular rule of Haile-Selassie's eldest son. The revolutionary charges that the imperial government 'covered up' the famine have a substantial basis of truth.[25] But what emerges from the episode is not simply or even mainly the callous abandonment of the peasantry to their deaths, but rather the total inadequacy of the mechanisms by which information about the disaster could be brought to the attention of the government in Addis Ababa, and any appropriate action obtained. It was necessary to cover up the government's inaction, because there was no way of producing action.

The result of this neglect was that when the crisis of the regime eventually erupted in 1974, not only was the imperial regime unable to call on the countryside to make up for its loss of support in the towns, but there were also a great many rural grievances which the new government could use to extend its own support to the countryside. Such grievances were often hard to mobilise, especially for a military government which inherited the centralising ethos of its predecessor. Sometimes they were mobilised against the regime rather than in its favour. In either event, they were a legacy of the way in which the old regime had cut itself off from the rural Ethiopia from which its own strength had originally derived.

THE DEBACLE

The events of 1974 which led to the collapse of the empire and its replacement by a radical military regime have often been described.[26] Far from constituting a *coup d'état* in the normal sense of the word, they consisted in a series of mutinies, strikes and demonstrations through which all of the elements in the potential urban opposition to the regime were progressively mobilised, and in a series of desperate countermeasures through which the imperial government unsuccessfully sought to stave off impending collapse.

The first and, throughout, most important of the urban groups was the armed forces. The first identifiable incident in the continuum that culminated in Haile-Selassie's overthrow was a mutiny by soldiers and NCOs in a small garrison at Neghelle in southern Sidamo in January 1974. Though the mutiny itself was simply over living conditions, the arrest by the mutineers of the senior officers sent to investigate it gave it political overtones, and indicated the powerlessness of the regime in the face of military dissent. The following month, the first demonstrations broke out in the capital. Teachers and students were alarmed by the implications of an education sector review which proposed an expansion of basic education in the countryside, and a relative restriction of secondary and university education in the towns. Taxi-drivers went on strike against the government's refusal to let them raise fares in response to the OPEC oil price rise – one of the few points at which upheavals in the international economy impinged on a generally domestic political process. Before the end of February, further and much more dangerous mutinies had broken out in the Second Division in Asmara, the Fourth Division headquartered in Addis Ababa, and the air force base near Addis Ababa. In part at least, these may have been fomented by aristocratic groups within the court, using their military connections – in a manoeuvre altogether characteristic of court administrations – to get rid of the prime minister, Aklilu Habte-Wold, an imperial protégé whom they saw as a threat to their own position.[27] If so, they had called up a monster which they were unable to control.

Aklilu was replaced as prime minister on 28 February by Endalkachew Makonnen, a liberal aristocrat who saw Ethiopia's constitutional development as lying, along broadly English lines, in the creation of a constitutional monarchy in which effective power would be devolved from the emperor to the aristocracy and gentry, and ultimately doubtless down to the people. He established a commission which set about drawing up a constitution on these lines. The effort was, inevitably, futile, and his brief tenure of office was entirely preoccupied with a losing battle for survival. Within days of his appointment there were large student demonstrations in Addis Ababa, and the trade unions – rather belatedly getting in on the act – declared a national strike.

The liberalisation measures which the new government declared were in these circumstances little more than an admission of its own loss of control, the hiatus between one dictatorship and the next. There were those who saw in the events of mid 1974 the genesis of a new, peaceful and democratic Ethiopia, aborted by the army's seizure of power and ruthless imposition of its own brand of centralising socialism. I cannot agree. The mobilisation of new groups with new demands was genuine enough, and set the context within which the military regime had to operate; but there was no sign at all of any political structure within which these demands could be peacefully settled. The imperial system was too thoroughly discredited in the eyes of most of the major urban groups to be acceptable even as a unifying symbol of national identity; and it was in any event unlikely that a purely titular monarchy could have been reconciled with the close connection in Ethiopian political culture between authority and the actual exercise of power. There was at no point any of that willingness to tolerate alternative viewpoints within an accepted set of political institutions which provides the essentials of liberal government. And beneath it all, there were real problems to be resolved, which were only intensified by the popular upsurge of 1974: problems of central political power, of economic control, and most basically of ethnic identity and national unity. It is certainly true that the military government which eventually came to power engaged in acts of gratuitous violence that exacerbated conflicts (especially in Eritrea) which might have been more skilfully and less brutally managed, given a willingness to compromise. But this brutality did not prevent the establishment of a liberal and democratic system of government – an option which was simply never available.

The armed forces were initially no more united or prepared than any section of the civilian population. Some, notably in the air force, were from the start bent on the overthrow of the monarchy and the establishment of a radical or even revolutionary regime. Others were concerned about the dangers of popular mobilisation – a large demonstration by Moslems in mid April, for example, indicated the threat presented to national unity as the government's hold slackened – and were prepared to suppress it. And in a situation in which every conceivable group was attempting to press its demands, the armed forces were ineluctably drawn into the conflict, both by other groups who hoped to use them for their own ends, and as actors in their own right.

The key question was then whether they would be able to achieve some kind of common front, or whether they would split apart (as had happened in the attempted 1960 *coup*) into different factions and units which would end by fighting one another. In the event, surprisingly, a common front was attained, through a device unique in the long history of military regimes.

This was the Derg – a little used Amharic word for committee – formed as a parliament of the armed forces, with representatives from each of the main units of the army, air force, navy and police, and a total membership of a hundred and eight. Though the date of its formation is now formally celebrated as 27 June 1974, it drew on various coordinating committees which existed before that date, and even after its formation acted not as a military government, but as a semi-clandestine power coexisting (and often competing) with the official regime. It soon began to act in ways which the government was powerless to prevent, especially in arresting some 200 leading figures of the old regime. On 8 July it issued its first policy statement, under the motto 'Ityopya tikdem' or Ethiopia First, though this was a vague and reformist document still promising loyalty to the throne. The armed forces were still as uncertain about what to do as anyone else, and the function of the Derg – riven as it was by personal, factional and policy disputes – was not so much to resolve differences, as to provide a forum within which these could be fought out without spreading to wider conflict between units of the armed forces as a whole. It likewise provided the setting for the emergence of a new revolutionary leadership, among whom Mengistu Haile-Mariam, then a major from the Third Division stationed in Harar, soon acquired a position of prominence.

Endalkachew's government, powerless to prevent the arrest even of its own members, was forced to resign on 22 July. His successor, Michael Imru, was an Oxford-educated nobleman from exactly the same social and educational background, who inherited much of the aura of radicalism and honesty attached to his father, Ras Imru. In the event, it did not make much difference. The Derg, acting increasingly like a government, proceeded to arrest the emperor's associated, nationalise his assets, and abolish the court institutions through which it believed his power to be exercised. On 12 September 1974, Haile-Selassie was formally deposed, and the Derg (which took on the title of Provisional Military Administrative Council) started to issue proclamations in its own name.

The process leading to Haile-Selassie's deposition was, it should be noted, entirely an urban one. The countryside neither came to his support, nor helped in his overthrow. The famine in Wollo was used to generate urban opposition to the regime – for example, by showing a television film which contrasted the starvation of the peasants with the luxury in which the emperor lived – rather than as a means of mobilising rural dissent, and the issue of what to do about the countryside was not confronted until after the military seizure of power.

3

The mobilisation phase, 1974–1978

The collapse of the old regime was one thing; the question of what would replace it was quite another. It is plausible enough to regard the fall of the imperial government as inevitable. It simply lacked the resources either of political organisation, or of political legitimacy, which it would have needed to withstand an uprising of urban discontent which could have been prompted by any number of issues, and which rapidly gained in intensity as the bankruptcy of the regime became ever more obvious. It was also predictable that it would be replaced by a much more radical regime, and given the position of the armed forces as the sole available source of organised political power, that this would be a military one. Ethiopia was classic territory for what Huntington has called a breakthrough *coup*, launched as in Egypt in 1952 or Libya in 1969 by a group of young officers with a strong nationalist ideology, determined to propel their country into a process of rapid modernisation which the old regime, in their eyes at least, had evidently failed to achieve.[1] It was at the same time far from inevitable that the new regime would take the course that it did. The officer corps of the armed forces, though certainly more radically inclined than the imperial government, nonetheless shared both social links and political and economic interests with it. Mengistu Haile-Mariam himself was brought up in the household of a Dajazmatch (second highest, after Ras, of the old titles of nobility) closely linked with the imperial court. Army officers as a class were one of the main beneficiaries of the imperial land-grant policy which gave them a vested interest in the existing structure of landholding in the south, and many of them also were drawn from neftenya or settler families. Haile-Selassie's basic goal of creating a centralised state structure was one which the military shared, since they owed their existence to it. The simplest explanation for why they eventually overthrew him was that they no longer needed his presence in order to achieve it, and sought to replace a process of nationalist centralisation which they regarded as outmoded and corrupt,

41

by a similar process, guided by themselves, which would instead be dynamic and efficient.

The early performance of the Derg, moreover, suggested little more than a fairly straightforward radical nationalism, stopping well short of revolution. Its slogan – it was far from a policy – of *Ityopya tikdem* (Ethiopia First) was nationalism of the vaguest kind, and the initial programme issued in early July 1974 was equally anodyne, combining commitment to the monarchy and to national unity with an attack on corruption and a call for 'lasting changes'.[2] The caution and gradualness with which the Derg co-ordinated its activities from June 1974 onwards suggested – however misleadingly, in the light of later events – that the young officers who managed it were willing and able to work with the more enlightened of the existing politicians on a programme of accelerated reform. Since they rode to power on an upsurge of strikes and demonstrations, they could easily be (and were) suspected of using popular discontent with the existing regime merely as a pretext for putting themselves in its place. The politicians who were progressively arrested from July 1974 onwards could be seen as the scapegoats of the Derg's drive against corruption, and were largely drawn from the group of courtier–bureaucrats who had been hand-picked by the emperor, and were left exposed by his failing ability to protect them. The selection of Michael Imru, a liberal aristocrat, as prime minister helped to maintain the façade of continuity; and even after Haile-Selassie's deposition, the man appointed to head the government was a senior and respected general, Aman Andom, who owed his reputation to his energetic handling of a brief frontier war with Somalia in 1964, and had participated in the liberation campaign of 1941. The Crown Prince, who was sick and in London, was named as titular king in his father's place. It is possible, and indeed with hindsight quite plausible, to argue that this transition – which in any event was handled with extraordinary skill – was part of a carefully orchestrated process through which a group of committed revolutionaries slowly worked their way into a position from which they could grasp unchallengeable power. But that position had not been attained by the time that Haile-Selassie was removed, and demands for revolutionary change came more from outside the military than from the people who actually held power. All the options appeared to be open.

A large part of the explanation for the course which the revolution took must lie in the mobilisation of the towns, and especially Addis Ababa, from February 1974 onwards. It was, ultimately, the revolution that made the Derg, rather than the Derg that made the revolution. Even though the particular course of events was often determined by rhetoric and manoeuvre within the group of military representatives who found themselves at the centre of events, the framework within which they operated was set by events outside. None of the policies which were to turn the Ethiopian experience into a revolution, rather than a radical military regime of the kind, say, that Nimairi formed in Sudan, appear to have originated within the Derg itself. Many of them, notably land reform, drew on the ideas which had gained currency among the student community over the previous decade. Others, such as the arming of the Addis Ababa kebelles, or the raising of a huge peasant militia, were desperate responses to an immediate crisis. Overwhelmingly the most important channel through which these policies were put onto the political agenda, at least in the early days, was through the personal contacts between radical intellectuals and individual members of the Derg. It was in this way that Derg members became familiar with Marxist ideas that they would certainly not have encountered in the course of their military training, and started to consider the possibility of far deeper changes than any of their early pronouncements envisaged. Senay Likie, a Marxist intellectual who had contacts especially in the air force, appears to have been particularly influential.

To understand how these ideas came to be accepted and implemented, it is essential to bear in mind that the Derg came to power in a situation in which the Ethiopian state appeared to be collapsing with the monarchy that had created it. In a society founded on a Hobbesian conception of the centrality of power relations to the maintenance of public order, the removal of a once-dominant authority figure always carried the threat of anarchy. In Addis Ababa, the failure of imperial authority unleashed an upsurge of demands which could not simply be suppressed, but for which some outlet had to be found. The more radical groups within the Derg were able to capitalise on these demands, at just the time when those who favoured reformist or even conservative solutions were left uncertain about whether anything could be salvaged from the old order to provide a basis for continuity. In the fullness of time, too, the weakening of central control was bound to spread to the regions and the countryside, whether this took the form of a resurgence of organised opposition – most obviously in Eritrea, where the guerilla secessionist movements were at rather a low ebb by 1974 – or of spontaneous resistance to central rule and to the landowning class in southern Ethiopia. Something had to be done, and from a reformist viewpoint, it was not at all clear what. So far from being imposed as part of a 'revolution from above', many of the measures which made the Ethiopian experience a revolutionary one appear to have been induced as *ad hoc* responses to pressures from below.

The period after Haile-Selassie's overthrow was marked by cautious manoeuvring between the formal head of government, General Aman, and the more radical groups inside the Derg. Aman was not a member of the Derg, and although he was both prime minister and minister of defence, his actual position was weak. He did not control the military, since the Derg had its own links with each unit, and on the two main issues of the day he favoured reconciliation while his opponents favoured force. In each case, indeed, his own position left him little alternative. He could scarcely support the execution of leading figures of the old regime, whom he had known in many cases for over thirty years; and as an Eritrean by origin himself

43

(though his own career in the Ethiopian government long predated the 1952 federation), he favoured negotiation with the Eritrean secessionist groups, and paid two successful visits to the region, where he appeared to be gaining wide support. He saw the change of regime as providing the basis for a settlement in which the Eritreans would receive a substantial measure of autonomy, while remaining part of a single Ethiopian state. It is by no means certain that he was right, even though the opportunity was a better one than had been presented before, or would be again. He would have had to win over or outflank the rival Eritrean liberation movements, and even had a settlement been agreed, the old issue of autonomy against centralisation remained to be resolved, and would have raised, in somewhat altered form, many of the same problems as the earlier federal arrangement after 1952. In any event, the option was never tried. The nationalism of the majority on the Derg was not prepared to allow, so soon after their takeover of power, the concessions to regionalist – and ultimately perhaps secessionist – political forces that Aman's approach would have required. Mengistu Haile-Mariam gained the Derg's approval for the sending of 5,000 additional troops to Eritrea – a move which would have nullified Aman's attempts at settlement – and on the night of 22 November, Aman was attacked and killed at his house. The possibility of a peaceful process of political accommodation, always a difficult option, died with him.

While the Eritrean issue was in some degree forced on the Derg, the issue of what to do with the old politicians was made by it, not presented to it. These people posed no threat of any kind. They were largely courtiers, and few, if any, of them had any base from thish they could, even if released, mobilise any opposition to the new regime. Their power had derived from the emperor, and disappeared with him. Their arrest had been treated with either indifference or satisfaction, and had aroused scarcely a ripple of popular dissent. It was widely expected that they would be imprisoned and their property confiscated, but that eventually they would be released into obscure retirement or allowed to make their way into harmless exile abroad. The Derg's announcement on 24 November to a stunned Ethiopian people, that fifty-seven former officials had been executed 'in accordance with its political decision' thus marked a critical point in the development of the revolution. Opinions differ as to what it was intended to achieve. From one viewpoint, perhaps the most plausible given the conditions of the time, the killings were an act of desperation, duplicating the action of the December 1960 *coup* leaders, who had shot their hostages at the moment when the failure of their attempt became clear: an assertion that, even if the whole revolutionary movement collapsed, some things would never be the same again. From another viewpoint, benefiting perhaps from hindsight, they might be seen as a calculated act of policy (behind which the hand of Mengistu Haile-Mariam would inevitably be discerned), designed to bind the squabbling members of the Derg into a shared complicity for bloodshed, and make it clear that they were set on a course from which there was no turning back. At all events, the crisis passed. The violent reaction, if one was expected, failed to materialise. The new chairman of the PMAC, Brigadier General Teferi Banti, was like Aman not a member of the Derg itself, but was brought in from his previous position as commander of the Second Division. Mengistu became the first vice-chairman, while the second vice-chairman, Major Atnafu Abate, was a Gojjami army officer who had played an important role in the Derg's original establishment.

THE GREAT REFORMS, DECEMBER 1974–JULY 1975

In the aftermath of the November executions, the political position of the new regime was nonetheless precarious. It had destroyed any possibility of reconciliation with the remnants of the old regime, or indeed with liberal reformists of any kind. It had equally rejected any compromise not simply on the possibility of secession, which could in any event have been excluded, but even on the establishment of regional autonomy of the sort that Aman had evidently been prepared to offer the Eritreans. Nor was its position secure with the politically mobilised groups in the towns which had opened the way to its own seizure of power. These were both suspicious of the armed forces, and anxious to gain the benefits from the overthrow of the imperial system which they saw themselves (justifiably enough) as having brought about. Within a few days of Haile-Selassie's overthrow, both a student demonstration and the annual conference of the Confederation of Ethiopian Labour Unions (CELU) had called for the formation of a civilian government.[3] A set of proclamations issued on 16 November, for the establishment of special courts martial, amendment of the Penal Code, and public order and safety, were clearly directed at the repression of urban dissent.[4]

The Derg's first attempt to formulate a policy, in the ten-point programme issued on 20 December 1974, sought a way out through the combination of nationalism and socialism appropriate to a radical military regime[5]

1 Ethiopia shall remain a united country, without ethnic, religious, linguistic and cultural differences.
2 Ethiopia wishes to see the setting up of an economic, cultural and social community with Kenya, Sudan and Somalia.
3 The slogan Ethiopia Tikdem of the Ethiopian revolution is to be based on a specifically Ethiopian socialism.
4 Every regional administration and every village shall manage its own resources and be self-sufficient.
5 A great political party based on the revolutionary philosophy of Ethiopia Tikdem shall be constituted on a nationalist and socialist basis.
6 The entire economy shall be in the hands of the state. All assets existing in Ethiopia are by right the property of the Ethiopian people. Only

a limited number of businesses will remain private if they are deemed to be of public utility.

7 The right to own land shall be restricted to those who work the land.

8 Industry will be managed by the state. Some private enterprises deemed to be of public utility will be left in private hands until the state considers it preferable to nationalize them.

9 The family, which will be the fundamental basis of Ethiopian society, will be protected against all foreign influences, vices and defects.

10 Ethiopia's existing foreign policy will be essentially maintained. The new regime will however endeavour to strengthen good-neighbourly relations with all neighbouring countries.

This programme remained the basic statement of the government's aims until the Programme of the National Democratic Revolution appeared nearly a year and a half later, and despite its radical nationalist tone concealed important ambivalences, which were to surface over the course of the revolution. The first article, in simply denying the existence of ethnic and related differences, obscured the conflict between an assimilationist nationalism (in which differences would be abolished) and the recognition of separate 'nationalities' on an equal basis, which would underlie the whole problem of national integration. The conservative provisions on foreign policy were to prove incompatible with the international implications of revolution, while in the management of the economy, the emphasis on the state was at odds with the references to regional autonomy and the idea of land to the tiller. In the event, neither of these last two principles was implemented, while the party, with which many of these contradictions were bound up, did not come into existence for a further ten years.

The most straightforward provision to put into effect was that on the nationalisation of private companies, and this took place almost immediately. Banks, insurance companies and other financial institutions were nationalised on 1 January 1975, and seventy-two other private commercial and industrial companies followed on 3 February. These measures accounted for all of the major foreign-owned concerns, though some companies owned by individual Ethiopians escaped. A Declaration on the Economic Policy of Socialist Ethiopia, issued on 7 February, laid down areas of the economy reserved for government, for joint ventures between government and private capital (in such areas as mining and tourism), and for private enterprise.[6] Since no compensation for nationalised assets was agreed for many years, and the government reserved the right to nationalise any other company at any time, it is not surprising that no new foreign private investment was forthcoming.

The nationalisations were a fairly standard measure of a kind adopted by populist socialist governments in many parts of the third world, and – in a country which had insignificant mineral resources and in which the production of export cash crops was largely in peasant hands – fell a long way

46

short of any seizure of the 'commanding heights' of the economy. The measure which, far more than any other, established the revolutionary credentials of the Ethiopian regime was, rather, the nationalisation of rural land which followed in March 1975. This abolished not only private owner-ship of land, but also all of the myriad tenures through which land had hitherto been farmed in Ethiopia, and with them the everlasting legal dis-putes to which land tenure was subject. In those parts of the country, notably the south, where large areas were owned by landlords, the entire economic basis for this class was removed at a stroke. Contrary to the implications of the ten-point programme, however, ownership of this (or any other) land was not then vested in the peasants who farmed it. Instead, formal owner-ship of the land was retained by the state, while its management was entrusted to peasants' associations, which were formed to cover areas of, in principle, at least 800 hectares each. The association was then responsible for allocating land as equally as possible to farming families within its area, subject to a maximum of ten hectares a family.[7] In practice this maximum was rarely if ever reached, and actual holdings were much lower, down to an average of only half a hectare in some places.

The basic provision under which all rural lands became 'the collective property of the Ethiopian people' had very different effects, and hence political implications, depending on the existing pattern of tenure. For tenant farmers and landless peasants, the abolition of land ownership removed a major source of exploitation in the one case, and provided guaranteed access to land in the other. They could obviously be expected to support the land reform, and the government which introduced it. Indeed, the effect of the proclamation was to provide them with a benefit which no opposition group could hope to outbid, and thus to secure the loyalty of much of the country – broadly speaking, the centre, south and west – during the critical period which the regime needed to consolidate its hold. The losers equally obviously included the former landlords, now abruptly reduced to a status no greater than that of their former tenants, and many of them took to the hills in violent opposition to the government; several of the great lords, notably Ras Mengesha Seyoum in Tigray, had already done so following the November killings. But more important, peasants who owned their own land, or who enjoyed customary tenures of one sort or another which gave them effective control over it, were also threatened by a measure which removed their security and put them on an equal basis with the land-less. A rough and ready guide to acceptance of the reform is therefore pro-vided by the percentages of farmers owning their own land in each region. This ranged from 83 per cent to 93 per cent in the four northern highland regions of Tigray, Gonder, Gojjam and Wollo, to a mere 27 per cent in Illubabor, with the remainder (apart from Bale and Eritrea, for which data are not available) lying between 41 per cent and 63 per cent.[8] These figures conceal both variations within regions (such as Shoa, which ranges from a pure 'northern' pattern in some areas to a pure 'southern' one in others), and

47

also the extent to which in some regions (such as Hararghe) owner–farmers were settlers from the north, rather than local peasants. Then again, in some regions (such as Gojjam) the new system might be fairly readily assimilated to existing institutions, whereas in others this was much more difficult. The results will be examined in later chapters; overall, however, land reform was critically important in defining who would be in favour of the new regime, and who would be against it.

This measure not only destroyed the landlord class, but had other far-reaching effects. The peasants' association became the base unit of local political power, replacing a system which had previously rested in part on landownership, in part on an amalgam of government office and local status. And the destruction of the landlord system also removed the means by which a surplus had been extracted from the peasantry for distribution in the towns. This was eventually replaced by a new marketing system controlled by the state; but in the immediate aftermath of land reform, peasants often ate better than ever before while the cities (and especially Addis Ababa) came close to starvation.

Land reform also affected agricultural production. The received wisdom of the pre-reform period had been that the peasantry, freed from landlord exploitation, would have the incentive to increase production from which they would now be the main beneficiaries. To some extent, this happened. Food production appears to have risen fairly sharply in the two years after reform, and recovery from the effects of the 1973–74 famine was rapid. In the longer term, however, other factors came into play. The guarantee of land to all peasants within an association resulted in still greater pressure on often overcultivated areas, leading to reductions in the size of plots, a lessening of the emigration which had previously helped to maintain a balance between local production and consumption, and an increase in agricultural and ecological degradation which was to culminate, under pressure of drought, in the catastrophe of 1984.

Areas which were already farmed as large single units, either by Ethiopian landowners or in a few cases by foreign companies, were excluded from break-up and redistribution, and turned into state farms. Smaller commercial farms were either divided up, or farmed as peasant cooperatives. Workers on state farms thus lost the chance to acquire their own land, and continued under state rather than private employment. The area involved was not very large – perhaps some 2 per cent of arable land – and was heavily concentrated both geographically and by crop. The major concentrations were in the Rift Valley, notably the foreign-owned sugar and cotton plantations, with some private grain farms in the Arsi highlands, and the large area of sesame cultivation around Humera on the Sudanese border.[9] Produce from these, of course, was directly available to the state. Peasant farmers, however, grew not only by far the greater part of the marketable food surplus, but also almost all of the major export crop, coffee. Land reform thus brought only a very small proportion of the agricultural surplus under the government's direct control.

The government had no administrative machine which was able, even had it been willing, to implement the land reform. The imperial administration at local level had been drawn from just those groups which had been most disadvantaged by it; and even though the new regime had by February 1975 changed all regional and provincial administrators, the new appointees, in addition to their inexperience, were at times politically unreliable as well. In any event, they lacked the capacity to conduct so large an operation at so detailed a level. Even at the lowest level of administration, the district or woreda, there were on average over 70,000 people, of whom the great majority were peasant farmers. In practice, land reform was therefore overwhelmingly put into effect by the peasants themselves, and this was probably in any event the most efficient way to do it.

By far the most important external involvement in rural transformation came, not from government administrators, but from students and teachers organised into the National Development Through Co-operation Campaign, which was generally known as the zemecha. Without student leadership, indeed, it is doubtful whether the peasants – still uncertain of the government's intentions, and fearful of the possible consequences of seizing their own land – would have implemented land reform at all. This was the regime's first attempt at revolutionary mass mobilisation, and set the pattern for other campaigns – such as the literacy and villagisation campaigns – in later years. First mooted in August 1974, it was formally announced in October and actually launched in December. It mobilised the entire body of some 50,000 secondary and university students and teachers to go out into the countryside, propagate the aims of the revolution, encourage literacy and, once the land reform had been decreed, explain it to the peasants. Since it offered students the chance to participate in spreading the revolution to the countryside which they had demanded, they could scarcely refuse to take part, and many did so enthusiastically. Some hoped in this way to create for themselves a rural political base. For the Derg, it not only offered a rural mobilising force which was vastly more committed to the revolution than the remnants of the old provincial administration, but also removed students from Addis Ababa and other cities where they could directly threaten the regime.

The effects of the great zemecha have been superbly discussed by Lefort.[10] Thrust into a countryside with which many of them – due to an overwhelmingly urban pattern of educational recruitment – were entirely unfamiliar, the zemecha participants found themselves at the sharp end of all the tensions and conflicts implicit in the land reform, the nationalities question, and the divisions between city and countryside. In northern highland areas, where there was no major problem of land alienation or of local class or ethnic conflicts, they were often regarded with suspicion by the peasantry as the representatives of a government which had destroyed the comforting symbols of Christian and Amhara supremacy, was widely regarded as being dominated by Oromos and Moslems, and most importantly seemed to threaten their tenure of their own land. In the south, the situation much more closely corresponded to the students' stereotyped view of the country-side as consisting of overbearing landlords and exploited peasants, and they often enthusiastically collaborated with the local peasantry in expropriating (and sometimes killing) landlords, and setting up peasants' associations. The problem was that in propagating the socialist goals of the revolution, they risked threatening its nationalist ones, especially in areas where the structure of local administration was closely bound up with that of land tenure, and where land reform therefore implied an attack on the represen-tatives of central government. In areas such as Wollamo in northern Sidamo, where the zemecha was led by a charismatic teacher of local origin, Solomon Wada, this swiftly raised the spectre of ethnic nationalism and potentially secession. Solomon Wada was shot, and many of the participants crept back to the cities, disillusioned with the regime and inclined to support the violently anti-military Marxist party then forming in Addis Ababa, the Ethiopian People's Revolutionary Party or EPRP.

The land reform and the zemecha marked a critical phase in the revol-ution: its extension from an essentially urban affair to one which spread throughout most of Ethiopia. It is this extension, more than events in Addis Ababa no matter how violent or spectacular, which places Ethiopia firmly in the category of revolutionary states. The effects, inevitably, were mixed, and often resulted in the mobilisation of rural as well as urban political forces against the regime rather than in its favour – though at the crisis of the revolution in 1977–78 they made it possible to draw on the countryside for the recruits who swelled the revolutionary army and militia. Equally important, the base units were put in place for the framework of organis-ation which was eventually to link city to countryside in a way that had never been possible under the imperial regime.

The last of the great revolutionary measures, the nationalisation of urban land and extra houses announced on 26 July 1975, completed the expropri-ation of all major forms of individual wealth, apart from trade.[11] As in many third-world cities, urban housing had become one of the main forms of investment and accumulation by a rentier class of noblemen and bureau-crats. This ranged all the way from the appalling hovels of the urban poor to elegant villas which found a ready market among diplomats and expatriate experts in a city which – as the headquarters of the United Nations Economic Commission for Africa and the Organisation of African Unity – was rapidly developing into the diplomatic capital of the continent. The proclamation, which allowed each family to retain only a single dwelling for its own occu-pation and transferred all rented property to the state, destroyed the economic basis for this class as instantly and totally as land reform had done for rural landowners. Unlike rural reform, moreover, some of the surplus thus expropriated could be diverted directly into the national budget, though rent reductions were used to pass on some of the benefits, especially to the poor.

A still more important consequence of urban land nationalisation was the establishment of local institutions to administer rents and, progressively, to take on other administrative and political functions within the towns, providing an equivalent to the peasants' associations in the rural areas. Formally called urban dwellers' associations, these were universally known as kebelles, from an Amharic word meaning neighbourhood, which denoted the lowest level at which the associations were organised. Each kebelle, with only a few thousand inhabitants, was small enough for its leaders to know and control the local population, and control of the kebelles became the vital battleground in the struggle for power in the cities which was shortly to break out. Kebelles were grouped into 'highers' or keftenyas, and these in turn, in the largest cities, into zones. Once the government had won the battle for control of the towns, kebelles served as the ubiquitous basic units of urban administration.

The key elements in the revolutionary transformation of the Ethiopian economy and ultimately political system were thus in place within a few months of the Derg's seizure of power. The remaining ingredients – the vast increase in the size of the armed forces, the creation of the party, the shift in foreign policy, the literacy and villagisation campaigns, and so forth – can be seen as corollaries of these initial measures. What remained in doubt was whether the Derg would be able to retain the control, either over the cities or over the countryside, which their goal of a revolutionary and centralised state required.

THE CONTROL OF THE TOWNS, 1975–1978

The revolution had been launched, in 1974, by a variety of urban groups which possessed no unity of leadership, policy or organisation. It had been brought under the precarious control of a military regime which, depending as it did on a body of about a hundred men drawn from different ranks, regions and units, was likewise riven by personal, factional and policy disputes. The process by which, over the next three or four years, this chaos gave way to the effective dictatorship of the group within the Derg led by Mengistu Haile-Mariam is complex, controversial and extremely violent. A description of this process is nonetheless essential to an understanding of the development of the revolutionary regime.[12]

The major groups involved in the fight for the cities, all of them divided, were the Derg and the armed forces, the ideologues, teachers and students who could loosely be described as the intelligentsia, the organised workers and trade unionists, and the city mob or lumpenproletariat. Even though the Derg had been selected from the armed forces by a reasonably democratic process, by a year or so after its formation it could scarcely be regarded as

51

fully representative of them. Units soon discovered that they could not recall and replace the delegates whom they had originally chosen, and the successive purges of different factions moved it further and further to the left. Equally, though much of the Derg's membership was drawn from ordinary soldiers and NCOs, political leadership was exercised overwhelmingly by the officers. Legesse Asfaw, who had been a sergeant under Mengistu Haile-Mariam's command in the Third Division in the Ogaden, was the only non-officer to reach the top political leadership; and as the Derg acquired a committee structure, with committees on different areas of government and an executive Standing Committee, the position of the officers (who tended to belong to the Standing Committee and to chair the other committees) was institutionalised. Not until February 1977, when Mengistu succeeded in killing the Chairman, Teferi Banti, in a shoot-out in the old palace, did even the Derg provide a reasonably stable and controllable core for the regime. Teferi himself was no more than a compromise chairman, brought in from outside the Derg after the killing of Aman Andom, and other members who, like him, sought to curb the influence of Mengistu, were purged at one time or another. Two prominent officers in the Derg, Majors Sisay Habte and Kiros Alemayehu, each of whom might have provided alternative leadership to Mengistu, were killed in July 1976. A further round of killings marked Mengistu's elevation to the chairmanship in February 1977, and vice-chairman Atnafu Abate, the last Derg member who represented any threat to Mengistu, was killed in November 1977. In assessing the behaviour of leading members of the Derg, it is always necessary to remember that they have emerged from a period of extraordinary tension, in which the penalty for being on the wrong side was almost always death. This has inevitably reinforced the sense of secrecy, suspicion and intrigue carried over from the political culture of pre-revolutionary Ethiopia.

The intelligentsia was far more divided even than the armed forces, which could at least be relied on to hold by the core values of national unity and strong central government. Its leadership was largely derived from Marxist intellectuals who during Haile-Selassie's time had stayed in exile in Western Europe and the United States, and its divisions incongruously reflected the squabbles of impotent student politicians.[13] Following the upheavals of 1974, many of these returned home (often not arriving until 1975), and proceeded in collaboration with those inside the country to establish a set of would-be communist parties, each of which regarded itself as the rightful Marxist–Leninist vanguard which should eventually succeed to power. The two main factions came to form the All-Ethiopia Socialist Movement (which was generally known by its Amharic acronym, Meison), and the Ethiopian People's Revolutionary Party (known by its English acronym, EPRP). These differed in their origins, leadership, ethnic balance, goals, tactics and, most important of all, attitude to the Derg.

The leaders of Meison were drawn from a fairly broad range of central and southern intellectuals, several of whom had been educated in Europe and especially France. The most prominent of them, Haile Fida, was an Oromo from Welega, and this helped to give the movement something of an Oromo identity, but others included Fikre Merid, a Shoan aristocrat and son of Haile-Selassie's minister of defence. Though like virtually all of the student radicals, they believed in 'self-determination' for Ethiopia's numerous ethnic groups, they did not see this primarily in terms of secession, and this made some accommodation possible with the rigid nationalism of the Derg. The policy which they adopted was one of critical alliance with the Derg. Though (in common with almost all Ethiopian intellectuals) they retained a deep suspicion of the military, they believed that it would be possible to adopt the Derg, educate it, and in due course take over from it. To some extent, this strategy worked. Meison leaders are credited with an important role in persuading the Derg to adopt the policies on the nationalisation of companies, land, and urban housing which laid the basis for revolution. Meison members also took over some ministerial and administrative posts, and formed the core of the various civilian political organisations set up by the Derg in the early years of the revolution, notably the Yekatit '66 Political School and the Provisional Office of Mass Organizational Affairs (POMOA) established in December 1975. The Programme of the National Democratic Revolution, issued in April 1976, was also largely of Meison inspiration and provided the authoritative formal statement of national policy until the issuing of the programme of the WPE in 1984. The Derg for its part was badly in need of civilian allies through which to divide, penetrate and control the urban intelligentsia; but though the divisions within the Derg during the Teferi Banti period gave Meison a bargaining power which it later lost, it is extremely unlikely that the Derg ever intended to hand over any appreciable amount of power to Meison.

The Programme of the National Democratic Revolution served several purposes.[14] Within the Derg, it marked a seizure of the political initiative by Mengistu, who announced it, at the expense of other factions and especially the chairman, Teferi Banti – though Lefort's claim that Teferi only learned of it over the radio seems implausible.[15] Among civilian groups, it similarly established the position of Meison, and helped to provoke the reaction by its main rival, the EPRP, which was to lead to the terror. In terms of its effects on external alliances, its references to 'scientific socialism' and to the need to form a true proletarian vanguard party, helped persuade the Soviet Union that the revolution was following a Marxist–Leninist path, rather than sub-siding into bourgeois nationalism; the Soviet Union had already identified Mengistu as the leader of the 'revolutionary democratic' nucleus within the PMAC, and Russian writers referred to the programme with approval.[16] From an American viewpoint, conversely, it could only be seen as threatening. The programme itself, couched in Marxist–Leninist terms though without specifically mentioning Marx or Lenin, abandoned most of the ambivalence of the programme of December 1974, though on the critical issue of nationalities it steered a course between the nationalism of the Derg and the much greater willingness to accept 'self-determination' which Meison shared with the other civilian groups. Nationalities were to be accorded regional autonomy within a united Ethiopia, and the role of the armed forces in safeguarding the country's territorial integrity was also emphasised. In this, too, it could be seen as following a Soviet model.

A number of other political groupings allied themselves with the Derg, and differed from Meison more on personality than on policy or ideological grounds. The Labour League (generally known by its Amharic name, Waz, or the hybrid Wazleague) was the personal creation of Dr Senay Likie, a former president of the Ethiopian Students' Union of North America. He was killed in the shoot-out which disposed of Teferi Banti in February 1977, and several members of his group later occupied high positions in the WPE. Echaat (the Amharic acronym for a group called the Ethiopia Oppressed Masses Unity Struggle) was an offshoot of Meison almost entirely composed of southerners, and suspect in the Derg's eyes as a source of southern ethnic nationalism. The smallest and least significant of the civilian parties, Emalered (Ethiopia Marxist Leninist Revolutionary Organisation) is said to have been drawn from EPRP members who decided to work with the Derg. All of these factions were grouped with Meison into the Provisional Office of Mass Organizational Affairs, which is discussed in the next chapter.

On the other side of the fence, those opposed to the Derg's continued tenure of power were more or less united in the EPRP. By comparison with Meison, its leadership tended to be younger, to have been educated locally or in the USA rather than in Europe, and to be drawn from the north, including quite a number of Tigreans (such as its leader Berhane-Meskel Redda) and Eritreans. To some extent ethnicity influenced membership in other ways: in south-western Shoa, for example, where Oromos were likely to support Meison, Gurages tended to opt for the EPRP, while in Harar it similarly gained some support from Aderes. These origins affected its stance over issues such as secession, which it was far readier to concede than any of the groups which worked with the Derg (though even some of these, including Meison, formally allowed for secession in their programmes). Most of all, however, EPRP drew on student hostility to the military, and strenuously denied that any military regime could be revolutionary. It drew support from disillusioned zemecha students, and although it is extremely difficult to find anyone who acknowledges membership, it was probably the best-supported party among the intelligentsia as a whole. Obituaries of its members show exactly the same preponderance of teachers and students as for Meison.[17]

The EPRP also had links with the trade-union organisation, CELU, which had called for a civilian government immediately after the Derg's takeover in September 1974, and repeated the call a year later, following an unsuccessful attempt by the Derg to suppress it in May 1975. EPRP sympathies were especially strong among employees of Ethiopian Airlines (EAL), who included a high proportion of Eritreans, and on 25 September 1975 seven

54

EAL workers were killed by the army at a demonstration at Addis Ababa airport. The CELU leadership then went underground and declared a general strike, which was countered by a state of emergency in Addis Ababa. The terms of the emergency proclamation,[18] which empowered the security forces 'to take a final measure' against (i.e. kill) anyone taking part in a strike, demonstration or illegal speech or distribution of printed materials, made it clear that it was directed against the urban workforce and intelligentsia, rather than the 'remnants of local reactionary forces' who were its ostensible target. CELU was dissolved and eventually replaced by a government-controlled trade-union structure, the All Ethiopia Trade Union (AETU), and a new labour law promulgated in December 1975 was even more restrictive than under the imperial regime.[19] However, though the treatment of CELU severely dents any claim by the Derg to represent the working class, not all trade unionists were opposed to the regime. The main industrial area of Addis Ababa, around Kalitti and Akaki to the south of the city, provided some of its most active and violent supporters. Less skilled than the Ethiopian Airlines staff, and more likely to be Oromo than Eritrean, workers at the Kalitti Knitting Factory, the Akaki Textile Mill and similar establishments were armed and took part in the house-to-house searches through Addis Ababa which destroyed the EPRP.[20] Workers at the Wonji sugar plantations, who were largely from Kambatta and Wollaita and constituted one of the most evidently exploited groups of Ethiopian wage labourers, also tended to support the regime.[21] To some extent, therefore, one may draw a distinction between less-skilled southern workers who tended to support the regime, and more-skilled northerners who tended to oppose it. The number of Amharas in the unionised labour force was in any case slight.

Lefort credits the Meison Minister of Public Works and Housing, Daniel Tadesse, with the realisation that the lumpenproletariat, organised into the kebelles, could become the defenders of Meison (and hence the Derg) in its struggle with the EPRP.[22] At all events, a proclamation in October 1976 greatly increased the powers of the kebelles, giving them direct control over the administration of their neighbourhoods, in place of their previous functions which, formally at least, were largely concerned with housing.[23] Public-safety committees within each kebelle were made responsible for public order, and recruited revolutionary guards who were often all too pleased to avenge themselves on the comparatively privileged strata who comprised the EPRP. Elections to these reformed kebelles took place in November 1976, and were largely controlled by Meison, though a fairly high proportion of soldiers among kebelle officials, especially NCOs, suggests that the armed forces also took a hand.[24] The EPRP had meanwhile launched a campaign of urban terrorism to coincide with the second anniversary of the revolution in September 1976, very largely directed against Meison, rather than the Derg itself. Several leading members of Meison were killed, and it in turn organised its own execution squads against the EPRP.

The outbreak of civil war between the civilian political factions coincided with a crisis within the Derg, and the two conflicts became enmeshed. On 29 December, in a move generally seen as curbing the power of Mengistu Haile-Mariam, the Derg was reorganised so as to concentrate power in a standing committee, while many of Mengistu's supporters were despatched to posts in the provinces. Mengistu however sought the support of the newly formed official trade union, the AETU, and of kebelle officials, and emerged as the backer of a counter-terror against the EPRP, at a time when Teferi Banti was seeking a reconciliation between the rival civilian groups in the name of national unity. A mass rally on 30 January 1977, ostensibly directed against the Nimairi regime in the Sudan, provided a platform for a speech by Teferi which, in sharp contrast to speeches by Mengistu in the same period, contained no reference to the EPRP and called in general terms for national unity. How anyone could have supposed a reconciliation to be possible between two organisations whose members were already killing one another in the streets is a mystery. At all events, Teferi never had a chance to put his programme into effect, since he and several of his supporters were killed on 3 February in the shoot-out at the old palace, which finally brought Mengistu Haile-Mariam to the unchallenged leadership of the Derg.

The worst excesses of the rival terror campaigns took place over the following few months. The EPRP broadened its assassination campaign to include kebelle officials and the leaders of the AETU, the first two chairmen of which were killed, along with several other leading officials and junior members of the Derg. The government responded to this by arming the revolutionary defence squads of the kebelles – essentially a matter of arming the lumpenproletariat against members of the urban intelligentsia and their followers in the university and the secondary schools. Urban guerilla warfare proved no more successful in this case than on any of the other occasions when it has been attempted against a sufficiently ruthless central government. On two occasions, in March and again in May 1977, house-to-house searches were carried out in Addis Ababa, and suspected EPRP members rounded up for execution. Attempts by the EPRP to launch a school strike were likewise countered by the execution of students who failed to attend classes. The press regularly reported the execution of 'anarchists' and 'paid assassins'. Along with the conflict between the rival political factions went the settling of personal scores, and gratuitous killings by psychotics on either side. The most notorious of these, Girma Kebede, was a Meison kebelle chairman in the Arat Kilo area of Addis Ababa, and the well-educated son of a former high official; he overreached himself by taking away for execution a group of 'reactionaries' from the Ministry of Education who included Mengistu's uncle, and was then shot on the charge of seeking 'to alienate the people from the Government and incite the broad masses against the revolution'.[25]

The EPRP was effectively destroyed by mid 1977, the remnants retreating in an attempt to launch a rural guerilla campaign from their home areas in the north. The urban terror, however, did not cease but merely changed targets, as the Derg sought to relieve itself from dependence on Meison. Meison's position of 'critical alliance' with the Derg was always an awkward one, since at the same time as working with the government, it kept its own separate organisation, and sought to build up a position through which it might eventually displace it, by placing its supporters in institutions such as the kebelles, POMOA, the media and the Political School. With the creation in mid 1977 of a peasant militia some 300,000 strong, it tried also to infiltrate that. At the same time, Meison's position *vis-à-vis* the Derg was weakening. Mengistu's assumption of the chairmanship of the PMAC in February 1977 replaced a collegiate military leadership, with its uncertainty of direction, by a single ruthless strongman; the destruction of the EPRP removed the need for the Derg and Meison to cling together against a common enemy; and the outbreak of war with Somalia in July 1977 prompted a nationalist reaction which the Derg was well-placed to profit from, but Meison was not. In common with other civilian political groups, it had called for self-determination for nationalities and flirted with secession, and its policy of supporting local peoples against 'Amhara' settlers in the south (and especially Hararghe) backfired when some of its appointees sided with the Somalis, and the Ethiopian war effort was impeded by the weakening of the settler communities who were committed to the national government. The goal of persuading the Derg to hand over power to a Marxist–Leninist party controlled by Meison became increasingly remote, especially after July 1977 when the Derg issued a proclamation to bring POMOA more directly under its own control.[26] In August 1977, the leading members of Meison disappeared from their posts overnight and went underground, as a prelude to launching their own attack on the Derg. Several of them, including Haile Fida, were caught and later executed. Others stayed with the Derg – at the price of betraying their own former colleagues. In the final phase of the red terror, culminating in December 1977 to January 1978, it was often hard to tell who was being killed by whom; assassinations routinely ascribed to the EPRP may well have been the work of rival factions of Meison, or even of the Derg seeking to rid itself of untrustworthy officials while blaming its opponents. By early 1978, the four-year period of urban upheaval had ceased. Effective – or even ineffective – opposition was ended, and the major towns were under unchallenged government control. The institutions, notably the kebelles, which had been formed during the period of conflict remained as structures of administration.

THE CONFLICT FOR THE PERIPHERY, 1975–1978

The conflict for control of the towns was essentially fought out between the participants in the 1974 upheavals. There were no 'traditional' forces, at any rate after the killings of November 1974, and the bureaucrats kept their

57

heads down as best they could. In the countryside, it was different. The revolution both threatened major interests which were in some position to defend themselves, and strengthened and encouraged longstanding regionalist and secessionist tendencies.

The first reaction came, understandably enough, from noblemen and landlords whose political position was swept away by the overthrow of the monarchy, and whose economic power was likewise destroyed by land reform. Since this opposition came from 'reactionary' groups, and has been almost entirely disposed of, it is easily overlooked by comparison with either Marxist or secessionist movements. It nonetheless provided the regime with its major source of opposition (outside Eritrea) in the early years of revolution, and fostered a pattern of anti-revolutionary mobilis-ation, especially in Tigray and Gonder, which was later to be taken over by other movements. At a formal level, the aristocratic opposition was organ-ised into the Ethiopian Democratic Union (EDU), founded in March 1975 under the leadership of two northern noblemen, regional governors and grandsons-in-law of Haile-Selassie, Ras Mengesha Seyoum of Tigray and General Nega Tegegn of Gonder. As its name implied, it was liberal rather than straightforwardly reactionary in formal political goals, and it gained tacit support from the Nimairi government in Sudan. During 1975 and 1976, it controlled much of Gonder region, especially the Humera area bordering Sudan, and the commander of the Ethiopian troops in the area defected to it in early 1977. This was however more a matter of filling the vacuum left by the collapse of central authority, than one of creating an effective local administration. The top leadership rarely came closer to the scene of action than the border town of Kassala in Sudan, and the enterprise as a whole seems to have suffered from that ambivalence and lack of commitment that afflicts *émigré* politics everywhere. Any major threat posed by the EDU collapsed in mid 1977, with its defeat at Humera and the regime's successful mobilisation of national identities against the Somali invasion.

In many parts of the country, and especially the north, noblemen and landlords simply took to the hills with bands of retainers, in unorganised resistance to the new order. Newspapers of the period regularly report the 'liquidation' of reactionaries or bandits, sometimes up to several hundred of them at a time.[27] It is often difficult to tell whether these were supporters of the old order, members of regionalist or secessionist movements, or mere bewildered peasants caught up in the settling of local scores or the paranoid brutality of some of the Derg's regional representatives. Most of this round of killings was over by 1978, though as late as December 1979 the 'notorious counter-revolutionary bandit' and former local governor Dajazmatch Kebede Bizunesh was killed near Addis Alem, only a few miles west of Addis Ababa, where he must presumably have been hiding out for the previous five years.[28]

Much of the rural mobilisation which followed the land reform was, how-ever, in favour of the government rather than against it. And since the old system of landownership had been most exploitative in the economically critical areas of commercial agriculture, including the coffee-growing regions and such grain-producing regions as Arsi, these were likewise the parts of the country in which the new regime was most assured of support. Since, equally, these were mostly Oromo areas, the effect was also (despite the increasing articulation of a specifically Oromo identity) to insulate the still fragile revolutionary regime against the one source of ethnic opposition that could have been fatal to it. In most agricultural areas (the exceptions being Eritrea, Tigray, Gonder and northern Wollo), peasants' associations had been set up within a year or so of the land reform proclamation, and soon provided the main source of recruits in the government's expansion of the armed forces. Peasants' association defence squads were set up – with impressive numbers, though extremely weak in armaments and training – and the PMAC vice-chairman, Atnafu Abate, spent much of the year before his execution in November 1977 travelling round the country presenting flags and arms to new peasant militias.[29] The first attempt to use the militias for anything but local policing was a total catastrophe. In June 1976 they were launched, ill-armed, ill-organised and unprepared, against well-entrenched guerillas in Tigray and Eritrea, and massacred in thousands – a sacrifice to that characteristic illusion in the early days of revolution that human masses can achieve tasks that lie beyond the capacity of technology or organisation.[30] By the time that the militia was relaunched a year later, the lesson had been learned, and it was to play a crucial role in the maintenance of both state and regime during the 'dark year' of 1977–78.

Though the government faced some armed challenge in virtually every region of the country, the major threats came – as under Haile-Selassie – from the north and south-east. In Eritrea, the rejection by the Derg of Aman's attempts at reconciliation, together with an attempt by the Eritrean guerilla forces to seize Asmara early in 1975 and its defeat by the Ethiopian army, helped to push the great majority of Eritreans (including notably most of the Christian educated elite) towards support for the secessionists. This was a process from which the EPLF, more explicitly Marxist, better organised, and less associated with Islam and Arab support, gained much more than its older rival, the ELF, whose strength lay largely in Moslem areas. The Derg's efforts to achieve a negotiated settlement, through its nine-point peace plan issued in May 1976, failed because essentially it had nothing to offer. Unable to concede either secession, or even any appreciable level of regional autonomy, it could offer only the opportunity of taking part in a national Ethiopian revolution on the same basis as other regions and nationalities, with no more than a few transitional provisions to take account of the 'difficulties' in what it always referred to (emphasising the similarity between Eritrea and other regions) as 'the Administrative Region of Eritrea'. Even the offer to recognise and negotiate with the EPLF (which in contrast to the ELF was implicitly treated as a 'progressive organisation') came from a position of weakness. From early 1977 onwards, the EPLF proceeded to take over towns throughout Eritrea, until by the end of the year no more than four strongpoints remained in Ethiopian hands.[31]

The Eritrean movements were greatly helped by the fact that Tigray region, immediately to the south, was also largely lost to central government control. Ras Mengesha Seyoum had set up a guerilla movement there during the first year of the revolution, as part of the EDU; this was unable to survive his own departure into exile abroad, but a strong sense of local identity, coupled with the government's inability to establish an effective administrative presence during the critical period of land reform, made it possible for a small group of radicals (with the help of the EPLF in Eritrea) to establish a Marxist guerilla opposition called the Tigray People's Liberation Front or TPLF. The long-term political goals of this organisation were ambivalent. Since Tigray, site of the ancient capital of Axum, has formed part of the Ethiopian state without a break for over two thousand years, it was difficult to present a convincing case for independence, and it has generally presented its aims in terms of regional autonomy. Regardless of ultimate goals, however, it formed an effective guerilla movement opposed to the central government which soon controlled most of Tigray apart from the main towns, and prevented the government from reinforcing its troops in Eritrea by road.

Equally, the Ethiopian revolution – like any other – placed in question the country's external relations, both with its neighbours and with the major industrial powers. Until 1974, the pattern of regional alliances had been fairly stable. The Ethiopian central government was sustained by the West, and especially the United States, while its regional rival, the Somali Republic, was allied with the Soviet Union. Following the Somali *coup* of 1969, which brought General Mohamed Siyad Barre to power, the level of contact with the Soviet Union was intensified, the Republic declared its adherence to Marxism–Leninism, and the level of arms imports sharply increased. Although American reluctance to match this increase with equivalent aid to Ethiopia alarmed the Ethiopians, there was no serious danger of Somali invasion so long as Ethiopia retained an effective central government with the backing of a major power. With the outbreak of the revolution, however, both of these conditions were threatened. Even though the United States had been preparing for Haile-Selassie's departure, and had been distancing itself from the imperial regime with that in mind, the relationship was unable to survive the upheavals from 1974 onwards. The initiative for the breach came largely from the Ethiopian side. The Derg and the civilian ideologues alike regarded the United States as bearing a large responsibility for sustaining Haile-Selassie, and were strongly drawn towards Marxism, in alliance with either China or the Soviet Union. Leading members of Mengistu Haile-Mariam's group inside the Derg started to go on extended visits to the USSR from 1975 onwards. Even though US arms supplies to Ethiopia increased in the first years after the revolution (though in the form of commercial sales rather than aid), the relationship was always under strain; American revulsion at the killings from November 1974 onwards, and President Carter's decision to make Ethiopia an example of the 'human rights' approach to foreign policy after his inauguration in January 1977, merely hastened a disintegration in the US–Ethiopian alliance which would have taken place in any event.

By the time of Mengistu's takeover in early February 1977, his relationship with the Soviet bloc was already well established. On the day after the killing of Teferi Banti, Mengistu held meetings with the Soviet and Cuban ambassadors, who expressed their support – a clear indication that they had already decided to back him against his rivals in the Derg. The alliance was cemented with a visit to Ethiopia by Fidel Castro in March 1977 (in the course of which he tried, unsuccessfully, to arrange a settlement with the Somalis), and a visit to Moscow by Mengistu in May. Numerous goodwill missions between Ethiopia and the socialist states helped to reinforce the new alliance. But although, on the diplomatic front, Ethiopia moved very quickly to replace one superpower by the other, the switch in alliances could not be so painlessly accomplished. For one thing, the Ethiopian armed forces were still equipped with American weapons, shipments of which were finally halted by President Carter at the end of April 1977, following the expulsion from Ethiopia of the US military mission. There was therefore bound to be a damaging hiatus before the new Soviet alliance could be turned into military strength on the ground. Still more important, the Soviet Union had for many years past – and especially since 1974 – been equipping the Somalis with very large quantities of weaponry, for which they could have no possible use save to attack Ethiopia.

The Somalis were thus left with a brief period during which they had overwhelming local military superiority, and could attack Ethiopia in the hope either that the Ethiopians would be too shattered and divided to provide effective resistance to the incorporation of the Somali-inhabited areas of the country into the Somali Republic, or that the USSR would at worst remain neutral or at best support its old ally against its new one, or even that the United States would join the Somalis to balance the Soviet switch to the Ethiopians. All of these calculations proved to be wishful thinking. Even though the Somali armed forces from July 1977 overran not only the Ogaden, but also many non-Somali inhabited areas of Hararghe, Bale and Sidamo regions, the invasion was doomed once the Ethiopian regime had proved able to coordinate an effective national resistance and secured the unconditional backing of the Soviet Union. The Somalis were decisively defeated in March 1978.

Most attention has been given – understandably enough in the international context of the conflict – to the level of Soviet military aid to Ethiopia, and the spearhead of some sixteen thousand Cuban troops which took part in the final assault on the Somalis. In understanding the Ethiopian revolution, however, the feats of domestic military and domestic mobilisation called for by the war are every bit as important. The most spectacular

61

of these was the formation of Tatek camp, a few miles outside Addis Ababa, where huge numbers of militia drawn largely from the peasantry – the official figure is 300,000 – were trained and armed. These forces can scarcely have been drawn entirely or even mostly from the northern highlands, and it is likely that a high proportion of them were Oromo, from the areas of southern and western Ethiopia where land reform had its greatest effect in binding the peasantry to the new regime. The Somali attack thus helped to evoke a sense of Ethiopian nationalism which went well beyond the highland core, and which enabled the Derg to establish itself as the representative of a national tradition. The main right-wing opposition, the EDU, collapsed as an effective force at about this time, and officers previously retired from the armed forces on political grounds were reinstated. The campaign against the regime's urban opponents was however maintained and even intensified, following the defection of Meison in August 1977.

After the victory over the Somalis, the government started an offensive in Eritrea from July 1978 onwards, and during the next five months recaptured almost all of the region, leaving only the town of Nakfa in the far north in EPLF control. The EPLF for the most part withdrew its forces in good order, recognising the futility of trying to hold the main towns in the face of overwhelming Ethiopian military supremacy. Although Nakfa remained in EPLF hands, and successive and very costly Ethiopian attacks over the following eight years failed to capture it, the situation in Eritrea was broadly stabilised. The EPLF retained Nakfa and hence its communications with the Sudan, and the ability to launch occasional offensives against Ethiopian government forces further south. The Ethiopians controlled the main towns and the roads between them, including almost all of the more economically developed parts of Eritrea, but lacked the ability either to cut off the EPLF from its base areas in Sudan, or to launch a successful assault on Nakfa. Much of Tigray remained in the hands of the TPLF. But from the central government's viewpoint, the separatist problem could be contained, even if it could never, apparently, finally be resolved.

By the end of 1978, the upheavals of the previous five years had thus given way to a new, and reasonably stable, political order. The conflicts within the Derg had been resolved with the supremacy of Mengistu Haile-Mariam. The conflicts on the streets of Addis Ababa had been resolved with the supremacy of the Derg, and those civilian ideologues who had stayed with it through the traumas of the terror. The terror in itself helped to ensure that no overt urban challenge to the government would emerge, at least over the following nine years. The conflicts in the countryside were not so clearly resolved. In Eritrea and Tigray, and to a lesser extent in some other regions, armed opposition to the government remained in being and continued to control fairly large tracts of territory. These opposition movements, however, had no plausible prospect of achieving secession, let alone of being able to overthrow the central government. The main productive areas of the country, including notably the coffee-growing and the main grain-producing regions, were under firm government control, as were the communications between these areas, the cities, and the coast. At the international level, the old alliance with the United States had been replaced by a new, and much more explicit, alliance with the Soviet bloc. Soviet arms sustained the greatly expanded armed forces, portraits of Marx, Engels and Lenin adorned the cities, and Ethiopia declared itself to be a Marxist–Leninist state.

The legacies of this period are crucial. Firstly, Ethiopia – in the country-side as well as in the towns – passed through a period of terror, in which at the very least several thousand people were killed and thousands more imprisoned, with a substantial proportion of these coming from the edu-cated sections of the population. This terror served, in gruesome fashion, the classic functions of violence in a revolutionary state: it produced a politi-cal *demobilisation*, matching the mobilisation of the early years, which made it possible for the new regime to organise and impose itself on a cowed popu-lation. Popular acquiescence in a multitude of later restrictions, from the institution of national military service to the compulsory wearing of uniforms, comes down to the fact that no one is prepared to go through such an experience again. Secondly, while the major organised urban groups opposed to the government were all destroyed, the Derg acquired at the same time a cadre of supporters who had committed themselves to it at the moment of truth, and who were held to that commitment by the fact that, in order to do so, they had often had to betray their former associates. The stand taken during the terror was to be the touchstone of revolutionary reliability, and was to leave many of those who passed it with blood on their hands. Thirdly, the government emerged with a single undisputed leader, Mengistu Haile-Mariam, who emphasised his dominance by having his vice-chairman and former rival, Atnafu Abate, executed in November 1977. Given the powerful role of dominant personal leadership in the Ethiopian political tradition, with its equal importance in the establishment of any revolutionary regime, this too was a major impetus to stabilisation. Finally, the regime had acquired the unequivocal backing of a major power, the Soviet Union, and through this not only a model of government, also an assured source of arms and diplomatic support.

But although a stable framework of political order had been reimposed, the essential task of institutionalising the revolution remained to be carried out. At the political level, a regime which claimed to be Marxist–Leninist still lacked any vanguard party to provide it, not simply with revolutionary legitimacy, but more importantly with an organisational structure linking a very small top leadership group with the rest of the country. The various groups which claimed or sought to perform this function had indeed largely been destroyed during the successive phases of the terror, which left the Derg without any organised civilian support. Administratively, though the new base units of government – the urban kebelles and the peasants' associ-ations – had been created, there was still no effective mechanism to link them into a single hierarchy. The economy, largely left to look after itself during the period of upheaval, needed to be revived within a Marxist–Leninist structure of planning, production and exchange. The organisation of the economy, like that of the party, thus raised questions both of the applicability of Eastern European models within Ethiopia, and of the kinds of linkage that would result with the Eastern European states (and especially the Soviet Union) themselves. Finally, there was a whole complex of questions related to the issues of nationality, integration, and regional autonomy. In a sense, the revolution could be said to have scarcely started.

4

The formation of the party, 1978–1987

Ethiopia has had no tradition of political party organisation and activity, either legitimate or underground. Under the imperial regime, members of the house of representatives ran for election on the strength of their local personal connections, and it was always tacitly accepted, though never formally decreed, that parties would not be permitted. Perhaps more surprisingly, the opposition to the regime which developed from the 1960s onwards never took the form of a party either, in sharp contrast to the well-organised clandestine communist party in neighbouring Sudan. This absence of parties is often ascribed by Ethiopians to cultural traits, and especially the pronounced lack of interpersonal trust, and the difficulty of organising any cooperative institution in a hierarchically structured society. It may equally be accounted for by the urban and government centredness of the opposition groups concerned. Mostly in or seeking government employment, despising the elected parliament as a set of ignorant countrymen, they had neither the motivation nor the opportunity to create any organisation going beyond their own small circle. The political factions which emerged after the revolution therefore originated not in any attempt to organise the Ethiopian masses, but in the rhetorical and highly introverted politics of Ethiopian student unions abroad.

Political parties played no role whatever in the outbreak of the revolution, and even afterwards the groupings which sprang up as the civilian intelligentsia returned from abroad and started to organise themselves were subordinate both to the army as the leading force in government, and to the social upheavals which the revolution had called into being. As Mengistu Haile-Mariam put it during a visit to Moscow in 1978, 'the historical uniqueness of the Ethiopian revolution' consisted in the fact that the army had assumed the vanguard role which was normally reserved for the communist party.[1] Nonetheless, the formation of a single national and socialist party was high among the goals of all groups from the earliest months of the revolution onwards. The ten-point programme of December 1974 called for 'a great political party . . . on a nationalist and socialist basis' – a formulation vague both as to the structure of the party, and as to what was meant by socialism. In the Programme of the National Democratic Revolution, issued in April 1976, the projected party took on a more explicitly Leninist form, with references to a 'true proletarian' and 'vanguard' party, and 'the principles of scientific socialism'.[2] This expressed the aim of all of the various revolutionary factions, including the EPRP, but since each group saw itself as the core of such a party, which it viewed as the means of establishing its own control over the new government, this unity of goal led to no corresponding unity of political action.

The Programme of the National Democratic Revolution formally announced the creation of the Provisional Office of Mass Organizational Affairs (POMOA), which had actually been established the previous December. As the name implies, this was not regarded as a party in itself, but rather as a 'popular revolutionary front' through which to co-ordinate the activities of the various factions. Even this apparently modest goal marked the decisive split between the EPRP and the factions led by Meison which were prepared to work within an organisation in collaboration with the Derg, and paved the way for the outbreak of the first phase of the terror a few months later. POMOA had a fifteen-man central committee composed of the leaders of its constituent groups, with Haile Fida of Meison as chairman, and his counterpart in Wazleague, Senay Likie, as vice-chairman. Several of the other members were university academics. It had an elaborate organisation, including committees for ideology, organisation, and the Yekatit '66 Political School, and branch offices reaching down to the regional and provincial, and in places even district, level;[3] its local representatives are reported in the press as organising such activities as ideological seminars for government officials. Membership of POMOA, as of virtually all political bodies at this period (including the Derg) was kept secret, not least in order to avoid the attentions of EPRP assassins, and its composition can only be inferred from its few known leaders on the one hand, and obituaries of assassinated representatives on the other. To judge from these, local representatives were almost invariably teachers or students, usually in their twenties, and were generally assigned to their own home areas or other places where they had personal connections.[4] They were in the front line of the vicious factional fighting of the period. The obituary of one assassinated POMOA representative in Gonder notes, entirely to his credit, that he had 'personally carried out the liquidation of numerous reactionaries'.[5]

Though shared exposure to danger, and complicity in bloodshed, gave POMOA members some incentive to hold together, they were riven both by internal factionalism and by the ambivalence of their relations with the Derg. Each of the constituent factions remained separate, its membership kept secret from the others. Each sought to infiltrate its rivals, and to post its own supporters in key positions in the umbrella organisation. The two main leaders, Haile Fida and Senay Likie, were personal enemies. Attrition among the top leadership of POMOA was high, and of the original fifteen-member central committee, only two – both of them academics, and neither in the upper ranks of the party leadership – remained in active politics by the time the WPE was formed in September 1984.

From the viewpoint of the Derg, POMOA was both necessary and threatening. It needed civilian political support, especially in the face of the assassination campaign launched by the EPRP, and also the countrywide political organisation that it could not create from its own limited military base. The programmes of political education or indoctrination that POMOA carried out equally served its own commitment to a Marxist–Leninist structure. The Yekatit '66 Political School, established under POMOA's supervision, became and remained the principal institution for inculcating Marxist ideology and later training party cadres. At the same time POMOA members, and especially Meison, had scarcely concealed political ambitions of their own. The Derg, and notably Mengistu Haile-Mariam, therefore used the obvious technique of playing on the differences between the POMOA factions in order to reduce them to its own control. Its main instrument for doing so was a further organisation called Abyotawit Seded, or Revolutionary Flame, which was formed in 1976 by a group of Derg members who had gone on political education courses to the Soviet Union from 1975 onwards. Its titular chairman was Mengistu himself, but its effective organiser was Legesse Asfaw, a former sergeant under Mengistu's command, who was the only non-officer among the Derg's members to rise to any major political leadership position. The admission of Seded into POMOA split the existing members; Meison and its ally Echaat strongly opposed it, seeing Seded (quite correctly) as a challenge to their own leading position in the organisation, while Wazleague and Emalered supported it for exactly the same reason. It was one stage in the process which was to lead to the eventual expulsion of Echaat and defection of Meison.

The breach with Meison took place in August 1977, following a long period of gradually deteriorating relations. Seded members were suspected of the assassinations of Meison stalwarts (such as Tewodros Bekele, the first chairman of the AETU) which were publicly ascribed to the EPRP.[6] Meison propaganda – including for example banners carried at the 1977 May Day rally – was increasingly directed against the Derg. Seded supporters were moved into places, such as the Yekatit '66 Political School, which had hitherto been almost exclusively Meison territory. The promulgation in mid July 1977 of two proclamations which brought both POMOA and the Polit-ical School more closely under the Derg's control, served as a final warning. However, although the top leaders of Meison went underground, and were soon exiled, imprisoned, or executed, a number of second-rank members sided with the Derg, and later emerged as leading members of the WPE. These included Alemu Abebe, later Mayor of Addis Ababa and a member of the WPE Politbureau. Echaat followed not long afterwards. It was especially vulnerable, since as an almost exclusively southern organisation which claimed in particular to represent the Oromo, it was suspect on national unity grounds, and in late 1977 its leading members were rounded up and imprisoned. As Mengistu later put it, 'instead of struggling for the unity and the common freedom of the masses, the so-called Echaat group embarked upon dividing the working people along ethnic lines. Some members of that organisation had openly joined forces with the reactionary regime of Somalia and began to fight against the revolution'.[7] Although POMOA continued to exist after Meison's defection, it came increasingly under military control. Its new secretary-general was a Seded member, Lt. Desta Tadesse, who was subsequently accused of receiving over 100,000 birr in bribes, and executed for 'espionage' in July 1980.[8] By the time POMOA was wound up with the formation of COPWE in December 1979, its representatives in Addis Ababa, Gamu Gofa, Shoa and Wollo, and doubtless others, were army officers.[9]

Despite the increasing artificiality of POMOA, as one member organisation after another was purged from it, Mengistu and the Derg persisted for a further two years in the attempt to establish a Marxist–Leninist party from the union of the existing organisations. A new grouping with the same members, Emaledih, or the Union of Ethiopian Marxist–Leninist Organisations, had come into existence in early 1977, and was designed to form the basis for the eventual Leninist party, while POMOA was largely concerned with political education. It published a journal, *YeHebret Demtse*, but although there were frequent references in the press to regional POMOA representatives, there was virtually no mention at all of Emaledih. Even with its membership reduced from five organisations to three, the problems were not solved. In Mengistu's words, 'Some members, particularly a few individuals among the leadership of Waz Ader and the Marxist–Leninist Revolutionary Organisation (Emalered), two of the three remaining organs, which were saying one thing while doing something else were caught red-handed thus creating further difficulties among revolutionaries'.[10]

Still more dangerously, these divisions opened the way for the infiltration of domestic politics by the regime's new socialist allies, a danger illustrated in May 1978, when an exiled Meison leader, Negede Gobeze, was smuggled on a South Yemeni passport into the Cuban embassy in Addis Ababa.[11] When this was discovered, Negede, the Cuban ambassador and his deputy, and the PDRY chargé d'affaires were all rapidly expelled. Mengistu was already coming under evident Soviet pressure to establish a full Leninist party, and in December 1977 two Soviet scholars had made the point clearly in a paper delivered to a conference on Ethiopian studies[12]

> Equally important for the creation of a people's democratic republic is the correct solution of the party question. Our conception of this question is that a vanguard party is indispensable, a party which is equipped with the revolution-

ary theory of scientific socialism and guided by the Leninist idea of the union between working class and peasantry, and embraces within its ranks all progressive members of the working class, the peasantry and the intelligentsia. Such a party should cement the unity of its ranks and maintain friendly ties with other vanguard communist parties.

This paper says nothing at all about the role of the armed forces, while the reference to ties with other communist parties indicates the importance of the party, in Soviet eyes, in binding Ethiopia much more closely into the socialist bloc than would be possible under a simple military dictatorship.

Even in September 1978, Mengistu still appeared to be trying to create a party out of the existing political factions. In his revolution day speech, he announced that 'the foremost slogan of the day is "Let the Common Front of Ethiopian Marxist–Leninist Organisations evolve into merger!" And this slogan echoes from the hinterland to the borders, from production centres to the war fronts'.[13] These echoes, however, soon died away, hastened by the discovery in the second half of 1978 that Wazleague had succeeded in infiltrating some of its own members into leading positions in Seded.[14] Some sources suggest that Waz had almost completed a takeover of the embryonic party structure which seriously threatened the position of Mengistu himself. This seems to me unlikely. Seded, with its largely military membership, was a difficult organisation to infiltrate, and its top leadership, including notably Legesse Asfaw, remained in place. In any event, though Mengistu at this period was the target of numerous assassination attempts, Emaledih was much too feeble an organisation to stand in any position to overthrow him. It may well be that the whole incident was fomented in order to expose anyone who still sought to displace him; some members of Wazleague were in any event executed, while others, said to have exposed the plot, were kept in positions of favour.

The lesson of the three-year period from the formation of POMOA late in 1975 to the dissolution of Emaledih in February 1979 was that no effective party could be formed from the merger of the existing political factions. Each faction had its own leaders, its own organisation and its own loyalties, and any attempt to group them into a single party broke down into a series of jockeyings for position. Furthermore, internal disunity opened up the party to the threat of infiltration by external forces, most obviously the Soviet Union. Exactly the same kinds of problem had arisen in Cuba, when Castro at first tried to form a single organisation from the union of his own guerila movement, the students, and the existing communist party, but had to abandon this in favour of a new communist party constructed on an individual basis.[15] In Ethiopia, the decision to proceed in this way was reached, according to Mengistu, in February 1979, and made public in early August.[16] It led to the formation in December 1979 of the Commission to organise the Party of the Working People of Ethiopia, generally known by its English acronym of COPWE.

COPWE

COPWE represented a deliberate process of party formation from above. Under the proclamation which established it, the chairman of the PMAC, Mengistu Haile-Mariam, was appointed as chairman of COPWE, and all of the powers and duties of COPWE were personally vested in him. He alone was given the power to appoint members of the Central Committee and Executive Committee (forerunner of the eventual Politbureau), and the secretariat; to issue regulations for the admission of ordinary members; to 'establish fraternal relationships with Marxist–Leninist parties, liberation movements, and other democratic organizations'; and to 'take all measures necessary to avert any situation which threatens the revolution, the territorial integrity of Ethiopia, or the dignity and welfare of the people in the course of the endeavours to establish the Party of the Working People'. All other political organisations and groups were prohibited.[17]

By December 1979, Mengistu had over five years experience as vice-chairman and then chairman of the PMAC. All those who had at one time or another been his rivals – Atnafu Abate, Kiros Alemayehu, Sisay Habte – were by this time dead. Other leading Derg members, such as Berhanu Bayih, Fisseha Desta or Fikre-Selassie Wogderes, had accepted their position as his subordinates. Nor had his career been confined to the internal politics of the Derg; he had also been involved in intricate alliances with civilian groups – with Meison against EPRP, with Wazleague against Meison, with Seded against Waz – in setting up the new trade-union organisation, and in arming the kebelles. Especially since his critical visit to the Soviet Union in May 1977, he had been very closely involved in foreign affairs. The establishment of COPWE nonetheless marked a deliberate movement into a wider political arena. All sources agree that it was very much his own creation, and that he spent many hours interviewing and selecting prospective members. This process was largely completed during the period between the formal establishment of COPWE in December 1979, and its first Congress in June 1980. By that time, the formal structure of the party – the Executive Committee, Central Committee, secretariat and regional organisation – was ready to be put in place, and the leadership cadre had been selected which was to carry through almost unchanged into the Workers' Party of Ethiopia, when this was ultimately formed in September 1984. The establishment of a new and stable political leadership was essentially a product of 1979 and the first half of 1980.

The core group in this leadership continued to consist of those members of the Derg who had followed Mengistu through the vicissitudes of the previous six years. Fifty-nine of the ninety-three founding members of the COPWE Central Committee were present or former members of the armed forces and police, as were twenty of the thirty alternates, and twenty-seven of these were members of the Derg.[18] The first ten members in order of seniority comprised the Standing Committee of the PMAC, and most of the members of the PMAC Central Committee were also included. The leading members of this group, comprising Fikre-Selassie Wogderes, Fisseha Desta, Tesfaye Gebre-Kidan, Berhanu Bayih, Addis Tedla and Legesse Asfaw, were to carry through unchanged into the Politbureau of the WPE. The other soldiers in the COPWE (and later WPE) leadership fall into four main groups. First, there were the senior officers commanding the main military units, including Merid Negussie, who had emerged as the most effective of the Ethiopian commanders in Eritrea, Tesfaye Habte-Mariam, the commander of the airborne division, the commanders of the air force, navy and police, and several of the leading army officers. Essentially career soldiers, these were brought in so as to maintain the links between the armed forces and the regime. The second group, with nine full members and six alternate members of the original COPWE Central Committee, were officers with specifically political responsibilities, as members of the directorate of military–political affairs. The existence of a political organisation within the armed forces predated, by several years, the formation of COPWE itself. For a long period it came under the control of Legesse Asfaw, who fought to retain it even after taking on the main role in the COPWE secretariat, but was later taken over by another of Mengistu's close confidants, Gebreyes Wolde-Hana. Thirdly, there were quite a number of former army officers who had by this time moved across into civilian administration, such as Goshu Wolde, at this time minister of education and later minister of foreign affairs. Finally, there were a few soldiers with personal ties to Mengistu, such as his old Holeta classmate, Nesibu Taye, who was ambassador in Moscow.

While the military formed some two-thirds of the top COPWE leadership, the civilians provide an interesting indication of the way in which the embryonic party drew on the various constituencies thrown up by the revolution. The sixteen government ministers were all included on the Central Committee (one only as an alternate member), several of these being former army officers. Two senior technocrats, Hailu Yimenu and Amanuel Amde-Michael, had been officials under the imperial regime, and had continued in office throughout all the upheavals since 1974. Amanuel, a lawyer and attorney-general under Haile-Selassie, was the sole Eritrean in any major central government post, and thereby acquired a protected and symbolic position. To these might be added the minister of industry and later finance, Tesfaye Dinka, and the relief and rehabilitation commissioner, Shimelis Adugna, who was one of the best-known Ethiopian officials in the West, especially effective as a fund-raiser. The more ideological appointees were mostly placed in the new COPWE secretariat. The four leading civilian ideologues – commonly known as the 'gang of four' – comprised Shimelis Mazengia, an Addis Ababa University dropout chiefly known for his rhetorical abilities; Alemu Abebe, a Soviet-educated veterinarian and Meison member; Fassika Sidelil, an American-educated economist who had come to Mengistu's attention while working in the Planning Council; and

71

Shewandagn Belete, a former Wazleague activist. Shimelis Mazengia was chiefly responsible for drafting Mengistu's speeches, and is credited with devising many of the new Amharic words and phrases needed for Marxist terminology. The only woman on the Central Committee, Tiruwork Wakoyo, had been a prominent though scarcely radical student at Addis Ababa University in the mid 1960s, and was married to Tefera Wonde, then minister of health.

None of these, however, had any substantial following in their own right. Some of them, indeed, were widely distrusted for the role they were said to have played in betraying their colleagues at the time of the terror. Nor did they represent any particular viewpoint or geographical area by virtue of their previous membership of one or other of the political factions. Like Haile-Selassie's appointees under the previous regime, they owed their status to the confidence of the leader. A few, including Tesfaye Tadesse, the deputy editor and later editor of the new party newspaper, were brought out of jail, and were thus especially dependent on the chairman who had released them.

In regional and ethnic terms, the COPWE leadership was heavily centralist – understandably enough considering the heavy representation of the military. There were only four Moslems among its members, two of whom were Aderes from the city of Harar, the minister of transport Yusuf Ahmed, and the director of the Yekatit '66 Political School Abdel Hafiz Yusuf. The others were the only Moslem member of the Derg, Ali Mussa, and a Somali brought up in Ethiopia. Though eleven members had identifiably Oromo names, only one, Amanuel Amde-Michael, was Eritrean, and only one likewise – Fisseha Desta, the third-ranking member of the PMAC – was identifiably Tigrean.

A party secretariat on the Soviet model also came into being with the first COPWE Congress, and by the time of the second Congress in January 1983 this had a staff of seventy-nine.[19] It consisted largely of civilian ideologues, under the supervision of senior Derg members. Fisseha Desta was nominally First Secretary, but in practice the main role was taken by Legesse Asfaw, who as Head of Organisational Affairs was responsible for recruiting new members. The regional COPWE organisation was entirely in military hands. By mid 1980, Derg members had been responsible for regional political leadership for several years. A statement of the powers and responsibilities of PMAC members assigned to the regions, published in early January 1977,[20] put first on the list the need to 'politicize, organize and arm the broad masses and coordinate the efforts of progressive forces to establish the proletarian party'. Other functions included the organisation of revolutionary defence squads, and the encouragement of co-operativisation in agriculture. The PMAC members at first operated outside the formal administrative structure, but this disjunction between political and administrative functions, foreshadowing the later distinction between party and state organs, was abolished when they were appointed as regional chief administrators from mid 1978 onwards. At the first COPWE Congress, these chief administrators, in every region except for Eritrea, then took over as COPWE representatives and chairmen of the regional COPWE committee. Twelve of the fifteen regional representatives were also members of the Derg, the sole exceptions being Dawit Wolde-Giorgis in Eritrea, former deputy head of the Ministry of Foreign Affairs and later RRC commissioner; naval commander Lema Gutema in Addis Ababa; and Mulugeta Hagos in Tigray. Only in one case, Melaku Tefera in Gonder, was the COPWE representative a native of the area which he governed, though Mulugeta Hagos' family had Tigrean origins. Beneath the representative, regional COPWE committees were composed of the local heads of organisational, ideological, cooperative, youth and women's affairs. The more important of these regional officials were already identified, in June 1980, by their membership of the Central Committee, and were members of a nationally circulating elite. In Hararghe, for example, where the top three COPWE officials under the representative were all Central Committee members, these were promoted within a few years to become respectively minister of education, vice-chairman of the National Control Commission, and ambassador to Czechoslovakia. Several of the other regional COPWE officials appear to have been little more than stopgaps, who soon dropped out of sight.

Every effort was made, at the first COPWE Congress, to convey the impression of a national organisation. Over 1,200 delegates attended, and delegations from each region were formally welcomed by leading PMAC members on their entry to Addis Ababa. Photographs taken of each delegation with the chairman make it possible to estimate the regional spread. By far the largest delegation was that of the armed forces, with over 230 members attending. The next largest groups were of 178 for Addis Ababa and 115 for Shoa, with the other regions accounting for between thirty-six (Illubabor) and eighty-five (Hararghe).[21] These will not by any means have all been natives of the region concerned, and it is likely that a large proportion were simply central officials who happened to have been posted there. The social spread of the membership was moreover very narrow indeed. In his report to the second COPWE Congress in January 1983, Mengistu stated that of the members and candidate members admitted up to the date of the third Central Committee plenary meeting in November 1981, nearly two years after COPWE's formal establishment, only 2.9 per cent were drawn from the working class and 1.2 per cent from the peasantry, with the remaining 95.9 per cent coming from teachers, civil servants, the armed forces and other sectors of society.[22] Despite its claims to represent an alliance of workers and peasants, therefore, COPWE was in fact drawn almost entirely from the ranks of state employees, and I have been unable to identify a single member or alternate member of the original COPWE Central Committee who was either worker or peasant. A recruitment drive took place after November 1981, and by October 1982 the percentage of

73

workers stood at 21.7 per cent and of peasants at 3.3 per cent, leaving exactly 75 per cent in the remaining categories. Many of these new members appear to have been officials of trade unions and peasants' associations, which were becoming increasingly hierarchical and bureaucratised, and few if any were actual workers from the fields and factories. In any event, coming into the hierarchy fairly late in the day, and after the main leadership cadre had been established, they served largely to pad out the numbers and provide the cannon fodder for party campaigns. Though COPWE, and later the WPE, was certainly more than a mere façade for the maintenance of military rule, it remained – like its Soviet model and counterpart – a party of the state apparatus.

Once established, the leadership of COPWE remained extremely stable. Of the ninety-three full Central Committee members appointed in June 1980, eighty-six still belonged to the WPE Central Committee elected in September 1984, though one of these, major-general Merid Negussie, had been dropped and reinstated in the interim. Between June 1980 and the second COPWE Congress in January 1983, only five full members and four alternates were dropped, and three new full members admitted; two of the new appointees were PMAC members (one of whom had been suspended from office in 1980, while the other had been on a political education course in Eastern Europe), and the third a civilian ideologue then serving as ambassador to Bulgaria. Three more full members and three alternates (one of whom had died) were left out of the WPE Central Commiteee elected in September 1984. Overwhelmingly the most important reason for dropping people from the Central Committee was personal misbehaviour. No public breaking of ranks was permitted. Merid Negussie, the regime's outstanding general, was demoted after getting into a public fight with a fellow officer, general Gebre-Kristos Bale, and reinstated only after his opponent had fled the country. The minister of finance, Tefera Wolde-Semait, defected while on a trip abroad. Two members are said to have been dismissed for corruption, one for drunkenness, and one for rape, though some of these allegations may well have covered personality clashes. The minister of culture was made the scapegoat when the lights embarrassingly failed during a state visit gala performance at the national theatre. But of the factional disputes which had riven POMOA and Emaledih, there was no sign. One incidental consequence of these dismissals was the reduction of the Moslem membership of the Central Committee from four to two, with the exclusion of Ali Mussa and Hussein Ismail, both of whom are said to have been jailed.

The COPWE period falls into three distinct phases. The first, lasting six months from COPWE's establishment in December 1979, was one of frantic though secretive preparation for the Commission's formal launching at its first Congress in June 1980. During that period, there was no public reference to COPWE membership, officials or organisation, and the first membership card was formally presented to Mengistu at the Congress. The twenty months following the second Congress in January 1983 were likewise devoted to preparations for the tenth anniversary of the revolution, and the metamorphosis of COPWE into the fully-fledged Workers' Party of Ethiopia. During the intervening two-and-a-half years, there was much less evident sign of activity, and it was often speculated that the whole exercise had stalled, and that the promised party might never see the light of day. At the time of COPWE's establishment, Mengistu raised the question of why the party itself, rather than merely the commission for organising one, could not be set up at once, and answered that while a party in name only could be announced immediately, the creation of a party which would do some justice to its name was inevitably a much slower business.[23] This argument had something to be said for it. Whereas over many issues, such as the resettlement or villagisation campaigns, the Ethiopian government has pressed ahead at very short notice and with little preparation, the process of party formation was carried out with extraordinary caution. Prospective members were carefully screened, and required to go through a process involving first participation in discussion groups, and subsequently candidate membership. Though in the early years of COPWE, a lot of people seem to have got in on the nod, and personal connections – especially with Legesse Asfaw and his protégés – were evidently important, as time went by recruitment became extremely cumbersome. Mengistu had warned early on that membership was 'not a special ticket for further promotion or the attainment of special privileges',[24] and (though a privileged party elite certainly emerged) members found themselves being plucked from their offices and sent out on campaigns such as the resettlement scheme.

The party was formed strictly along Soviet lines, and with Soviet participation and encouragement. Even before COPWE had given way to WPE, it reached party-to-party agreements with the CPSU, rather than participating in state-to-state agreements between Ethiopia and the Soviet government – an important distinction in the Soviet system, in which party-to-party agreements are normally reserved for established Leninist parties. COPWE cadres were trained in the Soviet Union and other socialist states.[25] The Soviet influence was evidently exercised in the direction of haste rather than delay. The Russians had ample experience in north-east Africa of setting up alliances with military leaders – Nasser and Sadat in Egypt, Nimairi in Sudan, Siyad in Somalia – which were renounced once they no longer served the leader's purpose, and they evidently saw the establishment of the party as promising some permanence to a relationship in which they had made a substantial military and diplomatic investment. Mengistu however seems to have regarded this Soviet eagerness as providing some reason for delay. Despite his own commitment to the Soviet alliance, he was extremely sensitive to any Soviet intervention in the domestic affairs of third-world Marxist–Leninist states. The Negede Gobeze incident had aroused a brusque reaction, and the Soviet ambassador left shortly afterwards, before the normal end of his tour.[26] A second Soviet ambassador also left prematurely early in 1982, and Korn suggests that this was due to his presumption in lecturing Mengistu on his relations with Western European states.[27] The Soviet invasion of Afghanistan, involving the violent replacement with Soviet military assistance of the head of a communist state, came only a few days after the proclamation establishing COPWE. Though the Ethiopian press took its coverage of events from Tass, it was not until over a fortnight after the invasion that the government announced its support.[28] The events in South Yemen in 1986 were to excite much more explicit Ethiopian disapproval. There seems every justification for the view that a passage in Mengistu's speech on COPWE's establishment, rebutting criticisms at the delay in forming the party, was directed against the Russians.[29]

Nonetheless, progress was made, even during the hiatus between the first and second COPWE Congresses. At the central level, the second plenary session of the COPWE Central Committee held in February 1981 marked the point at which the formal announcement of government policies started to come through the party organs rather than through the PMAC – though the PMAC continued to issue appointments and legislation until the formal establishment of the People's Democratic Republic of Ethiopia. The Central Committee issued resolutions on such matters as economic planning and the collectivisation of agriculture, which were then discussed and implemented by subordinate state and COPWE organisations.[30] A party newspaper, *Serto Ader*, was established, along with an ideological journal, *Meskerem*, which kept going for three years and produced fourteen issues up to June 1983. This is interesting largely for its attempts to rewrite Ethiopian history from the perspective of the new orthodoxy, and to provide official accounts of the early years of the revolution and contentious issues such as Eritrean secessionism. It lacked, however, any serious analysis of how Marxism–Leninism could actually be applied to Ethiopian conditions. As has happened in other socialist states, the status of Marxism as an official doctrine virtually precluded its use as a method of analysis.[31]

The COPWE organisation was extended down through the hierarchy of regional and provincial government. Although the regional COPWE representatives appointed in June 1980 were merely (except in Eritrea) the existing military chief administrators already in post, the posts of chief administrator and COPWE representative were separated late in 1981; this created the normal Leninist bifurcation between state and party offices which was to be carried through into the WPE after 1984. When this process took place, it was the old military bosses who continued as COPWE representatives, leaving subordinate officials – several of whom were also from the military, and a few of whom were members of the Derg – to take over the lesser job of chief administrator. This ensured that the party's supremacy over the state administration was established from the start, and since the COPWE representative usually continued in practice to run the regional administration, the new chief administrator became in effect his chief of staff. The price for the party's supremacy was then that the people who wielded it could scarcely be described as Marxist–Leninists at all. Their origins lay in the military, and the vicious factional conflicts within the Derg. Their role model was in effect that of the traditional Ras, imperiously wielding power with as much independence of central authority as they dared. Though they were all sent, at one time or another, on courses in the USSR and Eastern Europe, they were largely innocent of ideology, or specifically Leninist forms of political organisation.

Below the regional level, the COPWE organisation was gradually extended to the larger towns and to provincial, and in some cases even district, government. The first documented case is for Assab, the port at the southern end of the Red Sea which was administered separately from Eritrea as an autonomous province, where not only the COPWE representative but also the rest of the COPWE committee arrived from Addis Ababa to take up their duties in April 1981, clearly indicating their central rather than local origins.[32] The representative in this case was a junior Derg member and teacher at the Political School, Eshetu Aleme. COPWE organisations appear shortly afterwards in towns such as Jimma and Dessie, and had been set up in nearly half of the hundred-odd provinces by the time of the second Congress in January 1983.[33] The formation of COPWE primary organisations also accelerated after November 1981, and by June 1982 there were reported to be 436 of them – still not a large number, but including organisations in almost all the state-owned factories and all the state farms.[34] There were 162 of these basic organisations, or over a third, established in the armed forces, down to brigade level,[35] where they took over the functions of the previous Military and Political Affairs offices. The training of party cadres was also intensified. In the two-and-a-half years between the first and second Congresses, 2,845 participants graduated from courses at the Yekatit '66 Political School, in addition to those who went to Russia and Eastern Europe.[36]

The available evidence thus suggests that the period of nearly five years between the establishment of COPWE in December 1979 and its transformation into the WPE in September 1984 was due not to doubts about the enterprise itself, but to the time needed to ensure that the party would be effectively established, organised, and controlled. Loyalty rather than ideological commitment was, according to all reports, the principal criterion in its recruitment. This loyalty will certainly have included checks on the reliability of cadres educated in the socialist states, but equally important was the need to avert any resurgence of the conflicts between factions which had marked the period up to 1978. In this, COPWE evidently succeeded.

THE WORKERS' PARTY OF ETHIOPIA

In many respects, the foundation of the Workers' Party of Ethiopia, which formed the central point of the celebrations of the tenth anniversary of the revolution in September 1984, was merely a matter of relaunching the existing COPWE organisation under a new name. Care was taken to go through the formal rituals of democratic centralism, and from June 1984 onwards party founding congresses were held in primary party organisations, at local level and in the armed forces, at which resolutions were passed and delegates elected to go forward to the next stage of the hierarchy, up to the founding congress itself.[37] Huge amounts of money – Korn estimates between fifty and a hundred million US dollars[38] – were spent on the celebrations, including the beautification of Addis Ababa and the erection of numerous monuments and a new party congress hall. Thousands of people, including reluctant students and civil servants, were trained in mass marching and gymnastic displays. Intense and successful security precautions were taken to ensure that the occasion was not marred by any overt expression of terrorism or dissent, and the famine then reaching its height in northern Ethiopia was, so far as possible, concealed. High officials attended from all the accepted socialist states, along with somewhat incongruous delegations from often minuscule though politically acceptable communist parties in the West.

Formally speaking, the major difference between COPWE and the WPE lay in the replacement of a constitutional structure which gave total power to the chairman, by one which followed the standard procedures of a Soviet-style communist party, including the principle of the election of higher by lower organs. This change may in itself be seen as accounting for much of the caution and delay in establishing the party, in that now it would formally be possible for the chairman – or general secretary as he now became – to be constitutionally ousted from power by an adverse vote of the Central Committee. The organisation of the party closely followed the Soviet model, save that the federal structure of the Soviet party, which allows for a separate party organisation within Union Republics which have a technical right of secession, was replaced by a thorough-going centralism.[39] Primary party organisations were to be established on a workplace basis, and in turn organised at district, provincial and regional levels, culminating in the party Congresses held at five-yearly intervals. The Congress elects the Central Committee, which normally meets twice a year, and has the power to regulate its own membership between Congresses, and to elect the Political Bureau, the General Secretary, and the members of the party secretariat. A special chapter of the party rules regulated the structure and functioning of the party in the armed forces, which came under the control of the Main Political Administration of the Revolutionary Armed Forces, itself a department of the Central Committee secretariat. Though the detailed organisation of the party in the armed forces was left to regulation by Central Committee directives, the rules made it clear that this was to follow the military chain of command, and not be subject to the control of territorial party organs within the areas in which military units were operating. 'Close contact' with territorial party organs was enjoined, but the party organisation within the military remained completely distinct.[40]

Mengistu Haile-Mariam's position as general secretary, combined with his existing titles as chairman of the PMAC and commander-in-chief of the Revolutionary Armed Forces, made clear his position of total dominance. There was not so much as lip-service to the idea of collective leadership. The emphasis on Mengistu's personal leadership of the revolution, which had been growing during the COPWE period as he emerged from the semi-anonymity of the Derg, was greatly increased by the tenth anniversary celebrations and the founding of the party. The set of stamps issued for the occasion for the first time bore his portrait. Huge portraits were erected in Revolution Square and on the front of the party headquarters, and posters showed him leading a representative selection of Ethiopians (soldier, worker, peasant, woman) towards a glowing future. The slogan 'Forward with the Revolutionary Leadership of Comrade Mengistu Haile-Mariam' appeared on buildings and arches across the roads. Provided by the North Koreans, this display of official art also illustrated the growing relationship between Ethiopia and the most unashamedly personalist of all socialist regimes, though the cult of personality stopped a long way short of the adulation heaped on Kim Il Sung.

Mengistu could also draw on an indigenous tradition of leadership, and in many ways his model was neither Castro nor Kim Il Sung, but Haile-Selassie. His formal leadership style, on occasions such as state visits and meetings with Western ambassadors and delegations, was consciously modelled on that of the emperor. He also kept up the old imperial palace, with its large retinue of servants – perhaps just because he enjoyed it, perhaps because he felt it necessary to reassure either the populace or himself by reference to inherited patterns of leadership behaviour. The pronounced hierarchy of Ethiopian society, together with its strong sense of privacy, in any event maintains a distance between the supreme leader and the ordinary population which the replacement of the Elect of God by a Soviet-style general secretary does little to diminish. Popular art puts this continuity well. In the time of the imperial regime, it was common to see pictures in which Father, Son and Holy Ghost, enthroned in the clouds, projected a beam of light onto the emperor (symbolically situated at mid-point between heaven and earth), who in turn diffused it to a waiting people. At the tenth anniversary celebrations, along with the official decorations provided by the North Koreans, it was also possible to find home-made tributes in which the gift of grace, embodied in a celestial trinity of Marx, Engels and Lenin, similarly descended to the grateful masses by way of Mengistu Haile-Mariam.[41]

In other respects, however, Mengistu's leadership style stops well short of the imperial. In contrast both to North Korea and to imperial Ethiopia, there is no cult of the family; his wife occasionally appears at official events, but his children go to the French Lycee, along with those of many other Ethiopian officials. As is normal in Africa, the leader's portrait adorns all public rooms (and is sometimes seen in frames with a crown on top, from which the emperor's portrait had been removed); but after ten years in power, and in contrast to the huge number of schools, streets and so forth named after his predecessor, only a hospital in southern Shoa and a mountain in Bale bore his name, in each case applied by local officials anxious to ingratiate themselves. Nor does he have the status and appearance needed to project the imperial aura so carefully cultivated by Haile-Selassie. His dark skin and coarse features, which he shares with the emperor Menilek, would not necessarily count against him; but coming from an obscure southern background, he would have difficulty presenting himself in terms of traditional nobility, and does not seem to have any interest in doing so. His demeanour expresses power, rather than dignity. His speeches, however, are written (largely, as already noted, by Shimelis Mazengia) in the consciously fine Amharic which is one of the marks of the cultivated Ethiopian. One other important respect in which he falls well short of traditional conceptions of leadership is in his failure to live up to the ideal of generosity, by which leaders were expected to look after their people, and bestow gifts wherever they went. Haile-Selassie was accompanied on provincial tours by a retainer who scattered banknotes among the crowd; Mengistu by contrast is dour, and a reputation for grasping from the people, and having little to offer in return, extends from him to the government as a whole.

His exercise of power has grown steadily more aloof. Ethiopian officials have complained that the simple leadership style of the early years, when ministers could gain access to Mengistu fairly easily, and speak to him openly and informally, has been replaced by an imperial type of audience, in which they are expected to lard their submissions with fulsome compliments to his leadership. A new retinue of court officials is developing. But even if the forms are imperial, the content is very different; his ruthlessness and impatience were evident from the moment of his first semi-public appearance on the political scene, with the massacre of the leading officials of the old regime and the killing of Aman Andom in November 1974, for both of which he is generally ascribed a personal responsibility. Where Haile-Selassie liked to balance and manipulate factions, in order to keep his courtiers dancing attendance on himself and maintain a wide range of policy options, Mengistu appears to work with a small group of advisers, though even these may fall rapidly out of favour. In Jackson and Rosberg's terms, he is an autocrat rather than a prince,[42] a commander rather than a manipulator, with a willingness to go whole-heartedly for massive and risky schemes – from land reform through to villagisation – from which a cautious operator such as Haile-Selassie would have recoiled. His predecessor's favourite device of claiming the credit for any favourable outcome, while evading responsibility when things went wrong, is scarcely open to him.

Purposive leadership of this kind has been essential to achieve the transformation which Ethiopia has undergone under Mengistu's rule; but at the same time, it has introduced a rigidity into policy-making which Haile-

Selassie was able to avoid. Once government policies become personally associated with the leader, they cannot be questioned without seeming to challenge the leader's own authority. As Mengistu established his personal dominance over central decision-making in the decade after 1977, in consequence, he became surrounded not simply by flatterers (which is the common fate of anyone in a position of power), but by followers who could not proffer policy advice, because the major issues of policy had already been pre-empted by leadership decision. The resulting inability to alter unsuccessful policies has been evident across the range of government activities from the nationalities question to the collectivisation of agriculture. In each case, the response to failure has been to pump further resources into trying to implement the original policy, because it was scarcely possible to question the wisdom of the policy itself.

Mengistu's beliefs, like his personality, have to be inferred from his actions. There can be no doubt, either about his commitment to a centralised Ethiopian state, or about his hatred for the old regime and those who ran it. Never at any time has he shown any willingness to compromise over the essential structure of central control, and even the concessions which at one time or another he has been prepared to offer to regional or ethnic autonomy have been cosmetic. It is hard to suppose that he has regarded the provisions on the nationalities question, from the Programme of the National Democratic Revolution to the Constitution of the PDRE, as anything more than necessary palliatives. Nor has he ever raised the question of his own ethnic origins, or attempted to make political capital out of the general belief that he is at least partly of southern parentage. It is very much harder to discern anything that might be called ideological conviction, or indeed to surmise what 'Marxism' might mean to someone in Mengistu's position, except as a convenient means of aggregating anti-monarchical radicalism with the rigid organisation of central control. To ask whether he is a 'convinced' Marxist would seem to me, indeed, to be beside the point. He has certainly pressed hard for measures, such as the collectivisation of agriculture, which fall onto the Marxist agenda but which likewise permit the more efficient extraction of a surplus from the peasantry. He has pursued the Soviet alliance with a commitment which has led many Ethiopians to regard him as unnecessarily subservient to Moscow, and undermined his own standing as a national leader; but at the same time, he has been extremely sensitive to any threat that this alliance might present to his own power. While Marxism–Leninism is evidently a very useful doctrine to a leader in Mengistu's position, to speak of conviction would imply an idea of it as a view of the world to be implemented for its own sake, rather than as an instrument for achieving nationalist and statist goals, and of this I can see no sign.

The Political Bureau of the WPE, with eleven full members and six alternates elected in September 1984, was in a sense the lineal successor of the Standing Committee of the PMAC and the Executive Committee of

COPWE. Its members fall into three distinct groups: the surviving top leadership of the Derg, civilian ideologues, and career technocrats. The first seven members, all drawn from the Derg, precisely duplicate the two earlier bodies: Mengistu Haile-Mariam, Fikre-Selassie Wogderes, Fisseha Desta, Tesfaye Gebre-Kidan, Berhanu Bayih, Addis Tedla, Legesse Asfaw. All of these except for Legesse Asfaw had been officers in 1974, but only Tesfaye Gebre-Kidan, minister of national defence until 1987 with the rank of lieutenant-general, continued to be directly involved with the military and to use a military title. Fikre-Selassie, as secretary-general of the PMAC and deputy chairman of the council of ministers, was in the classic mould of the second-in-command who presents no threat to his leader. Fisseha Desta was formally first secretary in the WPE secretariat, and head of its department of defence, security, administration and justice, and was in that sense deputy to Mengistu in the party organisation, as Fikre-Selassie was in the state administration; Addis Ababa rumour has it that his role has been largely titular. Berhanu Bayih held an ordinary portfolio as minister of labour and social affairs, though as the most experienced member of the Derg in foreign affairs and chairman of a Politbureau committee on aid, he was also involved in various advisory and supervisory activities; he became minister of foreign affairs in November 1986. Addis Tedla, as deputy chairman of the National Council for Central Planning, was nominally in charge of planning and economic management. None of these, with the exception of Tesfaye Gebre-Kidan in his role as minister of defence, appeared to wield any great power or have any appreciable following, though Fisseha Desta had a distinctive position as the regime's only important Tigrean, and was often suspected of favouritism on his compatriots' behalf. Legesse Asfaw, on the other hand, as second secretary of the WPE in charge of organisational affairs, was generally seen as the key man in the party organisation, and the main dispenser of party patronage. He was also commonly, perhaps exaggeratedly, credited with close relations with the Russians. More than anyone else in the Derg, he has been Mengistu's protégé and hatchet man. After taking a course in political education in the Soviet Union in 1975, he established Abyotawit Seded in 1976, and was in charge of arming the kebelles for the red terror in 1977, and purging Wazleague following the infiltration plot in 1978. For three years after the killing of Teferi Banti in February 1977 he was responsible for military–political affairs in the armed forces, and thus for organising the military wing of what was to become the WPE. He remained the only member of the Politbureau with a political base of his own.

Of the other members of the PMAC, however, only Teka Tulu (a police-man with a distinctively Oromo name, largely concerned with security) became even an alternate Politbureau member. The remaining four members of the PMAC Standing Committee, though they retained their positions in the formal Central Committee ranking, were given less import-ant posts – as WPE sixth secretary, pensions commissioner, minister of interior, and party first secretary in Gamu Gofa. One other alternate Polit-bureau member, the minister of state and public security Tesfaye Wolde-Selassie, was a military/police officer but not a member of the Derg. Eighteen other Derg members were named as full members, and five as alternate members, of the Central Committee.

The formation of the WPE also provided the opportunity to promote the group of civilians who had already emerged through COPWE. Hailu Yimenu and Amanuel Amde-Michael, the two senior technocrats who had been in office throughout the post-revolutionary era, became full members of the Politbureau, with finance minister Tesfaye Dinka and the minister of construction Kassa Gebre as alternates. The two leading civilian ideologues, Shimelis Mazengia and Alemu Abebe, also became full members, and the two other members of the 'gang of four', Fassika Sidelil and Shewandagn Belete, were alternates. In the party secretariat, moreover, the civilian ideologues held a dominant position. All four of the 'gang' held major secretarial positions, with Shimelis in charge of ideology, Alemu of the Central Control Commission, Fassika of the department of economic affairs, and Shewandagn of the department of nationalities. Another civilian prominent since the early years of the revolution, Ashagre Yigletu, became secretary in charge of international relations; he had previously been minister of commerce and then ambassador to Bulgaria.

The actual processes of decision-making inside the WPE are entirely secret and, almost certainly, highly personalised. No one would doubt that Mengistu's word is law, and that any major decision would have to be made by him. Even such decisions as the siting of the government's new settle-ments after the 1984 famine were made by Mengistu during a helicopter tour of the south and west.[43] In so far as members either of the Politbureau or of the secretariat possess political 'power', this power derives from their close-ness to Mengistu rather than from anything inherent in their newly-established offices. Nonetheless, care has been taken to ensure not only that the forms of a Soviet-style Leninist party system are followed, but equally that those who do enjoy a substantial measure of influence and access to the general secretary are in party rather than state positions. The most striking example of the Politbureau being used as the forum for major policy decisions was at the very first meeting after its formation, in early October 1984, when it was used to announce the government's strategy for dealing with the famine. Until that moment, and through all the celebrations of the founding of the party, the famine had been entirely ignored in the govern-ment media. It was as though it could not be allowed to exist until the party was available to deal with it. Once it had been decided to open up the ques-tion, and to commit the government's resources to a whole-hearted cam-paign for relief and resettlement, the Politbureau was the body which reached the formal decisions and set up the necessary structures. Neither the PMAC, which remained in being as the supreme organ of state power, nor the council of ministers, took any public role.

83

There is likewise no doubt that the party secretariat is a great deal closer to policy-making than government ministries working in the same area. Two fields in which this has been particularly evident are agriculture and foreign affairs. In each case the relevant government ministry, staffed by bureaucrats many of whom were trained in the West, has been quite unable to influence policies made by party officials with an evidently socialist or Soviet stance. In the case of agricultural policy, this is evident in government measures to encourage the 'socialisation' agriculture, including the establishment of of state farms, strong inducements towards the co-operativsation or collectivisation or peasant agriculture, the introduction of a centrally directed agricultural marketing structure, and the concentration of peasants into centralised villages in place of the previous scattered homesteads. Most of these programmes antedate the establishment of the party, villagisation being the exception, but they reflect a pattern of policy-making totally at variance with technical advice which can be explained only in terms of the imposition of an ideology of state, or party, control. Similarly in the field of foreign policy, Western diplomats constantly bemoan the fact that they are obliged to deal with the ministry of foreign affairs, where the officials are articulate, skilled, and so far as possible helpful, but are entirely unable to influence the policies which they have to carry out; the representatives of socialist states, on the other hand, can gain access to the foreign affairs department of the party secretariat, which, even if it does not make policy, is far better placed to influence it.[44]

The Central Committee is in no sense a decision-making body, and its importance lies more in the status which membership confers, and in the recognition given to the posts whose occupants belong to it, than in anything which actually takes place in the committee itself. It differs from the COPWE Central Committee largely in the expansion of its membership. Of the ninety-one full members and twenty-six alternate members of the COPWE Central Committee appointed in January 1983, all but three members and three alternates (one of whom had died) were elected to the WPE Central Committee in September 1984. At the same time, however, the size was increased to 136 full members and sixty-four alternates, for a total of exactly 200. This expansion was due partly to the inclusion of the new holders of posts, such as ministers or army commanders, who would have been on the COPWE Central Committee had they been in post at the time, but mostly to the need to recruit some people – in a party which nominally represented the alliance of the proletariat and the peasantry – who could be referred to as peasants or workers. The new members, many of them only alternates, thus included the chairmen of the regional trade unions and peasants' associations (all of whom were administrators rather than actual peasants or workers), and a few leaders of peasant cooperatives.

A breakdown of Central Committee members by sex, post and name is given in table 1.[45] The figures by sex are complete, indicating the tiny proportion of women in leadership positions. Information on present or former

Table 1. *Composition of the Central Committee of the WPE, September 1984*

	Full members	Alternates	Total	%
By sex				
Male	135	60	195	97.5
Female	1	4	5	2.5
	136	64	200	100.0
By military/civilian origin				
Military/police	74	21	95	47.5
of whom Derg members	(30)	(5)	(35)	(17.5)
Civilian	40	8	48	24.0
Not known (mostly civilian)	22	35	57	28.5
Total	136	64	200	100.0
By post in September 1984				
Central WPE Secretariat, etc.	25	7	32	16.0
Regional WPE first secretaries	15		15	7.5
Other regional WPE officials	7	1	8	4.0
Ministers	21		21	10.5
Other central government officials	7	2	9	4.5
Regional administrators	5	1	6	3.0
Other regional government		1	1	0.5
Ambassadors	7		7	3.5
Armed forces command posts	16	4	20	10.0
Armed forces political	9	13	22	11.0
AETU and other 'workers'	9	4	13	6.5
AEPA and other 'peasants'	9	15	24	12.0
Other mass organisations		2	2	1.0
Not known	6	14	20	10.0
Total	136	64	200	100.0
By name				
Amhara/Tigrean/Christian names	116	52	168	84.0
Oromo names	15	10	25	12.5
Moslem names	3	2	5	2.5
Other names	2		2	1.0
Total	136	64	200	

Notes: WPE Secretariat includes Yekatit '66 Political School, Institute of Nationalities;
'other central government institutions' include Commissions, National Council for Central Planning, Council of Ministers;
'other mass organisations' include REWA, REYA;
'other names' are one Italian and one unidentified ethnic minority name.

membership of the armed forces is available for most full members of the Central Committee, though for far fewer of the alternate members, who are generally much less well-known. Over half of the full members have at one time or another served in the armed forces or police, with former Derg members making up a substantial minority. The breakdown by posts indicates the extent to which the party represents the state apparatus, all but a small number of Central Committee members (most of whom are low down on the list) belonging to the state and party bureaucracies, or the command or political administration of the armed forces. Though all government ministers in September 1984 were elected to the Central Committee, the same was true of only a small proportion of state (as opposed to party) administrators at the regional level. All regional first secretaries automatically became members, along with a number of other regional party officials, and this imbalance accurately reflects the supremacy of the party over the state organisation in regional government. The ambassadors on the Central Committee were mostly those to Socialist states, including the USSR, Cuba, Bulgaria and the PDRY. Since 1985, Central Committee members have been appointed to ambassadorships in non-socialist states including the United Kingdom, India and Japan; this should however be seen as providing comfortable posts in semi-retirement, rather than as indicating any upgrading in the importance of relations with the states concerned. Among those members who did not hold government or party posts, the increased representation of the workers and peasants was largely achieved by co-opting regional trade union and peasants' association officials. Of the other mass organisations, only the national chairman of the government youth association (REYA) and chairperson of the women's association (REWA) were included, in each case as alternate rather than full members, while there was no formal representation at all of the kebelles or urban dwellers' associations. Given the importance of the kebelles, both to the revolution as a whole and to the administration and political organisation of the towns, this omission is surprising.

The analysis of names, finally, must be treated with enormous care. This is in no sense a summary of the ethnic composition of the national leadership. Christian names, and Amharic and Tigrinya names, have, as already noted, spread over the years to the extent that they may for many purposes be regarded simply as Ethiopian national names. Central Committee members with 'Amhara' names include not only many who are ethnically Oromo, but also Kaffas, Kambattas, Gurages, Wollamos and doubtless others. By the same token, the ethnic or regional origin even of many leading members of the regime is mixed or uncertain. The significance of the high proportion of Central Committee members (over 80 per cent) with Amhara–Tigrean names is thus not to demonstrate the ethnic exclusiveness of the regime, but rather the extent to which it is drawn from people who have, over at least two generations, been associated with a central or national Ethiopian culture. The group most evidently excluded are the Moslems, a high proportion (though by no means all) of whom retain distinctively Moslem names. These will include Oromos, in such areas as highland Hararghe where the indigenous Oromo population is heavily Islamised. On the other hand, the proportion of identifiably Oromo names is high, given that many Oromos are not identifiable by name at all.

No figure has been given for the total individual membership of the party, and the sole reasonably authoritative estimate which I have been able to gain puts it at 30,000 towards the end of 1985. Since this would give a party membership equivalent to less than one in every thousand of the total Ethiopian population, it is clear that the WPE is very much an elite (or in its own terms 'vanguard') organisation. It is unlikely that the membership increased very much during the two years after its foundation, since the criteria for admission became increasingly rigorous, and even the enthusiasm of careerists to join it must have been dampened by the use of junior militants as the shock troops of the resettlement and villagisation campaigns. The party rules require would-be members to be vouched for by three existing members, and to go through a period of candidate membership. Though it is possible for applicants to seek membership on an individual basis, in practice members are co-opted; often indeed, it is made clear that they are expected to join the party whether they wish to or not. No breakdown of the social or professional status of the total party membership has been provided, but a summary was given at the founding congress of the origins of the 1999 militants who attended it, and this is reproduced in table 2.

These figures do not fully correspond with one another; the numbers of trade union and peasants' association members, for example, differ from those indicated by the percentages given for workers and peasants. The proportion of women (6.3 per cent) is markedly higher than their representation in senior party posts, and is probably largely composed of women's association (REWA) officials, and those concerned with 'women's affairs' in the party organisation; even so, it amounts only to a shade under half of the percentage of REYA members, representing youth. Unlike the first COPWE congress, there is no figure for the number of participants coming from the armed forces, but the high proportion of teachers, who include teachers in higher education, corresponds with the large numbers of teachers in all of the political organisations which grew up after the revolution, and is also confirmed by the number of former teachers among WPE officials encountered especially in regional and provincial government. The educational level of those attending, showing 87.5 per cent with at least some secondary education, indicates the heavy bias towards those qualified for state employment, and suggests that a very high proportion of militants identified as 'workers' and 'peasants' must have been drawn from the permanent officials of the AEPA and AETU; very few working peasants and wage labourers would have this level of education. The proportion, very nearly a quarter, of members with tertiary education but no degree may be assumed to consist largely of teachers and officers in the armed forces. The breakdown by salary should be set against basic salaries of 1,500 birr a

Table 2. *WPE militants attending the Founding Congress, September 1984*

By sex
Men	1873	93.7%
Women	126	6.3%

By social and class standing
Workers	19.26%	(385)
Peasants	11.81%	(236)
Army, government and other social sectors	68.93%	(1378)

By social and class origin (parents)
Workers	6.87%	(137)
Peasants	64.86%	(1297)
Others	28.27%	(565)

By age
18–30	Men	648	Women	57	Total	705	35.26%
31–40		676		84		760	38.01%
41–50		435		4		439	21.94%
51–60		79		0		79	3.96%
61+		15		1		16	0.80%

By level of education
Read and write only	1.65%	(32)
Elementary (grade 1–6)	10.88%	(217)
Secondary (grade 7–12)	46.82%	(936)
Tertiary (no degree)	24.82%	(496)
BA degree	9.01%	(180)
MA degree	4.70%	(94)
Doctoral decree	2.92%	(58)

By salary
up to 100 birr/month	9.18%	(184)
101–500 birr/month	40.27%	(805)
501–1000 birr/month	32.43%	(648)
over 1000 birr/month	9.27%	(185)

By political education
Received political education in Ethiopia	926	46.37%
Received political education abroad	565	28.26%
Belonged to Emaledih	1437	71.89%

By membership of mass organisations and professional associations
Trade unions	401	(20.06%)
Peasants' associations	276	(13.81%)
Youth associations (REYA)	255	(12.76%)
Urban dwellers' associations	633	(31.67%)
Teachers	212	(10.61%)
Medical associations	26	(1.30%)
Artists	15	(0.75%)
Musicians	12	(0.60%)
Journalists	14	(0.70%)
Health professionals	5	(0.25%)

Source: These figures were announced at the congress by Legesse Asfaw, and some of them are published in *The Ethiopian Herald*, 9.9.1984; the full figures are published in Cole, *Ethiopia: Political Power and the Military*, pp. 52–4.

month for ministers and regional administrators, and 800–1,000 birr for civil service department heads and provincial administrators. The great majority of civil servants have salaries which fall below 500 birr a month, while the official minimum wage is fifty birr.

At regional level, the old COPWE representatives for the most part simply exchanged their title for that of WPE first secretary. Of the fifteen regional first secretaries appointed in 1984, only two (in Eritrea and Illubabor) were not of military origin, while ten were former members of the Derg – a number increased to eleven when a former Derg member took over in Addis Ababa in 1986. This meant that COPWE's reliance on regional military bosses was perpetuated in the WPE. That one of the non-military first secretaries should be in Eritrea may seem at first sight surprising, but was due to the fact that there, as in Tigray, the regional army commander was also head of the regional administration, and with these dual functions, combined with membership of the WPE Central Committee, effectively displaced the first secretary as the regional boss. Tefera Wonde, first secretary in Eritrea, was a biologist and veterinarian whose family came from Gonder, and who had been minister of health for several years, before moving to Eritrea in 1983. His counterpart in Tigray, Mulugeta Hagos, was an army officer but not a Derg member, and had become chief administrator in 1979, and then in turn COPWE representative and WPE first secretary; he was however subordinate both in the military hierarchy and in the WPE Central Committee rankings to the regional army commander, Kefelegn Yibsa, and his appointment may be seen as reflecting the need to have a first secretary in so sensitive a region who could claim local origins, while at the same time (as an army officer brought up in the south) he could be acquitted of sympathies for the TPLF. The other civilian first secretary, Simon Galore, was a southerner (sometimes said to be Wollamo) who had worked his way up within the regional administration in the south, before transferring to COPWE posts in Kaffa, Sidamo and Illubabor.

Several of the regional first secretaries had emerged by the mid 1980s as men with considerable power, and a good deal of initiative in the management of both party and state administration in their own regions. The most independent of them all, Melaku Tefera in Gonder, earned international notoriety for ordering the burning down of the Ibnat famine relief camp in 1985; and although the adverse publicity surrounding the incident made it necessary for Mengistu to reprimand him, he was not at the time replaced or even effectively disciplined. However, his high-handed treatment of central government officials visiting Gonder, and the counter-productive brutality of his suppression of local dissent, eventually told against him, and he was recalled to Addis Ababa in January 1987. But while Melaku played his hand as a tough man, Debele Dinsa in Shoa was able to gain quite the opposite reputation, and to build up a measure of personal popularity by mitigating (or so it was widely believed) the harshness of government measures, ranging from the red terror on the one hand, to the enforcement of the firewood regulations on the other; he was also a Welega Oromo, often regarded as a spokesman for Oromo interests,[46] and that he could take charge of the central region of Shoa indicates the comparative unimportance of regional origins in making party appointments. Two of the other regional bosses, Kassaye Aregaw and Zeleke Beyene, were originally appointed in 1978 to Gojjam and Hararghe respectively, but were switched round in 1983, it was said because Hararghe, with its virtually open market for contraband goods, offered too great an opportunity for self-enrichment. As these examples show, first secretaries are always liable to be recalled or redeployed, and have not attained any position independent of central government. They have been kept in their posts for long periods, and given a wide degree of latitude, because the regime recognises the need for strong regional leadership, not because it could not dismiss them if it wanted to. Two other regional first secretaries, Endale Tessema from Gamu Gofa and Girma Habte-Gabriel from Sidamo, were recalled to posts in Addis Ababa in 1985 and 1986 respectively, in one case as minister of interior, in the other as vice-chairman of the WPE Audit Commission.

One indication of the autonomy accorded to regional first secretaries was the villagisation campaign from early 1985 onwards. There is general agreement that this originated, not from any central directive, but from a local initiative by Kassaye Aregaw in Hararghe, which was already well under way before Mengistu visited the region, and by his approval of the campaign indicated to other first secretaries that this was now the thing to do. Even then, individual first secretaries seem to have had some latitude in deciding when and how to adopt the campaign in their own regions, and not until September 1986 was it extended to the whole country. Before then, out of the five northern regions, only Zeleke Beyene in Gojjam had attempted to implement it at all, while in the south regions such as Sidamo and Gamu Gofa lagged behind Arsi or Welega. It is also possible to detect differences in regional style over matters such as revolutionary propaganda. In Arsi (popularly known as *YeLenin ager*, or Lenin's country), the roadsides are festooned with slogans, while in neighbouring Hararghe they are restricted to a bare minimum on official buildings.

Beneath regional first secretary level, the party organisation was considerably expanded. Each region acquired a WPE committee of some eight to ten members, most if not all of whom were permanent party functionaries in charge of the various divisions – ideology, organisation, women's and youth affairs, cooperatives, and so forth – in the regional party secretariat. The two leading party officials below the first secretary were the heads of organisational affairs, reflecting the emphasis in any Leninist party on the internal management of the party itself, and of ideological affairs, responsible for political education. There was no defined hierarchy among these officials, and either of them (or in one case the regional military commissar) might take over when needed as acting first secretary. The chairmen of the regional party control and audit commissions were concerned with checking on party members, while the heads of women's and youth affairs supervised their local REWA and REYA organisations. Other party officials covered agitation and propaganda, and economic and social affairs, while regional defence matters came under the military commissar – though he did not exercise direct control over the military, which as already noted had its own separate party organisation. A matching structure was extended down to the provincial level, and eventually to the district as well. At every level, the party boss was from the start recognised as the top official in the area, with the right to control the regional, provincial or district administrator who formally headed the state bureaucracy. This immediately became clear, for example, to relief workers in the famine areas, who had to secure party clearance for their activities, while party supremacy was also symbolised in the fact that party officials took over the main regional and provincial government buildings, relegating the state administrators to temporary accommodation until a separate party headquarters had been built.

These party officials constitute a national elite, though with a tendency to become increasingly localised at the lower levels of the hierarchy. A check on the names of officials noted in the press shows individuals moving from Welega to Bale, Eritrea to Arsi, Gojjam to Sidamo, Gonder to Kaffa, Gojjam to Tigray. It follows that many of them, at any rate, were not natives of their regions, and that they were primarily central government appointees, rather than serving as a channel for local representation. Nonetheless, there were quite a number of cases where party officials were assigned to their home regions, if not necessarily to their own province. In Eritrea and Tigray, where at least a working knowledge of Tigrinya is essential for effective administration, a high proportion of WPE officials have distinctively northern names. In the Gash-Setit province of Eritrea, the first secretary was a native of the area who had been successively POMOA and then COPWE representative, and who then ran the provincial WPE until he was killed when the EPLF captured Barentu in July 1985, but this was exceptional: in an area much of which was dominated by the secessionist movements, an active local leader committed to the central government was obviously worth sustaining.[47] In Hararghe, at least four of the WPE provincial first secretaries in March 1986 were Moslems from the region, though only one of these at most was running his own home province. It is likewise possible to detect a fair sprinkling of Oromo names among party officials in Oromo areas, though these may not have come from the region to which they were posted.

As these references suggest, even if the WPE can scarcely be regarded as a representative organisation, its local level leadership is by no means ethnically restricted to Amharas or other 'core' peoples. An analysis of the names of 228 regional and provincial WPE officials (excluding regional first secretaries) noted in the press over the two years after the party's foundation, shows fifty-seven or precisely a quarter to have distinctively non-Amhara/Tigrean names, with a further fifteen names which are distinctively

91

Tigrean or Eritrean. Of these sixteen were Moslem, and another twenty-one distinctively Oromo. Of the eighty-eight provincial first secretaries whose names are available, accounting for the great majority of the party bosses in the hundred or so provinces, 12.5 per cent each are Moslem and Oromo, while a further 8 per cent are distinctively Eritrean or Tigrean. These figures are of course subject to all the problems of analysing Ethiopian names already noted, and represent a minimum estimate of individuals drawn from non-Amhara peoples, the actual proportion probably being much higher. They indicate nonetheless that even though the WPE is dominated by people associated with the centralist tradition of the Ethiopian state, it contains a notably higher proportion of officials who are evidently drawn from non-Amhara groups than is found in comparable institutions such as the military or the civil bureaucracy.

It is also clear that, below the level of the regional first secretary, the military domination of the party apparatus drops sharply. Only twenty-two of the 228 party officials noted above are identifiably from the military (four of them former Derg members), and though this is certainly an underestimate, there is nothing to indicate the proportion of military membership found at Central Committee level. In Hararghe, for example – which as a sensitive frontier region and the main battleground in the Ethio–Somali war might be expected to have an exceptional military representation – no more than three of the twelve provincial first secretaries in post in early 1986 were former soldiers, while five were teachers and the remainder mostly lower-level civil servants. There was a similar preponderance of former teachers in Wollo, where (without being able to conduct a full survey) I was unable to find any former officers among the provincial first secretaries. A few local party officials were survivors from POMOA, while others were former provincial administrators who had moved across from the state to the party apparatus. At local level, much more evidently than at the centre, the party is more than the mere rechristening of a military regime.

THE PEOPLE'S DEMOCRATIC REPUBLIC OF ETHIOPIA

The establishment of the People's Democratic Republic of Ethiopia (PDRE) in September 1987, with the introduction of a new constitution, completed the formal creation of a new set of Marxist–Leninist institutions, taking over from the military regime. In principle, even though the party had been created three years earlier, state power remained until 1987 in the hands of the PMAC. The transfer of this power to civilian institutions based on popular election was very largely cosmetic. The same people remained in power, and guided the process by which they assumed the mantle of popular sovereignty. This process nonetheless provides some guide both to the regime's mode of operation, and to the type of political system which it sought to create.

The first step, in a sequence characterised by an extraordinary formalism, was the establishment in March 1983 of the Institute for the Study of Ethiopian Nationalities, which itself had been proposed in a resolution of the second COPWE congress held the preceding January.[48] The Institute was largely staffed by academics seconded from Addis Ababa University, and representing a variety of disciplines, including law, political science, sociology, history and economics. Its director, Yayehirad Kitaw, was a former teacher in the medical faculty. It was given the twin tasks of conducting studies on the nationalities question and on the projected constitution of the PDRE. In practice, though it accumulated a great deal of information about the various ethnic groups in Ethiopia, there was little specific use to which this could be put, and its most tangible task was in drafting the constitution. Formally, this was entrusted to a Constitutional Commission appointed in February 1986, with the institute as its secretariat; but with a membership of 343, the commission was much too large to serve as anything but a rubber-stamping body, and served largely to convey the impression of wide national participation in the constitution-making process.[49] It was inevitably dominated by the WPE leadership, with 122 full and alternate members of the Central Committee; but in including not only the Patriarch of the Ethiopian Orthodox Church and the chairman of the Supreme Islamic Council, but also the heads of the Catholic and Lutheran Churches in Ethiopia, it provided the regime's most explicit recognition of organised religion. A wide variety of other notables included artists, writers, doctors and Ethiopia's two surviving Olympic gold-medal winners. Eleven members bore traditional titles of nobility inherited from the old regime, and at least twenty-one were women. Thirty-one had recognisably Moslem names, and a further fifty-nine had non-Amhara/Tigrean names, many of them Oromo.

The draft constitution which this body formally approved followed a conventional Leninist pattern.[50] The preamble recites the struggles, both of Ethiopia against imperialism, and of the Ethiopian working people against exploitation, while emphasising that 'the Ethiopian state has, from the beginning, been a multi-national state'. Ethiopia is a state of the working people founded on the alliance of workers and peasants (art. 1.1), and based on the principle of democratic centralism (art. 4.1). The WPE is a vanguard political party guided by Marxism–Leninism, which determines the perspective for the development of the country, and is the guiding force of the state and the entire society (art. 6). The chapter on the economy, while stating that the ownership of the means of production is socialist (art. 12), and that the state shall guide the economic and social activities of the country through a central plan (art. 11), nonetheless allows for private ownership within the limits set by law (arts. 12, 15). A provision that 'In order to create favourable conditions for development, the state shall ensure that human settlement patterns correspond to the distribution of natural resources' (art. 10.2) clearly refers to the resettlement programme, just as the provision that 'The state shall encourage the scattered rural population to aggregate' (art. 10.3) refers to villagisation.

The chapter on defence states that the PDRE shall maintain a strong defence force (art. 25.1) and implement national military service (art. 26.3). Foreign policy is based on the principles of international proletarianism, peaceful coexistence and non-alignment (art. 27), the ambivalence between the first and last of these being clarified by stating that while the PDRE respects the right of states to pursue the social and economic system of their choice, it promotes all-round relations and cooperation with socialist states, and strengthens its relations with the international working-class movement (art. 28). The chapter on the freedoms, rights and duties of citizens includes the only change of any substance made in the draft originally published in June 1986: the removal of a prohibition on bigamy (draft art. 38.1). This reflected not only the need not to seem discriminatory as between Christianity and Islam, but also considerable difficulties in implementation; monogamy remains the government's goal.[51] There is also a guarantee of freedom of movement and residence (art. 48), which may conflict with the state's obligation to regulate settlement patterns.

The supreme organ of state power is the National Shengo (art. 62), a neologism evidently coined as an Amharic equivalent to 'soviet'. It is elected for a five-year term (art. 68), holds one regular session a year (art. 67), and enjoys sweeping powers to determine state policy, establish other national institutions, and elect officials from the president downwards (art. 62). Candidates may be nominated only by the WPE, mass organisations (such as kebelles), military units, and other bodies entitled by law (art. 64). The Council of State acts as the organ of the National Shengo between sessions (art. 81), and has the right to issue decrees (art. 83). The president of the republic – a post clearly destined for Mengistu Haile-Mariam – can manage the executive, appoint and dismiss ministers, and issue decrees (arts. 86, 87). The Council of Ministers, though formally the highest executive and administrative organ of the PDRE (art. 89.1), is evidently subordinate to the president, while the prime minister likewise has only subsidiary duties (art. 93).

In the critical area of nationalities and regional autonomy, the constitution is predictably centralist, with only token concessions to the idea of autonomy. The PDRE is a unitary state, which 'shall ensure the equality of nationalities, combat chauvinism and narrow nationalism and advance the unity of the Working People of all nationalities' (art. 2). Although it ensures the equality, development and respectability of the languages of the various nationalities (art. 2), state activities are to be conducted in Amharic (art. 116). The provisions on regional government allow for two kinds of subordinate territorial jurisdiction, the administrative region and the autonomous region (art. 59). Given that the administrative region already exists as the main territorial unit within Ethiopia, the autonomous region is implicitly available as an area for self-administration by minority nationalities, either within an administrative region, or directly responsible to the central government. Though each region is to have its own shengo (art. 95), these are subject to the National Shengo, which also establishes regional boundaries (art. 63.2). The basic powers of the regional authorities outlined in the constitution are identical for both administrative and autonomous regions (art. 97), but the autonomous regions may be given additional powers by law (art. 99). Any powers to be enjoyed by local self-governing areas are thus strictly delegated, and enjoy no constitutional protection.

Once the commission had approved the initial draft, this was submitted to a process of widespread organised consultation, after which a final draft was drawn up for approval by referendum. Within Ethiopia, this consultation took the form mainly of meetings of peasants' and urban dwellers' associations, other mass organisations and units of the armed forces, at which WPE representatives outlined the draft and sought comments and questions; it encompassed a very high proportion of the population. Any reactions critical of the basic framework were brushed aside, but considerable discussion took place on provisions such as the monogamy clause, and a lengthy statement issued with the final text explained issues raised during the discussions. Particularly striking were the efforts made to assess the views of Ethiopians living abroad, and Politbureau members spent several weeks addressing meetings of Ethiopians living in the socialist states, the Middle East, and the West. Although the government thus evidently hoped that the constitution could serve as an instrument for national reconciliation, it contained little that was likely to appeal to any of the organised opposition groupings. The final text was approved in a national referendum in February 1987.

Since state power was formally vested in the National Shengo, the election of the Shengo was the one step required before the constitution could be put into effect. The country was divided for the purpose into 835 single-member constituencies, and except for Addis Ababa, which was heavily over-represented with 12.3 per cent of the constituencies for only 3.4 per cent of the population, these were distributed broadly in proportion to the population of each region in the 1984 census.[52] Candidates, normally with three for each constituency, were nominated at kebelle and peasants' association meetings held in May. This process was entirely stage-managed. Kebelles within the same constituency simultaneously adopted the same list of candidates, and any nominations apart from the official ones were refused. In Addis Ababa, nearly two-thirds of the candidates were returned unopposed, but this was quite at variance with the pattern elsewhere in the country, where at least in principle a choice was almost always available. In almost every case, however, the candidate placed first on the list was evidently expected to win, whereas the other two were local worthies pressed into service in order to present an appearance of choice. In all but fifteen of the 702 contested seats for which voting figures are available, the first-placed candidate won, usually by a wide margin, and no prominent party figures were defeated. All of the leading members of the WPE Central Committee were elected, and those who had personal connections with particular areas of the country stood in their own home regions – Berhanu Bayih for example in Gojjam, Fisseha Desta in Tigray, Amanuel Amde-Michael in Eritrea. In several constituencies, especially in Eritrea and Hararghe, all of the candidates were army officers, and these were presumably specifically military seats. The other successful candidates included regional party officials and administrators, and officials of mass organisations such as peasants' and women's associations. Many, however, were unknown outside their home areas, and Shengo candidates were as far as possible of local origin. In Hararghe, for example, 55 per cent of the successful candidates had Moslem names, while in the Gambela province of Illubabor, all of the candidates were drawn from the local Nuer and Anuak peoples. Even though the Shengo would have no more than rubber-stamping functions, and the candidates must all have been of known loyalty to the regime, care was taken to present at least the appearance of representation.

The formation of the party involved a sustained attempt to create a new political leadership, with a structure through which its decisions could be communicated and implemented throughout the country. The seriousness of this enterprise should not be underestimated. This was no cosmetic repainting of a military regime in Marxist–Leninist colours, despite the retention of former military men in many of its leading positions, or the evident façade which formed much of the public face of the regime, complete with ubiquitous portraits of Marx, Engels and Lenin, and the coining of Amharic neologisms for Marxist terminology. By the time of the formal establishment of the People's Democratic Republic of Ethiopia in 1987, Ethiopia possessed an authentic Marxist–Leninist regime, obviously copied from Soviet models, but nonetheless effective and drawing on indigenous roots.

Granted the total absence of any kind of political party organisation at any previous period of Ethiopian history, the apparent effectiveness of the WPE may seem surprising. But it would be wrong to ascribe it simply to the organisational techniques of Leninism, without also drawing attention to the ways in which these could be grafted onto an existing Ethiopian political culture. In many respects, indeed, this culture can be seen as resembling the Russian original for which the Leninist party system was initially designed. Both countries were heirs to Byzantium, and the idea that a Leninist party state is peculiarly well adapted to the legacy of Coptic Orthodox Christianity is not to be dismissed out of hand. Both Orthodoxy and Leninism provide a model of absolute rule, sustained by an esoteric official ideology which the people are expected to accept, even if they cannot understand it, and which is sustained by a priesthood of the initiated. The formal structure of divinely (or ideologically) sanctioned authority is at the same time riven by factional conflicts and intrigues which, because they are confined to the initiated, need not fracture the façade of unity which surrounds the regime. Traditional conceptions of personal leadership, in which the leader represents ideological authority as well as actual power, can be adapted to the needs of a Leninist party system, in a way that would scarcely be possible in a liberal state.

The role of ideology, often regarded as a critical feature of Marxist–Leninist regimes, nonetheless appears to me to be largely a matter of iconography. At one level, it is all-pervasive, not simply in the slogans and portraits which adorn the streets – not just in the big towns, but in quite small settlements and on innumerable arches across the main roads – but equally in very widespread programmes of public instruction. Millions of copies of works of Marxist–Leninist literature have been imported into Ethiopia, and a large number of them, including *Das Kapital*, have been translated into Amharic. The literacy campaign, one of the regime's most impressive achievements, has had as a main goal the creation of a population which can be politically educated because it is literate. Marxist–Leninist instruction is provided at the most basic level through mass organisations such as the youth organisation, REYA, and through the schools. At a higher level, it is disseminated through compulsory courses at the university (where the disciplinary regulations for members of staff provide that academic freedom 'may not be exercised to the detriment of the propagation of scientific truths, findings and methodologies of research already accumulated in accordance with Marxism–Leninism),[53] and through an enormous number of seminars, meetings, discussion forums and the like in all government institutions, including of course the armed forces. The Yekatit '66 Political School has put thousands of people (mostly civil servants, army officers, party cadres and officials of mass organisations) through its three-month or six-month courses, and a substantial amount of attention is given to political instruction even at an institution such as the Agarfa peasants' training college. There cannot be any doubt at all that the Ethiopian regime has taken its Marxism–Leninism seriously enough to devote a large amount of its resources to propagating it, especially in terms of the time spent on it by everyone from school children to senior officials.

At another level, however, it is possible to question just what the effect of all this activity is. Firstly, there is the question of whether people's beliefs are changed by the new and sedulously inculcated ideology. There is much to indicate that – for most people at least – they are not, and that (as in many parts of the world) the atheism of the Marxist creed provides a fundamental barrier to acceptance. Even teachers in schools are greeted with derisive laughter when they claim that God does not exist. A further barrier is the depth of indigenous belief in the immutability of human nature: an acceptance that human beings are selfish, aggressive, and not to be trusted.[54] There is startlingly little reference, despite occasional rather duty-bound allusions in some of Mengistu Haile-Mariam's speeches, to any idea of the 'new socialist man', or to any supposition that the revolution or the construction of socialism will make people much different from what they are now. The

Utopian element often present in revolutionary rhetoric is almost entirely missing in Ethiopia. Finally, there is the question of how an ideology derived from industrial Europe can be applied to the vastly different circumstances of Ethiopia, and this remains very largely unanswered. 'Feudalism' can indeed be used as a blanket term of condemnation for the old regime, and serves, along with 'imperialism' and 'bureaucratic capitalism', to characterise the enemies of the revolution. But the use of Marxist ideas to analyse the revolution itself or the options which it faces remains at a very simple level. The phrase 'the broad masses' substitutes for any attempt at class analysis, while references to 'proletarian internationalism', which amounts in practice to an assertion of the Soviet alliance, similarly block any attempt to analyse the international relations of production in a state which maintains trading ties with the capitalist West. Marxism–Leninism has gone almost straight into effect as an official ideology, with the deadening effect that this implies, without passing through any but a very brief period in which people could use it to try to understand the universe in which they lived.

When ideology *is* important, this almost invariably relates to its functions as a means of control. Marxism is in this sense for the new regime what modernisation was for the old one: a means of legitimising an increase in its own power. Virtually all 'socialist' regimes use socialism as a means of justifying state control over the larger private corporations, and this was the first major measure taken by the new regime in Ethiopia early in 1975. A specifically Marxist regime, however, permits a much more intensive level of control, of which villagisation and the collectivisation of agriculture are the best examples. Equivalent opportunities are provided by the kebelles and peasants' associations, by the attempts to concentrate artisan production into cooperatives, and by the socialisation of the distributive sector. Proletarian internationalism similarly justifies the use of international resources to maintain domestic control. Most basically of all, the organisation of the party itself serves as a means for maintaining and enhancing government power, by establishing a cadre of people for whom obedience to central directives is the primary duty, and access (or the hope of it) to the benefits of power is the primary reward. Such a system, carefully instituted, offers the chance of harnessing an inherited organisational capacity and respect for leadership to create an institutional machine such as the old regime could never have produced.

While the ideological aspects of the party are elusive, its organisational ones are thus omnipresent. They have resulted in the formation of a party elite, enjoying some privileged access to the perks of office, though as yet without any public display of ostentatious wealth. The three Vs – villa, Volvo, video – have come into currency as a phrase to describe the lifestyle of the party leadership, and (as in many other African states) membership of the leader's entourage on visits abroad is prized as a means of acquiring duty-free luxuries; but compared with the gross abuse of public office found in many West African states, for example, the Ethiopian regime is positively Spartan. As the system becomes established, it is widely assumed that party membership will become increasingly necessary to achieve top positions throughout the government apparatus: the selection of a party stalwart as president of the Addis Ababa University in 1985 may be symptomatic, and was reflected in the closure of the university, a few weeks before final examinations and the end of the academic year, so that students and staff could be despatched to outlying areas of the country to help with the resettlement programme. At workplace level, party militants are expected to report on the attitudes and activities of their colleagues, thus creating an information network to supplement the government security services. The Working People's Control Committees, which duplicate the party hierarchy at workplace and territorial levels, are closely associated with the party and provide a conduit for complaints and allegations of corrupt or anti-revolutionary behaviour.

The available evidence thus points to the conclusion that an effective Leninist system of government is being, and to a large extent has been, established in Ethiopia. This conclusion is not invalidated by the fact that the WPE, in several respects, does not measure up to an idealised model of a Leninist vanguard party, since the same would be true of any other such party that one cared to name. The top leadership of the WPE is highly personalised, for example, and loyalty to the leader is the single most important criterion for membership and promotion; but this is a characteristic feature of almost any Leninist party during its early years in power, including the CPSU under Stalin, the CCP under Mao, or the PCC under Castro. Many high ranking members of the party, even up to Politbureau level, could not with any plausibility be regarded as committed Marxist–Leninists, and at a lower level it is likely that simple careerism is as important a criterion for joining the party as any other; but it is hard to believe that many governing communist parties, the CPSU included, are so very different. The various factions and tendencies that can, though without any great clarity, be discerned within the WPE – between military and civilians, ideologues and pragmatists, the surviving adherents of one or another of the old civilian factions – likewise find their equivalents elsewhere. What matters is that there is an organisation, constructed on Leninist principles and receiving strong Soviet backing, which is both determined and for the most part able to push through a thoroughgoing Leninist programme.

The major question that needs to be asked is then not whether such a party exists, but rather what it can (and cannot) do. The evidence to be considered over the rest of this book suggests that the institutions developed since the revolution may be highly effective in some ways, but ineffective or counterproductive in others. For tasks which call for straightforward administrative control, directed from above, the effectiveness of the new system is extraordinarily impressive – regardless of the inherent desirability of the ends which it is used to achieve. The villagisation campaign, requiring millions of unwilling peasants to knock down their houses and rebuild them elsewhere, is its most striking monument; but a similar control capacity is evident in the thousands of miles of hillside terracing constructed, in the urban rationing system, or in the annual call-ups for military service. But this capacity for organisation at the same time stifles any initiative or incentive which might be mobilised by the people themselves, a problem most glaringly illustrated by the inability to grow enough food.

5

The Ethiopian state: structures of extraction and control

The Ethiopian state, like any other, consists essentially in three interlocking elements: a structure of control, through which the power of the central government is maintained and if need be enforced over the people within its jurisdiction; a structure of extraction and distribution, through which resources are extracted from the economy, and distributed according to the priorities of the government – mostly, of course, for the maintenance of the state itself; and a group of people who, because they manage the state, acquire a special interest in its maintenance and power, as well as personal interests in acquiring benefits from it. If we want to know what the revolution has done to Ethiopia, a central question is therefore what it has done to the state itself.

The consolidation of the Ethiopian state structure during the 120 years preceding the revolution has been discussed in chapter 2. The first priority of the imperial state was the establishment of central control, a problem seen initially in terms of securing the obedience of regional lords and extending the national territory to the south and west, and subsequently – from the early 1960s onwards – in terms of containing the guerilla insurgency in Eritrea, and guarding against attack from the Somali Republic. The creation of a modern standing army dates from the 1940s, and by the time that the independence of other African states in the early 1960s made comparison possible, Ethiopia had substantially the largest armed forces in black Africa. This reflected partly the fact that the Ethiopian state had been created by the efforts of its own rulers and the armies at their disposal, rather than by the intrusion of alien colonial forces, and partly the political structure of the country, with its constant danger of peripheral resistance. But despite the Somali and Eritrean threats, the Ethiopian armed forces did not increase in size over the final decade of imperial government; and though Ethiopia spent a markedly higher proportion of its government budget on defence than did most of its neighbours, at 23.5 per cent in 1973 compared with a regional average of 13.7 per cent, defence spending (along with spending on

101

internal order and general administration) accounted for a decreasing share of budgetary allocations over the decade to 1973.[1] The threat to central government control was kept within manageable bounds – certainly, very much more manageable than was to be the case after 1974; and though it may plausibly be argued that there were inherent threats to central government control in Ethiopia, which may have been hastened by the revolution but which would in any event have erupted sooner or later, it was only in Eritrea, and to a lesser extent Hararghe and Bale, that these were evident before 1974.

Control was maintained secondly through the civil administration, and through the mechanisms available for transmitting a belief in the legitimacy of the regime. It has already been suggested that any conception of imperial legitimacy was wearing extremely thin by 1974, especially in the cities but also in the countryside, despite the enormous efforts made over the years to project a sense of the emperor's wisdom and benevolence. The bureaucracy, however, remained intact. Regional government had been systematised after 1941 to provide what eventually became fourteen regions of very approximately equal size, which were divided into about 100 awrajas or provinces, and in turn into nearly 600 woredas or districts. The key figure at each level was the governor (who at regional level usually received the title of imperial representative); though regional governors were usually from the central region of Shoa, provincial governors were often, and district ones almost always, men from the region itself, though not necessarily the province to which they were appointed. In southern regions, they were often drawn from the local settler community. Their functions were very largely the traditional ones of maintaining order and collecting taxes; only occasional governors were much concerned with 'development', though in the later years of the regime, governors took to raising local funds for ostensibly development purposes, which (as in many other parts of Africa) were largely appropriated for their own use.[2] Such governors had an armed police force at their disposal, supplemented by an auxiliary police force known as the *nech lebash*, and were linked with the population through local notables known as *balabbat*. It was a reasonably effective administrative system with a very limited range of functions, which worked largely because it did not try to do very much.

The central government bureaucracy expanded fairly rapidly over the last twenty years or so of the imperial regime, to accommodate an increasing number of graduates and school leavers. No consistent figures are available for government employment before 1974. Markakis quotes estimates of 35,000 in 1961 and 60,000 in 1968, which if both were correct would indicate an annual rate of increase of 8 per cent.[3] Official figures of 16,280 central government employees in Addis Ababa in 1966, as against 19,340 in 1971, indicate a rate of increase of about 3.5 per cent a year.[4] This rise in government employment was the main contributor to a steady increase in government spending, which grew at an annual average rate of 8 per cent at current prices during the decade before the revolution, compared with a GDP increase of only 5.5 per cent a year.[5] Since government tax revenues went up in proportion to spending, this meant that even before the revolution the state was extracting an increasing share of GDP, and (like many another African government) faced an imbalance between the growth rates of the productive base and of the government apparatus that relied on it.

But although the beneficiaries of government spending were mainly the wealthier residents of the towns, where not only civil service employment but also such services as health and education were heavily concentrated, so also were the people who paid for it. Well over half of government domestic revenues (55.5 per cent in 1973–74) came from a small group of taxes (income tax, import duties, excise taxes on petrol and alcohol) which fell overwhelmingly on urban consumers, and these taxes (especially income tax) were the most rapidly growing sources of revenue in the pre-revolutionary decade.[6] Export duties (almost entirely on coffee) were low, at 6.5 per cent of domestic revenue in 1973–74, and other taxes on rural producers were also light, though this did not prevent resentment at charges such as the Education Tax and Health Tax, which were levied on rural producers, ostensibly to pay for services which they did not receive. In contrast with many third-world states, Ethiopia had very little mineral extraction, and virtually no multinationals producing for export. It did share with other third-world states an inefficient parastatal sector. High profits were made by the Tobacco Monopoly, and by the government-owned Commercial Bank, but for state-owned manufacturing industry apart from tobacco, the ratio of profit to paid-up equity capital was a mere 1 per cent in 1972 (compared with 20 per cent for private industry), and many enterprises were running at a loss. In the two industries where state and private enterprises could be directly compared, textile manufacturing and printing, the private sector was markedly more efficient. In textiles, though workers were paid almost exactly the same in the two sectors, value added per worker was over twice the value of pay in private companies, and less than half in the more heavily capitalised public ones.[7] Though comparison with the private sector would no longer be possible, similar problems were to recur in the much larger public sector after the revolution.

One of the fastest growing areas of the pre-revolutionary economy was commercial agriculture, both for export and for the domestic market. This was by no means an unmixed blessing. In some areas (of which the Arsi highlands were the classic example, though similar developments could be found in northern Bale and southern Shoa), landlords were able to apply modern inputs such as tractors, fertilisers and improved seeds to the development of large commercial farms, in the process turning part of the local subsistence peasantry into an agrarian labour force, while evicting the rest to seek refuge in the towns or scratch a living from marginal land.[8] This form of agriculture, which was largely directed to food grain production, did succeed (at considerable human cost) in creating a surplus which could be marketed in the towns. In other areas, for example the Awash valley, government land grants could be obtained to establish irrigated plantations for fruit crops and the like on 'vacant' land which provided a dry season refuge for Afar and Kereyu pastoralists. In some cases, the shift to commercial agriculture created employment rather than destroying it, notably in the area around Humera on the Sudanese border, which was rapidly developed (especially for growing sesame seed) from the mid 1960s onwards. Large numbers of seasonal labourers (probably about 100,000)[9] were hired at harvest time, most of them Tigrean peasants seeking a cash income to supplement their precarious subsistence production. This process may be regarded, according to ideological taste, as a prelude either to agricultural take-off or to intensifying exploitation and rural class formation. At all events, it was aborted (or diverted to state control) at the revolution.

Government management of the pre-revolutionary economy was slight. A first five-year plan had been promulgated in 1957 and a second in 1962, but these were little more than indicative documents and no serious attempt was made to implement them. A third and more systematic plan was introduced in 1968, under the aegis of a newly created planning ministry, but its implementation was severely restricted by shortage of foreign exchange.[10] In any event, only a small part of the total national economy was under government supervision or control. A coffee board had been established in the 1950s, and this did an effective job in buying coffee from peasant producers (at a price directly related to the current world market price), cleaning and sorting it, and marketing it either directly or through private coffee exporters. A grain board, set up in 1950 for the same purpose, soon became redundant as Ethiopia moved from being an exporter to an importer of grain during the 1950s. Although an Ethiopian Grain Corporation was established in 1960, with a view to intervening on a large scale in grain marketing, it lacked working capital, market information and a pricing policy, and – with a market share never exceeding 5 per cent – was unable to compete with private traders.[11] A small capitalist class developed, much of it Armenian, Indian or Italian, but with Ethiopian participants who included leading government officials. Indigenous traders were mostly Moslem.

In summary, the extractive and control capacities of the pre-revolutionary Ethiopian state were limited in scope, but not evidently ineffective for those tasks which it sought to perform. It sought to maintain a basic level of order, and to extract sufficient resources from the economy to support an expanding state apparatus. Government development activities were largely restricted to the section of the population – in effect the urban population, and especially the middle classes – which came within its orbit. When it was called on to perform tasks outside this limited area, as for example in the Wollo famine of 1973, its inadequacy was dramatically exposed. But, in contrast to the political weaknesses of the regime which have already been discussed, it could not be said that there was any major crisis of the state itself at the time of the revolution.

THE IMPACT OF REVOLUTION

The revolution did not destroy the Ethiopian state structure, and ended by greatly strengthening it. In the short term, however, it both weakened the state and intensified the demands being made on it. The part of the structure most sharply affected was the local administration. This depended very largely on local notables and aristocrats in the northern highland regions, and on central appointees and settlers in the south; the position of the southern settlers was directly undercut by land reform, and even though the northern notables usually did not own large estates in the form found in the south, they nonetheless enjoyed a privileged status in the community which they felt, correctly, was threatened by the new regime in Addis Ababa. This regime rapidly replaced all of the previous regional and provincial governors, and within a short time a complete turnover had taken place in almost the entire personnel involved in local administration. In the other main parts of the state structure, the central administration and the armed forces, the turnover was not so complete, and a basic institutional continuity was maintained even though the top leadership was changed. In each case, the social and economic basis of the institution itself was not threatened in the same way as was the regional administration, and all that was needed was the removal of a fairly recognisable leadership cadre associated with the old regime. Most of this process took place as soon as revolution broke out in 1974, its most dramatic expression being the execution of the fifty-seven leading figures in the old regime (including several senior army officers, as well as civilian politicians) in November 1974. Several hundred other officials and senior officers were arrested, many staying in prison for up to ten years, or made their way into exile. Over the next few years these numbers increased as liberal and reformist officials lost faith in the new regime, and as the conflicts between revolutionary groups produced their own large crop of victims, prisoners and exiles. The clear-out of top and even middle-level officials from the old regime has been virtually complete. The two senior civilian technocrats on the WPE Politbureau, Hailu Yimenu and Amanuel Amde-Michael, are the only two officials who held posts equivalent to vice-minister (with the coveted title of Excellency) to survive the first few years of the revolution. A few others, such as Kassa Gebre, minister of construction and alternate Politbureau member in 1986, had reached the rank of assistant minister. Some officials of the old regime continued to be protected by their connections with the new one, a notable example being Kassa Kebede, son of Mengistu's patron Dajazmatch Kebede Tessema. But although the post-revolutionary administrative elite is almost entirely new, the changeover was achieved by promoting previously junior officials rather than by any wholesale transformation of the institutions themselves. This is a fact of which the new regime and its civilian allies were very much aware. During the early years of the revolution, 'bureaucratic capitalism' was ranked with 'feudalism' and 'imperialism' amongst the trinity of enemies of the revolution, and was used to denote the elitism and obstructiveness (often, in practice, the result of hesitation and confusion at a time of great tension and uncertainty) which were ascribed to the bureaucracy. Articles in the press referred to 'the hideous and anti-popular actions being taken by the bureaucracy in the current revolutionary period', and urged 'the fight for the elimination of the existing bureaucratic system'.[12] In practice, however, the bureaucracy was indispensable, and such attacks died down after the consolidation of the revolution in 1978, though its policy-making powers were sharply limited by the pre-eminence of the party, and many of its members had little sympathy with government policies.

An equivalent clear-out took place in the armed forces. Despite the size of the pre-revolutionary armed forces, no officers remained in post beyond 1977 who had reached the rank of brigadier general or above under the imperial regime, and very few who had reached the rank of colonel. The highest rank at which officers could become members of the Derg was major, and most of those above that rank were retired, even when they were not executed or in exile. However, the unity of the armed forces was maintained despite the tensions created by revolution – this being one of the major achievements of the Derg – and its institutional continuity was likewise preserved.

The tax base of the regime was not seriously affected by revolution, and was indeed broadened by new forms of government income which will be discussed shortly. Government domestic revenues rose at an average rate of 17 per cent a year in cash terms over the six financial years from 1974–75 to 1979–80.[13] Most taxes were in any event raised from foreign trade and from the urban areas which the government controlled, and it likewise consistently retained control over all the main coffee-producing areas. The main insurgent areas contributed negligible amounts to government revenue, and probably constituted a net drain on resources. The sole major cash-crop area lost to government control was Humera on the Sudanese border, where sesame seed production never recovered.[14] The marketing system, on the other hand, suffered badly. Though peasant agriculture quickly recovered from the 1973 famine (which was in any event limited in geographical impact), the available mechanism for removing a surplus from the peasantry had been destroyed, while the boom in private commercial agriculture was abruptly halted. The larger private estates were taken over as state farms, and a new distribution system was eventually constructed, but there were serious food shortages in Addis Ababa and other major towns which had to be met through imports.

The major effect of revolution was however not that the state apparatus was weakened, but that it was required to do much more. This in turn resulted partly from increased pressures from the population, partly from the regime's own insistence that the state should take responsibility for tasks which had previously been undertaken privately or not at all. One of the

106

effects of revolution – or more precisely, perhaps, of the kind of regime that opens the way to revolution in the first place – is that the political demands which inevitably build up as the result of social and economic change are released onto the political system over a very short period of time. The resulting chaos is what prompts the concern of post-revolutionary regimes for order and control. In large part, too, political demands are encouraged during the early years of revolution by new and insecure revolutionaries seeking to destroy the bases of the regime which they have just overthrown, by mobilising previously excluded sections of the population. In the Ethiopian case, there were three main ways in which political demands were increased, each with slightly different origins. The initial explosion in the towns was largely spontaneous, and led to the revolution itself; the new regime was put in place by urban upheaval, and in turn had to control it. The upheavals in the countryside which followed land reform were, in contrast, deliberately fostered by the new regime in order to destroy the rural bases of the old. The upsurge in regional and ethnic resistance, finally, was neither fostered nor intended by the regime, but nonetheless resulted from the general mobilisation of political identities which any revolution brings with it, from the weakening of central control which encouraged local opposition movements, and from particular circumstances in specific areas which led to mobilisation against the regime rather than in its favour, and encouraged external intervention on the opposition side.

But the increase in state power which follows from revolution is not merely reactive; it also follows from a characteristically revolutionary insistence that the state is the mechanism through which a general transformation of the conditions of life should be achieved. Sometimes, there is an early and short-lived faith in spontaneous popular action, though in Ethiopia this was almost entirely absent. Only the initial land reform could be said to have been left to 'the people' to implement by themselves, guided by the zemecha campaigners. Both the military basis of the government, and its origins in a society with a long-entrenched respect for hierarchy and order, militated against any belief in spontaneous popular activity; only the EPRP – whom the official press contemptuously referred to as 'anarchists' – had much faith in it, and even that, in all probability, was largely a product of their opposition to the Derg. The regime's own emphasis was consistently on the state, especially in the management of the economy, and this was apparent from the nationalisation of businesses and the establishment of state farms in the early months of the revolution. This reliance on the state rather than the market in running the economy, together with the increased level of surplus expropriation needed to sustain the new instruments of control themselves, required a level of detailed regulation which the old regime could scarcely have dreamed of, and would never have been able to achieve.

This increase in the power of the state, and its application to the various fields of government activity including urban administration, agricultural policy, and regional government, are what the rest of this book is basically about. The remainder of this chapter provides an overview of this process, and later chapters will then discuss some of its manifestations in greater detail.

THE STRUCTURES OF CONTROL

It goes without saying that any revolutionary state will possess unlimited formal powers for regulating the lives of its citizens. A Marxist–Leninist state has no place for a 'bourgeois' Western conception of human rights, any more indeed than did the monarchical state that preceded it – though the powers of the state have been much more explicitly set out and more brutally enforced under the revolutionary regime than under its predecessor. The first set of proclamations issued by the new government after its own establishment, in November 1974, amended the existing legislation in order to create new offences, increase the government's powers, and bring the judicial process more closely under its control.[15] Frequently amended, they established special penal and criminal procedure codes, and set up special courts to try people accused of offences against the revolution. They were supplemented as required by additional legislation, such as the State of Emergency Proclamation of September 1975, which made offences such as striking, issuing illegal pamphlets, or illegal public speaking, punishable by up to ten or fifteen years imprisonment, or in exceptional cases death.[16] Following the suspension of the existing constitution at the time of the military takeover in September 1974, there was no formal restriction on the powers of government until the promulgation thirteen years later of the new constitution of the People's Democratic Republic of Ethiopia. In common with other socialist constitutions such as that of the Soviet Union, this formally guaranteed a number of individual rights such as the privacy of the mail.[17]

A long series of reports by Amnesty International and other groups make it clear that not only have these powers been fully exercised, but that widespread executions and imprisonments without trial have occurred without reference even to the formal legislation.[18] This is indeed amply confirmed both from official sources and from other writings favourable to the Ethiopian government.[19] My purpose is not to add to the chorus of condemnation (which would equally have to take into account the means used by the regime's opponents), but simply to point out that government power, ruthlessly exercised, is one of the basic facts of Ethiopian political life. By the mid 1980s, that power was sufficiently well established for a Hobbesian framework of order to have been reimposed. Most areas of the country, outside the main insurgent regions, were peaceful, and it was possible to travel freely (with the necessary permits) in the countryside, while Addis Ababa was one of the safest cities in Africa. Though imprisonments, and indeed political executions, continued to take place, they were no longer gloried in as they had been earlier in the revolution, when the liquidation of 'anarchists' and 'anti-revolutionary elements' had been gleefully proclaimed. But this reflected the successful imposition of government power, rather than its relaxation, while the apparent acquiescence with which government policies were implemented continued to rest on the collective memory of the terror.

The regime's basic means of control is provided by the armed forces, which have expanded by between six and eight times since the revolution. Most estimates put the total number at about 300,000, though it is not clear whether this needs to be supplemented to allow for the number of national servicemen. The four-division army inherited from the imperial regime has been expanded to twenty-four divisions, which are grouped together as 'task forces' for specific operations. Probably nearly half of this total is stationed in Eritrea. It includes twenty tank battalions with about a thousand tanks, and four airborne brigades. The air force operates about 150 jet aircraft, in addition to helicopters and transports.[20] This enormous force, amounting in manpower to something approaching one per cent of the total national population, was raised in 1976–77 by requiring peasant associations to provide a quota of recruits from their own members. This both strengthened the power of the peasant association leadership, which inevitably took the key role in determining who should be conscripted, and also greatly lessened the cost of maintaining such a large army, since the association was also expected to pay and clothe its recruits, in addition to providing for the members of their families. Press reports refer to associations ploughing and harvesting land on behalf of members who had been sent to the front.[21]

The original militia raised for the peasants' march on Eritrea in 1976, and for the Somali war a year later, appears to have been run down progressively from late 1979 onwards. There are reports in the press of demobilised militiamen returning home between October 1979 and June 1981, and being received with organised welcomes in most of the regions of Ethiopia.[22] Local militia training has been maintained, however, and from time to time reports appear of a few hundred militiamen being given certificates by the regional military commissar in one or another area of the country. These include units drawn from the resettlement villages in frontier areas such as Asosa in Welega.[23] There has however been no further mass call-up of peasants equalling that of 1977. Its place has been taken by national military service, which was announced by Mengistu Haile-Mariam in his 1981 May Day speech.[24] The National Military Service Proclamation eventually issued in May 1983 provides for all Ethiopians aged between eighteen and thirty to undergo six months' military training followed by two years' active service, remaining on the reserve until the age of fifty.[25] In practice, this call-up has been selective rather than universal, with each peasants' association or urban kebelle being required to forward lists of eligible young men to the military commissariat established in the ministry of interior. In principle, the ministry then decides who to recruit, after which the kebelles or peasants' associations are required to ensure that the youths selected report for service. In practice, inevitably, much of the discretion has remained in the kebelle's or association's hands, while they in turn have been responsible for delivering a given quota of recruits on the due date. Recruitment takes place in a series of campaigns, with a first batch in May 1984 followed by a second in January 1985, each raising about 60,000 conscripts.[26] The first batch were said to have been used mostly on back-up duties, but most of the second batch were sent to Eritrea immediately after completing their training in July 1985, to help meet the crisis created by the EPLF capture of Barentu. Some of these fledgling soldiers were captured almost immediately by the EPLF around Nakfa, and the overall casualty rate appears to have been very high. The third round-up took place in December 1985, and partly because of the fate of its predecessor, partly because the size of the batch was apparently doubled to 120,000, proved harder to carry out; there was also a widespread rumour, emanating from a solidarity speech made by Mengistu at an OAU meeting, that the recruits were to be sent to fight in South Africa. At all events, young men disappeared like magic from the streets of Addis Ababa, many being sent to stay with relatives outside the kebelles where they were registered; even though their parents were liable to be imprisoned for a fortnight or so in the kebelle jail, most of these seem to have thought it well worth the price. Despite a newspaper report that 'the country's youth enthusiastically participate in the programme',[27] the reality was rather different, with lamenting relatives gathering round the keftenya head-quarters whence recruits were bussed to training centres in distant parts of the country. To prevent desertion, Addis Ababa conscripts were sent to camps in regions such as Kaffa and Welega, while Eritrean and Tigrean recruits were flown by Soviet aircraft to Addis Ababa.[28] These three batches of national servicemen, of which the first were demobilised in October 1986,[29] would by themselves add up to a total of close to a quarter of a million. A fourth batch was recruited in November 1986.[30]

The national military service programme is organised by regional military commissars, who are officers normally between the ranks of major and colonel, attached to the ministry of interior. These are not to be confused with the political commissars attached to units in the armed forces early in the revolution, a function subsequently taken over by the office for military–political affairs under Legesse Asfaw, and later by the COPWE and WPE organisation in the armed forces. Regional military commissars, however, usually come from the political administration of the armed forces, and are full or alternate members of the WPE Central Committee; a few of them are former members of the Derg. They sometimes take on wider responsi-bilities, as for example when the military commissar for Addis Ababa assumed the functions of the regional WPE first secretary when this indi-vidual was away for medical treatment in 1986.[31]

The network of political organisation inside the armed forces, which has been in place since well before the formation of the WPE or even COPWE, helps to emphasise the subordination of the military to political control. In the very early years of the revolution, factionalism in the armed forces was scarcely less than amongst civilian politicians, and near mutiny among Ethiopian forces in the Ogaden was responsible for the loss of Jijiga and the Karamara pass during the Somali war. Many officers were caught in a conflict between their Ethiopian nationalism on the one hand, and their distaste for the regime on the other; the overall effect of the Somali war was to consolidate the regime's control of the armed forces, by enabling it to call on the ultimate value of defending the national territory. Any assessment of political dissent in the armed forces since that time can only be speculative. It is to be expected that the long and costly war in Eritrea should have aroused resentments among those who have borne the brunt of fighting it, and from time to time there are rumours of the arrest or execution of suspect or dissident officers, sometimes in groups of up to forty or fifty. Mengistu Haile-Mariam himself is reported to have shot officers responsible for major losses, such as the destruction of aircraft in an EPLF raid on Asmara airport. But these are the products of a rumour network which thrives in the absence of reliable information. Thus far, at least, dissent has been within the government's capacity to control, and there has been no evident breaking of ranks. Military security procedures on Eastern European lines have been introduced with the aid of East German advisers, and dissent is in any event much harder to organise in an army of several hundred thousand than in one of only a few battalions. Even the takeover by a four-division army in 1974 was possible only because of the coordination provided by the Derg, and such a semi-clandestine organisation linking all the units of the armed forces would be inconceivable under the revolutionary regime. Such difficulties of organisation, allied as always to the memory of what the armed forces (like other sections of Ethiopian society) went through during the early years of revolution, may do more to account for the political quiescence of the military than do the Soviet and East German role in military security. Controlling the military security of another state is always difficult, not least one in which habits of secrecy are so well entrenched as in Ethiopia; and the outbreak of the civil war in South Yemen in 1986, which clearly took the Soviet Union entirely by surprise, showed how difficult it can be to control security even in a state much more closely under Soviet aegis than Ethiopia.

It is nonetheless possible to distinguish between career soldiers, often in command positions, whose commitment to Marxism–Leninism is evidently slight and may well be non-existent, and officers who have come up through the political administration of the armed forces. Even though senior officers in command positions are usually members of the WPE Central Committee, their functions are strictly military, and it is not difficult to infer the possibility of conflict between them and junior officers who have risen through the militarily disruptive channels of political connections and Marxist zeal. One reason why non-political officers retain high command must simply be the need for professional competence and organisational stability in an army continuously involved in warfare. This must in large part account for the reinstatement of major-general Merid Negussie, the best-known of Ethiopian field commanders and until 1987 commander of the forces in Eritrea, following his dismissal for involvement in a public brawl; he was appointed chief of staff in March 1987, in a move which put career soldiers into all the main positions in the ministry of defence. Another, however, is that such officers may provide insurance against too close a penetration of the military by a party organisation which might escape Mengistu's control. Originally set up by Legesse Asfaw, the political administration of the armed forces was later entrusted to another of Mengistu's close confidants, major-general Gebreyes Wolde-Hana. Like Legesse (and Mengistu) a Derg member from the old Third Division in Harer, but unlike Legesse an officer rather than an NCO, he is said to have cleared out many of Legesse's protégés from political positions in the army. However, any political organisation in the armed forces must be suspect, not least as a potential avenue for Soviet infiltration, and beneath the cover of a Leninist party organisation, Mengistu has in effect resorted to the same divide-and-rule policy as his imperial predecessor.

These tensions, held in check by the presence of a strong ruler, could well come into the open in a crisis over the succession, and in particular help to reduce the likelihood that Legesse Asfaw might be able to succeed Mengistu on the strength of his key role at the head of the party organisation and the assumed support of the Soviet Union. Legesse, the former sergeant catapulted into power through his association with the head of state, is generally regarded with deep hostility by the professional officer corps. So, despite their having come to Ethiopia's rescue in 1977, are the Russians, who are often credited with having encouraged the Somalis to attack Ethiopia in 1977, and with furnishing secret support to the EPLF (while restricting arms supplies to Ethiopia) so as to maintain the war in Eritrea. The continuation of a bitter war in Eritrea, which twelve years of fighting have failed to win, provides the main danger for a military reaction against the regime. The level of casualties in this war is horrifying – staggering, indeed, in relation to the virtual absence of interest or information about it in the outside world. An inconclusive Ethiopian offensive in November 1985 to January 1986, for example, virtually unreported outside, produced something in the region of 6,000 casualties; the toll for the much-publicised Red Star campaign of early 1982 was probably about 40,000. The disabled – including a large number who have lost their feet from mines – are not released back into the population, but are consigned to 'heroes' centres (with a showpiece centre at Debre Zeit, south of Addis Ababa, and other unpublicised ones elsewhere), where they are looked after but virtually imprisoned; the reintegration of these maimed and embittered veterans is a serious problem, and an earlier policy of making government offices accept a quota of them has been abandoned. One of the reasons for the use of national servicemen in Eritrea in 1985 may indeed have been to take some of the pressure off the regular army, but the release of demobilised national servicemen into a society with a high level of unemployment has caused problems in its turn.

A second means of control is the ministry of public and national security, established in 1979, together with the government's myriad information networks. The minister, Tesfaye Wolde-Selassie, is a professional intelligence officer trained in the West, and a close personal ally of Mengistu who is said to have been the best man at his wedding. In a country so riddled as Ethiopia with intrigue, suspicion and the fear of informers – and in this respect revolutionary Ethiopia differs little from its imperial predecessor – it is difficult to tell to what extent the universal belief in the existence of an all-pervasive security network is justified, to what extent the creation of popular culture.

A further control institution is the party itself, which provides its own intelligence network, through the obligation on its members to report any deviant or anti-revolutionary attitudes or actions to their superiors, and equally through the use of the party as a disciplined organisation for implementing government policies. Beneath the party, and subject to its supervision, are the various mass organisations through which virtually all Ethiopians are brought within a common administrative framework. As well as the organs of local administration – the kebelles and peasants' associations – these notably include the trade unions, and the women's and youth associations. The number of ordinary policemen declined sharply in the early years of the revolution from about 28,000 in 1971–72 to 17,000 in 1981–82, many of them being drafted into the army to meet the Somali invasion.[32] The numbers have however been much more than made up by the creation of revolutionary defence squads which provide a local police force in both peasants' and urban dwellers' associations.

Finally, the Working People's Control Committees, established on a Soviet model from November 1981 onwards, have been set up throughout the country, from central and regional down to workplace level.[33] Their functions – symbolised by a hand holding a disembodied eye, superimposed on a map of Ethiopia – are largely concerned with investigating economic malpractices and complaints of maladministration. From time to time, reports appear in the press, detailing cases of corruption, economic sabotage, misuse of public property, and the seizure of illicitly traded coffee.[34] The chairman of the national committee reported in September 1986 that 26,000 cases of corruption, involving the misappropriation of some 400 million birr, had been investigated since its inception.[35] At least for those who are not protected by political influence, the committees – which provide a legitimised channel for spying on colleagues and for the expression of grievances by government employees – may well serve as a deterrent to corruption, though local managers also complain that they have the effect of stifling initiative and responsibility.

Taken together with the ordinary agencies of state administration, these institutions add up to a control capacity vastly greater than anything that could have been provided by the personal networks of the old regime. To some extent, this increased capacity has been negated by an increased level of resistance; but over most of the country, it is reflected in an ability to organise the lives of Ethiopians by central direction in a way that had never been remotely possible before.

THE STRUCTURE OF PRODUCTION

From the very start of the revolution, the new regime was 'socialist' in the sense that it was committed to state control over the economy. Some businesses owned by the emperor and his family, including the main bus company, were nationalised even before the fall of the monarchy. Further nationalisations in January and February 1975 brought some 200 companies into public ownership, and were accompanied by the Declaration on Economic Policy of Socialist Ethiopia of February 1975, which in turn was incorporated into the comprehensively entitled Government Ownership and Control of the Means of Production Proclamation issued the following month.[36] This divided the economy into areas of exclusive government activity, activities which might be undertaken jointly by the government and foreign capital, and activities which were to be left to the private sector. The first category included financial services and basic industries, extending not only to large-scale enterprises such as iron and steel, petroleum, textiles, drugs and tobacco, but also to such areas of small-scale manufacture as leather goods and ceramics. The second encompassed sectors for which foreign expertise would evidently be needed, including mining, the manufacture of plastics, and tourism. The third left in private hands a wide variety of small-scale activities, but also import and export trade, wholesale and retail trade, and road transport. The nationalisation of rural land, and subsequently of urban land and extra houses, brought further major means of production under state control. Although some 98 per cent of agricultural land continued to be farmed by peasants, and administered through peasants' associations, the plantations and private estates formed the basis for a state farm sector which was rapidly expanded in the early years of the revolution, and will be examined in a later chapter. Other sectors of the economy which had previously been left in private hands were liable to be nationalised whenever the government felt the need to do so. In September 1979, for example, the Ministry of Transport announced that the Maritime and Transport Services Corporation would be the only legal operator for shipping agency and transport services, and that all other licences for these services were revoked forthwith.[37]

All of these nationalised resources were placed in 1975 under the management of a newly established Ministry of National Resources Development, which was divided into sections dealing with industry, agriculture, tourism, mining, properties and so forth; but this huge conglomerate proved unwieldy and was broken up. Separate Ministries of Industry and of Mines

114

and Energy were set up in 1976, and the agricultural properties were transferred to the Ministry of Agriculture. Finally, in May 1979, the old Ministry of Commerce was separated into Ministries of External Trade and Domestic Trade, enabling the government to take increasingly close control of areas which had been left in private hands in 1975, while a new Ministry of State Farms was created. The old Coffee Board was at the same time converted into a Ministry of Coffee and Tea Development, and in turn took over much of the coffee marketing which had previously been left in the hands of private traders. Since no compensation was paid for the foreign enterprises nationalised in 1975 (though in some cases partial compensation terms were agreed several years later), it was not surprising that the provision for joint government and foreign management failed to attract any new investment. The Joint Venture Establishment Proclamation eventually issued in January 1983 allowed for the foreign shareholding to be taken over at any time (though on payment of compensation) by the Ethiopian government.[38]

The early years of the revolution were a period of sharp economic decline, especially in the towns. The countryside was in contrast to some extent insulated from the economic disruption which is the almost inevitable initial consequence of revolution; peasants were still in a position to gain from the abolition of rent and the forced extraction of produce by landlords. These advantages were later to be whittled away by the increased pressure on land which the land reform eventually entailed, and by the creation of a new government extractive mechanism to replace the old private one. Apart from a short-lived increase in agricultural production in 1975 and 1976, due partly to land reform and partly to recovery from the 1973–74 drought, all areas of production declined. The clearest indication of increasing poverty is provided by the Addis Ababa retail price index, which rose at a rate of 17.1 per cent a year over the period 1974–79, compared with a rate of 2.5 per cent a year over the previous five-year period from 1969 to 1973.[39] Some allowance must however be made for the fact that house rents, which were reduced after the nationalisation of rented houses, were excluded from the index. The most important source of inflation (which was not accompanied by any increase in salaries) was the price of food, which rose at an annual rate of 20.4 per cent, with a 26.0 per cent inflation rate for food grains. This corresponded closely with a decline in the marketed agricultural surplus, which reached its lowest point in 1978.[40] Another major inflationary item was the price of firewood, with an average annual inflation rate of 32.9 per cent in Addis Ababa. Sharply diverging inflation rates for different towns reflect the increasing fragmentation of the economy over this period, with the breakdown of national distribution networks. The Eritrean capital of Asmara, unsurprisingly, had a particularly high inflation rate of over 40 per cent a year, as the insurgency both cut it off from its hinterland and led to an inflow of refugees.

Over the four years until 1978, the regime was too preoccupied with survival, and in 1977–78 especially with the Somali war, to be able to devote much of its attention to the economy. Mengistu Haile-Mariam's revolution day speech of September 1978 marks the shift in government priorities towards post-war and post-revolutionary reconstruction.[41] This speech is notable especially for its attack on 'the petty-bourgeois tendencies of the peasantry', and its whole-hearted commitment to collectivisation – issues which will be taken up in the discussion of the agrarian economy. A masthead slogan in *The Ethiopian Herald* at this time, 'We Will Liquidate The Evil Legacies of the Past and Place Nature Under Our Control',[42] perfectly expressed a revolutionary confidence in the achievements of centrally directed planning. The belief that for every economic problem, there was a political solution enforceable through administrative action, was to persist into the resettlement and villagisation campaigns of the mid 1980s. A proclamation to launch a National Revolutionary Production and Cultural Development Campaign and set up a Central Planning Supreme Council was issued in October 1978,[43] and the campaign itself was launched in February 1979, with a parade through Addis Ababa of tractors and representatives of the sixteen production task forces. The 'task force' imagery, adopted from the military formations in the Eritrean war, was pervasive – grain purchase task forces were to follow. 'Production cadres', selected initially from the Addis Ababa lumpenproletariat, were given three-monthly training courses in batches of 1,000 at a time, and sent off to supervise workers on the state farms and elsewhere.[44] A later report of a production cadre being sentenced to fifteen years imprisonment for killing a peasant, 'on flimsy pretext and in flagrant abuse of his authority'[45] must evidently have been an extreme case, but indicates the role of cadres in organising and controlling the peasantry.

The National Revolutionary Development Campaigns were indeed a matter of campaigning rather than planning. Although ambitious targets were announced, there was no comprehensive ordering of available resources to achieve specific goals. A more thoroughgoing attempt at planning was launched with the establishment of the Office of the National Council for Central Planning (in place of the Central Planning Supreme Council) in June 1984,[46] and the publication of the Ten Year Perspective Plan for the period 1984–85 to 1993–94. The Ten Year Plan projected an extremely ambitious annual GDP growth rate of 6.5 per cent in real terms – even this figure having been scaled down in drafting from an initial target of 10 per cent a year. Even before the whole process was effectively wrecked by the famine crisis which struck at exactly the moment when the plan was due to come into effect, it was abundantly clear that the plan targets (which envisaged annual average growth rates of 4.3 per cent in agriculture, 10.8 per cent in industry and 6.9 per cent in services) were little more than wishful thinking, and rested on extremely optimistic assumptions about everything from the weather to the availability of foreign exchange, and on a high level of internal inconsistency into the bargain. The projected balance of payments, for example, envisaged an increase in the current account deficit from 699 million birr in 1983–84 to 3576.8 million birr in 1993–94. This deficit would be balanced by an increase from 220.0 to 714.4 m.b. in official grants, from 516.0 to 1609.5 m.b. in net loans, and from nothing to 800 m.b. in joint venture investment, adding up to a total increase in investment capital inflows of 424 per cent.[47] Not only is it extraordinarily unlikely that such an increase could be obtained, but equally if it were, it would lead to a debt trap of unmanageable proportions, and even then could not be expected to generate the increases in output and employment needed to meet the plan targets.[48]

The Ten Year Plan was broken down into a number of sectoral plans, and was to be implemented through the launching of three medium-term plans respectively for two years (1984/85–1985/86), three years (1986/87–1988/89), and five years (1989/90–1993/94), each of which was to be further divided to provide annual targets. Seven zonal planning offices were established, covering small groups of administrative regions (normally two or three, though Hararghe had one to itself) which formed reasonably coherent economic units. These were to submit detailed zonal plans to the central planning office, and in turn supervise the implementation of the plan within their zones. Planning councils were also set up at provincial level, in order to involve local officials and the representatives of mass organisations such as peasants' associations, but in the first year (1985–86) for which zonal plans were drawn up, they appear to have consisted very largely of shopping lists of desirable investments sought by local administrators, and to have been almost entirely ignored at central level. Nor were local planning councils consulted over such vital issues as the implementation of the villagisation campaign in their areas.[49]

The arrangements for sectoral planning were no more successful. The sectoral plans, which accounted for nearly eighty per cent of the published text, consisted of little more than useful summaries of recent developments, accompanied by aspirations or shopping lists for the future. These ranged in length from just three pages for social welfare to fifty-one for education and sixty-two for trade and tourism; the key productive sectors, agriculture, manufacturing and energy, rated twenty-one, fifteen and ten pages respectively. These plans corresponded to individual ministries, and were often revealing as to bureaucratic priorities. The dedication of more than half of total manufacturing investment over ten years to thirteen large projects indicated the socialist gigantism which has equally characterised actual investment policy; and the ministry of information proposed to devote over 70 per cent of its planned investment to a single mass media centre.[50] They did not however add up to any coherent development strategy; and though this might have been rectified in the implementation process, the committees established to draw up annual sectoral plans were restricted to advising on the best means to achieve plan targets already laid down. When the targets were themselves well out of range, the issue of how best to hit them acquired an air of make-believe.

117

Just as, in imperial days, Ethiopia was sometimes described as a constitutional monarchy on the grounds that it possessed both a monarchy and a constitution, so it would be equally misleading in the middle 1980s to call it a centrally planned economy just because it had both an economy and a central plan. Nonetheless, the plan cannot be entirely disregarded. Not only did it provide a useful indication of government priorities, but also, where specific targets were laid down which could be achieved by administrative action, it was likely that the government would indeed seek to implement them. In this respect, the most important target in the whole document was the commitment to increasing the number of peasant households embraced by agricultural producers' cooperatives from 83,150 households (1.2 per cent of the total) in 1983–84 to 4,100,000 (52.7 per cent of the total) in 1993–94.[51] This objective foreshadowed a dramatic change in Ethiopian peasant farming over a decade which could not conceivably be implemented by the reasonably voluntary means used to encourage cooperativisation before 1985, and for which the villagisation programme was widely seen as laying the ground. The projected increase in the share of state farms in the total cultivated area of the country from 3.2 per cent in 1983–84 to 6.2 per cent in 1993–94, though large in its own right, was very much less important.

In contrast to the high growth rates projected in the plan, gross domestic product since the revolution has consistently failed to match the population growth rate of about 2.8 per cent a year, and a decline in per capita income was under way, even before the famine years of 1983–85.[52] A growth rate of less than one per cent over the three years to 1977–89 can be ascribed to the disruptions resulting from the revolution itself, including land reform, the nationalisation of private business, and the conflicts for political control which culminated in the urban terror, rural resistance and Somali invasion.[53] With the imposition of effective central government control over most of the country, and the launching of the National Revolutionary Development Campaigns from 1978, a recovery took place which produced GDP growth rates of 5.2 per cent in 1978–79 and 5.5 per cent in 1979–80.[54] This increase was due largely to reasonable weather conditions, and to a once-for-all increase in industrial output as factories left idle during the previous few years were energetically put back into production, and could not be sustained on a long-term basis. Over the next three years, the growth rate slowed to an annual average of 3.1 per cent, as industry reached full capacity and came up against increasing problems of spare parts and raw materials, while the agricultural economy ran into the intense difficulties discussed in a later chapter. The two drought years of 1983–84 and 1984–85 resulted in absolute declines of 3.7 per cent and 6.5 per cent respectively, and though the greatly improved weather of 1985–86 helped to produce a GDP increase provisionally estimated at 11.3 per cent, this only restored production to the level it had reached in 1982–83.[55] Coming during a period in which most African economies have been in severe difficulties, and several have experienced absolute declines in gross domestic product, the poor performance of the Ethiopian economy since 1974 cannot be ascribed entirely to the effects of revolution. At best, however, there has been none of that dramatic takeoff due to the dynamic mobilisation of previously underutilised productive resources which is sometimes expected from revolutionary transformation; and it is plausible to conclude that not only the disruption of the early years of the revolution, but also the policies pursued since that time, must have contributed to economic decline.

THE EXTERNAL ECONOMY

One familiar reason for the difficulties of economic planning (or economic management of any kind) in all third world countries is their high level of dependence on the industrial economies. This is, unsurprisingly, a weakness which Ethiopia shares; and though in some respects it is less dependent than quite a number of other third-world states, this in turn is largely a result of its lack of economic development. A comparatively low level of dependence on import/export trade, at 12 per cent of GDP in 1983, compared with an average of 18 per cent for the low-income African countries as a whole,[56] reflects the importance of the subsistence sector – though paradoxically, it was subsistence farmers' vulnerability to famine, rather than the role of multinationals or price fluctuations for primary produce exports, that most dramatically revealed Ethiopian economic dependence during the post-revolutionary period. The wholesale nationalisation of foreign enterprises in 1975 was possible, likewise, because these were so weak. The mining sector in particular accounted for only 0.3 per cent of GDP in 1983–84,[57] and this was derived from gold and platinum production which had been under government control even before the revolution. In two other respects, however, Ethiopia had a classically dependent economy: it derived over half of its foreign exchange from a single commodity, coffee, which was liable to price fluctuations on the international market; and it depended on foreign aid as its main source of investment finance. Both of these, moreover, bound pre-revolutionary Ethiopia (again like the great majority of third-world states) to the Western industrial economies. The United States was by far the major single recipient of Ethiopian exports, averaging 41 per cent over the period 1962–64, for example, while Western Europe and Japan provided the bulk of Ethiopia's imports.[58] The United States was also substantially the largest provider of bilateral development aid, and the major contributor to the main multilateral aid source, the International Development Agency of the World Bank.

Despite this dependence, and despite the post-revolutionary drying up of both foreign private investment and American development aid, there is no indication that either the international market mechanism, or the Western industrial states in particular, have hampered the economic development of revolutionary Ethiopia, and in some respects they have assisted it. Although the international market value of coffee has fluctuated sharply since the revolution, Ethiopia's terms of trade have generally been favourable. From a base of 100 in 1975, they peaked at 229.1 in 1977, when the Brazilian frost provided windfall gains to other coffee producers, which in Ethiopia's case providentially coincided with the Somali war. Thereafter, the index declined to a low point of 97.2 in 1981 (marking a slightly less favourable overall position than in 1975), before improving slowly in the first half of the 1980s.[59] Coffee prices surged again in 1985–86, following a drought in Brazil, but fell in 1986–87. In this respect, Ethiopia was merely lucky enough to market a primary product which, in contrast to many others, happened to do well during the decade in question. It nonetheless ran a large and increasing balance of payments deficit. A small current account surplus during the three years up to 1974 moved thereafter into a chronic deficit, which mounted from 178.8 million birr in 1975 to 569.7 million in 1980 and 1115.6 million in 1984. By 1984, the value of merchandise exports was no more than 41.6 per cent of imports.[60] This was however due to the failure of the total *quantity* of exports to keep pace with an increasing quantity of imports. In all but two of the eight years after 1975, indeed, the index volume of exports was lower than in that year; and the quantum index of exports divided by imports dropped from 100 in 1975 to 55.5 in 1980, picking up slightly over the following two years.[61] In short, Ethiopia's balance of payments problems were due, not to the international market, but to a failure of domestic production which will be examined in greater detail in the chapter on agriculture.

No substantial change took place in the direction of trade. As in the pre-revolutionary period, the greater part of Ethiopia's external trade continued to go to, and come from, the Western industrial states. There was also a flourishing export trade, in coffee and meat, but also in the narcotic chat, to the Arabian peninsula. Unlike Cuba, Ethiopia did not seriously consider reorienting its trade towards the CMEA, and unlike the other two African Marxist states which emerged from the continental traumas of 1974–75, Angola and Mozambique, it was from the start in 1975 a member of the Lome Conventions with the European Community. Ethiopian exports to Western Europe, North America and Japan amounted in 1984 to 68.4 per cent of the total, while imports from the same sources came to 61.9 per cent. The one major exception, apart from armaments which are excluded from the published figures, was oil, which from 1980 onwards Ethiopia imported from the Soviet Union. This accounted for by far the greater part of the 27.1 per cent of total imports in 1982, and 23.2 per cent in 1984, which Ethiopia received from the USSR.[62] It is paid for in hard currency, but at a long-term guaranteed price which is said to be rather less than average world market prices, and cushions Ethiopia against price fluctuations. In the early years of the revolution, Ethiopia made a few large but isolated coffee export deals with the CMEA economies, notably of nearly 20,000 tons (17.1 per cent of total coffee exports) to the GDR in 1976–78 in exchange for tractors, and 17,000 tons (10.5 per cent of the total) to the USSR in 1978–80.[63] These landed Ethiopia in the familiar problems of barter deals with the CMEA, both in reaching an appropriate rate of exchange, and in the resale of the produce on Western markets; the GDR deal, coming at a time of exceptionally high world market coffee prices, was especially disadvantageous – and in addition, the tractors received in exchange needed considerable modification for Ethiopian conditions. Bilateral trade between Ethiopia and the CMEA economies is regulated at annual meetings of joint commissions of the two countries; and since each side is largely concerned to find a market for export products which it cannot sell for hard currencies, both the level and the qualitative importance of these exchanges is low.

In addition to the published figures, there may be other exports to the Soviet Union, to be set against the cost of armaments. One such is gold, since the main Ethiopian gold mines at Adola in Sidamo are under Soviet management; and although their production was officially stated at nearly 500 kg in 1981–82, equivalent to an export value of $6,658,000, no figures were given for exports.[64] A second is fish, since Ethiopia's Red Sea coastline (especially the Dahlac islands, off Massawa, where the Soviet Union has a naval facility) is extremely rich in marine life, and fishing by local craft is severely restricted. A third, much more speculatively, is grain: local rumour has it, and many Ethiopians unquestionably believe, that both locally produced and relief aid grain is diverted to the USSR. This belief was publicised (under one of the classic headlines in the field of emotive journalism, 'Food for Starving Babies sent to Russia for Arms') in a British popular newspaper.[65] However, neither Korn, in his position as US chargé d'affaires, nor anyone else, has been able to discover any unequivocal evidence that these charges are true.[66]

Trade can usually keep flowing despite wide divergences in political outlook between the states involved. Aid is normally a different matter, allowing for a great deal of discretion on the part of the donor state, often in response to perceptions of political advantage. Ethiopia is not, and never has been, a major recipient of development aid. In 1982–83, it ranked no higher than forty-fifth among developing countries in terms of aid receipts as a percentage of GNP, at 5.9 per cent, and this despite one of the lowest per capita GNP figures in the world; the Somali Republic, by contrast, ranked fifth, at 24.3 per cent.[67] Ethiopian complaints that the country is neglected by aid donors are thus justified. However, aid receipts, and notably those from Western states and Western-dominated international agencies, have increased markedly since the revolution, and there is no basis for any claim that Ethiopia has been systematically discriminated against as a result either of its socialist policies or of its alignment with the Soviet Union. Although aid figures are often difficult to measure, and are notoriously subject to juggling for political purposes, all of the sources are in broad agreement. The Ten-Year Plan notes an increase in foreign assistance from an annual average of 76.7 million birr between 1970–71 and 1973–74, to one of 247.3 million birr between 1974–75 and 1980–81[68] – a 222 per cent increase in cash terms, and a substantial increase even in real terms. These figures include receipts from the socialist states, though the amount is not separately noted. The Ethiopian birr, surprisingly for a socialist state, has remained pegged to the US dollar, and while allowance must be made for global inflation, the exchange value of the currency remained constant. OECD figures, including aid from Western and OPEC donors and multi-national agencies, though not from the socialist states, show a series of leaps in aid receipts from an average of $53.9 million in 1971–73 to $124.5 million in 1974–78, and $227.9 million in 1979–82.[69] The proportion of total world development assistance going to Ethiopia increased from 0.7 per cent to 1.0 per cent over the period from 1970–71 to 1982–83, while aid as a per-centage of Ethiopian GNP rose over the same period from 2.4 to 5.9 per cent.[70] In every measurable respect, therefore, official development aid to Ethiopia increased after the revolution. While all of these figures exclude military aid, and also aid from non-governmental organisations such as private charities, some of them may include official aid for humanitarian purposes such as refugee assistance or famine relief. In any event, however, they all predate the immense increase in relief aid from 1984 onwards.

The one major aid programme affected by the revolution was United States development assistance, previously one of the largest sources of aid to Ethiopia, which was formally terminated in July 1979.[71] The Ethiopian government, however, bore quite as much of the responsibility for this as the American. The Americans would probably have been happy to keep aid going, if only as a source of political leverage, and annual disbursements of US aid indeed rose after the revolution from $19 million in 1973 to $30 million in 1976;[72] but the US administration then ran up against the Hicken-looper Amendment, a congressional requirement that aid recipients must compensate American citizens for nationalised assets. Such assets in Ethiopia were actually very small, amounting even at the complainants' valuation to no more than $30 million.[73] The only American company nationalised was a small concern buying spices from peasant farmers. The Ethiopian government refused compensation as a matter of principle, and thereby denied itself the much larger amounts that could have been avail-able as aid. This was, of course, a decision well within its sovereign rights; the point is merely that it was, in essentials, an Ethiopian decision rather than an American one. Compensation amounting to about $5 million was eventually agreed in December 1985, but although this served the purpose of improving Ethiopia's credit rating with international lenders, it did not lead to any resumption of US development aid. This was by then blocked first by a disagreement over a small ($2–5 million) but sensitive payment which the United States claimed was still due for arms supplied in 1976–77, and subsequently by a congressional provision explicitly excluding Ethiopia from eligibility under the 1985 Economic Assistance Act. Congress has con-sistently taken a much harder line over aid to Ethiopia than the US adminis-tration. American humanitarian aid was not affected, and though this led to difficulties in distinguishing what was 'humanitarian' from what was 'developmental', the American administration seems to have tried to shift as much as it could into the 'humanitarian' category.

The shortfall created by the ending of US development assistance was however more than made up by increases from other sources. One of the most important was the European Community. Aid receipts from the Community and member states rose from an average of $9.8 million in 1971–73 to $82.4 million in 1979–82, and Ethiopia became the sixth largest recipient of Community aid under the Lome Conventions, which came into effect from 1975.[74] Further large increases came from Italy, the International Development Agency, and the World Food Programme. In addition, Ethiopia qualified for aid from the Soviet bloc, and well-publicised assistance was received from the Soviet Union and other CMEA states, for projects which included the Combolcha textile mill, Mugher cement works, Nazret tractor assembly plant, and Melka Wakena hydroelectric project.[75] I am not aware of any detailed figures for CMEA aid, but different sources suggest a total of about $30 million a year, or 1.2 per cent of total CMEA aid for 1983.[76] Worldwide Soviet and CMEA aid is heavily concentrated on a very small group of socialist third-world states, among which Ethiopia is not included, and Soviet spokesmen have consistently made it clear that Ethiopia would have to gain by far the greater part of its capital requirements from Western sources.[77]

SURPLUS EXTRACTION AND GOVERNMENT SPENDING

The Ethiopian revolution, in common with socialist revolutions elsewhere, involved a sharp increase in the level of public employment, and a consequent need for an improved extractive capacity in order to maintain the enlarged state apparatus. The increase in the level of military manpower has already been noted, and although much of the burden of maintaining it was placed directly on the rural community by requiring peasants' associations to support their own militiamen, some of the expense fell on the national budget. Total current government expenditure increased by 246.8 per cent in cash terms between 1973–74 and 1982–83, from 529.5 to 1836.4 million birr.[78] The proportion of the total budget spent on general government expenses, by far the largest ingredient in which was defence, increased over the same period from 44.2 per cent to 55.3 per cent. In cash terms, this amounted to an increase of 333.9 per cent, as compared with increases of 143.5 per cent for economic services and 162.2 per cent for social services. The distribution of government current expenditure thus shifted markedly away from the service and developmental functions of the state, and towards its control functions. It should however be noted that the capital budget did provide increases in economic investment, though the great changes in the composition of the state sector before and after the revolution make these very difficult to assess.

123

There was a corresponding increase in civilian state employment. Although I have been unable to find any continuous statistical series comparing levels of government employment before and after the revolution, the available information indicates a sharp rise in the rate of increase in government employment after the revolution, and suggests a large increase also in the total level of employment. Between 1966 and 1971, the number of people employed by the central government *in Addis Ababa* rose from 16,280 to 19,340, at an average annual rate of increase of 3.5 per cent.[79] Between 1977–78 and 1982–83, the number of civilian employees *financed from the central government budget* rose from 109,322 to 167,860, at an annual rate of increase of 9.5 per cent.[80] The cost of these extra civil servants was reduced by keeping salaries pegged, at least until 1987, to the salary scales issued in 1972.[81] Only the very lowest salaries, which fell below the post-revolutionary minimum wage of fifty birr a month, were raised, while the largest salaries were subjected to greatly increased rates of taxation. The combination of level salary scales (though some upward 'creep' in grades can be detected) with the high rates of inflation already referred to meant a sharp decline in civil service living standards. In addition, there was a large increase in semi-state employment not financed from the budget, such as kebelle guards, at very low rates of pay; no figures for this are available.

Government revenues rose by 156 per cent over the period between 1973–74 and 1982–83, from 779.8 to 1996.6 million birr.[82] This was appreciably less than the corresponding rise in public expenditure, but nonetheless indicated an increased capacity to extract resources from the economy. Another indication is provided by the year-to-year increase in revenues. Over the last seven years of the imperial regime, revenues rose in cash terms by an average of about 9 per cent a year; for the first five years after 1974, the rate of increase doubled to nearly 18 per cent, with particularly sharp rises over the years 1976 to 1978. The subsequent fall-back to a rate of increase of about 5 per cent in the first half of the 1980s indicates both the depressed state of the economy, and the end of a once-for-all step-up in extractive capacity. Only some 5 per cent of revenue was derived from direct taxation on the peasant sector of the economy – a proportion very similar to that under the imperial regime; a collection of old taxes were swept away, and replaced by a land-use tax and an agricultural income tax which, though nominally progressive, amounted in practice to a fixed poll tax on peasant families. A hidden (and highly disincentive) level of taxation on the peasantry was however imposed through the pricing mechanism for cash crops, in addition to exactions by local officials on behalf of the government's almost continuous campaigns.

Almost exactly 75 per cent of the increase in government revenues over the nine years to 1982–83 – everything, that is to say, that cannot be ascribed merely to inflation – was derived from just four sources. The most important of these, producing additional revenue of 369.5 million birr, consisted in 'profits, interest and rent', or in other words, the profits from houses and businesses confiscated in 1975 which after the revolution accrued to the government rather than to private owners. This item alone accounted for 19.8 per cent of revenue in 1982–83. The second, bringing in an additional 259.7 million birr, was a six-fold increase in returns from business income tax, which, when account is taken of the fact that many areas of business managed both by Ethiopians and by foreigners had been transferred to the public sector, indicates both the extent of the revolutionary government's squeeze on private commerce, and also its capacity to survive. The role of private trade in revolutionary Ethiopia remains a politically sensitive subject, on which very little information is available. The third, bringing in an extra 157.8 million birr, came from a five-fold increase in returns from export duties, almost all of them on coffee. Since the volume of coffee exports remained roughly constant, this reflected partly an increase in world prices, but largely a sharp increase in the percentage of the value of coffee exports extracted by the state, which will be examined in more detail later. Part of this increase represents the profits extracted before the revolution by an exploitative class of landowning notables, but part of it also indicates an increased level of exaction from peasant producers. Finally, an additional 125.8 million birr came from a five-fold increase in alcohol excise taxes; the increase in production of alcoholic drinks has been one of the successes of the government's industrialisation programme, and has evidently been profitable too.

These additional revenues mark a once-for-all increase in extractive capacity from an economy in which growth rates have failed to reach the level of population increase since the revolution, and in which personal living standards even before the 1984 famine were in sharp decline. The Ten-Year Plan claims with characteristic optimism that 'the domestic revenue to GDP ratio which now stands at 20 per cent indicates that the tax effort of the country is still low even when compared to that of other developing countries at a similar level of economic development',[83] and that further revenues should thus be raisable. The stagnation in domestic revenues during the first half of the 1980s, coupled with ample evidence of the decay of the agricultural sector, indicate that this is unlikely. Indeed the level of taxation on private business and on coffee farming (as well as on grain farming, where the proceeds are channelled into low consumer prices rather than government revenue) is probably highly disincentive. The Ethiopian state, despite the enormous post-revolutionary increases in organisational efficiency and control capacity, appears to have come up against the limits imposed by the fragile and undeveloped agricultural economy on which it is perched.

THE STRUCTURES OF DISTRIBUTION

A further and vital element in the new political economy is the distribution system. Not only had the old structure of rural–urban marketing been severely undermined by land reform and nationalisation, but government control of distribution was also necessary for it to extract resources from the economy. In particular, the control of food grain distribution was needed in order to feed the army and other government employees and to keep down prices in the towns; and the control of the coffee trade was essential in order to enable the government to achieve the greatly increased share in the export value of the crop already noted, and in the face of declining production to restrict the supply of coffee to the domestic market so as to increase the amount available for export. The working of the new distribution system will be examined in more detail in the chapters on urban government and on agriculture, but as a significant aspect of revolutionary state formation it requires a mention here.

The key to the new structure of distribution lay in the fact that, with agrarian production heavily in the hands of individual peasant families, control of distribution was a much easier proposition than the control of production itself. Efforts were made to increase direct state production through state farms, and to extend state control of peasant production through cooperatives, but by the mid 1980s these still accounted for well under 10 per cent of agricultural production. The major agency of state intervention was the Agricultural Marketing Corporation, which was established in 1976 with duties which included the purchase of agricultural products for domestic consumption, the supply of agricultural inputs, and the maintenance of a national grain reserve.[84] Until 1978–79, it bought grain in local markets in competition with private traders – a task which inevitably condemned it to losses and ineffectiveness. With the launching of the National Revolutionary Development Campaign in 1978, however, it gained the much more basic task of regulating grain prices and production quotas at the rural level, and the transport of grain to the towns. Rather than being a mere adjunct to an open market, it exercised the state monopoly power needed to turn this into a controlled one. It purchased the entire output of state farms and collectives, and obliged peasants' associations to deliver given amounts of grain (determained at district level by grain purchase task forces) at fixed prices. Private traders were allowed to operate only under licence and AMC supervision, prior to the abolition of private trading altogether. An equivalent organisation for the coffee trade, the Ethiopian Coffee Marketing Corporation, was established in 1978; this buys coffee at a price geared to the international market value, rather than at a fixed price, but is no less punitive to producers.

Since both grain and export crops are bought by government at prices appreciably less than would be available in a free market, the government has to prevent such a market from forming or rigidly control it. This has led to one of the most distinctive features of revolutionary Ethiopia: the appearance (or reappearance, since they likewise characterised Ethiopian travel before 1935) of internal customs posts, with frequent searches to prevent domestic smuggling. When coffee can be bought at two birr a kilo in Gamu

Gofa, and sold for fifteen birr in Addis Ababa, the incentive for smuggling is all too clear.[85] A public bus on which I travelled from Sidamo to Addis Ababa in April 1986 was stopped and searched five times in the course of a 150-mile journey. Similar controls operate on the roads out of grain producing regions such as Gojjam, and (for imported goods) on the border between Hararghe region, where contraband is rife and uncontrolled, and Shoa. These checkpoints indicate, in the starkest manner, the level of physical control which is needed in order to achieve control over the economy; and by demonstrating the difference between open and controlled markets, they help to alienate both producers and consumers. Though corruption at checkpoints is only to be expected, however, the Ethiopian state is efficient and disciplined enough to be able to maintain a level of control which is not instantly corrupted into farce. The very difference in coffee prices between the producing areas and Addis Ababa is sufficient evidence of that, as is the difference in grain price levels between adjoining provinces.[86] Ostensibly intended to produce a distribution of resources which is 'rational' because it is directed by government, this system at the same time prevents, for example, the grain from food surplus areas from being redistributed through the market in neighbouring areas where grain is desperately short. A further government organisation, the Relief and Rehabilitation Commission with its attendant charitable agencies, is then called in to distribute grain through a centrally organised network. Famine, certainly, is not only or even mostly the result of government involvement in distributive trade; but it is equally certainly exacerbated by the agricultural purchasing system, as well as by the more general effects of revolutionary agricultural policy which are considered in a later chapter.

A further aspect of the 'socialisation' of distribution is the control of transport. Though small private transport enterprises continue to exist, both for goods and (at minibus level) for passengers, they operate subject to strict government control. There is an evident rationale for this. At times of crisis – to take the famine again as the most evident example – it enables the entire national transport network to be mobilised so as to take grain from the ports to the famine areas, or to take people for resettlement from the famine areas to the south and west. When university teachers and students were sent off to build resettlement villages in June 1985, they could be transported in busses withdrawn from ordinary services all round the country. The price to be paid is a cumbersome system of licencing and control, and (at normal times, anyhow) a distribution network that may well be less efficient than the market.

The revolutionary Ethiopian state is recognisably the successor to its disowned imperial progenitor. Even though its control apparatus has been vastly expanded, this apparatus is not only central to the attempt to construct a socialist system of government in Ethiopia, but is also an inherent consequence of the structure of the Ethiopian state itself. Though the revolution has greatly exacerbated the level of opposition, the regime is not gratuitously brutal after the manner of an Amin or a Bokassa, but has found itself obliged to resort to force as the logical consequence of the goal – a centrally commanded and organised state – which it has inherited and sought to extend. This goal of building a strong state has, paradoxically perhaps but consistently with normal third-world experience, entailed a dependence on external arms and alliances. This again duplicates, though in greatly intensified form, the experience of the old regime. Even the extension of state control over the economy can be seen as drawing, to some extent, on the means used by the imperial government to extract a surplus from international trade; but in this field the contrast with the old regime is generally at its sharpest. Despite its ineffectual attempts at planning, the imperial government had neither the intention nor the capacity to set up the centrally directed command economy which has been seriously attempted since the revolution. The people who run the state are not so very different from their predecessors. The trappings of monarchy and aristocracy have been swept away, and with them a political elite who had some interest in restricting the expansion of state power, if only because they owned the resources which a more powerful state would need to take over. Though part of the revolutionary state's increased extractive capacity has come from its greater control over the peasantry, most of it comes from the confiscation of assets individually owned by the old political elite. The new elite sustains itself directly from the power of the state, rather than by using state power to provide itself with private assets, and is thus more explicitly bureaucratic than its predecessor. Indeed it is the apotheosis of a process of increasing bureaucratic power which successive emperors had set in train for their own purposes. In no sense at all is it the workers' and peasants' state which it claims to be.

All the indications are, however, that this expanded and vastly more efficient Ethiopian state is running up against the limitations imposed by the society which it governs. The limitations in control capacity – though this is the area in which the revolutionary regime has been overwhelmingly at its most successful – are exposed by its inability to win the wars in the north, and the uncertainty aroused by the level and price of the Soviet commitment; and its increasing capacity to extract resources from the economy has come up against the limited and declining level of the resources available for extraction. Despite the state's evident power, the fragility of the base on which it rests is becoming increasingly obvious.

6

The control of the towns

According to the 1984 census (which was not a full census, but provided the best population data available), only 11.3 per cent of Ethiopia's total population of just over 42 million lived in 'towns'; and since towns were defined as settlements with urban dwellers' associations, many of which had under 1,000 inhabitants, this figure included a lot of small rural centres. 3,272,083 people, or 7.8 per cent of the national total, lived in towns of over 10,000, and of these 1,412,575 (3.4 per cent) were in Addis Ababa. The Eritrean capital of Asmara came next with 275,385, followed by Dire Dawa with 98,104, and nine towns with populations between 50,000 and 80,000.[1]

By the early 1980s, the upheavals which had shaken the towns during the early years of the revolution had ceased. The only demonstrations were those organised by the regime in support of official policies. Urban crime – never such a problem in Addis Ababa as in many large African cities – was kept well within manageable proportions. This state of peace was certainly maintained by a visible framework of public order. The curfew from midnight to five a.m. remained permanently in force, lifted only as a treat for major holidays, and curfew breakers were liable to be stopped and imprisoned. From nightfall onwards, armed kebelle police patrolled the streets in pairs. But this framework of order was accepted and may well have been welcomed. Nor were the functions of government limited to the simple maintenance of order. Housing, transport, much of the distribution system, employment and the activities of women and youth were regulated to an extent that would never have been possible before the revolution. Though at first sight, Addis Ababa might seem (save for the ubiquitous revolutionary slogans) almost unaltered since 1974, in fact the changes were profound.

One important underlying change was a decline in the rate of rural–urban migration. This has been noted in several studies,[2] and though urban growth rates must be derived from population estimates which vary widely in accuracy, the order of magnitude is indicated by figures for Addis Ababa showing population increases between 6.5 per cent and 8.7 per cent a year from 1961 to 1976, compared with 3.0–3.5 per cent from 1976 to 1984 – little more than the natural rate of increase.[3] These figures partly reflect changes in the relative attractiveness of rural and urban life which, at any rate for the first decade or so after the revolution, tended to favour the countryside. The most important factor keeping people in the countryside (or drawing them to it) was land reform. By guaranteeing land to farmers resident within their own peasants' association area, this removed the problem of landlessness which had previously been a major reason for the expulsion of people from the countryside; and in the first years after the land reform, this probably led to the return to the land of quite a large number of recent rural emigrants. This of course led to the converse problem of rural overcrowding. It was also at least in part responsible for an increase in the proportion of women in the urban population. Since rights to land were in practice vested in households rather than individuals, and since rural households were normally headed by men, land reform did not restrain the emigration of women to anything like the same extent. Women who had left (or been abandoned by) their husbands continued to seek refuge in towns, often maintaining themselves by prostitution. The proportion of women in the Addis Ababa population rose from 48.8 per cent in 1961 to 50.5 per cent in 1967 (indicating that a change was already under way before the revolution), and then to 52.4 per cent in 1976 and 52.6 per cent in 1978 and 1984. The discrepancy was especially great for the ages between fifteen and thirty-four.[4] The same imbalance occurred in other towns. By 1984, females accounted for 55.4 per cent of the population in Asmara, and though the total national population of the two sexes was almost equal, females made up 53.5 per cent of the urban population, but only 49.7 per cent of the much larger rural one.[5]

A second reason for the decline in urban growth was that immediately after land reform, the destruction of the old system of surplus extraction from the rural areas meant that the countryside enjoyed a sudden (though temporary) increase in standard of living, while the food situation in the towns on the whole grew worse. Two further disincentives to urban migration remain: the high level of urban unemployment, coupled with the declining real incomes of those who are employed; and the shortage of urban housing. Finally, there have been physical controls on movement, both of a regular administrative kind (since the permission of one's kebelle or peasants' association is required in order to leave it), and of an emergency kind; during the 1984–85 famine, road blocks and camps were set up to prevent peasants from the north flocking into Addis Ababa. This reduction in the rate of urbanisation has certainly helped to ease the problems of governing the towns.

THE KEBELLE

The distinction between city and countryside has been institutionalised by the revolutionary government, through the division between urban dwellers' associations on the one hand, and peasants' associations on the other. The kebelle, an Amharic word meaning 'neighbourhood', is properly speaking the base-level organisation of both a peasants' and an urban dwellers' association, though in practice the term has come to be used especially for UDAs. A single kebelle in Addis Ababa encompassed on average between 1,000 and 1,400 households at the time of the 1984 census, with a mean population of a little under 5,000 people.[6] Any town large enough to need two or more kebelles, of which there were 118 in 1982,[7] has a 'keftenya' (meaning simply 'higher') to supervise them, while the twenty-four towns large enough to have two or more keftenyas are administered by a city council. The only towns with more than four keftenyas, Addis Ababa (with twenty-five) and Asmara (with nine) have an intermediate administrative level, the zone, with five zones in Addis Ababa and two in Asmara. Kebelles are thus linked into a hierarchical structure of administration, governed by the principles of democratic centralism.[8]

Kebelles are entirely post-revolutionary institutions, but it is possible to trace their origins in the 'recognised idirs' which were involved in some government functions under the imperial regime.[9] 'Idir' is the Amharic name for the small mutual insurance societies which are almost universal in African cities, and which collect funds from their members which are then used to provide some minimal social security, and especially to meet funeral expenses. From the late 1950s onwards, they were used by candidates in parliamentary and municipal council elections as a means of organising support, and in 1966 the government issued regulations to enable them to be registered. By 1970, there were 395 officially recognised idirs in Addis Ababa with 50,723 member households, encompassing something in the region of one-third of the population of the city; these were organised into confederations covering each of the ten city districts. They were used for activities such as neighbourhood policing and getting out the crowd for official occasions such as state visits – two functions which were to be taken over directly by the kebelles. In 1972, the municipal authorities organised a conference of idir leaders, to orient them towards development objectives and encourage them to 'counteract adverse political processes' – the last of these evidently without much success. In the first year of the revolution, the Derg likewise used them to get out the crowd for demonstrations, but their leadership included too many landlords and other people associated with the old regime to make them suitable for the new regime's purposes, and after the urban land reform of July 1975, their semi-official functions were taken over by the new kebelles. Idirs, however, continue to flourish despite the government's tacit disapproval of them as institutions outside the official structure; probably most Addis Ababa households belong to one, and a study of two single mothers struggling to bring up families on a minuscule income in the city showed that each paid out 4 per cent of her earnings in idir subscriptions.[10]

Kebelles, which were established after the urban land reform, are, unlike idirs, straightforwardly official bodies, each covering a defined territory and responsible for all the people in it. Their boundaries follow physical lines of demarcation such as rivers and main roads, and (for Addis Ababa at least) were drawn up by an urban geographer, Dr Wondimu Abebe, who was to be gruesomely murdered (in *The Ethiopian Herald*'s phrase) at Debre Zeit in 1978.[11] The functions of kebelles laid down in the initial proclamation were largely concerned with rent collection, though they were also expected to establish judicial tribunals, and help provide health, education and similar services under government supervision.[12] These were expanded in a proclamation issued in October 1976, under the guidance of the Meison minister of public works and housing, Daniel Tadesse, to include the registration of houses, residents, births, deaths and marriages, and the collection of local taxes, while the public safety committee was empowered 'to carry on guarding and security activities in accordance with directives issued by the Ministry of Interior'.[13] At the time of this proclamation, which coincided with the outbreak of the terror, the kebelles were not under reliable government control. A later proclamation was issued in April 1981, by which time control was well established, and provided kebelles with somewhat extended powers and a much more elaborate committee structure, comprising a general assembly (of all kebelle residents), which elected a policy committee, which was in turn responsible for the election of the executive committee, the revolution defence committee, and the judicial tribunal.[14] This two-tier electoral structure, on the face of it highly elaborate for an area with no more than a few thousand residents, eased the task of controlling kebelle elections. As a further check, a separately elected inspection committee was empowered to inspect and report on the work of the other bodies. The most important change made by the new proclamation was, however, financial. Whereas the 1976 proclamation had allowed kebelles to keep their net receipts from house rents, save for 15 per cent which they had to hand over to the keftenya, the 1981 one required them to pay over their entire receipts from rents and fines to the central municipality, receiving in return the money needed to carry out their administrative functions.[15] The financial autonomy of kebelles was thus removed, and with it both the major opportunities for corruption, and the main means by which kebelles could carry out local development and improvement projects.

Each of these changes in the formal powers of the kebelles has coincided with changes in the people who have run them. The first elections after the establishment of the kebelle system in July 1975 were hurriedly organised, at a time when the new political parties of the revolutionary intelligentsia were only just getting under way. Although former landlords were prohibited from standing, the social networks which they had dominated remained in existence, and kebelle offices were often taken over by clients of the old elite, or indeed by the young intellectuals from fairly prosperous urban families who were to provide much of the leadership of the EPRP.[16] By the time of the next elections in November 1976, the situation had entirely changed. The kebelles had been identified as the key institutions of urban political power, notably by Meison and its then ally Mengistu Haile-Mariam, and the elections provided a means to place that power in the hands of a lumpenproletariat which could be used to exercise it against Meison's enemies in the EPRP. The foundation of the revolutionary defence squads, and the most horrifying examples of the abuse of kebelle power, date from this period. Kebelle leaders were themselves in turn the targets for assassination, and the newspapers of the period carry frequent reports of their deaths. This was equally the period during which the financial autonomy of the kebelles, and the general confusion of urban government, enabled their leaders to profit on their own account.

The proclamation of April 1981, together with the third round of elections which followed in June that year, marked a conscious effort to turn the kebelles into the obedient agents of central administration. These elections provided the first major test of the ability of the newly formed COPWE to exercise its role as an embryo vanguard party. 'The new proclamation', it was announced, 'placed urban dwellers' associations under the central leadership of COPWE in line with the principles of democratic centralism'.[17] Supervising committees were set up for the 1,260 kebelles in 315 towns across the country in which elections were to be held, in order to scrutinise the records of the candidates and screen out undesirables. The guidance provided by COPWE was constantly emphasised, and leading figures including Mengistu himself took a prominently advertised part in the proceedings in their own kebelles.[18] The people elected in this way, though they had to be residents of the kebelle in which they stood, were for the most part pre-selected from the centre. Some of the existing kebelle chairmen who had proved their competence and reliability were retained, but the new intake were generally better educated and better qualified for administrative tasks than their predecessors. Since kebelle office is both arduous and unpaid, and since many of the educated had been alienated from the kebelles in any case by the excesses since 1976, a lot of the new leaders (including a number of university academics) had to be virtually conscripted into office. The fourth round of elections, finally, took place in April 1986, as a prelude to the formation of the PDRE the following year. By this time, kebelle officials were effectively party or government nominees, and the genuinely elective element had almost completely disappeared. To some extent, this process may have served as a means of moving WPE cadres into kebelle office, though in many kebelles the party was still too thin on the ground to make this practicable. In any event, since individual party membership is not known, even residents in the kebelle would often be unaware of whether their officials were members or not. Nor does kebelle leadership appear to serve as a stepping stone to higher things. Urban dwellers' associations, as already noted, are unrepresented on the WPE Central Committee, and I am aware of only a single individual – Shimelis Alemu, chief administrator of Wollo – who has risen through the kebelles to high government office. I have been unable to identify anyone with strong kebelle connections even among the 104 Addis Ababa representatives elected to the National Shengo in 1987.

Even before the 1981 proclamation, kebelle incomes were generally not large. In one survey undertaken by a team from Addis Ababa University in February 1980, eight out of fifty-two kebelles reported monthly incomes of less than 1,000 birr, with twenty-one others at between 1,000 and 3,000 birr a month.[19] Eleven reported between 3,001 and 5,000 birr, with the twelve others going up to one with over 11,000 birr – quite a substantial sum in a city where the basic minimum wage was fifty birr a month. These are of course only reported incomes, and actual incomes may well have exceeded them. Kebelle incomes before 1981, overwhelmingly derived from rents, obviously varied widely in accordance with the wealth of the neighbourhood concerned, even though rents of over 100 birr a month were collected by a separate central agency. The new system in principle allowed redistribution of income from richer to poorer areas, and thus for a more even allocation of kebelle services. I have not, however, been able to find any figures for kebelle incomes after 1981.

The level of services provided by kebelles varies widely. In the survey already cited, just over half of the kebelles investigated claimed to have built new local roads, while rather less than half had built new houses and started co-operative shops. A quarter had built meeting halls, and the same number had provided land for football pitches. A much smaller number had laid on such facilities as reading rooms, infant day-care centres, public toilets, or bakeries. Since that time, kebelle shops have become universal, as kebelles have become responsible for administering the new urban food distribution system, and some of the more enterprising ones have started butcheries and even bars. All one can say is that kebelles provide an administrative mechanism through which urban development projects may be carried out, but that whether they are or not depends very much on the kebelle concerned.

The declining government interest in independent local action is illustrated by the preambles to the two urban dwellers' association proclamations. That of 1976 starts: 'WHEREAS, it is necessary . . . for urban dwellers to get organized in kebelle, Higher and Central Associations and run their own affairs, solve their own problems, and directly participate in political, economic and social activities'.[20] Its successor of five years later starts: 'WHEREAS, it is necessary to make urban dwellers' associations receive their guidance from one centre with a view to strengthening the solid foundation . . . enabling the broad masses of urban dwellers to organise into kebelle, higher and central urban dwellers' associations and administer themselves'.[21] Self-administration and central guidance have proved, unsurprisingly, to be incompatible objectives, and the development functions of kebelles have suffered as a result. All kebelle projects have to be submitted for central approval and funding, and the delays in the long bureaucratic process involved mean that projects rarely get approved in time for them to get carried out during the financial year to which the budget relates. A general decline in kebelle morale, and outside Addis Ababa, in development projects undertaken by local municipalities, to which the same constraints apply, has resulted.

When urban development is undertaken from above, however, the kebelle structure provides the essential administrative framework and information base. The kebelle itself forms a manageable unit of local administration, and its officials know their own residents, and can organise them to attend literacy classes, get themselves vaccinated, form work gangs, or whatever it may be. The most impressive urban development project in Addis Ababa has been carried out through the Norwegian Save the Children Fund (Redd Barna) in one of the poorest and most densely populated kebelles in the central market area. This comprises a series of interrelated activities, including health and sanitation (clinics, latrines, health education), house building and repairs, income-generating activities (food-processing, milling, weaving), and general social services (kindergarten, day care for the mentally retarded, training for school dropouts, and so forth).[22] But though the staffing of the project is overwhelmingly Ethiopian, the initiative came not from the kebelle itself but from outside, and its ability to carry on as a self-sustaining enterprise has yet to be demonstrated.

Inevitably, it is the control functions of the kebelles that are most highly developed. Each kebelle has its own court, its own police force (of revolutionary guards, normally with about thirty for each kebelle), and its own jail. Their powers are no longer so brutally or independently exercised as during the later 1970s; they serve, rather, as the normal agency for urban local administration. They organise attendance, for example, at the frequent demonstrations held to greet visiting notables, hail government measures, or express opposition to apartheid or the hostile actions of neighbouring states. Failure to attend may be punished by two or three days in the kebelle lock-up, or the confiscation of ration cards. Their role in conscripting young men for national service has already been noted, and their powers over housing and the distribution of cheap food will be discussed in later sections. The kebelle's permission is needed to move one's residence out of the kebelle area, and at any point when a citizen needs services from government, a letter from the kebelle normally has to be presented. One of the new street criers of Addis Ababa is the kebelle guard, equipped with mechanical loudhailer, who tours the streets (usually in the early hours of the morning) calling out the people for kebelle meetings, demonstrations, and the like. Whether or not it is resented, the kebelle has rapidly become part of the normal framework of urban life, to the extent that it is difficult to envisage life without it.

The role of the keftenya, and above that the zone, is much less evident. These are intermediate administrative echelons, not in direct contact with the people, and their function is largely to supervise the kebelle officials and transmit orders to them. One informant, asked what his keftenya did, simply quoted the Amharic proverb, 'a dog knows his master, but not his master's master'. The zone was initially established as a means of organising the party in Addis Ababa during the COPWE period, with a status equivalent to that of the province or awraja in the other administrative regions. The party organisation was extended after the formation of the WPE down to the keftenya level, which ranks on a par with the district or woreda. In due course, party organisations will presumably be set up in each kebelle likewise, and the job of kebelle chairman, who in 1986 was the undisputed leader of each kebelle, either merged with or subordinated to that of the WPE first secretary.

THE MASS ORGANISATIONS

The vanguard role of the WPE, and its consequently very restricted membership, leaves a need for organisations to provide a channel for mass participation for the rest of the population. In the countryside, the peasants' associations double up both as territorial administrative units and as work-based units for mass participation. In the towns, the kebelles serve only the first of these functions, while trade unions and professional associations provide the second. In both city and countryside, two specialised associations cater for women and youth.

An earlier chapter has already shown the difficulty which the PMAC experienced during the first years of the revolution in establishing control over the unions. Even after the PMAC had disbanded the Confederation of Ethiopian Labour Unions (CELU), inherited from the Haile-Selassie period, and set up the AETU in its place in early 1977, the new organisation continued to escape its control, especially through its links with Meison. Its leadership was frequently changed, partly as a result of assassination, and an article on 'the struggle of the Ethiopian working class' published in the COPWE journal *Meskerem* in May 1981 criticised 'its narrow and cliquish outlooks' and its preoccupation with trade disputes, and made clear the need for its thorough reorganisation.[23] This reorganisation took place in mid 1982, as part of the process by which COPWE, having dealt with the kebelles the previous year, set about establishing its control over other political organisations. This process started in April, with the holding of branch level meetings and elections, working up to provincial, regional, and finally national levels, and culminating in a national Congress at the end of June. Tadesse Tamrat, who as chairman of the Akaki textile workers' union had led the Derg's main source of industrial support during the terror, then became national chairman. He held office for the next four years, and was re-elected in 1986.[24] In the meantime, the legal structure of the AETU had been revised by the Trade Unions' Organization Proclamation issued in May 1982.[25] This was an uncompromising Marxist–Leninist document, emphasising the need 'to enable workers to discharge their historical responsibility in building the national economy by handling with care the instruments of

136

production and their produce, and by enhancing the production and proper distribution of goods and services'. It also noted the ideological responsibilities of the unions, and their provision of educational and sports facilities, but made no mention of strikes, which were already subject to heavy legal penalties. The name was changed to Ethiopia Trade Union (ETU) in 1986.

AETU membership grew only slowly from the total of 204,101 in 1976–77, though a membership drive at the time of the reorganisation brought the numbers up to 313,434 by 1983–84.[26] They were organised into nine industrial groups, of which manufacturing was the largest with 87,080 members (29.2 per cent) in 1982–83, followed by agriculture, forestry and fisheries (26.6 per cent), services (15.1 per cent), transport (8.1 per cent), construction (8.0 per cent), trade (6.2 per cent), utilities (3.7 per cent), finance (2.4 per cent), and mining (0.7 per cent).[27] The regional distribution of the membership shows the domination of the centre, with 35.6 per cent of the members in Addis Ababa and a further 18.0 per cent in Shoa; Eritrea accounted, together with Tigray, for no more than 7.5 per cent of total membership. 20.7 per cent of the members in 1983–84 were women – a marginal rise from the 18.9 per cent of women members in 1975–76. Although most of the chairmen both of the regional unions and of the industrial groups are full or alternate members of the Central Committee of the WPE, there is nothing at all to indicate that either they, or the organisation which they represent, have any policy-making role; they are seldom referred to in the press, save for their appearance at official functions. However, the political quiescence of the trade unions during the 1980s, compared with their activism during the later 1970s, presumably indicates their successful discharge of their main function. In the absence of pay rises, the unions have to encourage their members with symbolic rewards, and the press frequently records the distribution of certificates to meritorious workers. One star worker, at the main Addis Ababa printing press, was made a member of the WPE Central Committee.

The professions do not form part of the trade-union structure, but are organised into their own separate professional associations, by far the largest of which are the teachers. Others cover doctors, health workers, journalists and so forth, down to tiny associations of artists and musicians. They are not specifically represented on the WPE Central Committee, though the number of teachers at the WPE founding congress did not fall far short of the number of peasants. The Addis Ababa University section of the teachers' association may well be untypical, but contains a mixture of co-opted academics who enjoy the general respect of the community, and ambitious party members evidently seeking to work their way into political favour. Some effort is made to ensure that it does not simply look like a group of party nominees, but it is nonetheless firmly under party control. Congresses of the ETU and of all the professional associations were held in 1986, in preparation for the declaration of the PDRE; and the academics, who had previously had a section of the association to themselves, were then brought into the ordinary territorial structure of the association, subject to the regional and provincial organisations of wherever their institutions were located.

The Revolutionary Ethiopian Women's Association (REWA) and the Revolutionary Ethiopian Youth Association (REYA) are treated by the government as parallel organisations, in much the same way as are the ETU and the EPA. They were founded at the same time, in September 1980, and held their first Congresses simultaneously the same month. They have very similar constitutions,[28] acronyms (in Amharic as well as English), and mass memberships. Their national leaders rank together as alternate members of the WPE Central Committee – a ranking which marks their subordinate status to the EPA and ETU, which are much more strongly represented. Within the party organisation, officials at national, regional and provincial levels are responsible for women's affairs on the one hand, and youth affairs on the other, and have a superior status to their counterparts in REWA and REYA themselves. This parallelism between REWA and REYA is of course based on a false premise, in that womanhood is a permanent condition, whereas youth is something that one may with luck grow out of. Its effect is to move women into a separate set of institutions concerned exclusively with 'women's affairs', while virtually all ordinary government and party posts continue to be held by men. The heads of REWA branches are called 'chairperson', whereas their counterparts in other organisations are always referred to as 'chairman'.

In common with other revolutionary socialist regimes, the Ethiopian government emphasises the emancipating effect of the revolution on women. 'In mass and professional organizations, women enjoy equal and full rights to elect and be elected to the highest posts of responsibility. These days one can easily find women leaders on revolution defence squads, as cadres, on literacy campaign committees, in city councils, discussion forums, in production brigades and in various artistic and cultural endeavours.'[29] As is equally normal, the current liberation of women is contrasted with their exploitation under the old regime. In fact, though the status of women in pre-revolutionary Christian Ethiopia did not remotely approach equality with men, they did not suffer from many of the institutionalised inequalities found in Islamic societies and in many other parts of Africa. They were not secluded, they had equal rights of marriage, divorce, and property ownership, and they could at times reach positions of substantial political influence.[30] Haile-Selassie's immediate predecessor, the Empress Zawditu (1916–30), remains Africa's only twentieth-century woman head of state. The first woman vice-minister was appointed in 1966. Almost all of the women in prominent positions under the old regime benefitted from influential political connections, but there was at any rate some precedent on which the revolutionary regime could draw. By 1987, nonetheless, no woman in the post-revolutionary period had surpassed the

138

rank reached before the revolution, and the proportion of women in important positions remained at least as low as before 1974.

As already noted, there was only one woman among the 136 full members of the original WPE Central Committee; she was married to a WPE regional first secretary, and was in charge of women's affairs in the WPE central secretariat. Of the four female alternate members, two also worked in the WPE secretariat, one was national chairperson of REWA, and one was a vice-minister in the Council of Ministers' office; the fact that this last was the only one of the twenty-five vice-ministers to hold even alternate Central Committee rank suggests that her place on it may have been due to the need to boost the female membership. There have been no women Politbureau members or alternates, regional first secretaries or chief administrators, or ministers. Nor have I been able to find any women among the provincial first secretaries or administrators, or (save for those responsible for women's affairs) among the members of regional WPE committees. So far as the appointment of women to senior posts is concerned, there is thus no evidence of any improvement since the revolution. A very high proportion of the women in government, party or REWA posts, moreover, have Amhara/Tigrean names, reflecting both the pre-eminence of Amhara/Tigrean society in any event, and its comparatively favourable treatment of women; I have identified none with Moslem and few even with recognisably Oromo names.

Where the change has come, and it is an important one, is in the organisation of women. This reflects the enormous post-revolutionary changes in organisational capacity in the country as a whole. Official statements of REWA membership ran to 5 million in September 1980, and 5,041,960 in September 1985.[31] Even if these figures are inaccurate – and the first of them, produced for the founding REWA Congress, must have been grossly exaggerated – there are still a very large number of women organised both locally (into 20,787 basic chapters, according to the 1985 report) and into a national hierarchy. There were in 1982 153 full-time paid REWA officials, of whom all but eighteen were at regional level.[32] This hierarchy should, potentially at least, provide a means of transmitting information about such matters as sanitation and child care, though the limited information that I have been able to collect suggests that the organisation above local level is heavily bureaucratised, and that its own institutional structure effectively insulates it from foreign and even Ethiopian development agencies. There is no indication at all that the organisation is used to transmit women's views upwards to the party leadership. Local branches within kebelles vary from the moribund to the highly active; they may help to organise literacy classes for women, and some of them run kindergartens, playgrounds, and shops selling products such as home-made bread and handicrafts. Of the receipts from such shops, however, half have to be passed up to the keftenya or district level REWA, which in turn has to transmit half to the provincial level,

139

and so on up to regional and national levels; the women at the bottom who do the work can, formally at least, retain no profit from their activities at all. The same system applies to the membership dues of twenty-five cents a month. Local REWA branches are also looked to for contributions to producers' cooperatives, famine victims, and other official campaigns, and are expected to turn out their members for official occasions like the welcome of visiting notables. While the extractive and control functions of the organisation are clear enough, it is harder to discern ways in which it is of immediate benefit to its members.

The local REWA branches, though attached to kebelles and peasants' associations, operate as parallel units, and often, at least in the towns, have separate offices. These provide a centre for women, and enable them to feel part of an organisation which is recognisably their own. The price of control over a separate organisation is however exclusion from the main one. Although Addis Ababa in 1984 had over 52,000 more women than men, and 33.6 per cent of households had female heads,[33] the representation of women among kebelle leaders seems at least as meagre as on the Central Committee. The situation in the countryside is no different, since peasants' association membership is restricted to household heads, who are normally male, and I have discovered no cases at all of women association leaders.[34] Estimated unemployment for women, at 30.9 per cent in 1978, was two-and-a-half times as great for women as for men at 12 per cent.[35] Average pay for women workers in manufacturing in 1979–80 was two-thirds of that for men.[36] One problem which is certainly exacerbated by these conditions is prostitution. A survey carried out by the Ministry of Labour and Social Affairs in twenty-two towns in 1982 identified 37,115 full-time prostitutes, of whom 15,900 were in Addis Ababa, and this is almost certainly an underestimate;[37] the Addis Ababa total amounts to over 2 per cent of the female population of all ages. While some of these are educated girls working the tourist market, and commanding incomes way above anything that they could earn in other employment, the great majority are divorced women who have left (or been forced out of) their homes in the countryside, and for whom there is no other means of livelihood.[38]

The parallel youth association, REYA, is open to all youth between the ages of fourteen and thirty.[39] Since REWA is open to girls from the age of fifteen upwards, the effect is to channel them into REWA, and leave REYA as an overwhelmingly male organisation, save perhaps within specifically 'youth' institutions such as schools. At the first REYA Congress in September 1980, only fifteen of the 1,200 delegates were female.[40] The upper age limit serves in effect to allow young adult men to take leadership positions, and active mass involvement is largely a matter for boys in their teens and very early twenties. REYA membership at kebelle level calls for attendance at meetings, usually at weekends, and participation in physical exercises (in which it is not difficult to see a paramilitary element), Marxist–Leninist political education classes, and local community activities such as tidying the streets. REYA thus provides a convenient pool of free labour, and in my local kebelle, close to the main printing press, REYA members were sent to fold and staple exercise books on Saturday mornings, in preparation for the new school year. Total membership was given as 3 million in 1980, and as 3,800,000 (with 21,366 basic associations) in September 1985.[41] For ordinary members, REYA is policed by requiring any youth to present a letter from his local branch, certifying membership and satisfactory performance of his duties, in order to get a job, secure entrance to the university, or do anything else that requires official approval. In practice, such letters can be obtained for a few birr from complaisant kebelle authorities, and many youths, at any rate in towns, have virtually nothing to do with it. For organisers, REYA provides a potential channel for ambitious young men to work their way up through the tedious task of bear-leading the local youth, into the youth affairs section of the party, and thence into the ordinary party apparatus; they may also get onto political education courses in socialist states. REYA may thus serve as a recruiting mechanism for the party, whereas REWA is largely self-contained. In the university, REYA organisers are favoured in awarding graduate assistantships, and may thus work their way onto the academic staff. Political activity is an important and explicitly recognised criterion in making academic appointments.

I have no evidence that either REWA or REYA provide any policy input to the government, in the form of official consultation over policies which may affect their members, or any invitation to express their views. Organised as they are in accordance with the Leninist system of democratic centralism, they exist in order to socialise people in the manner that the government approves, and to provide a means of control over large sections of the population who are effectively excluded from the ordinary administrative structures of the peasants' associations and urban kebelles.

HOUSING AND THE CONTROL OF RESIDENCE

The control of housing is the basis of kebelle power. The mere numbering of houses imposed a pattern of official order on the chaotic urban structure of Addis Ababa and other major towns, with their villas, shacks and shanties crammed into higgledy-piggledy disorder along tracks and winding footpaths. The collection of rents was the kebelles' first task, and remains one of their main ones. But while the transformation of urban house ownership and administration provides one of the most dramatic illustrations of the expansion of revolutionary control, the chronic shortage of urban housing is an equally clear indication of revolutionary failure – an exact and by no means coincidental parallel to the combination of land reform and famine in the countryside.

Pre-revolutionary housing in Addis Ababa was broadly adequate in quantity, though grossly inadequate in quality.[42] On the one hand, one of the

141

most profitable uses for investment capital was building elegant villas for lease to foreigners (who were not permitted to own houses in Ethiopia), and the growing Ethiopian middle class. On the other, huge numbers of people were crammed into houses scarcely worthy of the name. A housing census of Addis Ababa carried out in August 1978, and largely reflecting the pre-revolutionary position (though further deterioration may have taken place during the intervening four years of upheaval), showed that 87 per cent of houses had non-durable walls (mostly of wattle-and-daub, known in Amharic as *chika*), 53 per cent had earthen floors, and 45.5 per cent had no foundations.[43] Only 6.7 per cent had piped water in the house, though half of the remainder had access to outside taps.

The housing reform of July 1975 did not nationalise all houses. It nationalised all land, but only 'extra' houses (i.e. those let out to rent), allowing each family to own one house for its own occupation. However, since only a small minority of houses were owner-occupied, most urban houses were taken over. According to an official report, 409,825 houses were nationalised across the whole country, of which 390,627 were adminis-tered by kebelles, while the remaining 18,858 had monthly rents of over 100 birr, and were therefore administered centrally by the Agency for the Administration of Rented Houses. Over 60 per cent of these centrally administered houses were in Addis Ababa.[44] Individuals who owned houses with a floor area of over 180 square metres, or valued at over 60,000 birr, were liable to have these taken over for public purposes, and would be allotted a smaller house in exchange. Larger houses were thus removed from residential use, many of them becoming kebelle or government offices, or leased to embassies or international organisations. Rents were reduced on a sliding scale, by between 50 per cent for the cheapest houses and 15 per cent for rents of 300 birr a month.

The results of the housing reform are for the most part entirely predictable and easily explained. On the one hand, it destroyed a rentier bourgeoisie, for which house rents provided a ready source of largely (but not entirely) unearned income, and greatly reduced the proportion of their meagre earn-ings which the city's poorest residents had to spend on rent. On the other hand, it reduced both the supply and the quality of urban housing, and led to an intense accommodation shortage. The housing census of 1984 showed very little change since 1978 in the percentage of houses with earth floors and non-durable walls, but a decline (from 6.7 per cent to 3.9 per cent) in the percentage with inside piped water, and an increase (from 20.0 per cent to 29.2 per cent) in those with no toilet facilities.[45] Less easily assessed is the general decay resulting from lack of maintenance. I have been unable to find any information on the maintenance of houses by kebelles, though there is a consensus of opinion that it has been slight or non-existent;[46] houses were for kebelles a simple source of income, rather than an investment to be managed – and after the reform of kebelle finances in 1981, they were not even that. The proclamation of April 1981, indeed, made no provision for kebelles to withhold money required for maintenance from the rents which they were required to pay over to the central municipality; the inference must be that this would have had to be specially sought through the cumbersome procedures already noted, and the easiest way out, in any event, would be to do nothing. Householders might carry out, at their own expense, limited repairs to their own dwellings, though building materials (such as the indispensable corrugated iron) were very difficult for private individuals to acquire. Properties looked after by the rented houses administration seem to have been better maintained, the main problems arising from the replacement of private landlords by a cumbersome centralised bureaucracy. Overall, there can be no doubt that the quality of the urban housing stock has declined, and with it, in a palpable everyday sense, the standard of living of its inhabitants.

In terms of quantity, the Ministry of Urban Development estimated in 1980 that 91,700 new 'dwelling units' were required in urban areas each year, of which 9,700 were needed to replace obsolete and uninhabitable housing, 24,000 to ease current overcrowding, and 58,000 to accommodate the growth in urban population.[47] About half of this total would have been required in Addis Ababa. Estimates of the number of houses actually built vary, but none come anywhere near this total. Official figures for the number of houses built in Addis Ababa from 1975 to 1981 range between 2,188 and 2,422 a year.[48] Estimates based on censuses of the housing stock in 1978 and 1984, on the other hand, yield an annual construction rate of 5,423 to 5,721, suggesting that houses have continued to be built outside government control.[49] While the upheavals of 1974–78 may have reduced the rate of house building, however, there is no evidence of any upsurge in construction during the 1980s. Indeed the increasingly cumbersome procedures imposed on would-be builders have made it difficult for private individuals, who accounted for three-quarters of the houses built in the five years to 1980, to get the necessary permits at all. Government policy has favoured house building by government agencies and housing cooperatives, but both these and private building involve an endless (and quite possibly fruitless) round of procedures. Over the seven years from 1976–77 to 1983–84, 23,019 Addis Ababa households joined housing cooperatives, but only 5,888 houses were actually built by these, and the numbers of cooperatives formed tended to fall over this period. About 70 per cent of these houses were built, moreover, for people in the top 31 per cent of the urban salary range, and at least 24 per cent for people in the top 3.7 per cent of the range.[50] The urban kebelles, on which the task of building low-cost houses for the mass of the urban population devolved, have done very little, and especially since the kebelle proclamation of 1981, have not even had the means to do anything. The Ministry of Urban Development itself built only 6,036 housing units (including hostel accommodation and flats) across the whole country in the ten years up to July 1985;[51] and though occasional low-cost housing projects were announced in provincial towns, an average cost

143

of 25,000 to 30,000 birr per dwelling put them well beyond the reach of most people, and indeed of most municipalities.[52] A 1984 report on the building materials industry noted that there had been virtually no investment since 1974 (with the single exception of the massive Mugher cement factory), leading to stoppages due to maintenance problems and lack of spares, and that the artificial prices imposed by the planning authorities led to further bottlenecks.[53]

The resulting shortages are felt at every level. At the top, embassies and high-ranking United Nations officials are housed in hotels because no other accommodation can be found for them. At the bottom, simple pressure on housing probably accounts for the increase in the average number of occupants per housing unit in Addis Ababa from 4.2 in 1967 to 5.2 in 1978 and 5.8 in 1984.[54] Conditions in the poorest areas rival Calcutta, with reports of eighteen people sharing an eighteen square metre room, and between ten and twenty families sharing a single kitchen.[55] One result, closely analogous to the effects of land reform in the countryside, is that residence is 'frozen' by people's simple inability to move. The market in private housing had almost dried up, before it was abolished altogether by the proclamation of February 1986 which required anyone selling a house to do so to the state. Kebelle waiting lists for accommodation are entirely out of proportion to the number of houses available, and further controls hamper population movement. One of the effects (and indeed probably one of the purposes) of this system is to discourage immigration, especially to Addis Ababa. One of the few ways to move house is to arrange a swap with someone in another kebelle; or, if a friend is for some reason moving out, to squat in his house until the kebelle accepts the new occupant. Shortage of a vital resource, the allocation of which is in official hands, almost automatically breeds corruption; and a large part of rumoured corruption relates to the housing market, at the level both of the kebelle and of the central agency for rented houses.

The government's reaction has been to blame shortages, in housing as elsewhere, on the activities of private speculators. In a series of measures announced in February 1985, Mengistu Haile-Mariam called for 'a stop to be made to the abuse of individual home building and selling through loans acquired through the banks and other sources, and to the sale of urban land, as these have been found to cause hardship to the broad masses'.[56] The effect was to place a complete stoppage on house building and finance for a full year, by both individual builders and housing cooperatives, which between them accounted for the great majority of houses built. Amid total uncertainty about what government housing policy would actually be, it was rumoured that all private house ownership and building might be abolished. The Construction and Use of Urban Houses Proclamation, issued in February 1986, stopped a long way short of this.[57] It allowed private individuals to build, own, and mortgage houses, and even to sub-let accommodation under an arrangement which, for ideological reasons, was termed 'co-dwelling' – disguising the return, in a limited and highly regulated form, of the private landlord. However, houses could be sold only to the government, which would resell to purchasers at a price fixed by itself; and the building regulations allowed for a maximum floor area of only seventy square metres (or 740 square feet) in any newly built house, with a minimum of seventeen square metres.

Most if not all major third-world cities suffer from chronic housing problems, and many of the problems of housing in Addis Ababa in any event predate the revolution. This is, nonetheless, an important area in which, despite the successful restriction of urban immigration, conditions since the revolution have deteriorated. This deterioration is due in large part to revolutionary policies, especially the abolition of private rented accommodation, but also other restrictions on house building, and the decline of the building materials industry. The experience of Ethiopia in this respect is similar to that of revolutionary socialist states the world over.

SOCIALIST DISTRIBUTION

The revolution has coincided with, and in part at least certainly caused, a large and steady increase in urban poverty. The real wages of low-paid workers fell by nearly a third during the six years after the revolution, and those of highly paid workers by over a half,[58] as prices (especially food prices) continued to rise, while wages stayed the same. The proportion of the Addis Ababa population unable to meet its minimum needs was assessed at 51.2 per cent in 1976, and estimated at over 67 per cent in 1982.[59] Since that time, increasing numbers of people have fallen into destitution, as the result especially of the food crisis. In one city centre kebelle, the proportion of 'marasmic' (a medical euphemism for 'starving') children under the age of five increased from under ten per cent of the kebelle total between August 1982 and December 1983, to between sixteen and twenty per cent between April and December 1984.[60] In this way, starvation in the countryside has filtered through, though at a greatly reduced level, to the cities.

The government has responded to this crisis by establishing a 'socialist distribution system', allocating goods through rationing at maintained official prices. One of the foreign companies nationalised in 1975, A. Besse and Company, was converted into the Ethiopian Domestic Distribution Corporation; but the system did not get properly under way until April 1980, when the Addis Ababa Basic Commodities Supply Corporation was established, and started distributing grain to the twenty-five city keftenyas, which in turn passed it down to the kebelles.[61] Each kebelle distributed grain, and subsequently other items such as sugar, pulses, and a small range of manufactured goods, through a rationing system to households within its area. Kebelles also set up shops which, through their right to buy goods direct from the state

145

manufacturing or distributive corporation concerned, could cut out middlemen and sell at less than the normal retail price – at ninety cents rather than one birr, for example, for a bottle of beer. The first point to be made is that this represents a remarkably effective system of urban distribution. Indeed the capacity to administer a reasonably fair and efficient urban rationing system is one of the most striking tributes to the level of organisation which the revolutionary regime has created. Each kebelle family is issued with a ration card (in 1985, three ration cards – one each for grains and pulses, bread, and other goods), which entitle it to a monthly allocation of the goods concerned at the controlled price. On the whole, this system works well. It enables households to buy at least part of their basic grain requirements at a price which, with the decline of national grain production, has amounted to a smaller and smaller percentage of the free market price. When the system started in 1980, kebelle prices for grain were at about three-quarters of the open market price; by the following year, the fraction had dropped to two-thirds;[62] and by the famine year of 1984–85 kebelle prices were a third to a quarter of the open market, though this discrepancy was greatly reduced by the good harvest and lower grain prices of 1986–87.

So marked a discrepancy between two parallel pricing systems provides obvious opportunities for corruption. There are rumours of kebelle officials selling goods on the side to private traders; and poor families, though they need all the cheap grain they can get, supplement their incomes by reselling their rations of less favoured goods.[63] On the whole, however, the system works, and corruption does not attain the level at which it would break down into farce. The problems lie elsewhere. The first is that cheap urban food supplies are possible only at the expense of low (and enforced) producer prices which exploit the peasantry, transfer income from the countryside to the cities, and at the same time provide a strong disincentive to surplus production. Insofar as the villagisation campaign, discussed in the next chapter, is intended to enable the government to extract a surplus more easily from the peasantry, it represents a high price in control, with almost certainly self-defeating objectives. A second problem is simply that the socialist distribution system cannot circulate enough of the basic commodities to avert reliance on the open market. In 1981–82, kebelle shops were able to supply about two-thirds of household staple grain requirements.[64] By 1985, with the decline in agricultural production accentuated by drought, and the need to import a large proportion of national grain needs (whether commercially, or as famine relief), the proportion had shrunk to probably between a third and a half. This in turn tended to increase the price differential between the kebelle and the open markets. A third problem, and the most complained about among the consumers, was that the kebelle shops provided only the least favoured types of grain. By far the favoured grain among Ethiopians is locally grown teff, which commands a substantial price premium over other grains in the open market. Though teff is bought by the Agricultural Marketing Corporation, it virtually never appears in the kebelle shops, and probably goes to feed the army (unless there is truth in the rumour that it goes to make vodka in Russia). Instead, consumers have to make do with whatever grain is available, such as the despised imported rice. Finally, the distribution system itself is subject to rigidities: amounts are allocated to each keftenya, for example, on the strength of population estimates which are rarely revised, while the number of people allowed for on each household ration card remains the same, despite changes in household size.

But despite all this, the kebelle rationing system has become an important means of mitigating the effects of fixed incomes and declining agricultural production on city dwellers. On the one hand, it thus increases the hold of the kebelles over the urban population; it is the single most evident benefit that the kebelle has to offer its residents, and for poorer people survival is almost impossible without it. This in turn helps to enforce obedience, since people showing dissent from the kebelle authorities may have their ration cards confiscated, and it likewise helps to control immigration into the major cities. A poor immigrant not registered with the kebelle, and therefore not receiving rations, would find it hard to survive. On the other hand, the system has become no less necessary to the government itself. The urban population has seen its standard of living fall dramatically since the revolution; it is controlled and restricted as never before, and outlets for dissent have been closed off. Unemployment is a major problem, while the real incomes even of those with jobs have dropped. Even a government with such a structure of control at its disposal, and the memory of the terror as always at its back, must be concerned about the effects of removing subsidies on food, and thus potentially moving starvation from the countryside into the towns. Nor indeed has it shown any sign of doing so; the shortages of food, and the discrepancies between prices in the controlled and open markets, are ascribed to anti-revolutionary collusion between the merchants and a section of the peasantry, calling in turn for further socialisation and greater control. In his May Day speech in 1985, an occasion generally devoted to urban affairs, Mengistu Haile-Mariam referred to the food shortage, and went on to say[65]

> The failure to stop the inhuman deeds committed by those merchants who run for exhorbitant profits by speculating on the basic necessities of the society, and who give priority to their individual interests rather than to the well-being of the country and the people, is absolutely inexcusable and in fact demands for firm popular justice. Especially with regard to food grain, it is no secret that such merchants consort with some weak elements among the peasantry under cover of darkness at the expense of the people . . . Hence the greedy merchants and their collaborators who are the major sources of this problem, must realise that they will no more be tolerated and must refrain from their vile activities.

In this way, the revolutionary government's attempts to control the market both create a shared interest in low prices between itself and the urban population, and arouse a corresponding alliance between farmers and merchants. An increasing level of physical control is thus required in order to police an increasing level of economic control.

INDUSTRY, EMPLOYMENT AND THE URBAN ECONOMY

Surprisingly for so underdeveloped a country, Ethiopia had 11 per cent of its gross domestic product in manufacturing in 1983, as against an average of 7–8 per cent for sub-Saharan Africa as a whole.[66] A large part of this manufacturing capacity is concentrated in Addis Ababa and a string of satellite towns – Kalitti, Akaki, Debre Zeit, Mojo, Nazret – along the road and railway line to the ports at Assab and Djibouti. These accounted in 1984 for 70 per cent of the value of industrial production, a proportion increased to 91 per cent with the addition of Asmara and Dire Dawa.[67] The revolution, which involved both the nationalisation of all major industries (most of which were foreign-owned) and upheavals in which industrial workers took a prominent part, resulted in a decline in production and a virtual halting of new investment. Only with the launching of the National Revolutionary Development Campaigns from late 1978 onwards was any sustained attempt made to revive the industrial economy, and much of this consisted in heroic but inevitably inadequate efforts to rehabilitate old and decayed machinery, while hampered by inexperienced management and a highly centralised system of bureaucratic control.[68]

No new foreign private investment has been forthcoming since the revolution, and industrial strategy has thus reflected both government priorities and the availability of capital and expertise, especially from the socialist states. This in turn has resulted in a small number of large showpiece projects, many of them marred by inappropriate technology. These include a textile factory at Combolcha in Wollo (with aid from East Germany, Czechoslovakia and Italy), a cement works at Mugher, west of Addis Ababa (East Germany), a tractor assembly plant at Nazret (USSR), a multipurpose weapons factory in Addis Ababa (Czechoslovakia), a hydroelectric scheme at Melka Wakena in Bale (USSR, Czechoslovakia), oilseed mills at Bahr Dar in Gojjam and at Mojo, and a substantial amount of new investment in alcoholic beverages, including a malting plant at Asela in Arsi, a distillery in Addis Ababa, and breweries in Addis Ababa and Harar. Many of these, including the tractor, cement, textile and weapons factories, were inaugurated during the build-up to the tenth anniversary celebrations in 1984, symbolising both socialist development and the alliance with socialist states that made it possible;[69] they have not been in operation long enough to show how well they have worked. This emphasis on a small number of large factories was however maintained in the Ten-Year Plan, which provided for just over half of all manufacturing investment during the period to be concentrated in thirteen projects, three of which were to be in textiles, with two each in sugar refining and caustic soda, and single factories for cement, an iron foundry, spare parts, fertiliser, pulp, and paper.[70]

This pattern of investment is characteristic of state socialist systems, reflecting the preferences of planners, the requirements of centralised management, and the availability of ready-made technology. The inappropriateness of such technology to underdeveloped third-world states has of course been the subject of a debate going well beyond its socialist examples, but is particularly evident in Ethiopia.[71] Since most of the investment capital for these projects has been Ethiopian – over 60 per cent for the textile factory, for example, and over 75 per cent for the cement works[72] – it has had to be diverted from other projects in which it might have been more usefully invested, especially for creating employment. The textile mill cost 222 million birr and was planned to employ 3,460 people,[73] an investment of some 64,000 birr for each job – an amount way beyond any rational allocation of resources in a country with a per capita income of some 220 birr.[74] The equivalent figure for the cement factory is a staggering 452,000 birr per job, while investments in large oilseed mills at Mojo and Bahr Dar, at 125,000–132,000 birr per job, threaten to destroy one of the main sources of small-scale industrial employment.[75]

This problem should be seen in the light of the fact that Ethiopia, like almost all third-world states, has suffered from an increasing level of urban unemployment, which has been exacerbated by the investment policies of the revolutionary government. Unemployment in African cities is notoriously difficult to measure, owing to the numbers of people in part-time and informal employment, and to the inadequacy of institutional mechanisms such as labour exchanges through which statistics can be collected. The Ministry of Labour surveyed thirty-one main towns in November 1978, revealing a total of 212,496 people unemployed, about half of whom were in Addis Ababa.[76] Since then, the position has deteriorated. An ILO report in 1982 notes that, although precise figures were not available, about twenty per cent of the labour force was unemployed in the eighteen largest towns, and also drew attention to a likely doubling of the urban labour force over the following eight years.[77] One effect of the post-revolutionary increase in education is that a much larger proportion of the unemployed are school leavers, including many with the Ethiopian School Leaving Certificate (ESLC) taken in the twelfth grade. The number of junior secondary school leavers seeking employment rose from 10,795 to 18,734 over the two years from 1978–79 to 1980–81, while the number of senior secondary school leavers looking for jobs rose over the same period from 19,245 to 44,718 – well over doubling in just two years.[78] The numbers have continued to increase since then, though exact totals are not available, and government ministries and corporations have been ordered to employ extra staff, in order to mitigate the problem.

The state sector accounts for some 95 per cent of industrial output and capital,[79] the remainder being spread through a large number of very small-scale establishments which have remained in private hands. These have come under the supervision of the Handicrafts and Small Scale Industries Development Association (HASIDA), which has attempted to organise them into cooperatives, in order both to increase productivity and to prevent the emergence of a capitalist class. 95 per cent of the workers who had been organised in this way up to mid 1983 were in the textile trades, especially weaving and tailoring.[80] A wide range of measures have been used to induce, or in some cases more accurately compel, individual craftsmen to join cooperatives. Tailors, for example, can only receive allocations of cloth through a cooperative, and cooperatives also monopolise official sources of credit. Just as in the case of agricultural cooperatives, however, these appear to be formed overwhelmingly in response to government pressures and inducements, and to attract, on the whole, the less able practitioners, who need official credit and other benefits to keep going. The price which they then have to pay is a higher level of government control, while cooperative officials are under a considerable temptation either to embezzle the funds, or to divert materials to the non-cooperative sector. A parallel sector then arises of, for example, private tailors, who have to obtain their cloth through the black market, but who are able to escape regulation.

EDUCATION AND LITERACY

A dramatic increase in education is a characteristic achievement of revolutionary regimes, which has certainly been realised in Ethiopia. One of the happiest sights of revolutionary Ethiopia is the large number of little children who can be seen each morning making their way to school. Total numbers of students in government schools nearly quadrupled from 811,114 to 3,076,948 between 1973–74 and 1983–84,[81] and are likely to have continued rising. The number of students in higher education has likewise roughly quadrupled.[82] This increase has been spread throughout the country, by a policy of trying to open secondary schools in every province in Ethiopia. In 1985, 40,907 students took the Ethiopian School Leaving Certificate examination at the end of the twelfth grade, compared with only 13,698 students in the twelfth grade eight years earlier.[83] These were drawn from schools in all but nine of the 102 provinces, seven of the exceptions being in the Ogaden provinces of Hararghe and Bale, one in the EPLF-controlled area of Eritrea, and the last on the Sudanese border in Kaffa. Though by far the greatest concentration of students taking the exam was in Addis Ababa and the surrounding region of Shoa, with 46 per cent of the candidates compared with 22.6 per cent of the national population, the best results in qualitative terms were achieved in the two insurgency affected regions of Tigray and Hararghe.[84] Both socially and geographically, the revolutionary government has made every effort to spread education much more widely than under the imperial regime.

This increase in the quantity of education has however been matched by a corresponding drop in its quality.[85] The number of students per teacher rose from 42.3 in 1975–76 to 58.4 in 1981–82.[86] The introduction of a shift system to cope with the increased numbers, with at times three shifts in each school per day (though by 1985 the number had generally been cut to two), means that each child in school normally receives only three hours of instruction each day. The resulting decline in quality is especially marked in English, which has in practice (though not in principle) been displaced by Amharic as the medium of secondary school instruction. The replacement of generally fairly high-quality instruction for a small number of people, by much lower-quality instruction for a much larger number, in a sense epitomises what the revolution is about. The decline in quality must likewise be set against the point, not only that more people get educated, but equally that the function of education may have changed. Rather than producing an elite, whose role was to mediate, in one way or another, between Ethiopia and the external world, it may be seen as supplying ordinary Ethiopians with the skills needed for life in a society where literacy in Amharic is more use than it would be in English. The effect of the decline in English in cutting Ethiopians off from the outside world may be positively welcomed by revolutionary nationalists bent on achieving 'socialism in one country', though at the same time the better-educated Ethiopian school leavers are often desperate to get out of a society which seems to have little to offer them, and join the large emigrant community in the West, and especially in the United States. As one interviews the articulate and highly qualified products of the imperial educational system who now hold high office in revolutionary Ethiopia, one is very much aware that, while the revolution has greatly extended the educational opportunities open to ordinary Ethiopians, it is nowhere providing the kind of education from which the present leadership has benefitted.

Though the overall effect of rising unemployment, especially among school leavers, has been to increase alienation from the regime – an alienation which is particularly evident, even if not openly expressed, in the universities – it may also help to provide recruits to the party. Party membership, despite the danger of being sent off to work in settlements on the western borders, does at least provide some guarantee against unemployment, and as party nominees are increasingly moved into leading positions in every sector in the state, it may form the most reliable avenue to a position of power. It also offers the chance of higher education in the socialist states, and although this ranks well below education in the West in the eyes of Ethiopian students, it does provide an opportunity for travel and gaining qualifications. Students entering the university are informed that scholarships to the socialist states are available, on the basis of political dedication rather than academic achievement, even to those who fail their Addis Ababa University exams. Since the revolution, opportunities for education abroad have been heavily concentrated in the socialist states, though with some renewed opening to the West since the early 1980s. Government figures show 93 per cent of Ethiopian students sent abroad in 1979–80 as going to the socialist states, with the largest numbers going to the Soviet Union, followed by Cuba and the GDR.[87] These figures exclude those going for specifically political training. Figures for later years are incomplete, but indicate a similar preponderance of students going to the Soviet Union and Eastern Europe.[88] Since language training has to be added to study time – there is enormous interest in English language learning in Ethiopia, but no evident enthusiasm to study Russian – such students are often away for many years. Periods of eight or ten years are not uncommon. I have been unable to detect any enhanced commitment to socialism among those who have undergone this experience.

The most spectacular example of revolutionary educational transformation is the national literacy campaign, launched in July 1979 and thereafter consistently pursued through successive twice-yearly 'rounds'. This draws heavily on the semi-compulsory services of students and school leavers, who make up some 90 per cent of the instructors,[89] and is organised so as to profit from slack periods in the school and farming year. It provides further evidence of the sheer scale of organisation that the government is able to achieve. This evidence obviously depends on official statistics, but allowing for some tendency to inflate the numbers, and a few cases where local officials have clearly invented figures which are way out of line with the rest of the country, these seem to be very broadly reliable. The first two rounds, in 1979–80, established 35,000 literacy centres and recruited 241,000 instructors.[90] By the end of the twelfth round, in 1985, 16,941,075 people (some 40 per cent of the total national population) had been enrolled for courses, of whom 12,037,542 had passed the end-of-course exam, and 10,070,102 had been enrolled in post-literacy programmes.[91] Plausibility is given to these figures by the fact that much lower totals are reported for the insurgency affected regions of Tigray and Eritrea than their total population would otherwise suggest, while these two regions also have an exceptionally high proportion of women among the participants. Some Moslem areas also report much higher proportions of men. This mania for numbers may indeed be one of the problems of the campaign: local literacy directors may be under pressure to report as high a total as possible, and even if the numbers themselves are not inflated, there must be a considerable temptation to sacrifice quality to the quantity of people put through the programme.[92] It is very basic literacy indeed, and many of those who achieve it are likely to lapse back into effective illiteracy because of the lack of widespread basic and intermediate literature to keep them within a literate environment. Figures for national literacy rates are untrustworthy, both because of this, and because of uncertainty about the size of the total population. Claims based on an assumed population of 30 million had to be abandoned when the 1984 census revealed a population 12 million higher.

The literacy campaign also provides one of the few assessable pieces of evidence for the revolutionary nationalities policy, under which the imperial government's policy of centralisation based on the core Amharic culture and language has, it is claimed, been replaced by a policy of equal treatment for all nationalities. The campaign has been conducted in fifteen 'nationality languages', starting with Amharic, Oromo, Tigrinya, Somali and Wollaita, and subsequently extended to include Sidama, Hadiya, Tigre, Afar, Kambatta, Gedeo, Kaffa, Saho, Kunama and Gurage.[93] Despite this impressive range, encompassing the native languages of a very high proportion (certainly well over 90 per cent) of the national population, the available evidence suggests that the achievement of literacy in the national language, Amharic, is a more important part of the programme than any encouragement for other and local languages. The Amharic script is used for all languages, with a few adaptations for languages such as Oromo which have sounds not found in Amharic, and even for Somali, which now has a Roman script used in the Somali Republic by the great majority of its speakers. This enables other groups to read the national language, but at the same time inhibits literacy from establishing contact with the outside world. In the towns, where a mixture of populations complicates matters, and use of different languages might well reinforce ethnic identity, Amharic alone is used; the different 'nationality languages' are thus used only in the countryside. Even there, officials claim, plausibly enough, that people prefer to learn to read and write in Amharic, both because there is more literature available, and because it enables them to have dealings with officials – which is one of the main functions of literacy in any event.

Oddly but doubtless symptomatically for a campaign so obsessed with statistics, there are no figures available for the numbers of people becoming literate in each language. The nearest substitute is provided by the number of books in each language delivered to literacy reading rooms.[94] Of a national total of 1,434,329 in 1985, 58.9 per cent were printed in Amharic, and 20.0 per cent in Oromo. Seven other languages – in descending order, Tigrinya, Wollaita, Saho, Somali, Afar, Gedeo, and Hadiya – accounted for between 4.5 per cent and 1.9 per cent apiece. Less than half of 1 per cent each were printed in Tigre, Kambatta, Kaffa, Sidama, Kunama and Gurage. A list of sixty-six locally produced literacy newspapers and magazines shows that 70 per cent were published in Amharic only, 18 per cent in both Amharic and a local language, and 12 per cent in the local language only; six of the eight publications in the last category were in Tigrinya, the language of highland Tigray and Eritrea, which already has a literate tradition of its own. Despite the large number of publications in Oromo, the overwhelming impression is that the literacy campaign serves to educate people in Amharic. This is, of course, an eminently defensible national goal. Literacy programmes on the radio are broadcast in Amharic, Oromo, Tigrinya and Wollaita.[95]

THE REACTION FROM CONTROL

Ethiopians are not North Koreans. The framework of public order imposed by the regime is accepted, even welcomed, and with it the deference and acceptance of authority which are needed to make it work; but this deference involves no total commitment or exaggerated obeisance to the new

153

order. The degree of ideological penetration achieved by hours of conscious political education appears to be slight, and the Amharic proverb, 'you bow in front – and fart behind', remains as apposite to the new regime as to the old. This state of affairs is accepted, perhaps for lack of choice, by the regime. Though correct public behaviour is insisted on, there is no evident attempt to monitor or control private behaviour or ideological commitment.

Expressions of public opposition are rare, and reports of them are usually circulated at second hand through a rumour network which may well exaggerate. By the mid 1980s, some demonstrations of discontent were taking place, none of them seriously threatening to the regime, but at the same time indicating a relaxation of the obedience inspired by the terror: peasants come to town for a religious festival chanting slogans against villagisation; parents lying down in front of the busses taking their children away for military service; and other minor incidents of this kind. But even if correctly reported, these were no more than isolated incidents. More general is a sub-culture of conscious detachment. Ethiopians had no need to learn from Eastern Europe the value of the subversive political joke. Myriad examples testify to Mengistu's supposed obsequiousness to the Russians; one, from the time of the famine, has atheist party cadres going to church to pray for rain – in Canada. Conspicuously Western dress provides another indication: youths in the streets display T-shirts with Western motifs, such as the emblems of (sometimes fictitious) American universities; 'Princeton University, California, USA' is for some reason particularly common. From late in 1985, people earning over 500 birr a month were required to wear uniforms of faintly North Korean cut, in khaki, or pale and brilliant blue; they did so, at least in Addis Ababa, but with many deprecatory comments. Efficient though the kebelle system is, some people are able (and prefer) to live outside it altogether, foregoing the benefit of subsidised food in exchange for freedom from organisation; in one case that came my way, two brothers each failed to attend a demonstration; the one who was registered with his kebelle received three days in jail, whereas the other who was not, escaped scot-free. But though this is a feasible strategy for unmarried youths, it is much more difficult for anyone with a family, who needs permanent accommodation.

One classic measure of alienation is the level of crime, which at first sight appears to have dropped sharply in the revolutionary era, from an average of 105,775 indictments a year over the decade preceding the revolution, to 43,915 for the six-year period from 1977–78 to 1982–83.[96] The later period covers a rise from about 34,000 cases a year in 1977–79 to 51,000 in 1981–83, but nowhere reaches even half of the pre-revolutionary average. This decline may readily be hailed as signalling the end of feudo–bourgeois injustices, and the institution of a fairer social order.[97] In a more practical way, the curfew and the regular nighttime patrols by kebelle policemen may well provide a real impediment to crime. However, differences between the pre-revolutionary and post-revolutionary eras make meaningful comparison difficult. The most important is simply that cases heard by kebelle and peasants' association tribunals are excluded from the statistics, and these are likely to have included many cases which would previously have been handled by the police. Crime may also have gone underreported between 1977 and 1979, due to the drafting of police into the armed forces, to meet the wartime emergencies in the Ogaden and Eritrea. But even if one cannot reach definite conclusions on the overall level of crime, there is ample evidence of changes in the *pattern* of crime, resulting from the new revolutionary order. Most striking is the increase in 'breaches of regulations' to become the commonest category of crime (overtaking both theft and assault), with just over a quarter of reported indictments; along with this goes a sixfold increase in cases of the misappropriation of public property, and a new category of 'crimes against the economy'.[98] Unsurprisingly, then, an increase in the regulatory and economic role of the state is reflected in the proportion of crime directed against the state rather than individuals.

But the most striking indication of detachment from the revolutionary order is the continuing (and perhaps increased) prominence of religion. The Marxist–Leninist regime has recognised religion as an obvious danger, and treated it with care. In the first phase of the revolution, the Derg – then anxious to dissociate itself from symbols of the imperial regime – abolished the special status of the Ethiopian Orthodox Church and raised Islam to formal equality with Christianity. Though the main Islamic feasts remain as public holidays, the early suspicion that the new regime favoured Islam has died away. The previous Patriarch was killed and replaced by a compliant old monk, and an administrator appointed, who serves in effect as a government watchdog over the Orthodox Church; but the Church itself has not been persecuted, and some efforts have been made to harness it as an agency for rural development.

The position of the mission churches was much more difficult, both because they could be regarded as alien rather than national, and equally because – seeking converts of necessity outside the main Orthodox areas – they inevitably became associated with regional interests potentially at odds with the central government. The Roman Catholic Church – despite much wider connections, including a longstanding mission in Harar – is strongest in Eritrea, where it was established during the Italian colonial period, and its relations with the government have been on both sides correct but unenthusiastic; there was no official reaction, favourable or hostile, when its head was created cardinal in 1983. The Lutherans were in a much weaker position; having established an autonomous Ethiopian church, called Mekane Yesus, they had the stigma of alienness without the protection of a prominent global hierarchy, and were most firmly entrenched in Welega, where some of their leaders were associated (if only by family ties) with the local Oromo liberation movement. Severe repression took place in the later 1970s. One of the side-effects of famine has however been to re-establish links between the mission churches and their Ethiopian counterparts, and thus to give them a measure of protection. Mekane Yesus leaders, for example, were allowed to receive publicly donations for famine relief from churches abroad. Both Catholic and Mekane Yesus leaders, along with the Orthodox Patriarch and the chairman of the Supreme Islamic Council, were also accorded official recognition by being included in the Constitutional Commission set up in 1986 to prepare for the establishment of the PDRE, and all of these except the cardinal were elected to the National Shengo.

The regime itself is nonetheless firmly atheist, and any public religious observance thus expresses independence of it, if not necessarily opposition to it. The great Orthodox festivals such as Maskal and Timkat continue to be celebrated with great enthusiasm, along with a mass of lesser occasions. It is hard to confirm the frequent claims that they attract an even larger turnout than before the revolution, and precisely because such attendance now has a quasi-political significance that it previously lacked, such claims may be exaggerated. At any event, enormous throngs of people attend, and church building continues even in Addis Ababa. The most spectacular demonstration of Christian fervour is the annual pilgrimage to Kolubi near Harar, which attracts hundreds of thousands of people each December and seems to be steadily growing in importance; despite the government's attempts to stem the flood by warning that transport will not be available, it has each year felt obliged to give way, and every available bus, train and aeroplane has been pressed into service to take pilgrims to Dire Dawa, whence most of them set out to walk the forty kilometres up the rift valley wall to Kolubi. The main Moslem shrine at Sheik Hussein in Bale is also very popular, but despite its large Islamic population, there has been no evidence in Ethiopia of the Moslem fundamentalist movements found in several of the neighbouring African and Middle Eastern states. Though religion provides a latent challenge to the regime at the level of popular belief, it does not provide an explicit one at the level of political action.

7

Rural transformation and the crisis of agricultural production

In the census of 1984, 88.7 per cent of Ethiopia's population was classed as 'rural'.[1] By far the greater number of these, in turn, were settled agriculturalists working in small family units and producing largely or entirely for their own subsistence – or in other words, peasants. Nomadic and semi-nomadic pastoralists, though they range over some 60 per cent of Ethiopia's land area, mostly in the east and south, account for probably no more than 10 per cent or so of the population.[2] Non-peasant agricultural production, in the former private estates which became state farms at the revolution, occupies no more than 1 or 2 per cent of the population. At a rough estimate, therefore, about three-quarters of all Ethiopians are peasants, and the centrality of peasant agriculture to the Ethiopian revolution thus becomes clear.

The land reform of April 1975 made all rural land the collective property of the Ethiopian people.[3] It abolished all existing forms of tenure, together with all dues on land and all litigation relating to it; it restricted the size of family holdings to a maximum of ten hectares (a maximum which, in practice, is seldom if ever reached), and prohibited the employment of hired labour on land. Peasants' associations were established to distribute land 'as much as possible equally', and were also empowered to set up judicial tribunals and market and credit cooperatives, and given minor local administrative responsibilities. A further proclamation, in December 1975, elaborated and extended the powers of the associations, including notably their right to establish peasant defence squads and agricultural producers' cooperatives.[4] It also established a hierarchy of district, provincial, regional and national Revolutionary and Administrative Development Committees to coordinate and control the work of peasants' associations. The All Ethiopia Peasants' Association (AEPA), established in December 1977 and reorganised in May 1982, set up an equivalent hierarchy which effectively replaced the Development Committees.[5] Its name was changed to Ethiopia Peasants' Association (EPA) in 1986.

157

Peasants' associations were established rapidly in the immediate aftermath of land reform. Within a year, 15,989 associations had been set up, encompassing 4,550,918 peasant households.[6] Comparison of regional membership figures with those for the early 1980s shows that most of central and southern Ethiopia was effectively organised into associations during this initial burst, including Arsi, Bale, Hararghe, Illubabor, Kaffa, Sidamo, Welega and most of Shoa. By 1980, the national total had expanded to 7,049,209 households within 23,506 associations, most of the increase being due to the organisation of the north-central highlands, especially in northern Shoa, Gojjam, and Wollo.[7] By 1982, the total had rather surprisingly dropped to 5,164,178 households in 19,579 associations,[8] but much of this change was due to the amalgamation of associations into larger units (especially in the Amhara highland areas where land had traditionally been allocated by the rist system, in which the initial associations were mostly very small), and to the weeding out of association members who had registered but could not maintain their claim to land, because they were too old or young, absentee, or had registered in more than one association. In some areas, however, the figures add up to a revealing admission of the loss of central control. Tigray had been fairly effectively organised in 1975–76, with 311,028 peasant households in 1,071 associations; by 1982, these numbers had sunk to 55,988 families in 157 associations. Eritrea, with a mere 38,537 member families in 1982, had never been properly organised at all. Throughout those areas which the government controlled, however, and these accounted for by far the greater part of cultivated Ethiopia, the organisation was both effective and complete. By July 1986, the numbers had increased again to 5,738,586 households in 20,396 associations, with 125,232 member families in Tigray, and the suspiciously round number of 130,000 in Eritrea.[9]

With an average membership of 281 households in 1986 (varying from a high of 546 in Wollo to a low of 177 in Welega), peasants' associations each contain only about a fifth as many people as urban kebelles, and are quite small enough for all their members to be known to one another and the association leadership. Their formal organisation is very similar to that of the kebelles, save that the policy committee (which in the kebelles serves as an intermediate body between the general assembly and the other committees) is dispensed with, and the revolutionary defence committee is elected by the executive.[10] All committees are in principle elected every two years, but unlike the urban kebelle elections, which are widely publicised and held simultaneously across the whole country, these are not usually reported, and Dessalegn found them to be held at varying intervals depending on central government policy and the views of local officials.[11] A series of elections, from individual associations up to the national AEPA, was however held to coincide with the reorganisation of the AEPA in mid 1982.[12] In practice, Dessalegn found, district officials exercised wide supervisory powers over the associations, including the management of elections, investigating complaints of mismanagement (which readily provided excuses for replacing association leaders with their own preferred candidates), redrawing association boundaries, and organising meetings, mass rallies, political education courses, and the like. He was writing before the extension of the party organisation down to district level, and it is likely that these powers have been taken over by the local party. At all events, the early period during which the associations were effectively self-governing has now given way to central management and control. This control is exercised through the state and party hierarchy, rather than through the hierarchy of the EPA, which nominally exists to enable peasants to participate in political affairs all the way up to national level. In practice, peasant participation in decision-making above the level of the individual association is nominal.[13] The EPA organisation is heavily bureaucratised, has no organic links with the peasantry which it is supposed to represent, and plays no role at all in rural development. 'Some of the Woreda (district) PA leaders we talked to were expensively dressed for peasants, and affected the worst mannerisms of civil service bureaucrats.'[14]

Little information is available on the leadership of the associations, but what there is suggests, unsurprisingly, that this reflected the structure of the existing society. In the north, association chairmen often seem to have been priests, whereas in the south they were likely to be younger than average (often in their twenties), and literate in Amharic.[15] At least in the early years, there was a rapid turnover in association leadership; and even at that time, when participation is likely to have been at its highest, leaders were dismissed much more at the behest of district officials than because of initiatives from the association members themselves.[16] Though both the administration and the association members would find it helpful to have local leaders who could communicate with the national hierarchy, the establishment of the associations in regions such as Hararghe marked the ending of the power of the settler class, and their replacement by men of local origin. It is likely that association leadership will have stabilised, as the system has become established, and as the leaders themselves have acquired their own interests and political connections. Though there has been no evident tendency for the associations to be 'captured' by the old ruling elites, there are some indications that association chairmen are developing into the revolutionary equivalent of the old village headman or *chika shum*, whose function is to implement orders from government, and who can in turn maintain themselves at least in part from levies on ordinary peasants. Land reform has resulted in a considerable equalisation of peasant holdings, and though inequalities remain, these are at least partly due to variations in family size and land productivity, as well as to inherent problems in dividing plots.[17] Dessalegn found that leaders did not have larger than average plots, though on the whole they were more likely than ordinary peasants to have plough oxen.[18] However, leaders can exercise considerable power over association members, in allocating land, selecting people for military service, or in some cases assigning them for resettlement or forced labour on state farms; and they may also profit from reselling goods, such as cloth, which they obtain at preferential prices from the EDDC. All the association leaders whom Dessalegn interviewed, and all that I have noted from other sources, were men. Because association membership is on a household rather than an individual basis, it is dominated by male household heads, and this is especially marked at leadership level. Across the country as a whole, only 12.72 per cent of association members in 1982 were women, with a tendency for the percentage to be greater in the Amhara-Tigrean plateau regions.[19] Two of the highest percentages were in Tigray (31.67) and Eritrea (27.00), where they were readily accounted for by the death or absence of men due to civil war. The only higher figure, of 34.81 per cent women members in Sidamo, is so far out of line with neighbouring regions that I am inclined to suspect a mistake in the statistics. On the whole, in peasants' associations as in urban kebelles, women are confined to REWA, which is regarded as of little importance.

Overwhelmingly the most important task of peasants' associations is the allocation of land. Following the initial allocation at the time of land reform, reallocations have been made every two or three years in order to take account of population changes; this is an occasion when (in contrast with the usual attendance) the association general assembly will be packed with peasants anxious to make their case for a land increase, or to protect themselves against a reduction. The opportunity for peasants to seek justice through their own judicial tribunal (rather than go to a government judge who would charge heavily for dubious services, as happened before the revolution) is also generally welcomed, though the tribunals are often regarded as being weighted towards the association leadership.[20] Associations, or groups of them linked together in service cooperatives, likewise run shops, through which to sell basic commodities and manufactured goods made available by the Ethiopian Domestic Distribution Corporation; the EDDC's distribution network is however restricted to relatively accessible areas, and elsewhere peasants continue to rely on private shops, which in any event are generally better stocked.[21] In 1985, the EDDC had distribution centres in only forty-six of the country's 577 districts, compared with a total of 120,869 licensed private traders.[22]

As the associations have come increasingly under governmental control, however, and as the government has sought to impose central policies on the countryside, so the associations and their leaders have had to transmit these policies to their members, and have lost enthusiasm and legitimacy in the process. A survey of the functions of the association leadership expected by peasants on the one hand, and by officials on the other, reveals a total divergence between their expectations.[23] The officials regarded collecting taxes and eliminating resistance to change as the two most important functions, neither of which received any support from the peasants; the main peasant objective of promoting rural projects likewise received no support from officials. The one function on which both agreed, strengthening links between the associations and government, was liable to very different interpretation from the two sides. To a large extent, then, the associations have become extensions of state power, rather than agencies for self-administration. All associations have defence squads, which are given arms by government, and which run the association jail; though the excesses of the early years, when (as in the towns) squads could be used to settle old scores and terrorise the population, now seem to be over, they are still available to enforce decisions of the government, or perhaps simply of the association chairman. During the height of the resettlement campaign, districts and in turn individual associations (especially in Wollo) were assigned target numbers of people to be resettled, and in some cases farmers would find themselves being rounded up at gunpoint by the local defence squad, and forcibly despatched to Pawe or Gambela. The most recent and dramatic expression of central policy, the villagisation programme imposed from 1985 onwards, likewise had to rely on the peasants' association to organise its members to destroy their houses, transport the salvageable materials, and rebuild them at a central site. Though resistance to villagisation has been reported, especially from highland Amhara areas, the most astonishing thing is that it has been so widely and effectively implemented. One indicator of the changing role of peasants' associations is that almost all of them have instituted penalties – fines, imprisonment, or compulsory labour – for failure to attend meetings, at which association leaders or government officials harangue peasants who would much rather (and much more productively) be working on their own farms.[24]

The role of government in extracting money, goods and services from its subjects is much more evident in the countryside than in the cities. In cash terms, peasants have to pay considerably more than their nominal taxes of twenty birr a year; one study of eight districts in Shoa indicated an average payment of nearly ninety birr, covering not only taxes but association fees, and contributions for various local development projects such as roads, schools, clinics, offices and public stadiums.[25] Compulsory unpaid labour was found in another study in Wollo to amount to up to forty days a year for adult men and women, inevitably interfering with farming needs.[26] The compulsory purchase of crops at substantially less than open market prices is another major form of surplus expropriation.

LAND REFORM: ITS IMPLEMENTATION AND EFFECTS

The first and central point to make about the Ethiopian land reform is that it was, on the whole, carried out successfully, fairly, and without a vast amount of local conflict. This is surprising. Land was after all the basic social and economic resource throughout highland Ethiopia. It was the subject of myriad court cases, intensively pursued over generations. The existing tenure systems which were abruptly abolished themselves varied widely,

161

even within quite small areas. Nor did the government have any means through which it could enforce, or in many areas even administer, its single most revolutionary measure. A review of a book about land tenure in Gojjam, published at the time of the reform, plausibly concluded that 'the byzantine complexity of the linkages between social structure and land tenure in Gojjam' indicated 'the possible futility of any reform not fine-tuned to the specific contours of numerous individual local communities throughout the country'.[27] In practice, precisely the opposite proved to be the case. Whereas 'fine-tuning' would have created endless scope for dispute and mobilising local interests, the imposition of a simple and uniform system presented peasants with a *fait accompli* which they could only accept or resist, and which overwhelmingly they accepted.

Obviously, there were exceptions. In some areas, especially those parts of the north where the local nobility and their supporters rallied to the EDU, the initial land reform was probably never implemented, though an equivalent and very similar reform has been carried out by the TPLF in those parts of Tigray which it controls, and equally by the EPLF in Eritrea.[28] There were some areas likewise where landlords violently resisted change, and as late as January 1977 one former landlord in Kaffa was still resisting, while another was imprisoned for trying to collect rent.[29] But the general success of the reform was indicated by the very rapid rate at which the peasants' associations were established.

Despite the absence of any official attempt to adapt land reform to the specific conditions of different areas, this success was only possible because different areas adapted it themselves. In the northern highlands, where peasants generally controlled their own land and landlords were not a problem, the new structure could often be adapted without great difficulty to the existing rist system. Very broadly, the right to cultivate land in northern Ethiopia derived from inheritance, through either male or female lines, from a founding ancestor in whom the original right to land was vested.[30] These rist rights did not confer title to a particular plot, but rather to a share of the land within a given area. Because the highly complex descent system allowed people to claim rights to undemarcated land over a wide area, the opportunities for dispute and litigation were endless, though in general peasants contented themselves with establishing their claim to an adequate amount of land within convenient reach of home.[31] The idea of people having rights to land periodically allocated within a given area was thus familiar, and where (as in Gojjam) the initial peasants' associations coincided with the old rist areas, the transition from the old system to the new could be accomplished without much difficulty. The main change was that whereas previously one could try to establish land rights in any area where one could claim an ancestor, one was now restricted to land within a single association; but though one was denied the right to seek land further afield, one was equally protected against incomers, and the abrupt ending of land litigation may well have come as a relief. In much of the south, land reform was in any case assured of a welcome because of its abolition of tenancy. In areas where the staple food was enset or false banana, a long-maturing root crop, land distribution did not affect each family's enset garden, which was planted immediately around the house.

Land reform inevitably had losers as well as gainers, and Dessalegn's survey of four different areas of Ethiopia enables one to gain some idea of the range of variation across the country.[32] The first point to emerge is that levels of tenancy varied widely, even in the south. In the single highland Amhara area surveyed, in Bahr Dar province of Gojjam, nearly 80 per cent of the pre-revolution cultivators had owned at least some of their own land, and thus had little if anything to gain from the abolition of tenancy. The same was true, however, for over 70 per cent of those in the enset cultivating province of Wollaita in Sidamo in the south; since enset supports dense populations, but is not commercially marketable, enset areas were not usually taken over by settler landlords, but were left in the hands of the local population. By contrast, nearly 70 per cent of cultivators surveyed in the coffee-growing province of Jimma in Kaffa, and over 80 per cent of those in the grain-growing province of Nekempte in Welega, had before the revolution been tenants, wage labourers, or landless. These people could only gain from land reform. Most of the former tenants in Welega had had to give up to a quarter of their crop, and most of those in Kaffa fully half of their crop, to the pre-revolutionary landlord. The removal of this imposition gave them an enormous relief, and a reason to support the revolutionary regime which no inducement from opposition movements could outbid. The position of peasants in Wollaita did not greatly change; they continued their self-sufficient enset cultivation much as they had done before. In Bahr Dar, two-thirds of the peasants had smaller plots after the revolution than before, largely it would seem due to population increase and the return of urban migrants; but in this particular area, where (unlike much of the northern highlands) land hunger was not a major issue, this reduction was manageable. A similar reduction of plot sizes has been found by other studies.[33]

One thing that land reform did *not* produce was any appreciable increase in the amount of land available for peasant cultivation. In some parts of the world, such as Zimbabwe or parts of Latin America, 'land reform' means the division of large estates among landless labourers or land-hungry peasants. In Ethiopia, there were very few such estates in the first place, and even these were not available for distribution. Mechanised commercial agriculture (apart from a few foreign plantations) had got under way only in the decade preceding the revolution, and accounted for only about 2.3 per cent of cultivated land.[34] The large estates were taken over intact as state farms, though small private farms, which would have been unviable as state farms, were distributed to the local peasantry.[35] The great majority of Ethiopian landlords did not farm land themselves, but merely extracted what surplus they could from their share-cropping tenants. The removal of the landlords lifted a burden from the tenants' backs, but left the same peasants farming the same land in the same way as before. Nor did the reform lead to any increased efficiency in the use of land. One surprising finding is that peasant plots in most areas remained little less fragmented than before reform.[36] Whereas previously fragmentation could be ascribed to the workings of the inheritance system (though even then perhaps reflecting a characteristic peasant strategy for minimising risk), after the reform it resulted from deliberate decisions by the peasants' association to assign land of different types (higher or lower, steeper or flatter, drier or boggier) to each of its members. This helped to provide both equality and insurance, but likewise meant that some of a peasant's land might be a few kilometres from his house. When this land might be reallocated after a couple of years, more-over, he had no incentive to improve its capital value or plant trees or long-term crops. The revolutionary government has undertaken impressive campaigns of hillside terracing and afforestation, but from a peasant viewpoint, these often involved a high input of forced labour, removed land from cultivation, and offered no immediate reward.[37]

These points are central to any appreciation of the effects of land reform on agricultural production. Tenant farmers in the south gained a once-for-all increase in income of up to 50 per cent,[38] due to the removal of rent, while conditions for other peasants continued much as before. The land reform proclamation had assumed that 'in order to increase agricultural production . . . it is necessary to release the productive forces of the rural economy',[39] and this accurately reflected the general feeling of the time. It was an assumption that proved to be entirely misconceived. The productive forces which had most evidently contributed, for better or worse, to agricultural change in the decade preceding the reform had been those of rural capitalism, and these had been stopped in their tracks. The reform ensured, by the nationalisation and even distribution of land, and the prohibition of hired labour, that no new development of private commercial agriculture could revive them. Even the minimum package programmes devised for peasant agriculture before the revolution depended on produce prices which were undercut by the new agricultural marketing system. But neither did any new socialist forces of production replace them. The original proclamation made provision for both state and cooperative farms, and referred to 'basic change in agrarian relations' in which 'through work by cooperation, the development of one becomes the development of all'.[40] State farms and cooperatives will be considered shortly, but in any event, since they comprised less than 10 per cent of productive land, they could not seriously affect the issue. What land reform actually did was thus to entrench peasants in their existing mode of production, under conditions that all but guaranteed their progressive impoverishment.

It was, as so often, the best-intentioned measures that had the worst long-term results. The land reform guaranteed land to all peasants within their own association area. In so doing, it abolished landlessness and (as the corollary of the decreased rate of urbanisation) encouraged peasants to stay on the land. The result (in the absence of population control) was an increase in pressure on land, with the inevitable decline in the size of plots, overcultivation, increased environmental degradation, declining yields, and ultimately starvation.[41] Land reform was certainly not the only factor leading to famine, as the experience of 1973 had showed, but it was in part responsible for a concentration of population on overcultivated northern farmland, from which famine was the ultimate outcome.

These policies not only encouraged peasants to stay on the land, but also impeded means that they had previously used to mitigate the effects of overcrowding. Peasants were not only guaranteed land in their own areas; they were denied it elsewhere. The process by which landless peasants had seeped southwards in search of land was halted. The resettlement programme undertaken at the height of the 1984–85 famine was in large measure an attempt to do something by government action which peasants had previously done, if only under severe economic pressure, by themselves.[42] The restriction on movement to the towns has already been noted. In addition, temporary emigration in search of seasonal work was limited by the prohibition on the private hire of agricultural labour, and by low rates of pay on state farms. A study of temporary inter-regional migration carried out shortly before the revolution, in 1969–70, showed substantially the largest net outflow from Tigray, with 31,100 temporary emigrants, followed by Wollo with 6,960.[43] Though the figures have to be treated with caution, and much temporary migration was within the region, they give some impression of the role of seasonal migration in mitigating the unviability of peasant agriculture in the most overcrowded highland areas. For Tigrean peasants, the nearest large source of temporary employment was at Humera on the Sudanese border, where some 100,000 labourers found work. The plantations in the Awash valley served a similar function for Wollo peasants, and provided permanent and seasonal jobs for about 150,000 highlanders.[44] Peasants from throughout the highlands moved to Kaffa and Sidamo to harvest coffee. Post-revolutionary policy, discussed in a later section, has deprived peasants of a useful source of income, led to severe harvest labour shortages, and resulted (most notoriously at Humera, but also in the Awash valley and elsewhere) in the forced conscription of workers at very low rates of pay.

In the absence of large-scale movement to the towns, or dispersal to other parts of Ethiopia, there was little option but for peasants to crowd onto their existing land. Dessalegn notes an increase varying from 9 per cent to 19 per cent in peasants' association membership in his four study areas between 1975 and 1980–81,[45] and this figure would have roughly corresponded to the rate of natural population increase. Though I have no long-term figures on changes in plot sizes, the Ethiopian Highland Reclamation Study carried out for the FAO indicates a decline in mean area (over a sample of highland peasants' associations across the country, though excluding Tigray and Eritrea) from 1.9 hectares per household in 1980 to 1.8 in 1982 – a 5 per cent drop over two years.[46] It likewise identifies a decline in average crop production per household of over 14 per cent in the same two years, from 940 kilos in 1980 to 805 in 1982, and found overcultivation to be overwhelmingly the most important cause, while in virtually all areas land degradation in one form or another was a major source of concern. This study, carried out shortly before the 1983–85 famine, takes too short a timescale to be altogether reliable as an indicator of long-term trends, but starkly illuminates the weakened state in which Ethiopian peasant agriculture faced the calamity which was about to strike the northern and eastern regions of the country. Viewed across the board at a national level, a 23 per cent increase in cereal production in 1975–76, due partly to recovery from the 1973–74 drought, was followed by stagnation over the next four years. Thereafter, production declined sharply even in absolute terms. Estimated cereal production fell from 6.4 million tons in 1979–80, to 5.6 million in 1980–81 and 5.4 million in 1981–82, picking up to 6.7 million in 1982–83 before dropping again to 5.5 million in 1983–84. In the disaster year of 1984–85, production fell to 3.9 million tons, recovering only to 4.4 million (on provisional figures) in 1985–86.[47] The 1986–87 harvest, following excellent rainfall, was much better, but no figures were available at the time of writing.

For the peasant farmer, this process of increasing population and declining yield adds up to what Dessalegn has termed agrarian involution – 'that is, a tendency, already in evidence, of being concerned solely with self-sustenance rather than involvement in the general exchange process.'[48] So far from inducing the dynamic agrarian development which the original proclamation envisaged, the land reform has, in the decade after its introduction, induced a retreat from the market into subsistence, and in turn into impoverishment and famine. Any assessment of Ethiopian agricultural policy has to start from this basic problem, which paradoxically coincides with the fact that peasant farming remains the most efficient mode of agricultural production, growing at least as much per hectare as other forms of farming, despite negligible inputs in terms of capital investment, machinery, fertiliser or improved seed.

One way of trying to resolve the problem – and one favoured, on the whole, by both Soviet and Western advisers and by aid agencies – is to try to build on the efficiency of peasant agriculture by providing peasants with inputs (such as fertilisers and seeds) through an improved extension service, while at the same time encouraging them to increase and market their output by means of improved producer prices. Such proposals often see a role for cooperative action in the provision of collective goods, such as hillside terracing or marketing, but would leave production itself in the hands of the peasant household. An unpublished memorandum of September 1985 by the team of Soviet advisers attached to the ONCCP stressed that 'it is now imperative to direct the bulk of efforts towards bolstering the production within . . . the individual peasant sector', while likewise emphasising that service cooperatives provided a much more promising strategy over the next few years than increasing the number of producers' cooperatives or collectives.[49]

An ambitious programme along these lines, the Peasant Agricultural Development Extension Project (or PADEP), was put forward by the World Bank and associated funding agencies from the early 1980s. Drawing on the experience of the pre-revolutionary minimum package programmes, and on the training and visit system which had operated successfully in India, this sought to identify potential surplus producing districts in which output could be raised through specialist advice, the provision of inputs such as fertiliser, and a pricing system which would provide an incentive to the farmer. Negotiations initially stalled on the government's refusal to concede the higher producer prices and lifting of restrictions on private agricultural trade which the donors regarded as essential to the success of the project. When discussions were resumed in 1986, following a two-year hiatus during which the energies of both government and international agencies had been preoccupied by the famine emergency, there was the additional obstacle of the villagisation campaign which, linked to the government's energetic promotion of agricultural producers' cooperatives, would have negated a programme based on the individual peasant farmer. When agreement, once again, could not be reached with the funding agencies, the government went ahead in January 1987 with its own project, which concentrated fertiliser and extension services on the previously selected districts, but without the concessions on prices, private trade and cooperatives which the external donors had demanded.[50]

At one level, the PADEP controversy raises critical issues about the relationship between domestic policy-making and external funding. While the government insisted on its right to make policy in keeping with its national priorities and ideological commitments, the external agencies conversely refused to commit their funds for a programme which they regarded as misconceived in terms of food production, and which might also have been directed towards the political goal of enforcing control over the peasant sector. In the domestic context, it could be seen in terms of a debate about the rival merits of smallholder and collective strategies for agricultural development, which itself raised major political issues.[51] Acceptance of a package such as PADEP would indeed have threatened the regime's own position, in a way not totally dissimilar from that in which land reform would have threatened the imperial regime. The package was incompatible with the establishment of central control over both production and marketing, and would also have shifted the rural–urban terms of trade against the urban areas, with potentially serious political repercussions. It raised the central issue of agricultural policy in a socialist state, which only the Chinese have been prepared to resolve in favour of the peasant producer. This was a step which an Ethiopian government bound to the Stalinist model, and obsessed with the issue of control, was not prepared to take. That being so, it was left only with the alternative response to the problem of agrarian involution: the

167

attempt to raise production, and haul the peasantry into the national market, through the 'socialisation' of agriculture. This in turn involved government control of agricultural trade, direct government production through state farms, and, most of all, the replacement of household production by producers' cooperatives or collectives.

AGRICULTURAL MARKETING

Most of the grain grown in Ethiopia is consumed on the farm or in its immediate vicinity. Official estimates suggest that only about 16 per cent of net cereal production, or 8 out of 50 million quintals, enter the market.[52] This marketed surplus is also geographically restricted, with between 75 and 90 per cent of marketed grain coming from the three regions of Gojjam, Shoa and Arsi.[53] This concentration greatly eases the government's task of managing and controlling agricultural marketing, while at the other end of the process the marketed surplus only has to be delivered to a small number of major towns, notably Addis Ababa, Asmara and Dire Dawa. But even though only a small proportion of the crop, and probably only a minority of Ethiopia's peasants, are directly affected by food-marketing arrangements, the surplus producing areas are also for the most part those where government measures can make the greatest difference to the level of food production, and where – much more than in the famine-affected northern and eastern highlands – there is the capacity to increase production to meet the needs of the population as a whole.

As already noted, the Agricultural Marketing Corporation (AMC) was established in 1976 to buy agricultural produce for domestic consumption, and from 1978–79 onwards became the key government agency regulating the domestic food trade.[54] It did not however acquire a monopoly over agricultural marketing, a task which in any event it lacked the capacity to carry out, but instead co-existed with private traders. This created two parallel systems, one regulated by the state, and the other by the market. In these circumstances, the state system would collapse unless state power was used to sustain it, both because of the greater flexibility, market awareness and general efficiency of the private traders, and because the AMC had as a basic objective the provision of cheap food to the cities and government institutions (including schools and hospitals, as well as the army), and therefore paid producers less than the going market rate. This power has been exercised in a number of ways. State farms and producers' cooperatives were brought directly into the system by requiring them to sell all their produce to the AMC, though at prices higher than those offered to ordinary peasants. Traders had to be licenced and to obey AMC regulations, including restrictions on the movement of grain from one region to another. They also had to deliver a proportion of their purchases, amounting to at least half in most regions from 1980–81 onwards, to the AMC at official prices. Eventually, they were required in the major surplus-producing areas to sell all of their purchases to the AMC, thus converting them into AMC agents or driving them out of business altogether. Private wholesaling was prohibited from 1982–83 in Gojjam, a surplus-producing region which, almost surrounded by the Blue Nile gorge and with only two bridges linking it to the rest of the country, is especially easy to police. Grain traders in Arsi and parts of Shoa were later required to sell all their produce to the AMC, and even though traders continued to evade controls, the effect was to increase the costs and risks of getting grain from farmers to consumers, to the disadvantage of both. Individual peasant producers were forced into the system by the establishment of quotas, allocated by grain purchase task forces at regional, provincial and district levels. These in turn were successively broken down into quotas for service cooperatives, peasants' associations, and individual households. On the one hand, service cooperatives are reported to withhold goods and money owing to peasants' associations until these have met their quotas; and one study notes that in one district of Gojjam in 1983, 30 per cent of farmers did not grow enough grain to meet their quotas, and had to sell animals in order to buy grain on the open market, which they then had to sell at a loss to the AMC.[55] There are also reports of AMC raids on private markets.[56] On the other hand, AMC figures show wide discrepancies between planned purchases, which indicate the total quota for each region, and the actual amount that it could get;[57] and in regions affected by famine, it is obvious enough that no grain could be extracted where none existed. For the four years from 1979–80 to 1982–83, the AMC came very close to achieving its overall planned purchases (save in 1980–81, when it reached only 89 per cent), despite a steady increase in the planned amount from 1,710,700 quintals in 1979–80 to 3,863,000 in 1982–83 (including pulses and oilseeds, as well as grain). Even then, however, the amounts bought in individual regions varied widely from the quota, whether above or below it, and the quotas themselves often fluctuated widely from year to year. In 1983–84, with the onset of drought, only 62.7 per cent of the quota was achieved, total purchases falling to 70 per cent of the preceding year. In the famine year of 1984–85, purchases at 1,148,000 quintals were no more than 30 per cent of the 1982–83 figure, and quotas ceased to have any meaning.

Save in 1979–80, when regional grain purchase task forces were allowed to set prices for their own regions, AMC prices have been centrally established by the CPSC or ONCCP. Though these have consistently been lower than open-market prices, the discrepancy steadily increased until 1986–87. Purchase prices were increased slightly between 1980–81 and 1982–83, but then remained constant for four years, at a time of rapidly increasing food prices. They have been heavily weighted in favour of state farms, and to a lesser extent cooperatives, and against individual peasants. From 1982–83, for example, peasants were paid thirty-four birr per quintal for white wheat, as against the thirty-nine birr paid to cooperatives and forty-seven birr paid to state farms for the same produce. Comparisons between the price paid to

169

peasants by the AMC, and the price which they could get on the open market, are difficult to make owing to the enormous fluctuations between market prices in different parts of the country. The average rural market price for teff, the favoured Ethiopian staple grain, rose from twice the AMC buying price in 1981 to three and a half times in 1985; but the 1985 market prices ranged from one and a third times the AMC price in the main producing areas in Gojjam, to over seven times in the famine areas of Wollo.[58] A study carried out in Arsi in 1981–82 showed that sorghum was selling locally for nearly four times the AMC purchase price, and maize and teff for over twice, with smaller discrepancies for maize and barley.[59] But despite the high level of variation between different places, periods and crops, and a drop in market prices after the good 1986 harvest, the central conclusion remains the same: that the government buys crops from peasants at a price which is well below what they can get on the open market, and which therefore has to be enforced by state power. Since much of the marketable crop is removed by the AMC, however, that part of the crop which does reach the open market is likely to reach higher, though more fluctuating, prices than if the whole crop had been marketed.

One feature of this system, already touched on, is that severe restrictions prevent the transfer of grain from surplus to deficit areas in order to take advantage of (and thus reduce) price differentials. The result is that Ethiopia has become progressively fragmented into local markets, which are increasingly insulated from one another. Local price variations are in any event to be expected, due both to differences in climate and to difficulties of transport, but these variations are greatly intensified by the effect of government action. Whereas in 1981, for example, the price of teff in the cheapest local market stood at 35.3 per cent of its price in the most expensive one, by 1985 the figure was 18.1 per cent.[60] The cheapest areas in Gojjam were adjacent, across the Blue Nile gorge, to the most expensive ones in Wollo. These differences give private traders an incentive to circumvent controls in order to make disproportionate profits, and there are some indications that they do so.[61] The effects on food production are much harder to assess but can only be negative, even though it may well be true that no large immediate production increase is to be gained from a rise in producer prices.[62] Raising the productivity of peasant farming is a complex issue, going well beyond simple questions of price, though one way in which prices are directly related to production is through the cost of fertiliser. Fertiliser was increasingly being used by peasant farmers during the pre-revolutionary period, especially in regions such as Gojjam which grew high-priced teff for the Addis Ababa market. The increasing cost of fertiliser, at a time when grain prices were low and constant, unsurprisingly resulted in a sharp decline in its use. One local study in Gojjam noted a 44 per cent drop in fertiliser use between 1975–76 and 1982–83.[63] In addition to price, there were also problems of distribution and severe restrictions on credit to individual farmers. Since 1983–84, the price of fertiliser has been held constant, and considerable efforts were made in 1987 to distribute it to peasants in potentially surplus producing districts.

AGRICULTURAL PRODUCERS' COOPERATIVES

There are two kinds of agricultural cooperative in Ethiopia. *Service* cooperatives are formed by groups of peasants' associations in order to buy and distribute inputs such as fertiliser and consumer goods through cooperative shops, and to market their produce – generally to the Agricultural Marketing Corporation. They thus form a link between the associations and the external economy. There are on average between four and five associations in each cooperative, and the great majority of associations – nearly 87 per cent in 1986 – belong to them.[64] Except in Eritrea and Tigray, they are almost universally established, and some development projects, like the PADEP scheme discussed above, would largely rely on them as a means of reaching the rural population.

Producers' cooperatives, as the name implies, are directly involved in agricultural production, and are composed of families within peasants' associations pooling their resources to produce in common. According to the government guidelines issued in July 1979, they fall into three types, at increasing levels of development: at the malba or primary level, members pool their land (save for 2,000 square-metre plots which they retain for private use), but retain individual ownership of oxen, ploughs and other means of production; at the welba or intermediate level, the means of production are likewise pooled, while the weland or highest stage consists of two or more welbas combined together.[65] Neither these names nor the institutions themselves (which are derived directly from Eastern European models) owe anything to indigenous origins; and since no weland had been formed by late 1985, all existing cooperatives fell into the first two categories. Welbas might be described as collective farms, though in practice the term cooperative is almost always used.

The producers' cooperative has consistently been the government's goal for the development of peasant agriculture, and numerous efforts have been made to enhance its attractiveness to peasants. The original land reform proclamation stated bluntly that 'the main function of the peasant association shall be to induce and organize peasants into co-operative farms',[66] a function subsequently neglected in favour of allocating plots between individual farmers, and carrying out the numerous other tasks with which the associations were loaded once they became the base units of rural government. This emphasis was considerably toned down in the Programme of the National Democratic Revolution, which referred (oddly, since all rural land was owned by the state) to 'the rights of individually owning farmers', and stated merely that the government 'shall encourage and shall provide the necessary moral and material support to all cooperative endeavours of the peasant masses'.[67] Mengistu Haile-Mariam's fourth anniversary speech of

171

September 1978 returned to the theme with a powerful attack on the individualism of the peasantry, and emphasised the need for collectivisation; he referred in this speech to collectives, rather than the usual term cooperatives, and promised them long-term loans, fertilisers, lower taxes, and low-cost services. The same message was constantly reinforced in Mengistu's speeches, resolutions of COPWE and WPE bodies, official publications, and the Ten-Year Plan.[68]

The inducements given to encourage peasants to form cooperatives were considerable. One of the most important was that a group of peasants forming a cooperative could ensure that they were allocated a single block of land, rather than the normal scattered plots, and that the best land available was allotted to them, evicting ordinary peasants, who might then be given greatly inferior land in exchange.[69] There is also evidence to suggest that cooperativised peasants may get appreciably larger allocations of land per head than those who continue to farm individually. In June 1984, land under producer cooperatives accounted, according to Ministry of Agriculture figures, for about 4.5 per cent of the total arable area of the country, although the number of peasants belonging to cooperatives was no more than 1.8 per cent of the total number of peasants' association members registered two years previously.[70] Though local differences in size of holdings and level of cooperativisation obscure precise comparison, the impression this conveys is confirmed by one study in Wollo, which showed the average holding of arable land to be 0.8 ha for cooperative members, as compared with 0.3 ha for ordinary peasants in the same area.[71] Cooperatives have virtually monopolised the Ministry of Agriculture extension services, gaining expert advice, fertiliser, high-yielding seeds, pest-control teams, and so forth. They also, virtually alone among peasant producers, have had ready access to capital, since rural credit agencies are encouraged to lend to them. These include service cooperatives, which may accumulate considerable amounts of capital from their marketing operations, but are forbidden to lend this to individual peasants, and the Agricultural and Industrial Development Bank; this was reported in January 1986, for example, as lending eleven tractors with ancillary equipment, valued at 634,000 birr, to eleven cooperatives in Gojjam and Gonder regions.[72] The annual land-use tax is only five birr for cooperative members, as against ten for other peasants, and they also, as already noted, receive higher official prices for their produce. There may be other inducements. The number of cooperatives in Wollo shot up from 108 with 5,654 members in June 1984, to 157 with 15,723 members in April 1985, and 250 with 34,757 members in July 1986 – a staggering increase of 515 per cent, compared with an increase of 75.5 per cent in cooperative membership for the rest of the country over the same period.[73] This may most plausibly be ascribed to the exemption of cooperative members from compulsory resettlement in the south and west of the country after the 1984 famine. Against these advantages, however, must be set one major disability: that cooperatives are expected to sell all

172

their produce at official rates to the Agricultural Marketing Corporation. Though some cooperatives get round this problem by paying 'wages' to their members in kind – i.e. as grain which they may then resell on the open market – it is possible that this one factor may in straightforward economic terms outweigh all of the inducements to join.

Whatever the reason, the campaign to get peasants to form cooperatives voluntarily was a failure. By June 1984 there were only 1,489 producers' cooperatives in the country, farming 313,085 hectares, and including under 2 per cent of peasants' association members.[74] By far the highest levels of cooperativisation were in Arsi and Bale, with 7.5 per cent and 5.0 per cent of peasants respectively belonging to cooperatives by June 1984. Elsewhere, the participation rate exceeded 1.5 per cent only in Gojjam, Illubabor, and Welega. These figures certainly confirm that participation was indeed for the most part voluntary, but likewise demonstrate that there was no possibility of creating the level of cooperativisation sought by the government by voluntary means. Indeed, the rate of formation of cooperatives fell off sharply after an initial burst in 1979–81. There was also some indication that cooperatives appealed especially to peasants who could not manage on their own, for reasons such as lack of oxen or physical disability.[75] Furthermore, figures may well have been exaggerated, because local administrators had an interest in reporting as high a total as possible, because some cooperatives (as in famine areas) were such in no more than name, or because cooperatives which failed, and collapsed back into individual farms, did not get reported.

From 1985 onwards, there were renewed official efforts at cooperativisation, associated with the Ten Year Plan targets and the villagisation campaign, which produced the 75 per cent increase in cooperative membership between 1984 and 1986 already noted, and which was still under way at the time of writing. By July 1986, 16 per cent of peasants in Arsi had been cooperativised, more than two and a half times the proportion in any other region, although an overseas mission visiting the area found marked hostility towards cooperatives among individual farmers.[76] The impression that I have gained from a number of regions, including Hararghe, Arsi and Wollo, is that cooperatives have spread not through coercion, so much as through the advantages that they have to offer to the peasants' association leadership. An association chairman who starts his own cooperative is not only assured of official favour, and hence tenure of office; he can use the combined positions to gain a disproportionate share both of the resources available within the association (such as more and better land), and of those coming in from outside (such as credit and fertiliser). So far from promoting equality among peasants, cooperatives may serve as a vehicle for state-aided class formation.

Any comparison of the efficiency of cooperatives with other forms of production is subject to all the uncertainties of Ethiopian statistics: it may be, for example, that cooperatives under-report their production, as a means of retaining produce which they would otherwise have to sell to the AMC. All the indications, however, are that – despite economies of scale, allocation of good land, and access to external credit and services – cooperatives are appreciably less productive than ordinary peasant farms. Gross nationwide comparisons show crop yield per hectare in cooperatives at about two-thirds of that on peasant farms,[77] and local level studies also tend to indicate the inefficiency of cooperatives. A survey of motivation shows peasants to be fully aware of the value of competition, material incentives and a sense of personal involvement in encouraging hard work[78] – or, as one peasant was reported to me as putting it, 'I is better than we'. Participation within cooperatives is slight, with decisions on production and the division of labour generally being taken by people outside them,[79] and there is little incentive for individual effort, with rewards poorly related to contribution.[80] The lack of any proper control system leads to ample opportunities for embezzlement by the leadership, and very few cooperatives abide by the official rules on investment and distribution of income.[81] Most dramatically of all, in two cooperatives studied in detail, income distributed to members amounted even in good years to much more than the total value of their net output – the difference being made up by borrowing and the sale of assets.[82] Instead of serving as a mechanism for accumulating investment capital, therefore, cooperatives have on this evidence provided negative accumulation, or a wastage of capital. This is important in the context of suggestions that cooperatives, despite their inefficient use of current resources, may nonetheless have the greatest potential for long-term accumulation.[83] Much however depends on what a cooperative actually does. The Ethiopian government has tended to treat cooperatives as a means of achieving large-scale production through the application of external inputs, duplicating in effect the functions (and also the problems) of the state farms, rather than taking advantage of their ability to mobilise labour for capital construction.[84] At all events, the capacity of Ethiopian producers' cooperatives in their present form to serve as agencies for agricultural development and capital accumulation must be doubted.

VILLAGISATION

Given the failure to achieve anything approaching the desired level of cooperativisation voluntarily, the government faced a choice between abandoning the policy or achieving it by other means. The first option does not seem to have been seriously considered. The control of the peasantry had been identified – in Mengistu's 1978 revolution day speech, and again in the Ten Year Plan – as a critical priority facing the regime. Although cooperativisation is publicly identified with growing agricultural productivity, the goal has not been abandoned in the face of the evidence that productivity in

174

cooperatives is actually reduced. It is in this light that one must see the villagisation campaign that got under way in 1985.

Villagisation – the concentration of scattered homesteads into centralised villages – had been one of the regime's goals since early in the revolution, and Mengistu Haile-Mariam had referred to it as a necessary step in providing government services to peasants in May 1979.[85] Producers' cooperatives were encouraged to build villages for their members, and up to June 1984, 232 of them had done so.[86] Following the Somali war of 1977–78, almost all of the highland area of Bale region was villagised, partly for security reasons, partly from a policy of settling shifting cultivators, many of whom had in any case been displaced during the war; unlike villagisation in other parts of Ethiopia, this did involve substantial change in local agricultural practices, but Bale, with a population of just on a million in 1984, was one of the smallest regions in Ethiopia, and the programme was confined to this single region. The model for villagisation was drawn largely from the 'Wabe villages' set up in Arsi and Bale to rehouse peasants evicted from new state farm sites in the Wabe Shebelle valley; these well-publicised showcase settlements were influential in presenting a picture of the ideal new socialist agricultural community, but their cost alone would prevent them from being effectively copied across the whole country.[87] There is no evidence that the experience of other countries, such as Tanzania, was taken into account.[88]

A more comprehensive campaign got under way in Hararghe early in 1985. Several reports put its origins in a local response to a single incident – the ambushing of a bus in Garamuleta province by Islamic Oromo Liberation Front guerillas, who killed the Christian passengers but released the Moslems; I can find no evidence that it was the result of any central directive. By mid May some 2,000 villages with 150,000 houses had reportedly been constructed.[89] The campaign did not extend to the national level until Mengistu Haile-Mariam visited the region early in June, and gave 'directives to create conditions conducive to the expansion of peasant producers' cooperatives in Hararghe'.[90] Thereafter, villagisation was accepted as national policy, and became the goal of a major government campaign from the end of the rainy season in October 1985 onwards. A set of official guidelines were circulated, drawing on the model of the Wabe villages, and a National Coordinating Committee for Villagisation was set up, with equivalents at regional, provincial, district and individual peasants' association levels.[91] The first meeting of the national coordinating committee was not held until June 1986, however, and much of this elaborate structure may have been a subsequent rationalisation of a process already under way.[92] The guidelines emphasised the role of villages in providing common services and assisting communal activities, but made no mention of cooperativisation. They suggested a maximum of 500 households per village, down to a minimum of thirty in rugged areas, and made eminently sensible recommendations about the need to site villages carefully (especially with regard to water supply), to avoid interference with the agricultural calendar, and to conserve resources, especially of wood. Unusually in an Ethiopian government document, it emphasised the importance of providing facilities for religious worship.

Shoa and Arsi were the first regions to get the campaign under way, followed by Kaffa, Welega and Illubabor, and in December 1985 the first steps were taken to implement it in one of the Amhara regions, Gojjam.[93] No further regions were involved until early 1987, when there were reports of villagisation from Gonder, Wollo and Sidamo.[94] There were no reports, up to July 1987, of villagisation in Eritrea, Tigray or Gamu Gofa. Once under way, the campaign went ahead with astonishing speed. Peasants were required to knock down their old houses, salvaging any materials (especially wood) which could be used for the new, and transport these to the site fixed for the new village. These sites were nominally decided after discussion with the peasants' association, and the level of consultation may well have varied from place to place, but the actual decision seems in practice to have been taken by officials. The houses were laid out on precise geometrical grids, and even though local variations in house types remained (and were often dictated by the reuse of timbers), the new villages were instantly distinguishable from the old informal clusters of buildings. Marked by a passion for revolutionary uniformity and order, the houses in each village were generally identical, save that in some places different types were available for those who did or did not have corrugated iron roofs. By September 1986, Mengistu was able to report that 976,084 new houses had been built, and 4,587,187 people moved.[95] By September 1987, the totals had climbed to over 1,300,000 houses for over 8 million people, representing an estimated 22 per cent of the rural population.[96] By that time, the process was virtually complete in highland Arsi and Hararghe, and in substantial areas of Shoa; in other regions, a large proportion of the population still remained in homesteads, though the campaign envisaged eventually villagising the entire rural population of close to 40 million. Some areas presented special problems. No steps were taken, at least in the initial phase, to villagise the Gurage people of south-western Shoa, whose magnificent houses normally take a year to build and may last for a lifetime, and whose staple food, enset, is planted immediately around the house and has to be very carefully tended.[97] Areas with major security problems, notably Tigray and Eritrea, were also excluded. Though villagisation has been reported from insurgency affected parts of Gonder,[98] the campaign has been basically concerned with economic control, rather than establishing 'strategic hamlets'.

Studies carried out by well-qualified foreign observers in Arsi and Hararghe indicate that the actual implementation of the campaign closely followed the official guidelines.[99] They found no evidence that direct physical coercion was used to make people move, though they moved only because the government ordered it, and many did so reluctantly. They also

176

found that the campaign was fitted in as well as possible with the farming year, and that harvests had not been affected; nor was it accompanied by any immediate pressure to form producers' cooperatives. These conclusions obviously applied only to the regions concerned, though the Hararghe study contrasted sharply with reports of gunpoint coercion from refugees in the Somali Republic.[100] Arsi especially provided optimum conditions for villagisation, with a cash-cropping peasantry already highly integrated into the national economy, an exceptionally high proportion of whom were already in producers' cooperatives. In most of Shoa, too, villagisation went ahead in a peaceful and orderly way, with some complaint but no resistance. There were rumours or reports of resistance elsewhere, most persistently from Gonder, but I have been unable to confirm them. Villagisation provides the most striking evidence of the revolutionary regime's capacity to reorder life in the countryside. Unlike the original land reform, which (in most areas, anyway) the majority of peasants could be relied on to support, villagisation involved a vast amount of work and disruption for what (despite all the promises) could only be very uncertain future benefits. The campaign was closely associated with the party, and though local government officials and peasants' association leaders were pressed into service, the party cadres played the main activating role. Some of these were evidently sceptical about its value, and distressed at the part which they were being obliged to play, but nonetheless the organisation held, and any opposition, at least in southern Ethiopia, was not enough to prevent its implementation.

Any attempt to assess the effects of villagisation must allow for a large number of imponderables, and a high level of variation between different areas of the country. It seems fair to conclude, for example, that the quality of housing must generally have deteriorated, even though many of the huts in which peasants were living before villagisation were wretched enough, and the guidelines allowed for more spacious houses than they often had already. The problem was that these could not be built without denuding an already often badly deforested countryside, while much existing wood must inevitably have been lost in the process of demolition and transport. Peasant homesteads had often been sited to take advantage of rocky land or sheltered corners, whereas the villages were usually in open sites on agricultural land. In highland areas where stone walls were an important defence against cold, thin wattle-and-daub ones replaced them. And while in some areas the new villages provided not only a house, but a separate kitchen, storehouse and cattleshed, this was evidently exceptional;[101] elsewhere they often had a dwelling house only, and lacked the cluster of agricultural outbuildings and compounds which had marked the old homesteads. Cattle then had to be herded together, and though initial panic selling of cattle (due to fears that they would be collectivised) died down, in a country where every pat of cowdung is collected for fuel, this produced problems of its own.

Despite Mengistu's original directives in Hararghe, the connection between villagisation and cooperatives was played down, and peasants continued to farm their individual plots, though an eventual shift towards cooperatives was taken for granted both by officials implementing the programme and by peasants themselves. Publicly, however, officials emphasised the advantages of villagisation in enabling the government to supply such benefits as roads, schools and clinics – and even, sometimes, telephones and electricity.[102] The government, however, did not have at its disposal anything remotely approaching the resources required to implement the promised benefits. The most basic benefit of all, water, may be taken as an example. Villagisation certainly made it easier to build wells closer to the population than when houses had been scattered, and some aid projects (including one funded by UNICEF) took advantage of this. But whereas water supply had been one of the key considerations in siting the old homesteads, villages were placed, where possible, close to roads, while a concentrated population put more pressure on available water resources than a dispersed one had done. In Bale, for example, even six years after villagisation the distance needed to travel for water had on the whole increased rather than diminished; the same was true of firewood, on which concentration had an even more adverse effect.[103] Equally, while there are several ways in which concentration may be expected to harm agricultural production, it is hard to envisage any in which it may improve it. The distance between farm and fields must inevitably increase, with especially disruptive effects in areas cut up by ravines, where moving plough oxen is extremely time-consuming, and the removal of the farmer from the immediate vicinity of the fields gives a free hand to monkeys and other pests. In some areas, such as the poor soils of the rift valley, concentrating a previously scattered population can only intensify land degradation, and pasturage in the vicinity of the village is likely to be heavily overused. In these respects, the traditional dispersal of homesteads was a rational peasant response to the distribution of resources.

Most important of all, however, are the consequences for the outlook of the peasants. The campaign was intended to increase peasant dependence, and the danger is that it may do precisely that, converting farmers from self-reliant household units looking for subsistence to their own efforts, into a 'captured' or cooperativised peasantry looking to government for services which previously they would have done without or sought to provide for themselves – and which in any event the government cannot provide. The services such as credit or fertiliser which have been directed towards the existing producer cooperatives have been available only because such cooperatives comprised a very small proportion of the farming population, and even then have done nothing to bring about any increase in agricultural productivity. One function of villagisation, even short of using it to induce the formation of producers' cooperatives, is to make it very much easier for the Agricultural Marketing Corporation to extract produce from peasants at controlled prices, and correspondingly more difficult for peasants to earn higher incomes by evading the official market. That indeed, from the government's perspective, may well be one of the major points in its favour. The more efficient extraction of a declining surplus characterises the revolution across the whole range of the Ethiopian economy. In equally characteristic fashion, the greatly increased control which villagisation gives the government over peasants is balanced by the likelihood of alienation and the possibility of revolt. Villagisation marks the disappearance of the autonomy conferred by land reform, and may lead to the very rural opposition which it was partly intended to prevent.

THE STATE FARMS

The state farm is, along with the peasant household and the producers' cooperative, the third major mode of agricultural production in revolutionary Ethiopia. The land nationalisation, as already noted, excluded large-scale commercial farms from distribution to peasants, and took them directly under government management as state farms. To these were added new farms, created by the large-scale clearance of bush or forest in sparsely populated areas; northern Bale, with 44,000 hectares under five huge farms, provided the largest concentration. The amount of land under state farms increased rapidly during the early years of the National Revolutionary Development Campaign, from 68,000 hectares in 1978–79 to 231,000 in 1981–82,[104] accounting at this point for 3.3 per cent of the estimated total of cultivated land in the country. The land cultivated by state farms then dropped to 178,000 hectares by 1983–84, and although the Ten Year Plan envisaged an increase in state farm coverage to 6.2 per cent of the cultivated area by 1993–94, the total had picked up only to 204,000 hectares by 1986.[105] The contrast with the Ministry of State Farm Development's plan in 1980 to develop a further 1 million hectares over the following decade, taking state farms to some 15 per cent of the total cultivated area, indicates a major reduction in the role of state farms, both actual and projected.[106]

By far the greater part of the state farm system is devoted to grain production, notably wheat in the Arsi and Bale highlands and maize in the rift valley, and grain accounted for about three-quarters of the total acreage in the first half of the 1980s. Next comes cotton, where the farms in the lower part of the Awash valley established by a British company, Mitchell Cotts, are the only state farms to make a consistent profit[107] – largely, it is said, because of the retention of the commercial management structure. A few fruit, dairy and coffee farms were taken over from private owners, and other farms include a large new coffee plantation at Bebeka in Kaffa, and the huge tract of former sesame cultivation at Humera. State farms are subject to a cumbersome and centralised management structure. From nationalisation until May 1977, they formed a department of the conglomerate Ministry of National Resources Development. They were then transferred to a State Farm Authority under the Ministry of Agriculture, which in May 1979 was converted into a separate Ministry of State Farm Development. This administers state farms through corporations (organised partly on a geographical and partly on a functional basis), which in turn supervise enterprises, which comprise groups of farms. The enterprise serves as the basic management and accounting unit, and both it and the corporation are sustained by levies on the income of the individual farms.

The central function of the state farms is to produce grain for urban consumption, while secondarily producing raw materials for domestic factories and a very limited amount for export. The entire output of the farms is sold to the Agricultural Marketing Corporation and other government agencies at controlled prices, and although they account for only some 3.4 per cent of total grain production, they provide about 35 per cent of AMC grain purchases.[108] This in itself ensures their indispensability, and also serves to indicate that the Ethiopian state farms are not an unmitigated economic catastrophe, and that simply viewed as mechanisms for growing an extractable harvest, they rank well ahead of either cooperatives or peasant farms. The problem is whether they represent an effective use of available resources of land, labour, or capital.

It is impossible to assess the efficiency of state farms in terms of standard accounting procedures. Even though the great majority of them make substantial losses, both the prices they pay for their inputs and the prices they receive for their output are so artificial that little can be deduced from any profit and loss account. Selling to the AMC, they are obliged to receive a fixed price, even though they are paid a substantial premium over the price offered to peasant producers. Targets are given in physical terms – the production of so much wheat or maize – rather than economic ones. In accounting terms, the problem is not so much that state farms make a loss, as that there is no means of knowing whether they use resources efficiently, and consequently no incentive for them to do so.[109]

The state farms absorb a very high proportion of the capital available for agricultural development. Between 1978–79 and 1982–83, for example, between 58 per cent and 64 per cent of government resources spent in agriculture were devoted to the state farms, with much of the rest also going to large-scale developments of one sort or another.[110] In the period 1980–82, they received nearly 80 per cent of the available supplies of improved seed, and over half of the fertiliser.[111] They are likewise highly capitalised in their use of machinery, with by far the greater part of the available tractors and combined harvesters. Almost all of the tractors received from the GDR in 1978–79 (in exchange for peak-priced coffee) were sent to the state farms. In a neighbouring state farm and cooperative which I visited in Arsi in 1984, the state farm had some twenty tractors and eight combine harvesters, the cooperative had one tractor, and ordinary peasants had no machinery at all. At the same date, the state farms of Shoa and Arsi regions had 593 tractors between them, of which however only 248 (or 41.8 per cent) were operational.[112] This was not entirely the state farms' fault: many of the tractors, especially those of East German origin, proved unsuited to Ethiopian conditions; but it nonetheless indicates the wastage involved in ill-considered overcapitalisation. The state farms, indeed, exemplify the attitudes likewise implicit in industrial investment policy: that large scale, centrally planned and heavily capitalised operations will inevitably produce success.

The actual success has been accurately described by Mengistu Haile-Mariam himself[113]

> While the yield of state farms should be an average of 25 quintals of wheat per hectare, the results so far achieved do not exceed a yield of 14 quintals per hectare, and this is not much superior to the amount produced in many areas by peasants using backward implements. Even the maize crop produced by the state farms is hardly higher than that produced by peasants in terms of yield per hectare. It is clearly recognisable that the lack of detailed studies of the sites of certain state farms has contributed to their operational inefficiency, low productivity, and diminishing sizes. The fundamental reason however remains to be the inherent defect in the utilisation of manpower and equipment and, as a whole, lack of control over the widespread inefficiency of management.

Other studies confirm that productivity per hectare is broadly similar on state farms with their massive technological inputs, and on peasant farms with the most limited conceivable technology. Though for grain, state farms generally do a bit better than peasants, for pulses and coffee they do considerably worse; both peasants and state farms do much better than cooperatives.[114] Even for grain, state farm yields have been substantially lower than (and for wheat only about half) those obtained on private mechanised farms before the revolution.[115] The reasons are likewise much as Mengistu identified them. Sometimes, as with the 10,000 hectare Sheneka farm in Bale, massive investments were made in areas which simply lacked the rainfall to support the crops[116] – a fact of which peasants farming in the area were perfectly well aware. Irrigation was another source of large-scale investment, understandably enough in a country where agriculture has been so devastatingly affected by drought, but (especially in the lower Awash) has led to extensive salination. But the major problem is indeed management, and this in turn is the result not merely of a lack of training and supervision, but also of the inherent difficulties of applying large scale industrial techniques, complete with a labour force working the statutory seven-hour day, to the unpredictable world of agriculture. A walk along a state farm boundary, with neatly tended little peasant plots on one side, and a vast and weed-infested acreage on the other, is often enough to make the point.

A further important problem for state farms is labour. They produce a higher surplus of food than peasant agriculture, not because they grow more per hectare, but because they do not have so many people to eat it on the spot. Regular employment on wheat farms, with nearly forty hectares per worker, compares with peasant farms in which two hectares or less support a whole household.[117] The clearance of peasants off the land, enforced by commercial agriculture in the pre-revolutionary decade, has likewise occurred in the establishment of new state farms, especially in Bale. But on the other hand, some state farms have also needed a large supply of temporary labour, especially at harvest time; and this has been achieved by conscripting peasants and other workers at very low rates of pay, and generally at a time when they most need to work on their own farms. Since state farm managers can pay labourers only 1.92 birr a day, corresponding to the national minimum wage of fifty birr a month, they are unable to compete for labour which (at harvest time, and despite the formal prohibition on the private hire of agricultural labour) may cost five birr a day on the open market.[118] The difference may be made up by imposing a quota of labourers on nearby peasants' associations, or by forced mobilisation of the urban unemployed, or by doubtfully voluntary campaigns among office workers, members of mass organisations such as REYA, or students. There are occasional references to such campaigns in the press,[119] while in November 1985, with the harvest on the point of starting, the Welega Agricultural Development Organisation announced that the workforce on its eight farms fell no less than 69,000 below what was needed.[120] Forced recruitment has been particularly evident at the Humera state farm on the Sudanese border, considered in a later section, but in one form or another it appears to be a standard practice for making up deficiencies in seasonal labour. It is one of the ironies of the revolution that the large-scale commercial exploitation of agriculture, which had been expanding fairly rapidly under capitalist farmers in the decade to 1974, should have been maintained and extended by a socialist state farm system which has proved both more exploitative of labour, and less efficient as a means of producing food, than its predecessor.

The inadequacies of the state farm structure to meet the needs of cash-crop agriculture have been recognised not only in the drastic scaling down of plans for their expansion, but also in the recommendations of the Soviet advisers attached to the ONCCP. These have suggested that 'it is advisable to consider the problem of developing . . . agriculture on a commercial farm basis by renting public land in sizes exceeding the ordinary plot and with manpower hired under the control of the state'.[121] This suggestion had not been taken up at the time of writing; but like the proposals for 'co-dwelling' which disguised the return of the private landlord to help meet the housing shortage, they reflected the need for some form of private incentive to make up for the deficiencies of the state.

THE EXPORT SECTOR: COFFEE, SESAME AND CHAT

Coffee consistently accounts for over 50 per cent, and in most years for over 60 per cent, of Ethiopia's published exports by value. It has already been shown that the revolution has made little difference either to Ethiopia's dependence on a single export crop, or to the direction of export trade, which (despite some barter deals) continues to be heavily directed towards Western hard-currency markets. It has likewise been noted that increases in the share of the value of coffee exports extracted by government have been one of the main contributors to increases in government revenues since the revolution. In managing the coffee market, therefore, the government faced the two potentially conflicting goals of maximising foreign currency earnings on the one hand, and domestic revenues on the other. The latter, in so far as it implied – at least in the short term – the extraction of an increasing share of the value of a fixed product, lent itself to the techniques for controlling producers which the regime in any case favoured. The former, in so far as it implied – at least in the long term – incentives to raise production, tended to favour a greater reliance on the market. Consistently with its actions in other fields, the government opted for policies of control which have ensured it an increasing share of a stable or declining production.

The two key features of the Ethiopian coffee business are firstly that it is overwhelmingly grown by peasant smallholders, and secondly that there is a strong domestic market, as well as an export one. Some 98–99 per cent of coffee is produced by smallholders, and the remainder by state farms.[122] This is a legacy of the pre-revolutionary structure of production, when, although coffee was a major source of enrichment for absentee landlords, these were generally content to raise their income by share-cropping, rather than by taking a direct part in production. A few small commercial plantations were converted to state farms at the revolution, but (in contrast to grain) their output has been dramatically inferior to that of smallholders; the available figures suggest that they achieve an average of some 240 kilos per hectare, compared with 400 kilos for peasant farmers.[123] Though this discrepancy can be ascribed to factors such as the age of trees, or the labour problems common to all state farms in labour intensive sectors of agriculture, the more basic reason must be the underlying weakness of state farm management in a sector where, unlike grain farming, this is not compensated by economies of scale or inputs of improved seed or fertilisers. One new state farm, at Bebeka in Kaffa region, has been cleared from virgin forest in a classic socialist attempt to crack the problem with a massive infusion of large-scale planned investment. Though this only entered into production in 1984 (and is excluded from the state farm figures given above), early results suggest that it will fall well short of its intended yield.

The indications are that coffee production since the revolution has declined. Coffee exports, at an annual average of 72,500 tons a year for the period 1962–67 and 79,800 tons for 1968–73, fell to 60,200 tons for 1974–78;[124] and although they then picked up sharply to an average of 81,500 tons for 1979–83, this was due more to a draconian squeeze on domestic consumption (normally reckoned to absorb about half of the crop) than to an increase in production. Peak exports of 97,900 tons in 1984 fell to 69,000 in 1985 and 73,200 in 1986.[125] The harvesting of coffee is hampered by the prohibition on the private employment of agricultural labour, even though this appears to be widely evaded by peasants prepared to pay two-and-a-half times the wage available on state farms.[126] Another reason must however be lack of incentive. Unlike many African states, the Ethiopian government does not pay a fixed price to producers, but pays instead on a sliding scale derived from the world market price, with the producer receiving a smaller share of the world price as this rises, and a larger one as it falls. This means that prices vary from day-to-day, but one carefully calculated study shows producers as receiving an average 62.3 per cent of the export value during the fifteen years to 1975–76, with a range from 45 per cent to 69 per cent.[127] This share dropped to 32 per cent in 1976–77, and 34 per cent in 1977–78, and though these were years of exceptionally high world coffee prices, the producer share over the six years from 1978–79 came to an average of 41.3 per cent.[128] This was the lowest share for any African coffee-producing country, and contrasted most sharply with the 93.7 per cent of export value paid to producers in neighbouring Kenya.[129] Equally revealing are studies showing comparative producer price movements as between coffee and other crops.[130] Relative prices of coffee and teff, at parity in 1977, had moved to 2.54:1 in favour of teff by 1981, though the benefits of grain growing may have been reduced subsequently by AMC buying prices. Relative prices of coffee and chat (of which more shortly) moved from parity to 2.25:1 in favour of chat over the same period. Reports that farmers have shifted from coffee to other crops, though I have not been able to confirm them, would reflect rational economic calculation on their part.

The low producer price is policed through strict physical controls on the movement and sale of coffee, which are chiefly intended to prevent it being sold on the domestic market.[131] Both the absolute level of Addis Ababa prices, which at fifteen birr a kilo in early 1986 were well above the then f.o.b. world market price (at the official rate of exchange) of nearly seven birr, and the discrepancy between these and the price of two or three birr for which coffee could then be bought in the producing areas, indicate the effectiveness of these controls. This difference between producer and consumer prices inevitably creates opportunities for corruption; late in 1985, for example, a senior regional government official was caught trying to smuggle five quintals of coffee from the south-west to Addis Ababa – an operation which, if successful, would have netted him a profit of some 6,000 birr. Further opportunities arise at central level, through the sale of some 20 per cent of exportable coffee by government to private coffee exporters, at what is nominally an auction but in practice amounts to an allocation by administrative discretion. In 1980, the official responsible for the auction section of the Ministry of Coffee and Tea Development was charged with receiving bribes of 186,600 birr[132] – a very large sum by Ethiopian standards. As in other areas of the economy, however, corruption is not widespread enough to seriously undermine control.

The coffee experience can usefully be compared with two other Ethiopian export crops, sesame seed and chat. Sesame is an oilseed, which in Ethiopia is almost exclusively grown in the Humera lowlands bordering the Sudan. This was one of the boom areas of commercial agriculture during the pre-revolutionary decade, and exports grew from 19,800 tons in 1967 to 84,600 tons in 1974, netting export earnings in the latter year of some 38 million US dollars. Ethiopia was then the second largest exporter in the world.[133] This crop demanded considerable managerial skill, both during the very short sowing season and at harvest time, when it had to be harvested at a precisely determined moment. Large numbers of short-term migrant harvest workers from the northern highlands – 100,000 is probably the best estimate, though some claims go as high as 300,000[134] – were able to earn rates of ten birr a day by exploiting the characteristics of the crop. These earnings, large by peasant standards, were of critical importance in helping to relieve the effects of land shortage and impoverishment in the areas of peasant agriculture from which the migrants came.

After the revolution, however, Humera found itself on the sharp end of the two main failures of the new regime: the failure of political incorporation of the northern highlands, and the failure of economic management, especially of labour intensive state-run agriculture. Politically, Humera was on the border between the main regional strengths of the EDU opposition in Gonder and Tigray, and its external support channelled through the Sudan. The area was lost to government control for much of the period between mid 1975 and June 1977, when the Ethiopian army decisively defeated EDU forces there; mopping up operations continued over the following months.[135] Serious attempts to revive production (which had continued, though at a dramatically declining rate, over the intervening period) got under way in early 1979, as part of the National Revolutionary Development Campaign which had then just been launched.[136] Valiant efforts to run Humera as a state farm continued until 1982, after which the attempt seems to have been abandoned, and much of the area came under TPLF control.

Economically, the attempt to grow a difficult crop such as sesame under the rigid conditions of state farm management proved a disaster. In 1979, nearly 4,000 members of the production task force – largely recruited from the Addis Ababa lumpenproletariat, many of them forcibly – were drafted to the area, along with some 50,000 peasants from Gojjam and Gonder.[137] In 1980, even larger numbers were employed, some of them coming from as far away as southern Shoa; these were kept away from their own farms for some four months, including the ploughing and planting seasons, though returning just about in time for the harvest.[138] These workers were according to one source paid 2.75 birr a day, though after compulsory deductions for food and other items, this was reduced to under one birr.[139] Export production had slumped from 84,600 tons in 1974 to a mere 3,400 in 1979; the development campaign got it up to 7,400–7,500 tons in 1980–81, and to 16,400 in 1982, after which it collapsed back to the 1979 level, and Ethiopia effectively ceased to be a sesame exporter.[140] The world price of sesame had doubled over the period during which Ethiopian production was collapsing, and remained at a high level of over $900 a ton throughout the first half of the 1980s.

Chat is a very different crop: a narcotic shrub, the leaves of which are

185

chewed throughout the lowland areas of the Horn and in the Arabian peninsula, inducing (it is said – I have not tried it) initial clarity of mind and loss of appetite, with a subsequent reaction; long-term addicts may have their mental faculties entirely blown, and wander about in a state of cheerful childishness. Most Ethiopian chat is grown in the highlands of Hararghe (though other producers, especially in south-west Shoa, are entering the market), and is both consumed locally and exported to Somalia, Djibouti and Arabia. Unlike any other cash crop, its production and marketing are virtually uncontrolled by the government, which exacts taxes at checkpoints and major markets, but leaves the trade itself to private entrepreneurs. Since the leaves must be chewed fresh for maximum effect, the crop places an enormous premium on speedy and efficient distribution, by air as well as by land, which a cumbersome government corporation would be ideally ill-equipped to manage. No figures are available for production or export, partly no doubt because this is outside government control, but equally because (though openly sold throughout the Red Sea region) it is classed as a narcotic. Claims that it is by some way the second largest Ethiopian export, after coffee, are however entirely credible, and it thus partly offsets the published Ethiopian balance of payments deficit.

Hararghe constitutes, to an extent impossible to appreciate without personal observation, an economy based on chat. The shrub grows throughout the region, above a height of some 1,800 metres, and is well-suited to the steep, terraced hillsides. Farmers can make about 3,000 birr a year from the crop, putting them well above the standard of living of highland peasants in other parts of the country.[141] Allied to the chat market, and financed by it, is a flourishing trade in contraband goods brought in from Djibouti, with the result that Hararghe forms a kind of free trade zone within a socialist state. The economic frontier of Ethiopia stands in effect on the Hararghe/Shoa border at Awash, and the region as a whole stands in the sharpest contrast to the problems of agricultural production and marketing in other parts of the country.

THE ORIGINS OF FAMINE

Famine provides both the dominant external image of Ethiopia, and its starkest domestic challenge. It should be made clear at the start, however, that any attempt to assign causes, or responsibility, for the decline in agricultural production per head which culminated in the catastrophe of 1984–85 is subject not only to a high level of emotive argument and political special pleading, but also to the impossibility of ascribing specific weights to any one of a cluster of interlocking environmental, social, economic and political variables. It is nonetheless possible to sort out the major elements involved, to dismiss a number of factors which evidently do not play a major role, and to sketch some of the relationships among the remainder.

First of all, highland Ethiopia, and especially the area from Wollo north to Eritrea, has been subject to devastating famines for as far back in history as records reach, some of them evidently worse than those of 1973–74 and 1984–85.[142] For those bred in societies where food arrives regularly in shops, and where serious shortage can only be the result of quite exceptional short-term factors, it is difficult to conceive of fellow human beings living in conditions where – as for virtually all other living creatures – natural changes in food supply bring, as an automatic consequence, corresponding changes in mortality and population. Such has however been the fate of the Ethiopian peasantry. A corollary is that famine cannot basically be ascribed, as it has often been elsewhere, to the incorporation of Ethiopia into the global economy, and the consequent diversion into export and urban consumption of resources previously used to sustain the rural population. There are some parts of Ethiopia, notably in the Awash valley, where irrigated plantations have taken away the dry season refuges of Afar and Kereyu pastoralists, and where this thesis does have some validity; but overwhelmingly the greater part of the famine has occurred in inaccessible areas of subsistence farming, producing virtually nothing for the world market. Access to the international economy has indeed eased famine, first by providing peasants with auxiliary incomes as harvest workers for cotton, sesame seed or coffee, and secondly through the provision of relief grain. Though there has been some concern about whether relief grain might itself encourage external dependence at the expense of peasant agriculture, this cannot be held responsible for the original famine itself.[143]

Secondly, Ethiopia has been suffering from a fairly steady decline in per capita food production over the forty years since the end of the Second World War – a decline, that is to say, which long predates the revolution. From being an exporter of grain in the 1940s (a situation which may itself have been the result of temporarily favourable circumstances), Ethiopia moved to a rough balance between supply and consumption in the 1950s, and became a net importer during the 1960s.[144] The only long-term study of which I am aware found that the annual rate of growth of agricultural output slowed from 3.3 per cent in 1957–61 to 2.9 per cent in 1963–67, and 1.2 per cent in 1968–73; from 1974 to 1980 there was virtually no growth at all, followed by an absolute decline from 1981 onwards.[145] This was due largely to the simple pressure of increasing population on resources, with consequent environmental degradation, especially in the north. It has in any event intensified since the revolution. Degradation is certainly a factor in the decline, and has been widely recognised as such by peasant farmers; in virtually all of the areas surveyed in 1983 as part of the Ethiopian Highlands Reclamation Study, land degradation in one form or another was a major source of concern.[146] The survey, moreover, excluded Tigray and Eritrea, where the problem is likely to have been even worse than elsewhere. But degradation itself is not simply a 'natural' factor, but may have been exacerbated by the effects of land reform in keeping people on the land within their own peasants' associations, and inhibiting population drift

187

either into the towns or to other agricultural areas. It may likewise have been checked, to some degree, by campaigns of terracing and afforestation carried out since the revolution.

The Ethiopian government has sometimes exaggerated the level of degradation, in order to gain support for its campaign to resettle famine victims in the south and west. One Relief and Rehabilitation Commission publication, for example, claims baldly that 'the highlands are barren' – an astonishing statement directly rebutted by much of the RRC's own published documentation;[147] the less-sweeping conclusion that many areas of the highlands held a population greater than they could normally be expected to support could however have been made with considerable force. Even more remarkably, Mengistu Haile-Mariam has turned the reasons for Ethiopia's existence neatly on their head by claiming that recurrent warfare in the past had compelled most of the population to live in highland areas which were comparatively unsuited for agriculture.[148] Equally misleading statements have been made about rainfall. The RRC's claim that 'there have scarcely been any real rains in the drought-prone areas since the 1972–74 catastrophe',[149] for example, is again directly rebutted by published official figures which show rainfall in northern Ethiopia in most years between 1975 and 1983 (despite considerable annual and regional variation) at average or above average levels.[150] Drought is certainly an important short-term precipitant of famine, but there is no evidence to suggest that, over a longer period, it has reduced the agricultural productivity of the Ethiopian highlands. Periodic shortages of rainfall merely expose a vulnerability created by other factors.

Thirdly, however, the considerable efforts which the revolutionary government has made to transform agricultural production, through land reform, cooperativisation, state farms, and the new distribution system, have evidently failed to improve the situation, and have in many respects been counterproductive. Even though the single most important factor in creating famine, population increase, is only very partially within the government's capacity to control, and that only over a long period, famine cannot be regarded as the inevitable result of the Malthusian pressure of population on resources. Particularly symptomatic are the comparative inefficiency of state farms as compared with pre-revolutionary commercial agriculture, and of producers' cooperatives as compared with household production. Basically more important, nonetheless, are the restrictions placed on peasant agriculture by government pricing policies, control of agricultural trade, and discrimination against the peasant sector in taxation, investment and credit. There has been no sustained government attempt to control the rate of population increase. Though the government has become increasingly aware of the effects of inexorably rising population on the whole range of development policies from agriculture to urban unemployment, any attempt to reduce the birth rate would require a large-scale campaign

188

which would tax its resources, and possibly bring it into headlong confrontation with peasant attitudes and religious convictions.

The steadily increasing scale of famine is graphically illustrated by the RRC's figures for the numbers of people 'affected' by food shortages during the first half of the 1980s.[151] These figures exclude both the whole of Tigray and Eritrea, which with Wollo were the regions worst affected, and also the pastoralist populations, being confined only to crop-growing districts. The number of people affected consists of the population of districts reporting serious food shortages in the year concerned. It rises from 1.9 million in 1980, to 2.4 million in 1982, 2.3 million in 1983, 3.2 million in 1984, and 5.8 million in 1985. Figures for grain imports provide complementary evidence, with an increase in the cost of food imports, overwhelmingly consisting of cereals, from 42.3 million birr in 1978, to 60.7 million in 1979, 90.9 million in 1980, and 112.7 million in 1981[152] – all years in which rainfall was generally adequate in most areas. From 1980–81 onwards, food aid displaced commercial imports as the main source of imported food. For the four years from 1980–81, cereal imports stayed roughly constant at about 250,000 tons a year, or 5 per cent of national requirements.[153] In the crisis year of 1984–85, they went up to 1.4 million tons, or 29 per cent of total consumption, while even following the good harvest of 1986, half a million tons were still needed. Regardless of weather conditions, Ethiopia has become a chronically food dependent country.

THE DOMESTIC POLITICS OF FAMINE RELIEF

Famine has presented the Ethiopian government, politically speaking, with both costs and opportunities. The costs are more immediately obvious, notably the challenge which famine presents to the government's claim to have provided a better life for Ethiopia's people, and the threat that a manifest failure to deal with it may undermine the revolutionary regime, just as the 1973–74 famine is often reckoned to have undermined the imperial government. The parallels which are often drawn between the potential political consequences of the 1973–74 and the 1984–85 famines may however, in my view, be misconceived. The earlier famine affected the regime not directly, but through its repercussions on an unstable urban population. The much greater level of control which the revolutionary government has been able to maintain over the towns helps to insulate it from any repeat of 1974. The long-term threat to the stability of any state which cannot feed its own people nonetheless remains, and many commentators (including notably defectors from the Ethiopian regime) have drawn attention to the role of Western famine relief in helping to maintain the government in power.[154]

More immediately significant, however, has been the government's capacity to use famine as a means of bolstering its political position, and pursuing its long-term programmes. At one level, famine relief provides an opportunity for the regime to demonstrate both its concern and its administrative capacity, as compared with the imperial government. The RRC, from this viewpoint, is a symbol of revolutionary effectiveness, and the newly formed WPE was likewise able to take up the banner of purposive action on behalf of the suffering victims of drought as its first major project after its formation.[155] At another level, famine victims are nothing if not dependent, and famine has helped to drive a previously autonomous peasantry into reliance on government for its most basic human need, and hence to make it available to serve political purposes, of which the resettlement programme is the most evident. The international effects of famine are likewise mixed, and closely duplicate the effects of civil war on the military capacity of the state. The very need for food, like the need for weapons, imposes an external dependence on the state's suppliers. But at the same time, the fact that food, like weapons, is distributed through the state and through agencies operating under its supervision, enables it to extend its control over the domestic population. The politics of famine relief thus has to be seen through the spectacles provided by the demands of socialist state consolidation.

Famine and its associated problems have been overwhelmingly the dominant focus of Western interest in Ethiopia in recent years, and have produced a considerable literature of their own, much of it concentrated on the nature and adequacy of the Western response.[156] It is certainly true that the Ethiopian government's capacity to organise famine relief is vastly greater than it was at the time of the 1973–74 famine, and greater also than that of many other affected states, such as Sudan. Nor is this surprising. Exactly the same emphasis on centralisation and command which accounts for some at least of the defects of revolutionary agricultural policy, and hence makes famine more likely, at the same time helps to produce a fairly efficient mechanism for coping with it when it comes. In part, this is the legacy of the longstanding capacity for organisation which distinguishes Ethiopia from much of Africa, reinforced by the removal of the constraints on centralised administration which existed under the old regime. The RRC also has very wide powers to co-opt people and materials for famine relief, and to co-ordinate the activities both of local government officials and of foreign relief agencies. Even though much of this co-ordinating role was taken over by the WPE after September 1984, it ensures a reasonably coherent chain of command, which is essential for example in managing the large number of non-governmental foreign relief agencies operating in Ethiopia, of which there were forty-five in March 1986.[157] At the same time, the role of the RRC as a buffer organisation between the Ethiopian government on the one hand, and the overwhelmingly Western sources of relief aid on the other, created strains which were illuminated by the defections of the RRC commissioner Dawit Wolde-Giorgis in late 1985, and one of the three deputy commissioners, Berhane Deressa, in mid 1986. The appointment as commissioner in 1986 of Berhanu Jembere, a longstanding personal colleague of Mengistu and former ambassador in East Germany, signalled the government's determination to bring the RRC under firm central control, even at the cost of weakening its relations with the donor agencies.

Three well-publicised aspects of the 1984–85 famine help to illuminate the relation between famine relief and the political priorities of the regime. The first arose from the cruel coincidence between the onset of a greatly increased level of famine from mid 1984 onwards, and the celebrations of the tenth anniversary of the revolution, together with the founding of the WPE. Unlike 1973–74, when part at least of the delay in responding to famine can be ascribed to the inefficiency of the bureaucracy at both central and regional levels, and the lack of any administrative machinery for dealing with a famine even once this had been identified, there can be no doubt that in 1984 both the RRC and the government were aware of the rapidly deteriorating situation. Famine was by this time a constant source of government concern, and the institutional mechanisms – notably the RRC's generally effective and accurate early warning system – were in place to identify and respond to it. Warnings had been given by Dawit Wolde-Giorgis in meetings with the aid community in March and again in early August.[158] The failure of the March appeal to generate any adequate international response lies partly in misplaced optimism on the part of the donor community, partly in the scaling down of requests to the level which the domestic distribution network was thought able to handle,[159] though even at that stage the government's response was muted. By August, there is more than adequate evidence of the official suppression of information about the famine, in order to ensure that the celebration of the benefits which ten years of revolution had conferred on the Ethiopian people would not be marred by the revelation that several million of them were dying for lack of enough to eat. Most striking is the complete absence of any reference to drought or famine in the official press for the months July, August and September 1984. Whereas all of the other meetings between the RRC and the donor community, including those of March and October 1984, received extensive coverage, there was no mention at all of the meeting on 6 August.[160] Reports which were published on productive performance and health services in the two main famine regions of Tigray and Wollo, in each case spoke of 'encouraging results', without reference to drought or famine.[161] Both journalists who were in Addis Ababa to cover the tenth anniversary celebrations, and officials of Western aid agencies, were refused the permits needed to visit the famine areas.[162] Nor did Mengistu Haile-Mariam's long speech at the WPE founding Congress make any reference to the problem.[163]

This was in startling contrast to the response from early October onwards. On 2 October, the second meeting was held of the newly formed WPE Politbureau, and this marked the occasion for the government to 'go public' on the famine. The Politbureau devoted the whole meeting to the issue, and decided that it should itself guide the emergency relief programme. There-

191

after, relief became the primary concern of the government and party, and the campaigning efforts previously devoted to the tenth anniversary celebrations were thereafter given to it. One of the features of centralised (and hence especially perhaps of socialist) political systems, extending well beyond Ethiopia, is that a political apparatus responding to initiatives from above has to be prompted by a series of campaigns, each of which directs the whole attention of the organisation for a limited period to a limited set of issues. The adoption of an issue for a campaign is then essential to secure an effective response. The limitations of this form of government are all too clear: each campaign is inherently temporary; it distracts attention from other tasks, and will in turn be abandoned itself; and it is liable to throw up disadvantages or abuses not considered at the time it was launched. As a short term response to a single issue, it can however be very effective. One consequence of the policy change of 2 October was to encourage the Western television coverage which in turn prompted an astonishing level of external response. This response, however, was not possible until the domestic policy change had taken place; and this change in turn resulted from the transformation of famine from an issue which could be used to undermine the post-revolutionary political structure, into one which could be used to maintain it.

The same rationale applies to a second aspect of famine relief, the choice of the resettlement strategy. Resettlement had been a favoured government response to a variety of social issues since the start of the revolution, and to a limited extent even before it. The first known planned settlement in Ethiopia was established in Sidamo in 1958, but only a few more were set up before the revolution. From 1975 onwards, the number grew rapidly, and by 1982 there were 112 of them, holding over 120,000 people.[164] The largest number, in western Welega, Bale, and even in the Ogaden, were established for migrants from the 1973–74 famine in Wollo. Others, especially in Shoa, were set up in an attempt to redirect the Addis Ababa unemployed (or 'lumpens', as they were called) towards agriculture, and dating as they did from the period of the terror, to help deal with the problem of urban security. Efforts were likewise made to settle nomads (especially Afar), and some settlements also resulted from the displacement of smallholders from newly established state farms. The experience of these settlements (which came under a Settlement Authority within the Ministry of Agriculture until 1979, and were then transferred to the RRC) was not encouraging. Their agricultural productivity did little to compensate for the high cost of establishing them, and almost all continued to depend on RRC assistance beyond the end of the three-year period during which they were expected to become self-supporting. Considerable social problems resulted from the practice of settling household heads alone, and only much later allowing their families to join them; large numbers of would-be settlers left the settlement sites soon after arrival.

This experience did not affect the resettlement campaign, however, any more than the experience of producers' cooperatives was to affect the subsequent campaign on villagisation. Resettlement offered an appealing model of purposive, large-scale government action, which would give a prominent role to the party, help to further the government's plans for transforming the structure of agricultural production by putting the settlers into producers' cooperatives, and at the same time promise a dramatic and permanent solution to the problem of famine. Despite an original target of moving a million and a half people to the resettlement areas, the actual number when the campaign came to an end in February 1986 was about 600,000 – in itself a very large-scale operation. Resettlement only very partially served the function ascribed to it by the various regional autonomist movements, of deliberately removing the population from the areas under their control; according to RRC figures, which may obviously be open to question, only just under 90,000 settlers were moved from Tigray, as against 107,000 from Shoa, and over 370,000 from Wollo.[165] It may better be seen as compensating by government action for the halting of the steady drift of peasants to the south and west which had been enforced by land hunger and stopped by land reform. Despite the halt in 1986, further resettlement remains on the agenda, and in March 1987 Mengistu spoke of the need to move at least 7 million people.[166]

Despite considerable international misgivings about the resettlement programme, the overall strategy of moving people from the northern highlands to the resettlement areas was approved by a wide range of external consultants. The most comprehensive survey of the highland economy, the FAO's Ethiopian Highlands Reclamation Study, argued that 'considerably more than 150,000 persons annually will need to be resettled or preferably migrate voluntarily, if present population growth and degradation trends continue'.[167] Another report commissioned by the ILO, the main conclusions of which were rejected by the Ethiopian government, nonetheless agreed with the claim in the Ten Year Plan that 22 per cent could be added to the total area of productive land over the ten-year period, and that most of this was to be found along the western frontier.[168] Three main areas were selected for the 1984–86 settlements. Just over a quarter of a million people went to western Welega, swelling the numbers already sent there in the earlier phase. Nearly 150,000 were settled south of Gambela in Illubabor, and just over 100,000 around Pawe in western Gojjam. In addition, 78,000 went to Kaffa, and much smaller numbers to Shoa and western Gonder.[169]

Much of the international response to the resettlement programme concentrated on whether it was voluntary, as the Ethiopian government repeatedly claimed, and much of this concern was in my view misconceived.[170] Voluntariness implies a decision-making autonomy simply not available to starving people in feeding camps, and the issue seems to have been raised in response to Western concerns, and accepted by the government owing to its urgent need for food. It might equally be argued that it was, under such circumstances, for the government to decide on the best solution, and direct the people accordingly. There were however ample indications that some at least of those chosen for resettlement by peasants' associations, rather than taken directly from feeding camps, neither wanted nor needed to be moved; peasants' associations in regions such as Wollo were given quotas of settlers which they were expected to meet, in much the same way as with military conscription, and some of these settlers eventually found their way back to their original homes.

More valid questions arise as to whether this was indeed a workable strategy, and as to how it was carried out. I find it hard to believe claims that some 50,000 people, or 8 per cent of the total number involved, died in the course of resettlement,[171] and know of no information on which the figure could plausibly be based; but shifting some 600,000 people, many of them very weak and in no condition to be moved, must greatly have increased the number of deaths. Likewise, the resettlement sites were hastily prepared, without any evidence of their capacity to support the people who were to be moved to them – that at Pawe in Gojjam, for example, was selected by Mengistu himself in the course of a helicopter tour,[172] and the same may well have been true of others. The climate and agriculture appropriate to settlements at about 1,000 metres above sea level would also (like the diseases, notably malaria and tsetse fly) have been entirely foreign to peasants accustomed to farm at about 3,000 metres. The long-term prospects for the settlements remain uncertain. Mengistu reported in March 1987 that the settlers had proved able to grow their own food requirements, and were to be directed increasingly to cash-crop production.[173] But at least some of the initial success was due to large-scale mechanised inputs which could not be maintained, notably a massive Italian investment in the Pawe scheme in Gojjam, or to the initial exploitation of thin soils which could not bear continuous cropping. It is difficult to see any basis for expecting the new settlements to be more successful than their predecessors.

A third issue in famine relief was the government's consistent refusal to permit relief to be directed to areas outside its control, despite pressure from both Kurt Janssen, the United Nations Assistant General Secretary for Emergency Operations in Ethiopia, and from the International Committee of the Red Cross.[174] The government likewise challenged any shipment of relief to Ethiopia through the Sudan, which in practice amounted to distribution under the aegis of the various regional opposition movements. From the Ethiopian viewpoint – and equally from that of the regionalist movements themselves – such operations offered the movements both a measure of international recognition, and a means to establish their control over the population. A similar attitude had been taken by the Nigerian government at the time of the civil war of 1967–70. More than any other, the issue symbolises the impossibility of separating the humanitarian aspects of famine relief from its consequences for state survival and political control.

8

The national question

Although Ethiopia is no less ethnically variegated than other large African states, the political role of ethnicity has, as already outlined in chapter 2, differed significantly from the pattern found in most of post-colonial Africa. A multiethnic state from the earliest times, it gave relatively little weight to issues of ethnic origin, and individuals from peripheral areas as well as from humble social backgrounds could reach positions not simply of power, but equally of authority and prestige. The price for this was however assimilation to a national political culture, which was largely (though not exclusively) defined in terms of the language, religion and values of the Amharic core, and was thus liable to induce revolt from those who were not prepared to accept the terms on which incorporation into the national political system was offered.

The impact of revolution on ethnic and regional identities has been characteristically ambivalent. Like virtually all revolutions, the Ethiopian had a strong nationalist component, which could successfully be mobilised to defeat external invasion. The new regime, while drawing on the sense of national identity inherited from the old, was however determined to expand this into a modern secular nationalism, divorced (though in practice this was scarcely possible) from the religious, social and cultural trappings which had restricted it in the past. But as with many revolutions likewise, and especially those which have taken place in decaying traditional monarchies, the temporary loss of central control and the upheavals in political identity and participation which accompanied the revolution, also encouraged the growth of peripheral nationalisms directed against the central core. In the crisis of identity and authority which followed the fall of the monarchy, there was widespread uncertainty among many educated Ethiopians, not only about what Ethiopia was, but equally about what *they* were. Was Ethiopia a 'Habsburg state' – a mere congeries of different nationalities held together by a dynasty, which had no further *raison d'être* once that dynasty was removed?[1] Was it an Amharic empire, sustained by the colonialist control of one people over their neighbours? If it was to be regarded as a 'nation', in what did its nationhood consist, and how was that sense of unity which must underlie any effective nationalism to be reconciled with the evident diversity of the peoples to be found within its frontiers? On the answers to these general questions depended immediate problems of personal identity, political action, and sometimes physical survival. These issues were often most acute for people with some affiliation to the largest and most amorphous of Ethiopian ethnic groups, the Oromo. Did the revolution mean that to declare oneself an Oromo was now practicable, or even profitable? What did 'being Oromo' actually entail? And what would be the relationship between this Oromo identity and the Ethiopian state or political system? In the early years of the revolution, some people – Amharic speakers, with Amharic names – surprised even their closest friends by declaring themselves to be Oromo, or as 'having an Oromo side'. In some cases this identity was maintained, in others shamefacedly suppressed as events took a course which placed increasing emphasis on centralisation and national unity. Sometimes, the contradictory demands of national and local or ethnic identity resulted in mental breakdown. The conflicts between centre and periphery, between nationalism, regionalism and ethnicity, were fought out not merely between rival programmes and political movements (each of which tended, naturally enough, to exaggerate the sharpness of the line which separated it from its opponents), but within the minds of many Ethiopians.

The institution which, more than any other, embodied the nationalist and centralist aspirations of the revolution was of course the armed forces. But the nationalism of the armed forces, and especially of the Derg, should not blind one to the ethnic diversity of their membership. Quite apart from Amharas and Tigreans, with a fair sprinkling of Eritreans, large numbers of Oromos joined the armed forces, along with members of the smaller ethnic groups. Senior officers (of the rank of brigadier general or above) with distinctively Oromo names serving since the revolution include Bahru Tufa (commander, Ground Forces, 1976), Kefelegn Yibsa (commander, Ground Forces, 1980), Demissie Bulto (commander, Eastern Sector, 1984), and Regassa Jima (commander, Eritrea, 1987). The ethnic identity of other senior Oromo officers (including, it is said, Merid Negussie, chief of staff in 1987) is disguised by their Amharic names. No Moslems have yet reached such top command positions, but three were promoted to brigadier general in the first half of the 1980s. There were likewise a large number of Oromos in the Derg, two of the most prominent being Teka Tulu, who was in charge of security and subsequently alternate member of the WPE Politbureau, and Debele Dinsa, WPE first secretary for Shoa; but only one identifiable Moslem, Ali Mussa from Wollo.

The need to use names to provide what is, even then, only fragmentary evidence of ethnicity helps to indicate a major difference in the role of

196

ethnicity in Ethiopia, as compared with most other parts of sub-Saharan Africa. Commonly in Africa, a politician's ethnic origins, all the way down to the clan or village level, are part of the social and political equipment which he carries around with him, and are readily accessible to anyone who wants to find out what they are; even military leaders are swiftly classified into the categories previously used for civilian politicians, and these categories in turn help to define their political constituencies. In the Somali Republic, for example, President Siyad's initial determination to stamp out 'tribalism', or clan identification, could not disguise his own identity as a Marehan, or prevent him looking to the Marehan and other clans to which he was related, as his national authority declined. In Ethiopia, leaders are often difficult if not impossible to place in ethnic terms, and the information may be of little immediate political relevance even if one discovers it. Before the revolution, politicians generally belonged to a well-established group of courtiers, whose origins could be traced through patronage or family links; but the post-revolutionary generation sprang from the anonymity of the armed forces, and their connections are less easy to discover. Similarly in regional and provincial government, the pre-revolutionary officials often had a status in local society which their successors lacked. This means that local residents, let alone foreign researchers, often simply do not know where they come from. One informant in Bale assured me, for example, that the regional chief administrator, Godana Tuni, came from Shoa; I was able to confirm, with reasonable confidence, that he was actually a Boran from southern Sidamo, the only member (to my knowledge) of this particular group to reach any post of prominence in the Ethiopian government. The label 'Shoan' denoted an outsider appointed by a central government which was associated with the central region of Shoa – or perhaps indeed, a person assimilated into a dominant national culture, who might more accurately be regarded simply as 'Ethiopian'.[2]

Similarly at the central level, some people can be classified, either because (like Teka Tulu or Debele Dinsa) they have distinctive names, or because (like two Politbureau members, Fisseha Desta from Tigray and Amanuel Amde-Michael from Eritrea) they have some tacit identification with a particular and politically sensitive region. Sometimes the information happens to emerge, for example that Petros Gebre, a junior Derg member and WPE first secretary of his native province in southern Shoa, is a Kambatta, or that brigadier general Tesfaye Habte-Mariam, the much decorated commander of the airborne division, is a Gurage. But Mengistu Haile-Mariam's own origins, as already noted, are largely conjectural; while those of such a key figure in the regime as Legesse Asfaw, the former sergeant and supposed Soviet protégé who took the major role in setting up the COPWE/WPE organisation, are virtually unknown. Although his name is Amharic, his pudding-faced features are the very antithesis of the classic highland type; some say he is a peasant's son from north-west Shoa, others that he is a tailor's son from Wollo. The chances are that he is Oromo. It does not much matter – but the fact that it does not matter in itself says a great deal about the role of ethnicity in Ethiopia.

Even the armed forces were not totally committed to an undifferentiated Ethiopian nationalism. Some of its members, especially Eritreans, recognised the need for some accommodation with regional identities and demands for autonomy. This was the issue which led to the death of Aman Andom in November 1974. Subsequently, most of the Derg's few Eritrean members defected to the EPLF, and with the assassination in Asmara in January 1977 of naval petty officer Michael Asgedom, not a single Eritrean member of the Derg remained.[3] Quite a number of other officers also defected, though much more often to nationalist opposition movements such as the EDU than to the ethnic or regionalist groups. But the coherence of the armed forces, in the face of political upheaval and continuous civil war, is nonetheless impressive.

The civilian political factions were generally much readier to take up the issue of ethnicity. For the student radical groups from which these factions sprang, the 'national question', as it was soon baptised, was one of the key points of difference from the imperial regime, and was pursued through the intense bickerings of the student organisations in Europe and North America.[4] Several of the leaders of these groups came from non-Amhara peoples (in Meison especially from Oromos, in EPRP from Tigreans), and the national question was a matter of defining their personal status, as well as seeking solutions to national problems. In terms of their common Marxist frame of reference, they could reach agreement on two broad themes. The first was that the repression of nationalities within imperial Ethiopia could be ascribed to the class basis of the regime, and that the removal of class exploitation, most obviously represented by land alienation in the south, was therefore the essential prerequisite for a solution to the problem. In this, there was certainly a good deal of justice, though whether ethnicity could so simply be reduced to class conflict was quite another matter. The second was that 'nationalities' should be recognised, and should be accorded a right to 'self-determination' and an equal place within the Ethiopian state. It was assumed that the removal of class oppression would make this second stage unproblematic. Where they differed was over the issue of whether 'self-determination' should include a specific right to secession. Nationalist Ethiopians, of all political persuasions, are extremely reluctant to concede that anyone, even the Ogaden Somalis, could actually wish to secede from the motherland; secession is almost invariably ascribed to a few malcontents and misled youths egged on by foreign powers. Nonetheless, all of the post-revolutionary political factions went a long way towards conceding a right of secession, at least in principle. Meison, in its programme of March 1975, stated bluntly that 'the right of nationalities to self-determination up to and including secession is recognised'.[5] Both Waz and Seded – particularly surprisingly in this last case, since it was a largely military movement chaired

by Mengistu Haile-Mariam himself – granted a right to secession in principle, while hedging it with practical restrictions. The EPRP proclaimed 'the
right of nations to self-determination without any reservation', the use of the
term 'nation', rather than the usual 'nationality', carrying the implication of
separate national independence.

The first of these themes, that the national question was no more than a
disguised form of class oppression, was one which the Derg could
wholeheartedly accept, and which it put into effect through the land reform
proclamation and the abolition of the cultural and religious trappings of
Amhara supremacy. It was perfectly compatible, after all, with its own
vision of a homogenised Ethiopian nationhood. The second was much more
problematical; it was implicitly opposed to the principles of 'Ityopya
tikdem', and, even if it did not lead to secession, risked the formal entrench-
ment of ethnic identities in a way that could only threaten national unity.
Yet, as the acceptance of the principle of self-determination by Seded
indicates, it was prepared to go a surprisingly long way towards conceding
Ethiopia's ethnic differences.

These concessions were incorporated into the Programme of the National
Democratic Revolution (PNDR), announced in April 1976, which sealed
the alliance between Meison and Mengistu Haile-Mariam's faction of the
Derg. This stated[6]

> The right to self-determination of all nationalities will be recognized and fully
> respected. No nationality will dominate another one since the history, culture,
> language and religion of each nationality will have equal recognition in accord-
> ance with the spirit of socialism. The unity of Ethiopia's nationalities will be
> based on their common struggle against feudalism, imperialism, bureaucratic
> capitalism and all reactionary forces . . .
> Given Ethiopia's existing situation, the problem of nationalities can be
> resolved if each nationality is accorded full right to self-government. This
> means that each nationality will have regional autonomy to decide on matters
> concerning its internal affairs. Within its environs, it has the right to determine
> the contents of its political, economig and social life, use its own language and
> elect its own leaders and administrators to head its internal organs.

This programme evidently stopped a long way short of secession, restricting nationalities to purely 'internal affairs', beneath the umbrella of a single
national government. Like any programme which defined nationality in
terms of culture and language, it also raised special problems in its application to Eritrea, an artificial colonial creation encompassing several
nationalities, the more important of which straddled the border into other
regions of Ethiopia. A rather different problem would accompany its application to Ethiopian Somalis, since the demarcation of a Somali-inhabited
territory would constitute recognition by the Ethiopian government of an
area which could then be claimed by the Somali Republic. Nonetheless, preliminary steps were taken to apply this programme to the Afar or Danakil, a

sparsely scattered people of the Red Sea plains whose territory spread over five administrative regions (Eritrea, Tigray, Wollo, Shoa and Hararghe), as well as the soon to be independent state of Djibouti. An Afar region had the combined advantages of providing a counter-attraction to Djibouti for Ethiopian Afars, and of separating the southern part of the Red Sea coast-line, with its vital port of Assab, from Eritrea. An eight-day meeting of Afar representatives was held at Gewane in April 1977, and called for the estab-lishment of an Afar region in accordance with the PNDR;[7] but the Derg member who chaired the meeting was assassinated on his way back to Addis Ababa, and with the Somali invasion three months later the idea of a separate Afar region was shelved, although Afars continued to serve as local administrators.

The invasion, with the simultaneous defeat of Meison in the internal fight-ing in Addis Ababa, dramatically altered the situation. It gave the Derg a monopoly of Ethiopian nationalism, and may well have proved a critical factor in forging a new sense of nationhood. Although the PNDR remained the authoritative statement of government policy, the pressure to achieve a negotiated solution to the nationalities problem was greatly reduced. Some residual recognition of ethnic and linguistic differences remained, but did not detract from the overwhelming emphasis on centralism. The National Literacy Campaign, though it provided for literacy in other languages, at the same time served especially as a medium for transmitting Amharic. Rep-resentatives of 'minority nationalities' – generally small and distinctive groups, with a hint of the picturesque – received some media coverage on occasions such as the annual Revolution Day celebrations.[8] But talk of regional autonomy, let alone of secession, dropped almost out of sight. Earlier hints of a negotiated settlement to the war in Eritrea were silenced, as the government sought to impose a solution from the centre. The new Workers' Party was organised on strict hierarchical lines; and the resettle-ment programme, which moved hundreds of thousands of people from one side of the country to the other, undercut the whole idea of regions within which the indigenous nationalities could regulate their own affairs. In western Welega and Gojjam, the indigenous peoples were soon heavily out-numbered by settlers.

No further formal approach to the issue of nationalities occurred until the procedures got under way for the establishment of the People's Democratic Republic of Ethiopia, starting with the establishment of the Nationalities Institute in 1983, and the appointment of the Constitutional Drafting Com-mission early in 1986. The Institute was expected to help 'resolve minor contradictions among nationalities', on the principle that 'chauvinism and narrow nationalism must be eliminated',[9] and as these phrases suggest, the latitude open to it was slight. Although the Constitutional Commission's 343 members were heavily dominated by the WPE, they included a sprinkling of individuals who tacitly represented the various nationalities. The use of the constitutional drafting process as a means of trying to reconcile the government's opponents was demonstrated by the widespread consultations over the draft, and especially the enormous amount of effort invested in consultations with Ethiopian communities abroad, which monopolised the attention of leading members of the Politbureau for weeks at a time. The constitution introduced in September 1987 nonetheless had very little to offer, and the 'autonomous regions' for which it provided were entirely subordinate to the national government, which could at will change either their frontiers or their powers. Amharic was denied the formal status of national language, but was designated as the language in which state activities would be conducted.[10] The provision for local autonomy under any 'democratic centralist' system of government is in any event likely to be slight, but the Ethiopian constitution stopped a long way short of the constitution of the USSR, which formally concedes the right of union republics to secede from the Soviet Union. There has been no indication that the Ethiopian government's fundamental commitment to central control might be open to dilution.

REPRESENTATION AND CONTROL IN REGIONAL ADMINISTRATION

The formal structure of local government in Ethiopia did not change in the thirteen years following the revolution, though some changes, notably the establishment of the 'autonomous regions' discussed above, are to be expected following the formal establishment of the PDRE. The existing structure, set up by Haile-Selassie in 1942 after the liberation of the country from Italian occupation the previous year, imposed a uniform hierarchy of administrative units in place of the previous patchwork of traditional provinces. At the top was the administrative region (or *kifle hager*, known until the revolution as a governate general or *teklay gizat*), of which there were fourteen in 1974, excluding Addis Ababa which counted as a region of its own. These varied in size from Hararghe with 254,800 square kilometres (just over the entire land area of the United Kingdom) to Arsi with 24,600;[11] and in 1984 population from Shoa with 8,090,565 inhabitants to Illubabor with 963,327, with a mean population (excluding Addis Ababa) of just over 2,900,000.[12] These were in turn divided into provinces (or awrajas), of which there were 102, with a mean 1984 population of nearly 400,000, varying from 1,330,345 in Sidama province in Sidamo, to 56,127 in Maji and Goldiya in Kaffa. The lowest level of the hierarchy was the district or woreda, of which there were nearly 600.

Like colonial governments in other parts of Africa, the imperial regime found it necessary or expedient to govern at least some of its provinces through dynasties which enjoyed some local authority. In northern Ethiopia, the province of Wag was virtually a hereditary fiefdom under its own ruling family; and in some parts of the south, notably Welega and Jimma, previously independent rulers accepted Ethiopian overlordship in the late nineteenth century, in exchange for recognition of their local status.[13] The Afar sultanate of Awsa remained virtually autonomous until the revolution. This recognition of practical necessities did not, however, develop into a colonial-style ideology of indirect rule. Appointment to governorships was the prerogative of the emperor, which after his restoration in 1941 Haile-Selassie was able to exercise in far less restricted fashion than before. The only important exception to a policy of centralisation which placed Shoan governors over almost every region was in Tigray, which until 1960 was ruled (for much of the period in fairly titular fashion) by the leading member of the regional dynasty, Ras Seyoum, and after his death, much more dynamically, by his son Ras Mengesha. Much of the south, and especially the coffee-growing regions of Kaffa and Sidamo, was ruled in ruthlessly extractive fashion by Addis Ababa noblemen and courtiers, aided by officials who were again largely of Shoan origin.

After the revolution, this policy of central appointment was regarded, with justice, as a form of exploitation which discriminated against the oppressed peripheral nationalities, and alienated them from the national government. The new regime, under the influence of Meison with its high level of Oromo membership, sought to reform regional government by appointing chief administrators (the title which had replaced the old governor general or imperial representative) who originated from the region itself. Many of these, obviously enough, were members or supporters of Meison. Most of them, too, were educated young men of regional origin who had made their careers in Addis Ababa, rather than truly local figures who could be seen as deriving their authority from the indigenous communities themselves. For at least part of the period between 1975 and 1977, all of the major southern regions were governed by chief administrators of local origin: Ahadu Saboure and Abdullahi Bedi in Hararghe, Haile-Yesus Aba-Hassen in Sidamo, Abiyu Geleta in Welega, Ababiya Abajobir in Kaffa – this last being the grandson of the Sheik Abajifar who had governed Jimma before the Italian invasion. A similar process occurred at provincial level, where a high proportion of the administrators appointed from 1975 onwards had names indicating local origin, and presumably at district level as well. In some cases, the Derg found itself appointing to posts in the southern regions men who had been recognised as local leaders by the old regime, and given traditional titles of nobility as a means of binding them to the central government. While in most of the north, traditional titles virtually disappeared as the regional nobility were swept away or discreetly abandoned their titles, in the south (and in Eritrea) they testified to the need of both imperial and revolutionary governments to appeal to the same stratum of local notables. In Hararghe, for example, Dajazmatch Ugaz Hassen Hirsi was recognised as 'representative of the Issa nationality', a Somali clan which the Derg sought, in time-honoured fashion, to win over by according it special privileges vis-à-vis other Somalis.[14] In Illubabor, former Senator Fitawrari Zewde Otoro became regional deputy administrator. In Eritrea, four of the six provincial administrators appointed in 1975–76 had traditional titles of nobility, one of the others being a Moslem.

In Tigray, by contrast, where the regional aristocracy was closely associated with the emperor's grandson-in-law Ras Mengesha, who had taken up arms against the new regime, the new appointees were all commoners. There as in Eritrea, however, they were of local origin, and the same seems to have been true of most of Gonder and Gojjam.

In both north and south, these local appointees were caught between the centralism of the regime on the one hand, and the intensification of local opposition on the other. The great majority lost their posts. Of 169 officials holding posts at regional or provincial level between the outbreak of the revolution and the end of 1976, I have been able to identify only 27, or 16 per cent, as holding any kind of government appointment after the beginning of 1979. Even allowing for natural wastage, and for those who may have escaped notice, the turnover during the traumatic years up to 1978 was enormous. In the north, many of the more traditionalist officials defected to the EDU, including Colonel Imru Wonde, chief administrator of Gonder region in 1976–77. (It is worth noting that this defection did not prevent his brother, Dr Tefera Wonde, from holding high office under the Derg, and becoming WPE first secretary in Eritrea in 1984; it is characteristic not just of the present Ethiopian regime, but of a political structure held together less by kinship than by hierarchical ties between leaders and subordinates, that the defection of an individual does not automatically taint the members of his family.) Others joined the EPLF or TPLF, or were assassinated by them, or were imprisoned by the government because of doubtful loyalties. The EDU had little backing in the south, but the pressures of centralism against localism were no less intense. In Wollaita in Sidamo, the organiser of the land reform campaign was a radical local schoolmaster, Solomon Wada, whose efforts to mobilise the local population against settlers from the centre were interpreted by the government as 'attempts to disturb the revolution', and led to his execution.[15] Many of the local administrators appointed in Oromo regions were associated with Meison, and either fled or were imprisoned or executed once the breach between the Derg and Meison occurred in mid 1977; some joined the Oromo Liberation Front. The outbreak of war with Somalia intensified the pressures, especially on administrators who had favoured local peoples over central immigrants to an extent that was then seen as weakening national resistance and central control. The killing of the chief administrator of Hararghe, Abdullahi Bedi, during a visit to the Ogaden in July 1977, is often ascribed to Ethiopian soldiers rather than the Somali infiltrators on whom it was officially blamed; and the following month the head of POMOA in Hararghe, Abdullahi Yusuf, who was notoriously hostile to Shoan Christian settlers in the region, was assassinated during a visit to Addis Ababa. Here and there, one finds a survivor; Godana Tuni, a meteorologist from Sidamo, became a provincial administrator in Bale early in the revolution, moved after the war to his home province of Borana, and subsequently returned to Bale as chief administrator. But the experiment of trying to marry centralism to localism by appointing administrators to run their own home areas ended abruptly in 1977.

In their place, members of the Derg were from 1978 appointed as chief administrators in every region, save only Eritrea and Tigray which came under direct military administration. One of these, Ali Mussa in Gamu Gofa, was of Moslem origin, while at least one other, Debele Dinsa in Shoa, was Oromo, but their appointment owed nothing to local connections; only in Gonder was a Derg member of local origin, the notoriously brutal Melaku Tefera, put in charge. This regularised the previous system under which Derg members had been 'assigned' on roving commissions to different regions, and in some cases, local men like Beshir Sheik Abdi in Hararghe stayed on as deputy administrators. The overall shift was nonetheless decisively towards the centre. The origins of provincial administrators are much harder to ascertain than those of their regional superiors, since they are generally far less well-known, but a sharp decline can be noted in the proportion with evidently 'ethnic' names.

To some extent, provincial administration continues to provide opportunities for an attenuated form of local representation, as for example in Hararghe where four of the twelve WPE first secretaries in March 1986, and seven of the thirteen provincial administrators, were natives of the region, if not necessarily of the province itself. On the whole, as this example suggests, provincial administrators are more likely to be of local origin than their superiors in the party apparatus, who form part of a nationally circulating elite. In the National Shengo, for example, where some care was taken in the 1987 elections to choose members who had some link with the area they represented, I have been able to identify twenty-one provincial administrators but only eight provincial WPE first secretaries – quite the reverse of what might have been expected. Afars have been appointed to administer Afar areas such as Awsa and Assab, while in Tigray and Eritrea, the need to speak Tigrinya imposes (in addition to more strictly political reasons) a strong incentive to appoint local officials. Even when such officials are not indigenous to the region where they work, they have often lived there for many years, moving around from one government job to another. The administration as a whole is nonetheless centralised, and the bureaucracy in the regional capital is assigned from the centre, with little if any concern for the regional origins of its members. There is thus little base on which a structure of regional autonomy could be built, and little reason to suppose that the 'autonomous regions' provided for by the PDRE constitution could achieve anything but the most formal and symbolic expression of local self-government.

REGIONAL OPPOSITION: THE NORTH

This book does not attempt any detailed analysis of the various resistance movements which, normally under the title of 'liberation fronts' for the ethnic groups or regions concerned, have proliferated both before and since the revolution.[16] Its purpose is simply to place them within the context of the revolution, and more generally the structure of the Ethiopian state. It has already been suggested that the high level of armed opposition to the Ethiopian state derives most basically from the structure of that state itself, intensified by the process of mass political mobilisation which necessarily accompanies revolution. It is nonetheless paradoxical that this opposition should be greatest in northern Ethiopia, including especially the Tigray region which has formed part of the Ethiopian state continuously since the earliest times, rather than in the recently incorporated regions of the south and west. This must in itself cast doubt on explanations of regional conflict which ascribe it simply to ethnic opposition to an Amhara internal colonialism; but it equally makes it necessary to look at the pattern of political incorporation of northern Ethiopia itself, and at the reasons for the evident failures of incorporation in, especially, Eritrea and Tigray.

The Tirginya-speaking areas of northern Ethiopia have historically possessed an intensified sense of regional identity, expressed not only in language, but in differences in customary land tenure, and in adherence to distinctive doctrines within the Orthodox Church. Strategically, the area was a frontier region, since it was there that the Ethiopian highlands came closest to the Red Sea, and to the main Islamic centres of the Sudan. Politically, it was governed very largely through an indigenous aristocracy, which intermarried with the Amhara aristocracy to the south, and intervened readily in national politics, but maintained both a distinctive identity and a high level of factionalism among its own members. Ethiopian emperors normally maintained an indirect control over the area through the manipulation of these local conflicts, a technique which became increasingly difficult with the incursion during the later nineteenth century of successive invaders – British, Egyptian, Mahdist, Italian – whom local lords could look to for support in attempts to retain their autonomy from the central authority.[17] The creation of the Italian colony of Eritrea in 1890 split off the northern tip of the Tigrinya-speaking Christian plateau, which had formed part of Ethiopia since the first emergence of a recognisably Ethiopian state some 2,000 years previously, and joined it to neighbouring Moslem areas, along the Red Sea coastline and across to the Sudanese border near Kassala, which had come under Ethiopian control at some periods but not at others.

Despite its historical and strategic importance, however, the entire northern part of Ethioia has become increasingly peripheralised over the last century. The southward shift of the empire's centre of gravity, from its foundation at Axum to the medieval centre of Lalibela and the late nineteenth century capital of Addis Ababa, is a commonplace of Ethiopian history. The death of the Tigrean emperor Yohannes in 1889, and the division of the Tigrinya-speaking area with the creation of Eritrea, converted a region which might (once in a while, anyhow) provide an emperor, into one in which local notables squabbled for local prizes, and in the process rendered themselves increasingly dependent on either the colonial authorities in Asmara, or the Shoan emperor in Addis Ababa.

Economically, too, the balance shifted, despite the Italian efforts to develop a modern colonial infrastructure in Eritrea. The increasing importance of cash crops for export reduced the role of the northern regions in favour of the forest zones where coffee could be grown, while the centralisation of the transport network on Addis Ababa, with the railway line from there to the coast at Djibouti, undercut the traditional role of the trade routes to Massawa. Eritrea gained from its comparatively high provision of education, and under Haile-Selassie ranked second to Shoa in the number of leading officials which it provided for the central government,[18] but for the most part these simply took the road south, and had little political base in the region they had left. The historic vulnerability of the area to famine, with the post-war decline of highland agriculture and an exceptional level of land degradation, left it increasingly dependent on imported food, while peasants had to travel in search of seasonal work in order to supplement the produce of their own inadequate plots. Continuous emigration, especially from Tigray, was a feature of the area from the later nineteenth century onwards.

This marginalisation of what had once been the core region of Ethiopia goes a long way to explain not only its opposition to central government, but also why the subsequent insurgency has been, from the central government's viewpoint, so manageable. Possessing few if any resources, astride no major trade route, and culturally and politically cut off from the rest of the country, Eritrea and Tigray have been the battlefield of major insurgencies, in one case for over twenty years and in the other for over ten, without seriously threatening the stability or survival of the state. A comparable insurgency in the surplus-producing Oromo regions of the south and west would have been a very different matter.

During Haile-Selassie's reign, it was possible to draw a sharp contrast between the patterns of political incorporation of Tigray on the one hand, and Eritrea on the other. Tigray showed the emperor at the peak of his manipulative skills. Before the war of 1935, he held a balance between the two rival dynasties descended from the emperor Yohannes, matching a similar strategy pursued by the Italians in Eritrea.[19] After it, he was able to oust the faction which had sided with the Italians, defeat a rebellion raised by its supporters with the help of British aircraft, and bring the region under increasing central control, while leaving it under the governorship of its local dynasty. By the later years of the imperial regime, with a dynamic governor drawn from the regional dynasty and married to the emperor's granddaughter, Tigray was politically more stable and quiescent than at any time in the previous eighty years – a success witnessed by the effective insulation of the region from the increasingly violent conflicts in neighbouring Eritrea.[20]

The incorporation of Eritrea was always much more difficult. About half of the population had the historic links with Ethiopia expressed through the

Tigrinya language and the Orthodox Church, while the other and Moslem half did not. The successful campaign to reunite the region with Ethiopia during the postwar disposal of the former Italian colonies drew not only on Haile-Selassie's diplomatic skills – including the exploitation of European guilt over the League of Nations' failure to prevent the Italian invasion of Ethiopia from Eritrea in 1935, and the lease of an important communications base to the United States – but also on the creation of an effective unionist political party, which, though obviously supported by the Ethiopians, had authentic local roots. No formal vote was taken in Eritrea on the United Nations proposal to federate the territory with Ethiopia (under a constitution which provided for a high level of local autonomy, but placed the all-important sovereignty over the area explicitly in Ethiopian hands), and a United Nations mission sent to ascertain the wishes of the inhabitants reached varied conclusions which reflected quite as much the preconceptions of its members as anything which they discovered on the spot. But the unionists won nearly half of the seats in the Eritrean Assembly, and there appears to have been broad support for federation in the highlands, and despite considerable misgivings elsewhere, no sign of violent opposition or the emergence of any composite Eritrean nationalism.[21]

The conversion over the two decades following federation in 1952 of this initial acceptance and partial support for union with Ethiopia, into an armed insurgency which controlled much of the Moslem area and even threatened the highlands, provides the sharpest illustration of the political incapacity of the imperial system of government. Partly, it was the result of a foolish choice of instruments, notably the selection of Ras Andargatchew Massai, a Shoan nobleman with a hectoring manner and no connections with the area, as the first imperial representative in Eritrea. This, however, was no more than the expression of an imperial determination to undermine the locally elected administration and bring the region under central control, rather than (as in Tigray) working through local authority figures and accepting the limitations which this placed on central initiative. And this in turn reflected an unwillingness or inability to do business with party politicians, having at least some electoral base and local organisation, rather than the familiar dynasties of Tigray. In many respects, the Ethiopian destruction of Eritrean autonomy after 1952 mirrors the post-independence assault on federal systems and opposition parties in other African states; the maintenance of separate and potentially competing political authorities calls for a constitutionalist approach to political conflict which no African state has yet been able to establish. The imperial regime, however, was even less able to incorporate a potentially dissident area into the national political system than were the party states in other parts of Africa; while the age-old tensions between centre and periphery in the Ethiopian state itself, coupled with the availability of military and diplomatic support from nearby Moslem states, made armed guerilla opposition a much more viable option than in most of post-colonial Africa.

The revolution not only failed to improve the situation in Eritrea, but also destroyed the linkages between the central government and Tigray. The failure in Eritrea was closely associated with the initial conflicts within the Derg, and the execution of Aman Andom. Even though it was uncertain, and even possibly unlikely, that Aman's proposals for reconciliation in Eritrea would have succeeded, they came at a moment when the new regime had a policy initiative which it was never to regain. Subsequent attempts to resolve the problem, though they were couched in more or less conciliatory terms depending on the relative strengths of the central government and the various Eritrean movements, could only offer a prospect of participation in a centralised system, which the movements could only reject. The conciliatory approach is exemplified by the nine-point peace plan for Eritrea, issued on 16 May 1976.[22] This refers throughout to 'the Administrative Region of Eritrea', making it clear that Eritrea was to be viewed simply as one of the fourteen regions, and does not refer at any point to 'Eritreans', speaking instead of Ethiopians who had, for example, lost property or gone into exile as a result of 'the absence of peace in the Eritrean Administrative Region'. It then offered 'progressive groups and organizations in Eritrea' the opportunity to participate in building an Ethiopian national revolution – a form of words signalling a readiness to make common cause with the EPLF, as the more explicitly 'progressive' of the Eritrean movements, against the more Islamic and Arab-supported ELF. But what was offered was a role in an Ethiopian revolution, rather than any form of autonomy which would give the EPLF the chance to construct an Eritrean one, and even the boundaries of Eritrea itself were not guaranteed, but would be liable to alteration in accordance with the decision of 'the entire Ethiopian people'. Small wonder, then, that the plan was immediately rejected by those to whom it was intended to appeal.

Following the end of the Somali war, and the Ethiopian offensive in the second half of 1978 which brought most of Eritrea (and especially the more densely populated highland areas) back under government control, the idea of reaching any settlement with the EPLF was abandoned. For a time in 1978–79, it seemed that the government offensive might succeed in reoccupying the entire territory, and by June 1979, under the appealing headline 'Days of Remnants of Secessionist Bandits Lurking in Bushes Numbered', the Ethiopian army chief of staff was predicting the imminent end of the war.[23] The government forces were however held up at Nakfa, the EPLF stronghold in the very north of the region, where they remained stuck for the following eight years, while the EPLF (which after 1978 had established itself as overwhelmingly the most effective of the Eritrean movements) launched occasional counter-offensives towards the western lowlands. The most ambitious of the government offensives, the Red Star Multifaceted Revolutionary Campaign, was launched with great publicity in January 1982, and in contrast with the nine-point programme's reference to 'progressive groups', lumped all of the Eritrean movements together as 'anti-freedom, anti-unity, anti-people and anti-peace bandit gangs'.[24] The Red Star campaign sought to combine the military defeat of the EPLF with large-scale rehabilitation and economic development programmes.[25] It seems to have consolidated government control over the highland areas, where the EPLF retains the capacity to make guerilla strikes, though not to maintain permanent control; but it failed in the symbolically important task of taking Nakfa, and the blow to the prestige of the government (and especially of Mengistu, who had taken a prominent personal part in the campaign) was such that no publicity was attached to later attempts to win the war.

There has been no adequate examination of the process by which, during the critical early years of the revolution, political mobilisation in Tigray was directed against the government in Addis Ababa rather than in its support. Such writing as there has been on post-revolutionary Tigray has often been so naively partisan as to fail to recognise that there is even a question to be answered.[26] Some of the ingredients can nonetheless be assembled. The first is that Tigray, like Brittany in the French revolution, remained under the rule of a local petty nobility which lived among the people, and enjoyed an authority which was reinforced by the overlordship of the regional dynasty. It was, in contrast to Eritrea, politically unmobilised territory, and the outbreak of a revolution which threatened not only the political but the religious order as well, could be expected to arouse a hostile response. As in other areas of the northern highlands, land reform would not have led to any substantial improvement in the economic condition of the peasantry, or have aroused mass support for the new regime. But unlike other areas, Tigray had an effective local leadership, in the form of Ras Mengesha and the lesser nobility under him, which immediately declared against the new regime.

This reactionary phase of the Tigrean opposition was however short-lived. Much of Ras Mengesha's authority must have been lost when, with other leaders of the EDU, he took refuge in the Sudan; political authority in high-land Ethiopia characteristically depends both on a leader's ability to protect his followers, and on a high level of face-to-face contact. The EPLF in Eritrea was anxious to spread the insurgency into Tigray to provide a buffer zone for itself, and assisted the formation of a sister organisation, the TPLF, with arms and training. Some of the Marxist ideologues of the EPRP, shattered by the red terror in Addis Ababa, retreated to their home areas in Tigray to start a guerilla insurgency and, failing to sustain themselves as a separate organisation, were defeated and absorbed into the TPLF. Heavy-handed government reaction helped to alienate young educated Tigreans, and to drive people in the countryside into support for the TPLF, which could likewise of course call on the appeal of a separate Tigrean identity.

It may however be a mistake to regard the post-revolutionary political mobilisation in Tigray, and even in Eritrea, as having created a regional nationalism, irrevocably set against any reincorporation into Ethiopia. It is hard to suppose, despite the claims of the opposition movements, that such a nationalism can have entirely displaced a deeply entrenched political culture, nurtured in the factionalism, conflict and warfare which have marked the area over many centuries. Central to such a culture is a need to survive, and hence to accept, for the time being, the authority of whoever is currently able to provide protection. From the fragmentary evidence which I have been able to gain, peasants appear to adapt themselves without great difficulty to a situation in which they may find themselves under the control at one moment of the TPLF, at another of the Ethiopian army. Educated Tigreans, too, are caught in a deep ambivalence between regional and national identities. This is expressed within the TPLF itself in the insistence that the movement is not a secessionist one, but is seeking only regional self-government within Ethiopia. Among Tigrean local administrators working for the national government, it is conversely expressed in sympathies for the TPLF, which lead to frequent purges of officials by the central regime – as in September 1984, when some members even of the Tigrean delegation to the founding congress of the WPE were arrested as suspected TPLF sympathisers. In Eritrea, too, even though the alienation of the population from the regime has lasted longer and drawn on deeper differences than in Tigray, it has still been possible to construct a local administration which is largely Eritrean, and to draw on support for union in at least some areas, such as Seray in the highlands or Barentu in the west. The structure of conflict is very much more fluid than the claims of either side would allow. At the same time, however, the rigid centralism of the national government has prevented it from recognising and responding to this fluidity in the way which the Haile-Selassie regime's treatment of Tigray (though not Eritrea) showed to be most effective.

The regionalist movements, too, have been caught up in the complexities of northern Ethiopian politics, in ways which have affected both their internal unity and their ability to define clear and practicable goals, thus severely limiting their effectiveness. The claims of both Eritrean and Tigrean movements, in contrast to the Somali and Oromo movements of southern Ethiopia, are formally defined in terms of territory rather than ethnicity; each claims to represent the administrative regions of Eritrea and Tigray respectively, and (with some exceptions in the Tigrean case) recognises their existing boundaries. In Eritrea, these boundaries are those of the former Italian colony, and the various Eritrean movements all seek (at least as an optimum solution) the 'normal' post-colonial settlement of independent statehood within the existing colonial frontiers, setting aside in the process the decision of the United Nations General Assembly which assigned sovereignty over the area to Ethiopia. The problem with this solution, and indeed one of the reasons why it was not implemented by the United Nations in the first place, lies in the political, ethnic and economic fragmentation of Eritrea. Intended by the Italians merely as a jumping-off point for the control of the entire Ethiopian plateau, it had no economic rationale independent of Ethiopia, and contains, even for an artificial colonial creation, an exceptional level of ethnic diversity. This in turn has been reflected, not only in the readiness of part of the region to accept incorporation into Ethiopia, but also in intense divisions among the groups seeking independence. It was these divisions which led to the failure of the independence movement at the critical moment, in 1977–78, when success seemed to be within its grasp.[27] Since that time, the Eritrean resistance has been consolidated by the victory of the EPLF over its local rivals, but the opportunity to gain independence has simultaneously disappeared.

The Tigrean movement does not have the same level of internal division, because of the greater ethnic coherence of the area which it claims, though it is not entirely free of the endemic factionalism of Tigrean politics. At the same time, it is obliged to base its claims on the established administrative boundaries, rather than on any idea of a historic Tigrean nation, because any such ethnic appeal would entail inclusion of the Tigrinya-speaking people of Eritrea, and thus lock it into an irreconcilable conflict with the much more powerful Eritrean movement, to which it has historically been subordinate; it would also deny it the large area of Tigray region which is inhabited by non-Tigrinya speakers. This in turn creates a 'national problem' within Tigray itself, due to the presence of minority groups such as the Afar and Saho which the TPLF seeks to incorporate into a Tigray nation – a local example of an inherent problem which has afflicted African secessionist movements from Biafra onwards.[28] The uneasy relationship with Eritrea likewise underlies another problem for the TPLF, derived from the fact that the Tigray region has no external boundaries, either to the Red Sea or to the Sudan, but is entirely surrounded by other regions of Ethiopia. At a practical level, this means that EPLF acquiescence is required to move people and material through Eritrea to Tigray, and intensifies TPLF dependence on its northern counterpart. More generally, the TPLF needs to define Tigray in such a way as to gain external access, and the two geographically most appropriate ways of doing so, by claiming a corridor to the Red Sea at Tiyo or Merse Fatma on the one hand, or to the Sudan between the Gash and Setit rivers on the other, are both closed off because they form part of Eritrea. The TPLF has therefore instead claimed part of northern Gonder, asserting entirely fictitiously that for a couple of years in the early 1940s this was administered as part of Tigray.[29] It has claimed Wag in northern Wollo on the same grounds.

But the major problem for the TPLF derives from the ambiguity of its aims. As already noted, it does not formally seek secession, and since Tigray has formed part of Ethiopia since antiquity, it could not claim that post-colonial independence which the EPLF seeks for Eritrea. At the same time, it is engaged in continuous warfare with the Ethiopian government in the name of a regional autonomy which cannot be defined, and which it is extremely hard to envisage being realised. On the other side, differences of objective, of tactics and implicitly of territorial definition involve it in an uneasy relationship with the EPLF, which at times breaks into open conflict. The EPLF, for example, strongly disapproved of the TPLF decision to respond to the 1984 famine by evacuating the population *en masse* to the Sudan – a decision no less ruthless than the Ethiopian government's resettlement scheme, and dictated by the need to retain control over a population which would otherwise have had to seek food from the Ethiopian authorities. More general differences have been raised by the role of the Soviet Union, and the issue of self-determination for nationalities (such as the Afar) within Eritrea. By 1986, the breach between the two movements was open and intense.[30] Whether or not this was to prove permanent – and reconciliation could equally result from the requirements of a changing situation – it reflected conflicts inherent in northern Ethiopian politics.

A further important aspect of the conflicts in northern Ethiopia derives from the juxtaposition of a Marxist–Leninist regime originating in a seizure of power at the centre on the one hand, with Marxist–Leninist opposition movements seeking to gain power through rurally-based guerilla warfare on the other. It is, as much as anything, the opposition to it of movements recognised as Marxist–Leninist which has led many Western Marxists to deny such recognition to the central government. This study is not concerned to award points for authenticity or ideological correctness to any of the contestants, all of which take their Marxist credentials very seriously and seek to implement them in practice. Its interest is in the points of divergence and convergence which result. The most evident divergences come from obvious differences of political situation. Controlling a national power structure, and enjoying the privileged access of a formally constituted government to external support, the Ethiopian regime is able to reach its decisions by central diktat, and implement them through the military, the bureaucracy, and a highly centralised Leninist party. Lacking such advantages, the regional movements can only maintain themselves through much closer links with the peasantry. Such links cannot be assumed to be voluntary or democratic. The regional movements need to recruit soldiers, extract what surplus they can in goods and services, and discipline opponents, no less than the central government. The EPLF especially is noted for the ruthlessness of its internal security apparatus.[31] Their leadership – as seems to be universal in such cases – is drawn from a comparatively educated group of Tigreans and Eritreans who have set about organising the local population in accordance with their own ideological precepts, rather than springing spontaneously from the peasantry themselves. But they must be much closer to the local population than is the central regime, because they are much more dependent on it. They are able to adapt their programmes, such as land reform, to the values and requirements of their specific population, rather than seeking to implement national plans on a uniform basis from a distant centre. Most of all, they are able to present themselves as authentically indigenous, and to cement their alliance with the population through constant contact and common exposure to government reprisals. The capacity of the EPLF and TPLF to survive in the face of an Ethiopian army several hundred thousand strong, and backed by the Soviet Union, is sufficient evidence of their effectiveness. Even though they rely on their supply lines through the Sudan, and their fortunes tend to rise and fall with the level of Sudanese support or acquiescence, their organisation on the ground must be, by far, the most important source of their strength.

At the same time, the points of convergence between Eritrean and Tigrean Marxism–Leninism on the one hand, and the Ethiopian national version on the other, are also very marked. Both draw on the organisational capacities of a hierarchically ordered society based on arable agriculture. The contrast between the EPLF's explicit Marxism–Leninism and the rival ELF's tendency to turn to Islamic and Arab nationalism, may be due not only to the latter's need for Arab financial support, but also to the highland peasantry's greater willingness and capacity to operate a tight Leninist organisational structure. The EPLF's insistence on organisation is as great as the Ethiopian government's.[32] In formal ideological terms, the two sides appear to be remarkably similar, with differences springing largely from an evident need to adapt a common rhetoric to opposing political positions. Lefort describes the soldiers on each side in the Eritrean trenches listening with interest to the ideological indoctrination being broadcast across no-man's-land.[33] Even more striking is the similarity between the programmes which each side seeks to implement in the areas under its control. Each has its land reform, which inevitably involves the more or less equal distribution of existing land among a given population, and seeks to overcome the problems of small-scale peasant agriculture through cooperativisation.[34] Each has its peasants' associations, though the capture by one side of territory previously held by the other involves the dissolution of the old associations, and the erection of new ones. Each has its health and literacy programmes (with similar problems of minority languages), and its public works for soil conservation. Most strikingly of all, each has reacted to agrarian degradation in the highlands, by introducing resettlement schemes to move peasants to more sparsely inhabited lowland regions towards the Sudanese frontier; and just as one aim of the Ethiopian government's programme is to bring such frontier districts under closer government control, so too the regional movements use resettlement to bring their strategically vital borderlands under the occupation of their core highland supporters. But convergence is one thing; compromise is another. And if the key function of Marxist–Leninist organisation is to establish and reinforce control over a centralised state structure, then similarity of policies serves only to entrench political conflict.

Opposition to the central government in the Amhara areas of the highland plateau has attracted much less attention than that of the Tigrinya-speaking areas. This opposition has not been so great, and has nowhere reached the level of sustained organisation and territorial control found in Eritrea and Tigray. It has however been far from absent, providing further confirmation

213

that opposition cannot be seen simply in terms of the stereotype of ethnic resistance to Amhara government. From the viewpoint of the northern Amhara, indeed, especially in Gonder, the dominant Shoan political centre is scarcely regarded as Amhara at all, and Shoans are often referred to contemptuously as 'Galla'.[35] The marginalisation and sense of alienation of an area which until the later nineteenth century itself formed the core of the Ethiopian political system is scarcely less than that of Tigray. The most active of the opposition movements in Amhara territory has been the Ethiopian People's Democratic Movement, or EPDM, which represents a southward extension of the TPLF, just as that in turn had been set up with the help of the EPLF; it likewise drew on refugees from the EPRP.[36] This operates in much of Gonder, and across into northern Wollo, with a lower level of activity in Gojjam and even northern Shoa. It claimed in mid 1985 to control about a million people, and though this total may well be highly exaggerated, its influence could be greatly increased as the result of government attempts to extend the villagisation programme into the highland regions.

REGIONAL OPPOSITION: THE SOUTH

Paradoxically, the issue of 'nationalities' has been much less immediate and intense in southern Ethiopia than in the north. Although most of what is now southern Ethiopia was definitively incorporated into the Ethiopian state only about a century ago (Jimma, the key commercial centre of the southwest, was conquered in 1881, Harar in the south-east in 1887), although much of the area is Moslem and thus sharply differentiated in religious terms from the Christian core, and although the Ethiopian occupation in most areas was unquestionably exploitative, its incorporation into revolutionary Ethiopia has for the most part proved much less problematic than that of the northern provinces which formed part of historic Ethiopia, and which had no such history of exploitation or religious subordination.

In attempting to explain this phenomenon, and in turn the survival of Ethiopia through its post-revolutionary traumas, the pastoralists must be treated separately. Thinly scattered over a large part of Ethiopia's territory (some 60 per cent, if all of the various groups are put together), they simply cannot muster the force to challenge a state based on the areas of settled agriculture, unless they receive substantial external help and the central government is itself severely weakened. Both of these conditions were met at the time of the Somali war of 1977–78, but since the Somali defeat, the guerillas of the Western Somali Liberation Front (WSLF), supported at times by the regular Somali government forces, have presented no serious threat. The Somalis are not only, by far, the largest pastoralist group, but are also the only one with access to an independent state governed by their own people. Although no Ethiopian government can expect to secure permanent Somali allegiance, the Derg has made efforts to favour the Issa clan, in the area bordering Djibouti, and has promoted a number of other Somalis to high (if titular) positions. Following the Somali defeat in 1978, and the emergence of clan-based domestic opposition to the Siyad regime, the Ethiopians lent support to both the Somali National Movement (SNM) and the Somali Salvation Democratic Front (SSDF), which counterbalanced Somali government support for the WSLF.[37]

The Afar have a more tenuous link with the Republic of Djibouti, which has a large Afar population but an Issa-dominated government. The Ethiopian government has attempted both to sedentarise the Afar, and to incorporate them into the national political system through indigenous party representatives and local administrators, whose willingness to cooperate with the regime derives in large part from divisions within Afar society. The former Sultan of Awsa and traditional Afar leader, Ali Mirah, took refuge abroad after the brutal suppression of a revolt in the mid 1970s, and Afar guerillas occasionally attack the state farms in the Awash valley, or mine the vital road to the port of Assab; an Afar Liberation Front was set up by Ali Mirah's son, with Somali support. The central government has however exploited both traditional divisions, and the uneasy relations between the Afar and the Eritrean movements to the north and the Somalis to the south. It used the sons of a former sultan, deposed by Ali Mirah, to provide a counterweight to the ousted ruler, and induced some of the younger radical Afars, gathered into the Afar National Liberation Movement, to seek an autonomous Afar administration within the Programme of the National Democratic Revolution. This was of vital importance in securing Afar acquiescence, and hence access to the port of Assab, during the war of 1977–78. It also provided a buffer against the EPLF, whose insistence on the territorial integrity of Eritrea would subordinate Afars in the coastal zone to control from Asmara. The Afar-inhabited Assab province was separated from the rest of Eritrea, and an ANLM leader appointed as its adminis-trator.[38] The third major pastoralist group, the Boran in Sidamo, were driven into the arms of the Ethiopian government by their opposition to Somali expansion, exacerbated by harsh treatment at the hands of the Somali invaders in 1977–78; it was for this reason that the government was able to appoint a Boran as governor of the Borana province after the defeat of the invasion.

In the agricultural areas of the south, land reform must obviously be ascribed a vital part in retaining local allegiance, especially during the critical early years of the revolution. During that period, too, with the Oromo-dominated Meison enjoying considerable influence in Addis Ababa, the regime was often regarded as an Oromo one, and this must have helped to secure Oromo support, just as its anti-Christian reputation and the defeat of the EPRP helped to foster opposition in Tigray. But an equally important reason was the difficulty of finding any social or political base on which a coherent opposition movement could be founded. The Oromo are by far the most important ethnic group in southern Ethiopia, and are represented in every region of the country save only Eritrea and Gonder; they are the single most populous group in most of the regions from Welega, Shoa and Hararghe southwards, and indeed in Ethiopia as a whole. Oromos have a common history of central domination and exploitation; they have some sense of common identity, which in turn was intensified by the revolution; and they have at least the makings of a guerilla opposition movement, the Oromo Liberation Front (OLF). If Ethiopia were to break apart, or if any serious insurgency was to operate in the southern regions, Oromo opposition in one form or another would have to be at the base of it.

From the mid 1960s onwards, attempts were made by educated Oromos to articulate this awareness of domination into an Oromo ethnic nationalism. In 1966, an attempt to establish an Oromo cultural and development association, called Metcha Tulama, had been suppressed by the imperial regime, and for several years in the late 1960s, an insurgency with at least some elements of Oromo identity occurred in northern Bale under the leadership of a local notable called Wako Guto. A document entitled *The Oromos: Voice against Tyranny* was published clandestinely in Addis Ababa (called by its original Oromo name, Finfine) in 1971,[39] and the OLF dates the start of its own armed struggle from an incident in the Chercher province of Hararghe in 1974.[40] Over the next few years, indigenous Moslems, including the chief administrator Abdullahi Bedi and the POMOA leader Abdullahi Yusuf, took over as government representatives in Hararghe, and by disarming the Christian settlers in the region and pursuing land reform, carried out many of the policies which the OLF had been formed to fight for. The result, however, was not to produce that loyalty of equal nationalities to a common Ethiopian identity which proponents of the reform had expected. Both of the Abdullahis were widely (though perhaps falsely) suspected of collusion with the Somalis, and at the time of the war the Kotu Oromo people in the area around Harar were said to have sided, initially at least, with the invaders.[41] At the same time, however, the Ethiopian army which contained and ultimately defeated the invasion itself had a very substantial Oromo component.

Underlying this absence of any united Oromo action at the time of the crisis of the regime in 1977–78 was the difficulty of identifying any politically coherent Oromo identity, and the same problem has likewise reduced the effectiveness of the OLF since that time. Any national or ethnic identification, obviously enough, means different things in different contexts. But these differences have, for the Oromo, been such as to prevent any effective organisation from emerging at all. In Wollo and Tigray, the Oromo are largely Moslem and occupy a buffer zone between the Amhara and Tigreans of the highlands and the Afar of the Red Sea plains; but the religious differences are not acute, an appreciable amount of interreligious and interethnic marriage takes place (it is not unusual to find people in Wollo with a Christian name and Moslem patronymic, and vice versa), and there seems to have been little articulation of a separate Oromo political identity; Oromo

Wollo leaders under the imperial regime enjoyed equal access with Christian Amhara to the highest positions of power, and since the revolution Ali Mussa, one of the most ruthless of the Derg's regional bosses, has likewise come from this area. In Shoa, the social and economic subordination of Oromo to Amhara has been more marked than in Wollo, and from this viewpoint the potential for Oromo nationalism is greater; but at the same time, the central position of Shoa in the modern Ethiopian state has given local Oromo (who comprise by far the greater part of the region's population) an opportunity to benefit from that position on something approaching equal terms. Mostly Christian, and often possessing Amhara names and patronymics, they may be all but indistinguishable from Amhara, and often intermarry with them. They have sometimes been referred to as Oromo-speaking Amhara, and when in regions such as Hararghe, Oromos on the one hand are contrasted with 'Shoans' on the other, these Shoans are much more likely than not to be Oromo themselves, though they readily identify themselves as Amhara.

Hararghe in turn presents the starkest picture of a Moslem Oromo peasantry, which can be sharply divided from a class of Christian central settlers; in so far as a 'Northern Irish' model can be applied to Ethiopian ethnicity, this is the closest approximation to it. Anyone with a Moslem name in Hararghe will probably be indigenous, whereas anyone with a Christian name will certainly be an immigrant, and little of the mingling found in Wollo has taken place. Something of this pattern may be found in the neighbouring regions of Arsi and Bale, and across into Kaffa and Illubabor; but, speaking very generally, these were mostly regions of landlord rather than settler agriculture, in which the distinction between 'Oromo' on the one hand, and 'Amhara' or 'Shoan' on the other, broadly corresponded to one between local cultivators and low-level notables, and the agents of the state, including virtually all government employees, the agents of Shoan landlords, and the Church.[42] Even poor Christian Oromo tenant farmers from the north, however, became increasingly differentiated from local Oromo pastoralists, and no common Oromo identity resulted.[43] The connections between Islam and Oromo ethnicity become weaker as one moves westward across southern Ethiopia, though in some areas a process of Islamisation has occurred in very recent times. Finally, Welega in the far west provides a different pattern again; incorporated into the Ethiopian empire under the control of local rulers, it was spared the more extreme forms of central exploitation, and maintained its own local landlord class, which intermarried with the rest of the population.[44] Since religious control had been pre-empted neither by Islam nor by the Ethiopian Orthodox Church, it was also the major region for foreign missionary activity, which led both to an exceptionally high level of education and to the foundation of the Ethiopian Lutheran church, Mekane Yesus, which was particularly strong in the region. This social and educational background meant in turn that Welega provided a high proportion of the identifiably Oromo officials

217

in central government, and ranked in that respect way ahead of the other southern regions.[45]

Translated into political terms, these regional differences account both for different relationships with the central government, and, even where it is an important force, for different conceptions of Oromo nationalism. For a start, it is clear that any Oromo nationalism, like its Somali equivalent, must be based on some concept of common ethnicity, and (unlike Eritrea or Tigray) cannot draw on claims for the autonomy of any existing adminis-trative unit. Although Oromo are spread across twelve of Ethiopia's administrative regions, only the smallest of them, Arsi, has an exclusively Oromo indigenous population. Historically, the intellectual leadership of Oromo nationalism has tended to come from Welega, and to press for some kind of Pan-Oromo political unit. While Oromo identity was often locally associated with Mekane Yesus (one of the main OLF leaders in Welega was the brother of a Mekane Yesus pastor), this was not a connection of any value beyond the region itself, and religion was for Welega Oromos some-thing that divided Oromos rather than uniting them. The northern Oromos (those from Welega, Shoa and Wollo) also have something of the Tigrean ambivalence towards the Ethiopian state. Not only is secession a much less evidently viable proposition for them than for Oromos further south, but they have occupied leading positions in the state (and indeed continue to do so), and have to balance the advantages of separatism against those of participation.

The sense of alienation from Ethiopian government has in contrast been most intense in Hararghe, where the lines of ethnicity, religion and exploitation have coincided, and where the religious factor has not only differentiated the indigenous from the settler population within the region, but also provided a link with external assistance from across the Somali frontier. Despite these connections, though, the relationship between Oromo and Somali is ambivalent, and any common cause that the two peoples can make against the central government is easily dissipated by their rivalries with one another. Wako Guto, leader of the Bale revolt in the 1960s, started an organisation in 1975 called the Somali Abo Liberation Front, which coined the artificial 'Somali Abo' identity, referring to the Oromo of Bale, Sidamo and Arsi, in order to emphasise the similarities between them and the Somali, and appeal for Somali support.[46] But this label, which clearly subordinated the Oromo to the demands of Somali expansion, was rejected by most of the south-eastern Oromo, for whom Somali expansion had been no less of a threat than central Ethiopian domi-nation. Any initial sympathies which the Oromo people of the area felt for the Somali invaders in 1977–78 were dissipated both by the behaviour of the troops on the ground, and by Somali claims that 'Western Somalia' extended north to the Awash river and into the Bale highlands, thus encompassing large areas inhabited by Oromo and Afar.[47] After their defeat, the Somalis moderated their demands and allowed the OLF to open an office in

Mogadishu, but the alliance was no more than tactical, and the office was later closed. Even those Oromo groupings which oppose both the Somalis and the Ethiopian central government are divided among themselves. The best known of the Hararghe Oromo opposition leaders, Sheik Jarra, split away from the main Welega-led OLF to press for a Moslem Oromo state, reaching only as far north as the Awash river and including Hararghe, Bale and Arsi, while excluding the Oromo of Welega, Kaffa and most of Shoa. This group is said to have been responsible for occasional hit-and-run incidents in the Habro and Garamuleta provinces of Hararghe. Other Oromos are caught not simply between these rival tendencies, but between them and the central government, in which as already noted a large number of Oromos occupy positions at every level from the Politbureau downwards. In these circumstances, it is not surprising that the OLF has failed to achieve either the military organisation or the territorial control of its counterparts in Tigray and Eritrea.

The Oromo threat cannot, nonetheless, be entirely dismissed. Ethnic solidarity has a persistence as a political rallying cry which can never be discounted, and which is always liable to be mobilised in response to some often fortuitous set of political circumstances. It would have been difficult to predict, for example, that the Eritrean resistance movement could have attained the strength which it has shown since the revolution, in a territory lacking historical, ethnic or religious unity. Oromo resistance must ultimately depend on the balance between alienation and control in the countryside of southern Ethiopia, and hence as much as anything on government agricultural policy. Once again, the villagisation campaign, which seeks to increase control at the expense of an inevitably increased alienation, may well prove to be the touchstone of central government success or failure.

9

The external politics of revolution

Revolution inevitably threatens and involves the international as well as the domestic political order. Revolutionary states cast their appeal in terms of universal values – the rights of man, the workers of the world, even Shi'ite Islam – which extend beyond their frontiers. The initial period of uncertainty and upheaval, coupled with the revolution's threat to their own stability, often prompts invasion by neighbouring states. And in a world characterised by superpower alliance systems drawn up partly at least on ideological lines, revolution has an almost automatically destabilising effect on global alignments.

The role of the international system in the Ethiopian revolution has been critical, though it has nonetheless been secondary. It has been critical, in that at certain key moments, and notably at the time of the Somali invasion of 1977–78, and the great famine of 1984–85, the revolutionary regime has been sustained, and in all probability saved, by a massive infusion of resources from abroad – in the one case of Soviet arms, in the other of Western food. It has however been secondary, in that these external resources have been subordinated to domestic political control, and used to maintain a revolutionary process and political organisation, the origins of which have again been very largely domestic. Pre-revolutionary Ethiopian rulers had similarly used external support to maintain a domestic political structure.

All African states ultimately depend for their maintenance on their relationships with the outside world, and Ethiopia is no exception. Like other African states, it depends on the revenue generated by the sale of its primary products on the international market, and on the corresponding import of the goods and expertise which are needed to maintain the state structure. Where Ethiopia differs sharply from other sub-Saharan African states is in the indigenous origin of the state itself, and the control of its incorporation into the global economy and the structure of international alliances by an indigenous ruling group.[1] Whereas other African states came to independence as artificial units created by an external colonialism, the Ethiopians were able to expand and consolidate their own state, by using external aid in conjunction with an existing political structure and its capacity for large-scale military and political organisation. The most important form of aid was of course military. As long ago as the 1540s, the Ethiopians ultimately defeated a catastrophic Moslem invasion, with the help of a small contingent of Portuguese soldiers armed with matchlocks – the Cubans of their day. In a more systematic way, the expansion of Ethiopian territory in the second half of the nineteenth century, with the matching increase in the power of the central government over its provincial subordinates, was directly derived from the ability of the Ethiopians, and within Ethiopia of the emperor, to establish the diplomatic contacts with the outside world which led to the import of arms. But this acquisition of fire-arms would not in itself have led to the consolidation of the modern Ethiopian state, without the indigenous capacity to organise and control large numbers of men; and the import of Soviet weapons in 1977–78 was likewise able to save the regime, only because of its own ability to raise the huge armies which were to use them. Without access to external weapons, however, as at the time of the Italian invasion in 1935–36, even a high level of organisational capacity has not been enough.

On his return from exile in 1941, therefore, Haile-Selassie set about con-structing a set of military, diplomatic and economic linkages through which the Ethiopian state could be sustained. The key to this system was the American alliance. Under wartime and immediate post-war conditions, Ethiopia needed a counterweight to the United Kingdom, which then con-trolled all the territory surrounding Ethiopia (save only Djibouti), and posed a threat both through the British administration of Eritrea, and through proposals to unite all of the Somali peoples into a common political unit, which would have included the large Somali-inhabited area of Ethiopia which was then under temporary British administration. Haile-Selassie cemented the American alliance by sending Ethiopian troops to fight in the UN force in Korea (in accordance with the doctrine of collective security to which he had vainly appealed in 1936), and by leasing the vital Kagnew com-munications base near Asmara to the United States; he received in return the essential American support for the union of Eritrea with Ethiopia. Shortly afterwards, a set of military assistance agreements provided for US training and weapons for the Ethiopian army.[2] The military relationship was supplemented by US development aid, by a large American presence in the educational system (especially from the early 1960s, when the secondary schools became heavily dependent on Peace Corps volunteers), and by the position of the United States as the principal market for Ethiopian coffee. But although Ethiopia became by far the largest recipient of US military aid in sub-Saharan Africa, the United States did not attain a level of penetration

221

which in any way matched the role of the ex-colonial metropoles in their former African colonies. This was due partly to the inherent impenetrability of Ethiopia itself, partly to the absence of any serious economic stake in the country, and partly to deliberate efforts on the part of the Ethiopian government to diversify its sources of external dependence.

When from the early 1960s onwards Ethiopia once again faced an external military threat, through the emergence of a Somali government bent on the unification of all Somali peoples into a single state, this was slotted into the pattern of external alliances already established. Since the Somali project challenged the existing political order not only in American-protected Ethiopia, but also in British-protected Kenya and French Djibouti, the Somalis faced a combined Western commitment to the territorial status quo, which could only be countered by an alliance with the Soviet Union. From 1963 onwards, the Russians armed and trained the Somali army. This alliance was intensified after 1969, when the Somali *coup* brought to power a government based on the section of Somali society, the army, with which the Russians already had the closest connections, and led to the formation of a regime which proclaimed itself to be Marxist–Leninist. From the mid 1960s, the Ethiopians were also threatened by the Eritrean separatist movements, which were not formally supported by the Soviet Union, but which received aid from radical Arab states allied with the Russians, and from a few other socialist states including Cuba. Nonetheless, so long as the regionally dominant superpower, the United States, remained allied with the regionally dominant African state, Ethiopia, the underlying situation was stable.

This stability was reinforced by the extraordinary success with which Ethiopia responded to the eruption onto the African diplomatic scene of a mass of newly independent post-colonial states. At first glance, these states might have been expected to have far less in common with the anachronistic Ethiopian empire than with a Somali state using the rhetoric of unity, anti-colonialism and self-determination. Certainly Haile-Selassie could draw on a general African pride in Ethiopia's achievement as the sole African state to retain its independence through the colonial era, as well as on his own prestige as the elder statesman of the continent, dating back in particular to his resistance to Italian aggression in 1935–36. But more than that, he was able to recognise Ethiopia's shared interests with the great majority of the newly independent states in maintaining national sovereignty and the territorial status quo, in opposition both to the Somali attempt to redraw the existing boundaries, and to Nkrumah's aspirations for continental government.[3] His success was embodied in the Organisation of African Unity, founded and headquartered in Addis Ababa, and based on the principles of respect for existing boundaries and non-interference in the domestic affairs of other states. Ethiopia's military alliance with the United States was thus backed by her position at the core of the African diplomatic consensus.

REVOLUTION AND THE REVERSAL OF ALLIANCES

The dramatic series of events which culminated in the reversal of super-power alliances in the Horn of Africa and the Ethio–Somali war of 1977–78 have been the subject of an enormous literature, and will not be examined in any detail here.[4] I am concerned only to outline the pattern of events, and to fit this into a general analysis of revolutionary Ethiopia. Even before the revolution, the Ethio–American alliance was already under strain. The intensification of Soviet–Somali relationships after the 1969 *coup* had led to a sharp increase in Soviet arms supplies to Somalia, which called in Ethiopian eyes for a matching escalation in US military support. The United States was extremely reluctant to give this support, in the climate of withdrawal from global commitments associated with the Vietnam war, while the value of the bargaining counter provided by the Kagnew communications base was being rapidly reduced by the advent of satellite technology. In addition, the Americans had to make provision for their position in Ethiopia after the demise of Haile-Selassie, whose reign by the early 1970s was evidently coming to an end. This led them to press for reforms, especially in agriculture, while trying to reduce their overt support for the regime, so as not to prejudice their position with its successor. It also meant that in the initial phases of the revolution, which in one form or another they had certainly expected, American hostility to the new regime was muted. One result of the secrecy, obscurity and factionalism which accompanied the first years of the revolution was that the ultimate course which the regime might take was very hard to predict, and all the normal canons of diplomacy suggested that it was wiser to try to build up working relationships with the new regime, than to take a stance of overt opposition which might drive it into the arms of the Soviet Union. In any event, since Ethiopia continued to rely on the United States for arms with which to defend itself against a potential enemy which was already closely allied with the USSR, it could plausibly be supposed that the Ethio–American alliance would be sustained for reasons of simple national security, regardless of the change of regime in Addis Ababa; US arms supplies to Ethiopia sharply increased from 1974, though much of this equipment came in the form of cash sales rather than outright grants, and also included deliveries of material ordered by the imperial government.[5] The strains in the relationship were nonetheless demonstrated by hostile American reactions to some of the measures taken by the new Ethiopian government, notably the execution of the leading members of the old regime in November 1974, and the disastrous peasant march on Eritrea in mid 1976 – reactions interpreted from the Ethiopian side as unwarranted interference in Ethiopia's domestic affairs. These strains were inevitably exacerbated by the increasing concern for 'human rights' issues in American foreign policy, culminating in the election of President

Carter in November 1976. Despite American efforts to cling on to the alliance, notably through the supply of sophisticated military aircraft, it was doomed by the contradictory demands being made on it from each side: the Ethiopians wanted a level of armaments that the United States could not provide; the Americans wanted concessions on domestic policy which the Derg could not accept.[6]

At the same time, the links which were eventually to be decisive were being built up with the Soviet Union. These links date from very early in the revolution; they were heavily oriented towards the military; and the initiative for them seems to have come largely from the Ethiopian side. Even though much of the early Marxist rhetoric of the regime came from civilian ideologues, few of these had any connection with the Soviet Union, one of the exceptions being Alemu Abebe, a Russian-trained veterinarian, Meison member, mayor of Addis Ababa during the red terror, and subsequently member of the WPE Politbureau; a few others, including Ashagre Yigletu minister of commerce from 1977 and subsequently WPE secretary for foreign affairs) were Yugoslav-trained. Many of the civilian Marxists were attracted more to China than to the Soviet Union, on the reasonable grounds that the Chinese experience might have more to offer to an agricultural country, and as late as September 1976 the death of Chairman Mao evoked fulsome tributes in the Ethiopian press.[7] Nonetheless, the faction within the Derg associated with Mengistu Haile-Mariam established connections with the USSR at least from late 1974, when Soviet sources referred to Mengistu as the leader of the 'revolutionary democratic' nucleus within the PMAC;[8] early in 1975, a group including three subsequent WPE Politbureau members (Fikre-Selassie Wogderes, Addis Tedla, and Legesse Asfaw) went on the first political education course to the Soviet Union.[9] It is certainly possible that personal links between Mengistu and the Russians may date back to the foundation of the Derg. By the end of 1977, several thousand military personnel had been on training courses to the USSR and Eastern European states, including East Germany, Bulgaria, Czechoslovakia and also Yugoslavia. These formed the core of the Seded group organised by Legesse Asfaw.[10]

The Russian connection was also strengthened by the ruthless purges inside the Derg. Aman Andom was a familiar and moderate general, who had been working with Western military advisers for over thirty years, and could only be reassuring to the West. After his death in November 1974 the position was much more uncertain, but the Americans seem to have pinned many of their hopes on Major Sisay Habte, a leading figure in the Derg who is sometimes regarded as one of its first and most committed Marxists, but who also evidently tried to prevent any close alignment with the Soviet Union;[11] he was executed in July 1976. Finally, the killing of Teferi Banti in February 1977 replaced an uneasy triumvirate, with its opportunities for international as well as domestic manoeuvre, by the unchallenged control of the Ethiopian leader most evidently committed to the Soviet alliance. There is no convincing evidence of direct Soviet bloc involvement in any of these deaths, but the fact that Mengistu received the congratulations of the Soviet and Cuban ambassadors on the very day after Teferi's death, and before he had even been formally elevated to the chairmanship of the PMAC, indicates that he was already well-established as a Russian ally.[12]

But while the Ethiopians evidently needed the Soviet Union, as the only plausible alternative to an American alliance to which the leadership of the Derg was becoming increasingly hostile, it was by no means clear that the Russians needed Ethiopia. Essentially, three issues were at stake. The first was whether Ethiopia could be regarded as a state of authentically 'socialist orientation'. The second was whether both the Ethiopian state itself, and the current leadership of it, could be expected to survive, and if so, to maintain a reliably pro-Soviet stance. The third was whether an alliance with Ethiopia would endanger the Soviet Union's close relationship with the Somali Republic, and if so, whether it was worth making the switch. The answers to all these questions proved to be positive. The issue of socialist orientation was evidently not resolved with the great reforms of 1975, but seems to have been considerably eased by the issuing of the Programme of the National Democratic Revolution in April 1976.[13] The Russians were also struck by the numerous parallels between the experiences of Ethiopia and those of Russia itself; with its Orthodox and imperial inheritance, its hierarchical social structures and Byzantine political processes, even its agrarian and national questions, Ethiopia provided much more reassuring and familiar ground than the nomadic and egalitarian Somali alternative.[14] Nonetheless, a critical obstacle remained, in the absence until 1984 of any Marxist–Leninist party. Likewise at the leadership level, though Mengistu Haile-Mariam's dominance was established by February 1977 (save for the far from negligible possibility of assassination), the Russians already had unhappy experience in both Egypt and Sudan of backing a radical military leadership which subsequently turned against them.

But the main risk posed by an alliance with Ethiopia was to the Soviet presence in Somalia, which had established itself by the mid 1970s as the leading Russian ally on the continent. The Somali government declared its commitment to 'scientific socialism' in 1970, and signed a treaty of friendship and cooperation with the Soviet Union – a key step in the bureaucratised structure of Soviet alliance formation – in July 1974. The USSR, which had by then been closely involved in training the Somali armed forces for over a decade, also gained important military facilities in Somalia, notably a naval base at Berbera, and long distance reconnaissance flights from Kismayu.[15] What remains astonishing, however – and it is easily the most puzzling aspect of Soviet policy in the region over the whole period – is the level of Soviet arms shipments to Somalia in the years leading up to the Somali invasion of Ethiopia in July 1977. In constant US dollar terms,

Somali arms imports, overwhelmingly from the Soviet Union, grew from $8 million a year in 1970–71, to $30 million in 1972, $57 million in 1973, and an average of $104 million between 1974 and 1976.[16] From 1972 onwards they were consistently more than double (and in 1974 nine times) the value of Ethiopian arms imports, even though Ethiopia had substantial military commitments apart from defence against Somalia, notably the war in Eritrea. It is quite clear, first that the level of Soviet arms supply to Somalia increased sharply after the outbreak of the Ethiopian revolution (although it was already on an upward trend), and secondly that these weapons could only be used to attack Ethiopia. Although the Soviet Union never formally endorsed the Somali claim on the Ogaden, it was thus prepared to provide the Somalis with the means needed to realise it.[17] The reasons for this policy have never been satisfactorily explained, and with the shift in alliances in 1977, each side gained an interest in playing it down. It seems most unlikely that the Somalis held a strong enough bargaining position to be able to insist on this aid as the price for permitting the Russian base facilities; certainly they were unable to sell the same facilities to the Americans for any remotely comparable price after 1978, though they tried to do so. A secondary puzzle is that the Somalis could scarcely have launched their attack in July 1977 without Soviet foreknowledge, and possibly also planning and logistical support. And though some Ethiopians argue that the Russians encouraged the Somalis to attack Ethiopia, so that the Ethiopians would then have to turn to the Soviet Union, this too seems unlikely, since it was effectively the Soviet arms supplies to Somalia which prevented the Russians from achieving their preferred solution of imposing a *Pax Sovietica* over the entire region. At all events, the Somali invasion and the crisis of the Ethiopian revolution in 1977–78 derive from a Soviet readiness to destabilise the existing power balance in the region by pumping in a level of armaments to which the Ethiopians could have no immediate counter.

In the face of this, the Derg – or at any rate Mengistu's group within it – persisted in the desire for a Soviet alliance. They may have reckoned that the American alliance was in any case bound to collapse, especially after Carter's election in November 1976, and his ending of military aid to Ethiopia in February 1977. At any rate, the Ethiopian attempt to gain Soviet backing is much more evident than any Russian support for Ethiopia. The Russians seem to have believed that they could maintain alliances with all the states in the region at the same time, and in March 1977 arranged a meeting in Aden, chaired by Fidel Castro, which was intended to lead to some kind of confederation, including Ethiopia, Somalia, Eritrea and PDRY, which would at the same time secure autonomy for the Eritreans and the Ogaden Somalis, under the aegis of the USSR.[18] This initiative failed. The immediate reason was that the Somali leader insisted that both Eritrea and the Ogaden Somalis should be able to participate in the confederation as separate units, following the exercise of self-determination. This in turn reflected the fact that both the EPLF (then rapidly mopping up Ethiopian garrisons throughout Eritrea) and the Somalis (with their huge superiority in weapons) felt themselves to be in a position to demand concessions which the Ethiopians were not prepared to make. Most basically of all, neither the commitment to Marxism–Leninism of all the parties concerned, nor the regional predominance of the USSR, provided the basis for resolving the intense divisions between them.

After the Aden summit, Mengistu continued to bid for Soviet support, demanded the closure of the Kagnew communications base in April (to coincide with the celebrations of Lenin's birthday), and visited Moscow in early May. An Ethio–Soviet joint declaration on friendly relations was signed, with an agreement for arms deliveries, but without the treaty of friendship and cooperation which would have placed Ethiopia's relations with the Soviet Union formally on a par with Somalia's.[19] *The Ethiopian Herald*, in an article headlined 'We Are Not Alone', referred to Ethiopia's 'international socialist allies including the first socialist state in the world – the Soviet Union',[20] but the joint communiqué contained nothing that could be interpreted as hostile to Somalia. The Somalis for their part increasingly hedged their bets by seeking support from the USA and conservative Arab states. However, the Russians continued to supply arms to the Somalis up to, and even after, the invasion of the Ogaden in July 1977, and not until late in August did they decisively opt for the Ethiopian side, while Siyad Barre waited until mid November before renouncing the treaty of friendship and cooperation with the USSR, and expelling Soviet advisers (many of them military) from Somalia. By that time, the Soviet commitment to Ethiopia was beyond question, and the Somalis' only hope of gaining any compensatory arms supply was by ousting the Russians and seeking aid from the West.

This series of events decisively changed the balance of power in the region, enabling Ethiopia to re-establish itself as the regionally dominant state, and to restore a stable alliance pattern in collaboration with the Soviet Union as the new regionally dominant superpower. Many aspects of it remain controversial or obscure, notably the level and nature of the Carter administration's assurances to Somalia, and the extent to which Siyad relied on them in launching his attack. My own judgement would be that these played a fairly minor role: it was to Moscow, after all, and not to Washington that Siyad went in search of arms in August 1977; and it was not until November that he broke with the Russians, whereas Mengistu had made his equivalent break with the Americans as far back as April. The decisive relationship was that between the Ethiopians and the Russians, and it is remarkable how far even this was the result of Ethiopian rather than Soviet initiative; the Russians did not withdraw from Somalia, for instance, but held on until they were expelled. More generally, the events of 1977, notably the virtual exclusion of the Americans from the arena and the rejection, even then, of the Soviet confederation plan, show that African states – even in a highly conflictual situation imposing a desperate need for arms – are very far from remaining pawns in the hands of the superpowers.

THE FOREIGN POLICY OF PROLETARIAN INTERNATIONALISM

The alliance with the Soviet Union and its associates, which is generally referred to under the slogan of 'proletarian internationalism', has since 1977 replaced the previous alliance with the United States as the keystone of Ethiopian foreign policy. It is in many ways a highly visible relationship. Visitors to Addis Ababa are immediately struck by the huge portraits of the Marxian trinity – Marx, Engels and Lenin – in Revolution Square, and by the statue of Lenin outside Africa Hall.[21] Exchanges of delegations between Ethiopia and socialist bloc states are frequent and well-publicised, and Mengistu Haile-Mariam usually travels at least once a year to the Soviet Union; his moment of greatest glory was in 1980, when he shared a place with the top Soviet leadership on the reviewing stand of the Lenin Mausoleum for the October Revolution parade.[22] He never in the ten years after assuming power visited any Western state, and his first visit to any non-socialist and non-African state was to India in 1985. In votes at the United Nations, and on other occasions when a symbolic declaration of allegiance is required, Ethiopia reliably sides with the Soviet Union. Korn, who at the time was United States chargé d'affaires in Ethiopia, recounts with evident frustration his unsuccessful attempts to induce Ethiopia to attend the Los Angeles Olympic Games in 1984, and to get Mengistu to make the normal OAU chairman's visit to the UN General Assembly in New York.[23] In some ways, the closeness of the relationship is deliberately exaggerated. The annual meetings of the joint commissions regulating trade between Ethiopia and the CMEA states are prominently reported, for example, even though the volume of trade is very much less than that of unpublicised commerce with the West. The contributions of socialist states to famine relief were likewise publicised out of all proportion to their actual importance, without in any way altering a universal public awareness that such aid was over-whelmingly Western. But behind the rhetorical hyperbole which inter-national alignments of this kind normally give rise to, there is a solid relationship based on an interlocking set of mutual interests.

The most obvious aspect of this relationship is the military one. Even though the inevitable upheavals of the immediate post-revolutionary period have now died down, and Ethiopia is safe from any evident threat of external invasion, the state continues to rely on external supplies of arms, and the revolutionary combination of mobilisation and centralisation has perma-nently lifted the need for arms well above its pre-revolutionary level. The scale of Soviet arms supply to Ethiopia has easily outweighed either previous American supplies, or pre-war Soviet aid to the Somalis. Maximum pre-war annual arms imports of $19 million in the imperial period (1968) and $50 million in 1976, compare with imports worth $440 million in 1977, $1,100 million in 1978, and $210 million in 1979.[24] They have since continued at something in the region of $200 million a year. There may be as many as 3,000 Soviet advisers, about half of them military,[25] and uniformed Russians are commonly seen in Ethiopian army vehicles and barracks. So long as no plausible alternative source of supply is available, the Soviet alliance is likely to enjoy the same basic stability that the American one displayed up to 1974. In exchange for this support, the Soviet Union gains diplomatic and strategic advantages analogous to those previously available to the United States: a reliable ally strategically placed at the southern end of the Red Sea, which is at the same time one of the established diplomatic leaders of Africa. While the USA had its communications base near Asmara, the USSR has a naval facility in the Dahlac Islands (also in Eritrea), which provides an excellent though desolate anchorage immediately adjacent to the Red Sea shipping lanes.[26]

This level of dependence breeds inevitable strains. The proverbial Ethiopian suspicion of foreigners derives not from any inherent xenophobia, but from an understandable dislike of dependence, especially on any single foreign power. The Italians, British and Americans have in turn earned this distrust, and that the Russians should inherit it along with their own succession to regional dominance is only to be expected. The very visibility of the Soviet relationship, and Ethiopia's all too obvious dependence on it, exacerbate the problem, and are reflected in jokes directed not simply at the Russians, but at Mengistu's supposedly demeaning subservience to them. Indeed, to an external observer, Ethiopia's foreign policy often seems gratuitously pro-Soviet, prejudicing both the regime's domestic popularity and its relations with the West to an extent that can scarcely be compensated by additional Soviet support. Popular dislike of the Soviet connection is almost universal, and the problems carry through into the official relationship. The Ethiopian arms debt, which is generally reckoned at one and a half billion US dollars for the 1977–78 war, and which has probably increased to some two and a half billion since then, imposes a financial obligation which there is no possiblity that Ethiopia can ever repay, while Soviet attempts to extract payment can only intensify Ethiopian resentment. Mengistu on his frequent visits to Moscow is reduced to pleading for more arms, which the Russians may well deny – especially since the accession of Mr Gorbachev, with whom the Ethiopian leader is said to have a poor personal relationship. At the day-to-day level, resentment is intensified by irritating instances of Soviet meanness and distrust. Whereas Ethiopian air force technicians were able to service all the aircraft which Ethiopia obtained from the United States, the Soviet Union insists that maintenance work on the MiGs which it has supplied must be carried out by Russian technicians, though at Ethiopian expense.[27] This was one factor in persuading the Ethiopians to purchase a new generation of Boeings for Ethiopian Air Lines in 1984 (since EAL has not only serviced its own Boeing fleet for many years, but also provides training and facilities for other African airlines), instead of the Ilyushins urged on them by the USSR. The fact that the Soviet Union continued arming the Somalis right up to, and even after the outbreak of war in July 1977 remains a source of resentment, and strengthens the suspicion that the invasion must have been launched with Soviet connivance. Many Ethiopians likewise believe that the Russians may secretly be aiding the EPLF in Eritrea, so as to hedge their bets and ensure that Ethiopia continues to need the arms which only they can supply. Whether such suspicions are well founded or not is only of secondary importance: the point is that they derive almost automatically from the tensions inherent in a dependent relationship.

A second aspect of the relationship is organisational: organisation, rather than ideology, is the key feature of the Marxist–Leninist system that the Ethiopian government has adopted, and it carries with it a commitment to the Soviet Union as a political model, and an extensive set of linkages with the socialist states. This is evidently an aspect of the relationship to which the Russians themselves attach particular importance; nothing else could account for the open and continuous Soviet pressure on Mengistu to form a Leninist political party. This in turn must reflect the Soviet view that an approved organisational structure provides the essential basis for a regime which is not only stable in itself, but can be relied on to maintain a stable relationship with the USSR, transcending both leadership opinions and changes, and immediate military requirements. The major contribution to this process from the Soviet Union and its allies has been in training party cadres. Much of this has taken place in Russia and Eastern Europe, though the Yekatit '66 Political School in Addis Ababa is said to include some Soviet instructors.[28] There are no figures for the number of party cadres trained in the socialist states, but the total must run at least into several thousands, or enough to man the party apparatus down to provincial or even district level. Nor is it possible to gain anything but entirely subjective impressions of the effect which this training has had on those who have undergone it. On the one hand, it is hard to imagine that any course of training could remove a fundamental sense of Ethiopian identity; and in so far as it induced any clash between the requirements of Ethiopian nationalism, as against those of communist solidarity, the former would in the great majority of cases be likely to prevail. On the other hand, however, such training may well help to reinforce an already present sense of the importance of organisation in its own right, and the need for directed and centralised management along Soviet lines. Those who are trained as cadres thereby acquire a vested interest in the system which they come to form part of, and the highly impressive apparatus of the Soviet state may well provide a model which they genuinely wish to implant in Ethiopia. In some areas, such as economic planning, training in Soviet techniques is reinforced by the presence of a team of Soviet advisers on the spot.[29]

But if reliance on Soviet arms breeds the inevitable reaction against military dependence, reliance on a Soviet organisational model fosters an equivalent reaction against domestic political penetration. The brusque Ethiopian response to the Negede Gobeze incident in 1978, and Mengistu Haile-Mariam's evident reluctance to form a Marxist–Leninist party until he could be sure of keeping it tightly under his control, indicate that this is a danger which the regime takes very seriously. It also accounts for the two recorded cases of Ethiopian dissent from the Soviet position in the foreign policy field. The first amounts to no more than a two-week delay between the Soviet intervention in Afghanistan in December 1979, and the issuing of a statement supporting the Soviet position in January 1980.[30] Though the intervention, which also involved the killing of the existing communist leader and his replacement by a more pliant Soviet nominee, provided an alarming example of Soviet takeover of a third-world communist state, it was not an issue over which it was worth stepping out of line. The second, the civil war in South Yemen (PDRY) in January 1986, was much more serious. PDRY was a near neighbour, with which the Ethiopian regime had exceptionally close relations. It was not only the first state to send troops and arms to Ethiopia's assistance at the time of the Somali invasion in 1977, but remained the only Moslem and Arab state to do so, at a time when most of the Moslem world supported the Somalis. Mengistu exchanged frequent visits with the PDRY leader, Ali Nasser Mohammed. The background to what was in essence a highly complex dispute inside the Yemeni Socialist Party was that Ali Nasser had taken over the leadership in 1980 from a rival, Abdul Fatah Ismail, who had then retired to Moscow. The Russians evidently induced Ali Nasser to accept Abdul Fatah back into the party leadership in 1985, and seem to have been taken entirely by surprise when Abdul Fatah's group launched a *coup* attempt in January 1986. This in turn led to bitter and bloody fighting between the rival factions for about two weeks. Although Abdul Fatah was killed in the fighting (or possibly beforehand), the Russians did not support Ali Nasser, but sided with the rebels.[31] At all events, they then recognised a new government, led by the prime minister, Hayder Abu Bakr El Attas, who had taken refuge in the Soviet Union during the fighting, and whose appointment was announced from Moscow.

The Ethiopians, and in such a crisis this could only mean Mengistu, consistently supported Ali Nasser. The government issued a statement on 16 January, regretting 'the problem caused by reactionary and counter-revolutionary forces' in PDRY, and reiterating 'its readiness to extend every assistance to those who stand for the development of socialism under the vanguard leadership of the Yemeni Socialist Party headed by Comrade Ali Nasser Mohammed'.[32] An Ethiopian force was put on stand-by to intervene, but did not do so. Still more strikingly, the WPE official newspaper *Serto Ader* continued to refer to Ali Nasser as party leader in its issue of 30 January, five days after the new regime of Hayder Abu Bakr had been recognised by Moscow. After Ali Nasser's eventual defeat, moreover, he was given refuge in Ethiopia, and although relations with the new regime in

Aden were gradually normalised over the following eighteen months, they did not regain their former closeness; the Ethiopian delegation to the Yemeni Socialist Party congress in June 1987 was led only by the deputy head of the foreign relations department of the WPE secretariat.[33] At one level, Mengistu may have over-hastily taken sides in a domestic dispute which he would have been wiser to stay out of. But at another, he may also be seen as displaying an extreme sensitivity to Soviet meddling in the politics of a third-world socialist state with which Ethiopia had much more in common than with Afghanistan.

The same sensitivity has affected the Soviet Union's role within Ethiopia. The then Russian ambassador left shortly after the Negede Gobeze affair, and another ambassador was recalled prematurely in 1982, apparently after telling Mengistu to consult him before inviting Western officials to visit Ethiopia.[34] Since 1982, Soviet ambassadors have been chosen from senior CPSU officials rather than from career diplomats: an indication of the way in which, under the Soviet system, relations with other socialist states are managed through the party rather than through the state bureaucracy. All three of these new-style ambassadors (Konstantin Fomichenko, Gennadii Andreev and Valentin Dmitriev) have had precisely similar career patterns: a long apprenticeship in local party work in the Russian Soviet Federal Socialist Republic, followed by a spell in the Central Committee apparatus in Moscow, and then appointment as second secretary in one of the smaller Union Republics – Khirgiz, Armenia and Latvia, respectively.[35] None has had any previous diplomatic experience, even in Eastern Europe; and the distinctive functions of the Union Republic second secretary, who is almost invariably an ethnic Russian, and runs security matters and the party organisation beneath the titular leadership of a first secretary, who is normally a native of the republic concerned, give some indication of the role expected of Soviet ambassadors in Ethiopia. That ambassadors should be drawn from men holding such critical control positions within the Soviet party apparatus, and holding alternate membership of the CPSU Central Committee, also suggests the importance of Ethiopia to the Soviet Union.

It is often speculated that Soviet penetration of Ethiopian domestic politics is reflected in an internal division between 'pro-Soviets' on the one hand, and 'Ethiopian nationalists' on the other, with Mengistu sometimes seen as holding an uneasy balance between the two. This all-too-easy dichotomisation seems to me to reflect the preconceptions of Western policymakers, quite as much as any actual differences within the Ethiopian leadership. Mengistu's style of government does little to suggest the kind of balancing act which came easily to Haile-Selassie; and both the need for the Soviet alliance on the one hand, and the dangers of it on the other, must be sufficiently clear to everyone in the Ethiopian leadership to impose considerable restraints on the range of policy debate or choice. Nonetheless, there are variations in approach which may partly reflect differences in attitude or ideology, but which equally derive from the value or threat of the

Soviet connection to the people concerned. One example would be the divergence in attitude between the Ministry of Foreign Affairs, under its minister Goshu Wolde before his defection in October 1986, and the international relations division of the WPE secretariat under Ashagre Yigletu. Under a Soviet-style system, the secretariat is the main agency involved in advising the party leader on foreign policy issues, and Ashagre as the secretary responsible had an accepted position in contacts with other socialist states. The ministry, on the other hand, is no more than the governmental agency responsible for implementing decisions already reached by the party, and this is indeed the role that it has played. A further important aspect of the relationship between the two organisations is that the ambassadors and other officials of the socialist states have direct access to the decision-making apparatus of the party, whereas Western diplomats are restricted entirely to formal contacts with the ministry, and thus have little ability to influence policy-making.[36] In these circumstances, a division between a more 'pro-Western' or at any rate 'neutralist' ministry, and a more 'pro-Soviet' secretariat, is an almost inevitable function of the distinction between the two institutions; and this in turn may prompt a Western diplomatic reaction designed to strengthen the hand of the 'moderates' within the ministry, at the expense of the 'ideologues' within the party secretariat. In practice, however, there is no indication that the ministry has played any significant role in foreign policy formulation at all. The appointment as foreign minister in November 1986 of Berhanu Bayih, a Politbureau member and one of the survivors of the Derg in the top party leadership, may signal a greater role for the ministry, though at the expense of closer party control.

Another area where an analogous distinction in institutional and ideological attitude might be suggested is in the armed forces, between career officers who have been promoted within the normal command structure, and political appointees who have worked their way up within the political administration of the military. This is a familiar division within the armed forces of socialist states, including the Soviet Union, which in Ethiopia must be expected to promote a greater commitment to the Soviet alliance among those whose status depends very largely on the maintenance of a Soviet-style system. Even then, however, such a commitment would have to remain secondary to the much more important one of loyalty to Mengistu himself. The same goes for the duplication of party and state structures throughout the whole of the Ethiopian government, and the protected and privileged position which the party appointees thereby acquire.

A third potential aspect of the Soviet–Ethiopian relationship, economic and social interaction, remains extremely weak. Economically, with the single though important exception of Soviet oil supply, Ethiopian external trade remains almost as closely oriented towards the Western market economies as during the imperial epoch. Soviet bloc aid has been heavily directed into a small number of large-scale projects, such as the armaments factory in Addis Ababa, the Mugher cement works, the Nazret tractor assembly plant, and the Melka Wakena hydroelectric project; and quite independently of the value of these projects in their own right, therefore, they have not permitted anything approaching the level of penetration of the Ethiopian economy that characteristically results from colonial and post-colonial relationships with Western capitalist economies in many other African states. The large number of Ethiopian students sent to the Soviet Union and Eastern Europe provide a further source of penetration, and this may become more salient as the generation of mostly Western-educated Ethiopians in high positions comes to be displaced, with the aid of party patronage, by their Soviet-educated juniors. Many Ethiopians, moreover, spend a very long time in the Soviet educational system, and even twelve years after the outbreak of the revolution, it may be too early to assess their effect. But at a popular level, the generation of urban Ethiopians who have grown up since the revolution seem to be more Western-oriented than their pre-revolutionary predecessors, for whom the West was associated with the maintenance of the old regime. In short, the Soviet connection is almost exclusively geared to the maintenance of the state and party apparatus. Within that apparatus, it has helped to build up a group of people whose interests are at least in part associated with the Soviet alliance. These interests, in turn, provide the most important means by which a Leninist party structure is able to keep itself in power.

Ethiopia's relations with the Eastern European states have been little more than supplementary to those with the Soviet Union, and symptomatically, it has been those states which are closest to the USSR within the Eastern European setting, notably East Germany and Bulgaria, which have also had the closest connections with Ethiopia. These two countries have, with Cuba, provided the largest training programmes outside the Soviet Union, and the East German ambassador in the mid 1980s, like the Soviet ones, was a high party functionary.[37] The Ethiopian ambassadors in both Moscow and Berlin for several years up to 1986 were former army officers who had been at the Holeta military academy with Mengistu, though the Bulgarian post was given successively to two leading civilian ideologues – one of whom, Ashagre Yigletu, subsequently became WPE secretary for international affairs. The Czechs have been involved in several of the major socialist bloc aid projects, notably the Combolcha textile mill and the Melka Wakena hydroelectric scheme,[38] but relations with Poland, Hungary and Romania have been slight.

Relations with other socialist third-world states are similarly selective. With many of them, including Vietnam and Kampuchea, Afghanistan, and the former Portuguese colonies in Africa, Ethiopia does not have very active diplomatic links, though formally friendly relations are maintained. Relations with the Asian states for the most part follow simply from the Soviet link; in 1978–79, for example, Ethiopia took Vietnam's side following Vietnamese takeover in Kampuchea and the subsequent Chinese invasion of Vietnam.[39] The three major exceptions, states with which Ethiopia has maintained a distinctive relationship in some measure independent of the Soviet Union, are South Yemen, North Korea, and Cuba. The South Yemeni connection has already been discussed, and gains added importance from the fact that this is the only state among any of its near neighbours that the Ethiopian regime has been able to regard as an ally. No such considerations apply to North Korea (DPRK), a regime which appears to exert a strong personal fascination over Mengistu Haile-Mariam; Mengistu has been treated royally on his visits to Pyongyang, and the DPRK must offer an intoxicating mixture of personalism and disciplined mass organisation to any visiting socialist leader. The North Koreans took an important role in organising the celebrations for the tenth anniversary of the Ethiopian revolution in September 1984, both drilling the population for the mass parades, and putting up celebratory placards and monuments which have proved impressively durable. The uniforms which officials were required to wear from 1985 onwards were likewise of North Korean inspiration. A mineral prospecting team was sent to Ethiopia, announcing the discovery of 'ample' deposits of iron ore in Welega to coincide with the visit of one of the DPRK vice-presidents in November 1985,[40] and Korean experts have started developing a vast state farm, with a projected quarter of a million hectares, in the lower Omo valley.[41]

Cuba played the spearhead role in the victory over the Somalis in March 1978, and the name of the battlefield at Karamara remains an oft-invoked symbol of Ethio–Cuban solidarity. A large contingent of Cuban troops remained after the war, and although most of these were withdrawn in 1983–84,[42] at least one brigade remained in the Dire Dawa area in 1986, along with instructors at the Harar military academy. By the time of their withdrawal, the position of the Cuban troops had however become something of an embarrassment, especially in the Harar/Dire Dawa/Jijiga area, where the presence of a large number of soldiers with very low pay and easygoing Caribbean sexual habits led to unfortunate incidents with the local womenfolk. With the disappearance of the Somali threat, they had outlived their military usefulness, and they were mostly stationed too far from Addis Ababa to serve as a praetorian guard for the regime. Cuba has also provided economic and technical aid, appropriately enough for the sugar plantations which were previously run by a Dutch multinational, and also medical teams in provincial hospitals – where they led a lonely life, and the local population were extremely reluctant to avail themselves of their services. Another source of Cuban involvement is the mass education of Ethiopian children, by Ethiopian instructors, at the 'Isle of Youth' off the south coast of Cuba. Two shiploads each of 1,200 Ethiopian children were reported leaving for Cuba in June and November 1979, and the total number of Ethiopians passing through the programme amounts to several thousand.[43] The sheer scale of this operation indicates the regime's determination to train the cadres needed to put a fully socialist system into effect, even though the problems involved in transferring these cadres from the institutionalised seclusion of a tiny Caribbean island to the actual management of such a system in Ethiopia must be enormous.

Much unnecessary speculation has been devoted to the question of whether the Cuban presence is in any sense 'independent' of the Soviet Union. The basic parameters of the relationship are, first, that the level of military and other assistance which Cuba has provided would have been impossible without a genuine determination on the part of the Cuban regime to export the benefits of its revolution, reflecting a belief in the internationalism of the systems which it sought both to overthrow and to establish, quite at odds with the overwhelmingly domestic preoccupations of Ethiopian revolutionaries; but secondly, that this level of external activity would have been quite impossible without the support of the Soviet Union, and could not run counter to Soviet interests and priorities. The only occasion on which it has been suggested that Cuban policy in Ethiopia differed in any important respect from that of the USSR, was over the supposed refusal of the Cubans to help the Ethiopian attack on the EPLF in Eritrea, immediately after the Ogaden campaign in 1978. Ethiopian sources claim that Cuban aid was not sought in any event, on the grounds that it would have been inappropriate in dealing with a domestic conflict. Nonetheless, the Cubans helped to provide back-up facilities, and to secure the Ogaden while Ethiopian troops were transferred to Eritrea, and their non-involvement was thus little more than symbolic.

THE WESTERN RESPONSE

In principle, Western states have faced a choice between two alternative approaches to the Soviet role in Ethiopia. They might either take a 'hard' response, which would treat Ethiopia as a committed Soviet ally, and seek to build up countervailing regional forces, or possibly try to destabilise the regime internally; or they could take a 'soft' response, which would treat it only as a Soviet ally of convenience, and thus maintain correct relations, while seeking in the long term to lure Ethiopia away from the Soviet bloc by demonstrating the advantages of neutralism or alignment with the West. In practice, despite Ethiopia's very public commitment to Marxism–Leninism, and despite a dependence on Western food supplies which matches that on Soviet arms, the 'hard' option has scarcely been available. In the absence of any effective central opposition to the regime, any destabilisation strategy would involve providing aid (and especially arms) to its external and peripheral opponents, notably the Somali Republic or the regional separatist movements. Western states, however, have been little less committed than the OAU, and rather more so than the USSR, to maintaining the existing structure of African states and boundaries. Nor have they had any evident interest in supporting secessionist movements, most of which (and notably the two most effective of them, the EPLF and TPLF) have been every bit as socialist as the central government which they oppose. And while support for the Somali Republic could be brought within the established principle of maintaining an existing state, any substantial rearmament programme directed against Ethiopia could be relied on not only to strengthen the Ethio–Soviet alliance, but also to arouse opposition from Kenya, in which Western economic interests are vastly more important than in either Somalia or Ethiopia. At some points, and notably during the early months of the Carter administration in 1977, the ambivalence in Western policy has been great enough to cause real confusion. As a serious option, however, support for Somalia against Ethiopia has scarcely been available, at least so long as the Ethiopians refrained (as they have generally done) from attacking Somalia in retaliation for Somali attacks on themselves. Economic support has been provided to the Somali government, together with a limited quantity of 'defensive' military aid, but the Western states have provided no military assistance at a level which could threaten Ethiopia, or raise Somali aspirations. Support for the varied separatist groups has likewise been left to local allies or clients, notably Saudi Arabia and Sudan. And while dependence on relief aid in principle provides enormous leverage to the Western states which supply it, in practice this leverage has been extremely difficult to apply.

A low-key American response has also been helped – in contrast, say, to Central America – by the comparative distance of Ethiopia from major centres of US strategic interest or popular concern, and by the virtual absence of any American economic interests in the country. Nor has the large Ethiopian refugee community in the United States taken any effective role; indeed many of its members have integrated themselves extremely well into a variety of professions, from employees of international organisations to taxi drivers and restaurateurs. Ethiopia was nonetheless excluded from US development assistance in 1985, as a result of Congressional hostility to the regime; and potentially much more serious (especially as there was no US development aid to Ethiopia anyhow), Congress also inserted into the 1985 International Security and Development Cooperation Act a clause which would have prohibited all commercial trade between the United States and Ethiopia, had the President determined that the Ethiopian government was pursuing a deliberate policy of starvation against its people. President Reagan decided, however, that there was no evidence of such a policy.[44] Ethiopian relations have been far worse with the United States than with other Western countries, and the Ethiopians have, despite some US overtures, maintained relations at the frigid level indicated by the refusal to exchange ambassadors. The Soviet alliance has a much more sensitive effect on relations with the US than with other Western states. Trade relations have however continued unaffected, and as in the case of the Boeing purchase in 1984 have occasionally taken on a political dimension, while the United States has remained a major market for Ethiopian coffee.

As frequently happens in Western relations with socialist third-world states, the European Community countries have filled some of the gap left

237

by a breach with the US; European Community aid has as already noted helped to more than make up the shortfall created by the withdrawal of American assistance. The major European role has in turn been taken by Italy, which has continued to maintain something of its historic interest in the region. The Italian foreign minister was the first ranking Western official to visit Ethiopia after the revolution, though even then the visit did not take place until 1981; and the Italian ambassador is generally credited with making it clear to Mengistu in early October 1984 that Ethiopia could not continue to suppress information about the famine, but must publicise it in order to attract Western relief.

The famine was the major factor in expanding Ethiopian relations with the West. Though some Western relief agencies had worked in Ethiopia continuously since the 1973–74 famine, from October 1984 there was a massive increase in the Western presence in the country, much of it through the activities of non-governmental agencies, which aroused among Western diplomats the hope that Ethiopia's dependence on Western food might help to counterbalance the dependence on Soviet weapons, and – even if it could not entirely wean Ethiopia away from the Russian alliance – might at any rate provide the basis for a more even relationship between East and West. This did not happen. The Ethiopians were well aware of the influence of Western public opinion on official as well as unofficial relief supplies, and were adept at using the Western media and relief agencies in order to appeal directly to Western opinion over the heads of Western governments. Nor could these governments use the threat to withhold food from starving people as a weapon to compel any change in diplomatic alignment. They had instead to make it clear that such aid came with no political strings attached, while at the same time hoping that the contrast between Western and Soviet bloc capabilities would not be lost either on the government or on the population as a whole.[45] So far as the population goes, this strategy certainly worked; there was universal recognition that the aid was overwhelmingly Western, and at a popular level in the countryside it was often associated simply with 'America'. But at the official level, the Ethiopian government retained a freedom of action which was conspicuously demonstrated first through the resettlement campaign and later through villagisation. The defection of the foreign minister, Goshu Wolde, in October 1986 provided an indication from one of the people best placed to judge that no change in the government's attitude was to be expected.

The long-term problem of food dependence nonetheless remains. For so long as Ethiopia continues to depend on imported food – and regardless of year-to-year changes in weather conditions, there is nothing in the long-term pattern of agricultural production to suggest that this dependence is likely to diminish – it will likewise depend on the Western grain-surplus states to provide it. The government's economic development strategy equally depends on a level of capital inflow which only the West can provide. If donor fatigue and disenchantment reduce the level of voluntary aid to Ethiopia, and especially if continuing agricultural failure is ascribed not so much to weather conditions as to government policies such as villagisation or low produce buying prices, then the political costs of food dependence may become very much more evident.

The Ethiopian revolution has led to a dramatic change in alliances, to a resulting reversal of superpower strengths in a strategically sensitive part of the world, and by way of internal and regional conflicts which have attracted external involvement, to a very sharp increase in militarisation. The relationship between domestic revolution and the international order has nonetheless differed significantly from that found in regions such as Southeast Asia, southern Africa, and the Caribbean and Central America. One important difference is that there has been no attempt to export it. Ethiopia is surrounded by states with very different social and political systems, and Ethiopians have regarded their revolution as the outcome of specifically indigenous factors, rather than as a challenge to the global order, or as something which might be applied to a range of similar societies. Revolution has intensified, rather than changing, the long-held perception of national distinctiveness; and though Mengistu has sometimes pledged Ethiopian military aid to the southern African liberation movements, this has derived more from a desire to make an impression within the Organisation of African Unity, than from any conviction of the exportability of the Ethiopian revolution.

A second important difference lies in the reaction to revolution by external powers. Revolutionary regimes commonly have to establish themselves in the teeth of a hostile international environment, in particular through attempts by major powers which favour the existing international order to curb or destabilise the revolutionary regime, by means ranging from economic blockade through support for opposition groups to outright intervention. This danger is all the greater when, as for Cuba and Nicaragua in the Caribbean basin, or Angola and Mozambique in southern Africa, the revolution occurs within the sphere of influence of a regional power which views it as a threat to its hegemony. The Ethiopian revolution has aroused no such response. The involvement of external states, and especially of the major powers, has on the whole been very much in its favour. The sole important exception, the Somali invasion of 1977–78, was in essence a local conflict triggered into open war by the temporary failure of control within Ethiopia; and even though the level of Soviet arms supplies to the Somali Republic was all that made it possible, this was subsequently much more than compensated for by the supply of Soviet weapons to Ethiopia. The shift in Ethiopia's international allegiance from the United States to the Soviet Union was accomplished without any serious reprisals from the Western side. And on two major occasions, the Somali crisis of 1977–78 and the famine crisis of 1984–85, the regime has been saved from disaster by external aid. In each case, indeed, the revolutionary government was able to call on

239

international support in order to make up domestic deficiencies, of military control or food production, which were certainly not entirely caused by the revolution, but which were exacerbated by it.

This success owes something to historical accident, but it owes a great deal also to the intractability of conflicts within the Horn to external manipulation. In this situation, Ethiopian policymakers have benefitted from control over an established and internationally acknowledged state with a strategically dominant position within the region. In this, the elements of continuity from the old regime are very strong. It was just this advantage which nineteenth-century emperors used to maintain Ethiopia's independence during the colonial scramble for Africa, and which Haile-Selassie helped to build into the ground rules of the African diplomatic system. Despite overthrowing and vilifying Africa's most respected elder statesman, the revolutionary regime was able to maintain African support in its conflict with Somalia on the basis of the principles of non-interference in domestic affairs and respect for existing boundaries which Haile-Selassie had done much to establish. Here fortunate coincidence played a part, in that the independence of the former Portuguese colonies in 1975, and the Soviet–Cuban intervention in the Angloan war of 1975–76, both strengthened the 'radical' group of OAU states to which Ethiiopia belonged, and provided a precedent for their involvement in the 1977–78 war.

Fundamentally, then, the international system has continued since the revolution to play the same role as it had done before, in providing the essential military and economic resources needed to enable a domestic ruling group, controlling the state, to establish its control over a perennially fractious society. The intensification of state control since the revolution, and the intensified level of reaction from it, have called for a much increased level of international commitment – and one which the Ethiopian regime has, so far at least, been able to obtain. This has entailed a switch in international allegiance to a new patron which is better able to supply armaments than the old one; but which is less able to provide economic benefits, and also demands a much higher level of ideological and organisational commitment, and thus presents a greater threat to the autonomy of the domestic government. So far, the Ethiopian government has been able to manipulate the international system for its own purposes, though in the process it has run up a level of dependence from which it is likely to find it increasingly difficult to escape.

240

10

Conclusion

Since 1974, and especially since the stabilisation of the revolutionary regime in 1977–78, Ethiopians have found themselves part of a highly effective, disciplined and centralised state system. The origins of that system stretch well back into Ethiopia's past, and build on the economic foundations of ox-plough agriculture, on the central role of authority relations within highland Ethiopian society, and on the success of the Ethiopian empire in drawing these into a multiethnic political structure, held together by a recognition of hierarchy and at least an embryonic conception of Ethiopian nationhood. Under the imperial system, the capabilities of this state were always inherently limited, impressive though it was within the setting of a technologically backward Africa. The first steps in converting it into an effective modern state were taken by its late nineteenth- and twentieth-century emperors, through the development of a cash-crop economy geared to external markets, and the import of the military, organisational and educational technologies required for increased state control. But the culmination of this process required the destruction of the outdated and increasingly ineffective political formula on which the old regime had rested, and the ruthless reorganisation of subordinate economic relationships, especially of landholding, by the new wielders of state power.

Along with this came a new political formula, which not only emphasised centralisation and control, but also embraced a broader and less discriminatory concept of nationhood than the old. The new state institutions were turned, much more dynamically than in the past, towards the goal of national unity and integration, but also towards social and economic development under the aegis of the state. The organisational effectiveness of this system is beyond question, attested not only by its ability to put through impressive campaigns such as literacy and villagisation, but equally by the matching organisation, ideology and policies of the only movements, in Eritrea and Tigray, which were able to resist it. The problem is that the goals which this system so single-mindedly set out to achieve have stayed beyond its grasp, and in some respects indeed have receded further into the distance. Famine is of course the starkest indicator of failure, for a regime

241

which itself came to power in the midst of famine, and set agricultural transformation as the first of its development priorities. But this is no mere isolated disaster – and in a society so directly dependent on agriculture for survival, let alone for development, it is inconceivable that it could be. The failure of agricultural production is immediately reflected in falling living standards in the towns, despite the government's attempts to protect them. This is no case of a surplus being extracted from the countryside, however harshly, in order to promote development elsewhere. The surplus is indeed extracted, but goes very largely to support the state itself, and especially its massive military requirements, though also in some part to implement agricultural and industrial investment policies which, on the evidence so far available, appear to be badly misconceived. The capacity of the countryside to produce that surplus continues to decline. The Jacobin determination with which the regime has pursued its goal of national unity has been effective over much of Ethiopia, but has aroused a level of resistance in the north which its vastly expanded army has been unable to overcome.

Here, as at many points in previous chapters, it is necessary to point out that the traumas of post-revolutionary Ethiopia are not simply ascribable to the policies followed by its government, or indeed to 'revolution' as a process in itself. Ethiopia before the revolution was one of the poorest states in the world, and it remains so still. The relentless pressure of population on resources would have placed great strain on any society and system of government. The imperial government had failed to manage the political incorporation of Eritrea, and even though the rest of the country was generally quiescent, it could well be argued that Eritrea was merely the precursor of analogous problems which would have arisen throughout Ethiopia with the inevitable eventual explosion of political awareness. In defusing the 'southern problem' through land reform, the revolutionary government can be credited with settling the major issue of national unity, in a way that its predecessor could never have managed. But even though the failure to solve deeply seated problems of agricultural production and national unity can surprise only those who held grossly inflated preconceptions of revolution as a magical political formula, the means which the government has used to attack all its problems – the relentless application of centralised state power – has in each case had seriously counterproductive consequences.

It will be clear from the whole tenor of this book that Ethiopia is not to be regarded as a 'model' implicitly replicable, for either good or ill, in other parts of Africa or the third world. The revolution came about as the result of local conditions which, though they have parallels in the experience of other revolutionary states such as France or Russia, are not duplicated among the great majority of formerly colonial third-world states. It did not result from conditions, such as incorporation into the global economy, which Ethiopia shares with other parts of the third world. The capacities of the post-revolutionary regime likewise follow, not from the application of Leninist or revolutionary organisational techniques which can be implemented in any state where a revolution has taken place, but from the marriage between these techniques and specifically Ethiopian historical legacies. Even other African revolutionary regimes, such as Angola and Mozambique, may try to use similar techniques with very different results.

But the coincidence in Ethiopia of one of Africa's most powerful states with one of its poorest economies (perhaps *the* most powerful, and probably *the* poorest) does raise questions about the adequacy of the state as a motor for development which may be more widely relevant. It is easily assumed, especially by the leaders of third-world states, that the state is a kind of machine which can be used, in the hands of dedicated ruling elites, to achieve a wide variety of tasks, of which 'development' in one form or another is the most salient. In Ethiopia, the machine is in place, together with the determination to use it. It is run for the most part efficiently, and often indeed with dedication. But the construction and operation of such a machine requires the subordination of all else to the needs of the machine itself, and especially its demands for control, in a way which – despite the goals of 'unity' and 'development' to which it is directed – often impedes production and fosters resistance. This is the impasse into which the Ethiopian state appears to have forced itself, at the moment when it celebrates the culminating achievement of revolutionary statehood with the declaration of the People's Democratic Republic of Ethiopia in September 1987.

Notes

Full references are given in the bibliography.
The following abbreviations are used in the notes:
EH   *The Ethiopian Herald*
NG   *Negarit Gazeta* (the Ethiopian government official gazette)

Preface

1 UNDP and World Bank, *Ethiopia: Issues and Options in the Energy Sector*, p. ii.
2 Relief and Rehabilitation Commission, *Combatting the Effects of Cyclical Drought in Ethiopia*, pp. 14, 16.
3 From the well-known series of engravings by Henry Salt (1780–1827), reprinted by the Ethiopian Tourism Commission, Addis Ababa, 1984.
4 R. E. Moreau, *The Bird Faunas of Africa and its Islands*, pp. 207–8, 220–2.

1 Revolutions

1 This account of revolution draws on C. Clapham, *Third World Politics*, ch. 8, and draws much of its inspiration from S. P. Huntington, *Political Order in Changing Societies*, ch. 5; since completing the original draft, I have also benefited considerably from reading T. Skocpol, *States and Social Revolutions*.
2 Such a view of third-world revolution is suggested by J. Walton, *Reluctant Rebels*; P. Chabal, *Amilcar Cabral*, pp. 196–7, has, however, argued convincingly that socio–economic incorporation and exploitation cannot be used to account for differing levels of revolutionary mobilisation against the Portuguese regimes in Africa.
3 See J. C. Scott, *The Moral Economy of the Peasant*.
4 In addition to Huntington and Skocpol, see also Barrington Moore, *Social Origins of Dictatorship and Democracy*.
5 Skocpol, p. 47.
6 Huntington, pp. 266–8.
7 Skocpol, p. 167.
8 Skocpol, p. 167.
9 Skocpol, pp. 168–71.
10 See, for example, C. Legum, *Ethiopia*, and B. Thompson, *Ethiopia*.
11 See, for example, F. Halliday and M. Molyneux, *The Ethiopian Revolution*;

244

R. Lefort, *Ethiopia: An Heretical Revolution?*; and J. Markakis and Nega Ayele, *Class and Revolution in Ethiopia*.

12 See, for example, P. Gill, *A Year in the Death of Africa*; G. Hancock, *Ethiopia: the Challenge of Hunger*; P. King, *An African Winter*.

13 This is a criticism which may be brought against Lefort, and Halliday and Molyneux, but not against Markakis, whose *Ethiopia: Anatomy of a Traditional Polity* provides the most comprehensive account of the late imperial political system.

14 A. de Tocqueville, *The Ancien Regime and the French Revolution*, first published in 1856; as Tocqueville argued (p. 50), the first aim of the revolution was 'to increase the power and jurisdiction of the central authority'.

15 At least until villagisation got under way in late 1985, replacing scattered homesteads by regimented rows of houses.

16 J. Markakis, *National and Class Conflict in the Horn of Africa*, chs. 8 and 9.

17 Halliday and Molyneux, *The Ethiopian Revolution*, pp. 25–31.

18 See B. and S. Webb, *Soviet Communism*; I have been unable to trace the original quotation.

19 The most uncritical account is P. Schwab, *Ethiopia: Politics, Economics and Society*.

20 Michael Chege, 'The revolution betrayed'; Markakis and Nega, *Class and Revolution in Ethiopia*, p. 191.

21 See, for example, *Review of African Political Economy*, No. 30, September 1984, with its persistent references to the 'state capitalist' character of the Ethiopian regime.

2 Monarchical modernisation and the origins of revolution

1 Workers' Party of Ethiopia, *Ethiopia – A Decade of Revolutionary Transformation*.

2 Despite the existence of several excellent studies of individual periods, there is no remotely satisfactory general history of Ethiopia; the best political history is probably still Margery Perham, *The Government of Ethiopia*.

3 D. N. Levine, 'Ethiopia: identity, authority and realism', p. 250.

4 See G. Steer, *Caesar in Abyssinia*, for accounts from the war of 1935–36.

5 See D. N. Levine, *Wax and Gold*, ch. 5; A. Hoben, *Land Tenure among the Amhara of Ethiopia*.

6 See S. Rubenson, *King of Kings Tewodros of Ethiopia*.

7 See Zewde Gabre-Sellassie, *Yohannes IV of Ethiopia*.

8 See H. G. Marcus, *The Life and Times of Menelik II*.

9 For Haile-Selassie's accession to power and early reign, see H. G. Marcus, *Haile Sellassie I: The Formative Years, 1892–1936*.

10 See C. Clapham, 'Ethiopia', in R. Lemarchand, ed., *African Kingships in Perspective*.

11 R. Booth, *The Armed Forces of African States 1970*.

12 H. G. Marcus, 'The infrastructure of the Italo–Ethiopian crisis'; C. Clapham, 'Ethiopia', in T. M. Shaw and O. Aluko, eds., *The Political Economy of African Foreign Policy*.

13 See M. Stahl, *Ethiopia: Political Contradictions in Agricultural Development*.

14 For the workings of the old regime, see C. Clapham, *Haile Selassie's Government*; and J. Markakis, *Ethiopia: Anatomy of a Traditional Polity*.

15 See R. Balsvik, *Haile Selassie's Students*.

16 See Levine, *Wax and Gold*, ch. 5.
17 Markakis, *Ethiopia*, p. 176.
18 See P. Schwab, *Decision-Making in Ethiopia*.
19 See Clapham, *Haile Selassie's Government*, pp. 142–3.
20 See P. T. W. Baxter, 'Ethiopia's unacknowledged problem: the Oromo'.
21 H. Ehrlich, *The Struggle over Eritrea, 1962–78*, p. 8.
22 See Ehrlich, *The Struggle over Eritrea*.
23 Markakis, *Ethiopia*, pp. 369–71.
24 Markakis, *Ethiopia*, pp. 376–87.
25 See Relief and Rehabilitation Commission, *The Challenge of Drought*.
26 See Lefort, *Ethiopia*, ch. 2.
27 Lefort, *Ethiopia*, pp. 51–5.

3 The mobilisation phase, 1974–1978

1 S. P. Huntington, *Political Order in Changing Societies*, ch. 4.
2 R. Lefort, *Ethiopia: An Heretical Revolution?*, p. 65.
3 Lefort, *Ethiopia*, pp. 70–1.
4 See the Special Courts Martial Establishment, Special Penal Code, Special Criminal Procedure Code, and Public Order and Safety Proclamations, *NG*, 16 November 1974.
5 Lefort, *Ethiopia*, p. 84.
6 PMAC, *Declaration on Economic Policy of Socialist Ethiopia*, which is embodied in the Government Ownership and Control of Means of Production Proclamation, *NG*, 11 March 1975.
7 Public Ownership of Rural Lands Proclamation, *NG*, 29 April 1975.
8 Cited in J. Markakis, *Ethiopia: Anatomy of a Traditional Policy*, p. 128.
9 Dessalegn Rahmato, 'Moral crusaders and incipient capitalists'.
10 See Lefort, *Ethiopia*, ch. 3.
11 The Government Ownership of Urban Lands and Extra Houses Proclamation, *NG*, 26 July 1975.
12 The most detailed account is in Lefort, *Ethiopia*, chs. 4–7.
13 See Getachew Wolde-Mikael, 'The scope and limits of a student movement'.
14 The text of the Programme is published in Provisional Office of Mass Organizational Affairs, *Basic Documents of the Ethiopian Revolution*.
15 Lefort, *Ethiopia*, p. 166.
16 See, for example, the favourable reference in G. Galperin, *Ethiopia*, pp. 17–18; and R. G. Patman, *Intervention and Disengagement in the Horn of Africa*, pp. 193, 222.
17 See *EH*, 13 March 1977, 19 March 1977, 23 April 1977, 11 June 1977.
18 Declaration of State of Emergency Proclamation, *NG*, 30 September 1975.
19 Labour Proclamation, *NG*, 6 December 1975.
20 See *EH*, 10 March 1977, 13 March 1977, 29 March 1977, 1 November 1977.
21 See *EH*, 8 March 1977, 1 October 1977.
22 Lefort, *Ethiopia*, p. 171.
23 Urban Dwellers' Associations Consolidation and Municipalities Proclamation, *NG*, 9 October 1976.
24 Lefort, *Ethiopia*, p. 173; there are several references in *EH* at this period to kebelle officials with military titles.
25 *EH*, 3 April 1977.

26 Provisional Office for Mass Organizational Affairs Organization and Operation Improvement Proclamation, *NG*, 14 July 1977.
27 See, for example, *EH*, 5 May 1977, 12 May 1977, 14 May 1977, 17 May 1977.
28 *EH*, 30 December 1979.
29 Lefort, *Ethiopia*, pp. 203–4.
30 Lefort, *Ethiopia*, p. 178.
31 For accounts of the conflict in Eritrea, see H. Ehrlich, *The Struggle over Eritrea, 1962–1978*, and J. Markakis, *National and Class Conflict in the Horn of Africa*.

4 The formation of the party, 1978–1987

1 P. B. Henze, 'Communism and Ethiopia'.
2 Programme of the National Democratic Revolution, in POMOA, *Basic Documents of the Ethiopian Revolution*, pp. 9–17.
3 Tamiru Endale, *Political Organizations in Post-1974 Ethiopia*.
4 *EH*, 22 January 1977, 15 April 1977, 1 June 1977, 9 June 1977, 20 July 1977. 5 August 1977.
5 *EH*, 15 April 1977.
6 Lefort, *Ethiopia*, p. 223.
7 Mengistu Haile-Mariam, *First COPWE Congress Report*, 16 June 1980.
8 *EH*, 7 September 1979, 22 February 1980, 12 July 1980.
9 *EH*, 7 August 1979, 25 August 1979, 25 October 1979, 16 November 1979.
10 Mengistu Haile-Mariam, *First COPWE Congress Report*, 16 June 1980.
11 *The Times* (London), 29 May 1978; Henze, 'Communism and Ethiopia'.
12 A. Kokiev and V. Vigand, 'National democratic revolution in Ethiopia'.
13 Mengistu Haile-Mariam, *Speech on the Fourth Anniversary of the Ethiopian Revolution*, 12 September 1978.
14 Mengistu Haile-Mariam, *First COPWE Congress Report*.
15 See C. Clapham, *Third World Politics*, pp. 171–2.
16 *EH*, 4 August 1979.
17 Commission for Organizing the Party of the Working People of Ethiopia Establishment Proclamation, *NG*, 26 January 1980.
18 The list of Central Committee members is published in *EH*, 25 June 1980.
19 From a photograph in *EH*, 9 January 1983.
20 *Addis Zemen*, 21 Tahsas 1969 (1 January 1977), translated and cited in Civil Service Commission, *Organization of the Provisional Military Government of Socialist Ethiopia*.
21 *EH*, 14 and 15 June 1980.
22 Mengistu Haile-Mariam, *Second COPWE Congress Report*.
23 Mengistu Haile-Mariam, *Towards Party Formation*.
24 Mengistu Haile-Mariam, *Towards Party Formation*.
25 Mengistu Haile-Mariam, *Second COPWE Congress Report*.
26 D. A. Korn, *Ethiopia, the United States and the Soviet Union*, p. 167.
27 Korn, *Ethiopia*, p. 167.
28 *EH*, 29 December 1979, 5 and 9 January 1980.
29 See M. Ottaway, *State Power Consolidation in Ethiopia*.
30 See *EH*, 7 March 1981, 1 and 16 April 1981.
31 *Meskerem: A Marxist–Leninist Ideological Journal*, published by the Ideological Department of the Central Committee of COPWE; the first issue (vol. 1 no. 1) was published in September 1980, and the last (vol. 3 no. 14) in June 1983.

32 *EH*, 9 April 1981.
33 Mengistu Haile-Mariam, *Second COPWE Congress Report*.
34 *EH*, 19 June 1982.
35 Mengistu Haile-Mariam, *Second COPWE Congress Report*.
36 Mengistu Haile-Mariam, *Second COPWE Congress Report*.
37 Tamiru Endale, *Political Organizations*; *EH*, July and August 1984.
38 Korn, *Ethiopia*, p. 124.
39 Workers' Party of Ethiopia, *Rules*.
40 WPE, *Rules*, ch. 7, 'Structure and functioning of the WPE in the revolutionary armed forces'.
41 There was an excellent example near Addis Ababa railway station.
42 R. H. Jackson and C. G. Rosberg, *Personal Rule in Black Africa*.
43 *EH*, 3 November 1984.
44 See Korn, *Ethiopia*, ch. 3 and *passim*.
45 Information on posts held by Central Committee members is taken largely from *EH*, supplemented by personal informants.
46 Pliny the Middle-Aged, 'The life and times of the Derg'.
47 See *EH*, 11 July 1985, for his obituary.
48 Institute for the Study of Ethiopian Nationalities, *Documents*.
49 The membership of the Commission was published in *YeZareyetu Ityopya*, 22 February 1986.
50 See C. Clapham, 'The constitution of the People's Democratic Republic of Ethiopia'; the initial draft text was published in *EH*, 7 June 1986, and the final text in *EH*, 30 January 1987.
51 See Constitutional Commission, 'Explanatory statement', supplemented by information from the Institute for the Study of Ethiopian Nationalities.
52 The information in this paragraph is taken from official but unpublished voting figures for 799 of the 835 constituencies; I do not know why no information is available for the remaining thirty-six constituencies, and there is no evident shortfall in results for potentially insurgency-affected regions such as Tigray and Eritrea.
53 Addis Ababa University, *Duties, Code of Conduct and Disciplinary Regulations of Academic Staff*, art. 3.
54 See D. N. Levine, *Wax and Gold*, pp. 80–1.

5 The Ethiopian state: structures of extraction and control

1 W. I. Abraham and Seilu Abraha, 'Ethiopia's public sector'.
2 See J. Markakis, *Ethiopia*, pp. 305–6; and for pre-revolutionary regional government in general, J. M. Cohen and P. H. Koehn, *Ethiopian Provincial and Municipal Government*.
3 Markakis, *Ethiopia*, p. 240.
4 *Ethiopia Statistical Abstract*, 1972.
5 Abraham and Seilu, 'Ethiopia's public sector'.
6 *Ethiopia Statistical Abstract*, 1972, 1975, 1977.
7 Abraham and Seilu, 'Ethiopia's public sector'.
8 For a review of the debate on commercial agriculture in pre-revolutionary Ethiopia, see Dessalegn Rahmato, 'Moral crusaders and incipient capitalists'.
9 Dessalegn, 'Moral crusaders'.
10 Markakis, *Ethiopia*, pp. 335–7.

11 Alemayehu Lirenso, 'Grain marketing in revolutionary Ethiopia'.
12 *EH*, 1 January 1977, 14 January 1977.
13 *Ethiopia Statistical Abstract*, 1977, 1982; National Bank of Ethiopia, *Annual Report*, 1980, 1982, 1983.
14 See discussion in ch. 7.
15 Special Courts Martial Establishment, Special Penal Code, Special Criminal Procedure Code, and Public Order and Safety Proclamations, *NG*, 16 November 1974.
16 Declaration of State of Emergency Proclamation, *NG*, 30 September 1975, art. 7.
17 Constitution of the People's Democratic Republic of Ethiopia, art. 49.
18 Amnesty International, *Human Rights Violations in Ethiopia*; and *Report*.
19 See, *EH* throughout 1977 for continuous references to the 'liquidation' of anarchists and reactionaries; P. Schwab, *Ethiopia*, pp. 40–2.
20 Cole, *Ethiopia*, p. 61.
21 *EH*, 25 December 1977.
22 *EH*, 16 and 24 October 1979, 17 and 19 June 1981.
23 *EH*, 22 and 23 September 1984, 2 October 1984.
24 *EH*, 3 May 1981.
25 National Military Service Proclamation, *NG*, 4 May 1983.
26 *EH*, 11 November 1984, 10 January 1985.
27 *EH*, 31 December 1985.
28 *EH*, 7 January 1986.
29 *EH*, 15 October 1986.
30 *EH*, 1 November 1986.
31 *EH*, 16 March 1986.
32 Andargatchew Tesfaye, 'Patterns and trends of crime in Ethiopia'.
33 Working People's Control Committee Establishment Proclamation, *NG*, 5 November 1981; Hailu Asefa, *People's Control Committee of the USSR*.
34 *EH*, 20 February 1985, 16 February 1986.
35 *EH*, 24 September 1986.
36 Government Ownership and Control of the Means of Production Proclamation, *NG*, 11 March 1975.
37 *EH*, 25 September 1979.
38 Joint Venture Establishment Proclamation, *NG*, 22 January 1983.
39 Shiferaw Gurmu, 'An empirical analysis of recent price trends in Ethiopia'.
40 ILO, *Socialism from the Grass Roots*, p. 234.
41 Mengistu Haile-Mariam, *Speech on the Fourth Anniversary of the Ethiopian Revolution*, 12 September 1978.
42 *EH*, 1 April 1979.
43 National Revolutionary Development Campaign and Central Planning Supreme Council Establishment Proclamation, *NG*, 29 October 1978.
44 *EH*, 1 July 1979, 30 December 1979.
45 *EH*, 25 February 1981.
46 Office of the National Committee for Central Planning Establishment Proclamation, *NG*, 7 June 1984.
47 Office of the National Council for Central Planning, *Ten Years Perspective Plan*, p. 53.
48 See ILO, *Socialism from the Grass Roots*, pp. 10–13.
49 For a set of official views on regional planning, see papers by Asmerom Beyene, Getachew Asfar and Solomon Bellete, Second Regional Development

Seminar, 1987; see also P. Treuner *et al.*, *Regional Planning and Development in Ethiopia*.

50 ONCCP, *Ten Years Perspective Plan*, p. 315.
51 *Ibid.*, p. 64.
52 See C. Clapham, 'Revolutionary Socialist Development in Ethiopia'.
53 ONCCP, *Ten Years Perspective Plan*, p. 20.
54 *Ibid.*, pp. 20–1.
55 GDP from 1983–84 to 1985–86, from unpublished official figures supplied to the author.
56 World Bank, *World Development Report 1985*, p. 182.
57 ONCCP, *Ten Years Perspective Plan*, p. 108.
58 *Ethiopia Statistical Abstract*, 1965, p. 129.
59 These terms of trade figures have been calculated from the import and export value indices, in National Bank of Ethiopia, *Quarterly Bulletin*, vol. 10 no. 1, 1984, tables 22 and 23; other calculations of Ethiopia's terms of trade show slightly different figures, but follow the same trend.
60 *Ethiopia Statistical Abstract*, 1984, pp. 218–19, excluding transfer payments.
61 Import and export quantum indices, NBE, *Quarterly Bulletin*, vol. 10 no. 1, 1984, tables 24 and 25.
62 *Ethiopia Statistical Abstract*, 1982, 1984; NBE, *Quarterly Bulletin*, vol. 10 no. 1, 1984.
63 Ministry of Coffee and Tea Development, *Coffee Statistics Handbook*, table E5.
64 *Ethiopia Statistical Abstract*, 1982, p. 64.
65 *The Sunday Times*, London, 27 March 1983.
66 D. A. Korn, *Ethiopia, the United States and the Soviet Union*, p. 104.
67 OECD, *Twenty-five Years of Development Cooperation*, p. 128.
68 ONCCP, *Ten Years Perspective Plan*, p. 317.
69 OECD, *Geographical Distribution of Financial Flows to Developing Countries (1971–77)*, and *Geographical Distribution of Financial Flows to Developing Countries 1979–82*.
70 OECD, *Twenty-five Years*, p. 121.
71 Korn, *Ethiopia*, p. 53.
72 OECD, *Geographical Distribution*, 1971–77 and 1979–82.
73 Korn, *Ethiopia*, p. 52.
74 OECD, *Geographical Distribution*, 1971–77 and 1979–82.
75 *EH*, 25 December 1981, 30 January 1985, 29 March 1985.
76 F. Halliday and M. Molyneux, 'The Soviet Union and the Ethiopian revolution', pp. 180–92; P. Mosley, *Overseas Aid*, p. 30.
77 Halliday and Molyneux, 'The Soviet Union and the Ethiopian revolution'; V. Vigand, 'Problems of Ethiopia's socio–economic development'.
78 National Bank of Ethiopia, *Annual Report*, 1977, 1980, 1983; *Ethiopia Statistical Abstract*, 1984.
79 *Ethiopia Statistical Abstract*, 1972.
80 Ephrem Asebe and Ashenafi Belayneh, 'Analysis of employment and wage structure of employees administered under central personnel administration'.
81 Public Service Position Classification and Salary Scale Regulations, *NG*, 1 June 1972.
82 *Ethiopia Statistical Abstract*, 1975, 1977, 1982; National Bank of Ethiopia, *Annual Report*, 1980, 1982, 1983.
83 ONCCP, *Ten Years Perspective Plan*, p. 317.

84 Agricultural Marketing Corporation Establishment Proclamation, *NG*, 20 November 1976; Alemayehu Lirenso, 'Grain marketing in post-1974 Ethiopia'.

85 These were the prices current in January 1986; the Addis Ababa price had declined with the world market price by 1987.

86 Relief and Rehabilitation Commission, *Food Situation in Ethiopia, 1981–1985: Trend Analysis Report*, October 1985.

6 The control of the towns

1 Population and Housing Census Commission, *Ethiopia 1984 Population and Housing Census Preliminary Report*.

2 Dessalegn Rahmato, *Agrarian Reform in Ethiopia*, p. 63; ILO, *Socialism from the Grass Roots*, p. 378.

3 Solomon Mulugeta, *Meeting the Housing Shortage in Addis Ababa*, p. 36; Hadgu Bariagaber and Asmerom Kidane, *The Dynamics of the Addis Ababa Population*, p. 11.

4 Population and Housing Census Commission, *Analytical Report on Results for Addis Ababa*, table 1.1.

5 PHCC, *Ethiopia 1984 Census Preliminary Report*, p. 16.

6 *Ibid.*, p. 66.

7 National Mapping Agency, *National Atlas of Ethiopia*.

8 Urban Dwellers' Associations and Urban Administration Proclamation, *NG*, 25 April 1981, art. 10.

9 Fecadu Gedamu, 'Urbanization, polyethnic group voluntary associations and national integration in Ethiopia'; see also E. and P. Koehn, 'Edir as a vehicle for urban development in Addis Ababa'.

10 Sara Wolde-Mikael, *The Culture of Poverty*.

11 *EH*, 16 February 1978.

12 Government Ownership of Urban Lands and Extra Houses Proclamation, *NG*, 26 July 1975, art. 24.

13 Urban Dwellers Associations Consolidation and Municipalities Proclamation, *NG*, 9 October 1976; see Lefort, *Ethiopia*, p. 171.

14 Urban Dwellers Associations Proclamation, *NG*, 25 April 1981.

15 Urban Dwellers Associations Proclamation, *NG*, 9 October 1976, art. 9 (18); Urban Dwellers Associations Proclamation, *NG*, 25 April 1981, art. 13 (1).

16 Lefort, *Ethiopia*, pp. 142–3.

17 *EH*, 8 May 1981.

18 *EH*, 19 May 1981, 5, 9, 13 and 16 June 1981.

19 Makonnen Bishaw *et al.*, *Social Development Needs in Addis Ababa*.

20 Urban Dwellers Associations Proclamation, *NG*, 9 October 1976.

21 Urban Dwellers Associations Proclamation, *NG*, 5 April 1981.

22 Jember Teferra, *Case Study of the Health Component of Kebelle 41*.

23 'The struggle of the Ethiopian working class', *Meskerem*, vol. 1 no. 4, May 1981.

24 *EH*, 3 July 1982, 2 May 1986.

25 Trade Unions Organization Proclamation, *NG*, 24 May 1982.

26 Ephrem Asebe, 'Analysis of employment and wage structures of members of the All Ethiopia Trade Union'.

27 *Ibid.*

28 Revolutionary Ethiopia Youth Association Establishment Proclamation, and

Revolutionary Ethiopia Women's Association Establishment Proclamation, *NG*, 9 August 1980.

29 *EH*, 23 August 1984.
30 I know of no survey of the role of women in pre-revolutionary highland society; on kinship, marriage and divorce, see W. A. Shack, *The Central Ethiopians*, pp. 28–37, or G. A. Lipsky, *Ethiopia*, pp. 74–82; on inheritance, see A. Hoben, *Land Tenure among the Amhara of Ethiopia*; on political influence, see C. Prouty, *Empress Taytu and Menilek II*; see also *Ethiopia Observer*, vol. 1 no. 3, 1956.
31 *EH*, 3 September 1980, 10 September 1985.
32 ILO, *Socialism from the Grass Roots*, p. 318.
33 PHCC, *Analytical Report on Results for Addis Ababa*, p. 154.
34 See Tegegn Teku and Tennassie Nichola, *Rural Poverty Alleviation*, and also ch. 7.
35 ILO, *Socialism from the Grass Roots*, p. 257.
36 *Ibid.*, p. 308.
37 *Ibid.*, p. 328.
38 *Ibid.*, p. 334.
39 REYA Establishment Proclamation, *NG*, 9 August 1980.
40 See *EH*, 2 September 1980.
41 *EH*, 2 September 1980, 8 September 1985.
42 Solomon, *Meeting the Housing Shortage*, p. 40.
43 PHCC, *Housing Census of Addis Ababa, August 1978*.
44 *EH*, 1 March 1979, 13 October 1979.
45 PHCC, *Analytical Report*, pp. 297–307.
46 ILO, *Socialism from the Grass Roots*, p. 215.
47 *Ibid.*, p. 217.
48 From Ministry of Urban Development figures in *EH*, 23 July 1980; Shito Mersha, 'Urban development and housing planning in Ethiopia'.
49 Solomon, *Meeting the Housing Shortage*, p. 80; PHCC, *Analytical Report*, p. 323.
50 Solomon, *Meeting the Housing Shortage*, p. 92.
51 *EH*, 26 July 1985.
52 *EH*, 2 and 17 April 1985.
53 M. A. Cappiello, *Draft Report on the Study of the Building Materials Industry*.
54 Solomon, *Meeting the Housing Shortage*, p. 58; PHCC, *Analytical Report*, p. 320.
55 Jember, *Case Study of the Health Component of Kebelle 41*.
56 *EH*, 10 February 1985.
57 Construction and Use of Urban Houses Proclamation, *NG*, 17 February 1986.
58 ILO, *Socialism from the Grass Roots*, p. 238.
59 *Ibid.*, p. 242.
60 Jember, *Case Study of the Health Component of Kebelle 41*.
61 *EH*, 23 March 1980, 3 May 1980.
62 ILO, *Socialism from the Grass Roots*, p. 245.
63 Sara Wolde-Mikael, *The Culture of Poverty*.
64 ILO, *Socialism from the Grass Roots*, p. 244.
65 *EH*, 3 May 1985.
66 World Bank, *World Development Report 1985*, p. 178.
67 Melisachew Mesfin, 'Towards a strategy of industrial location policy'.
68 See Cappiello, *Building Materials Industry*; and, for aluminium pans, *EH*,

4 October 1980; on central control of nationalised industries, see Makonnen Abraham, 'Pricing policy', and Leikun Berhanu, 'The management of industrial enterprises'.

69 *EH*, 1, 19, 22 and 26 August 1984; 1, 2 and 4 September 1984.

70 ONCCP, *Ten Years Perspective Plan*, p. 104.

71 See Eshetu Chole, 'The impact of industrial development on employment generation in Ethiopia', and Gizachew Shiferaw, 'The choice and development of manufacturing technology in Ethiopia'.

72 *EH*, 22 and 26 June 1984.

73 *EH*, 26 August 1984; ILO, *Socialism from the Grass Roots*, pp. 148–9.

74 Calculated from a GDP of 9067.8 million birr (National Bank of Ethiopia, *Annual Report 1983*), divided by an assumed population of 41 million.

75 From unpublished official figures supplied to the author.

76 *EH*, 2 February 1980.

77 ILO, *Socialism from the Grass Roots*, p. 16.

78 *Ibid.*, p. 271.

79 ONCCP, *Ten Years Perspective Plan*, p. 97.

80 Ministry of Industry, 'The evolution of manufacturing industry'; see also M. K. Sethi, 'Small-scale enterprises in socialist Ethiopia'.

81 *Ethiopia Statistical Abstract*, 1982, 1984.

82 ILO, *Socialism from the Grass Roots*, p. 358.

83 *Ethiopia Statistical Abstract*, 1982; Ethiopia School Leaving Certificate results, Ministry of Education, Addis Ababa, 1985.

84 Ethiopia School Leaving Certificate results, 1985.

85 ILO, *Socialism from the Grass Roots*, pp. 207–16.

86 *Ethiopia Statistical Abstract*, 1982.

87 *Ibid.*

88 *Ethiopia Statistical Abstract*, 1984.

89 WPE, *Ethiopia – A Decade of Revolutionary Transformation, 1974–1984*.

90 *EH*, 12 September 1980.

91 National Literacy Campaign Coordinating Committee, *14th Round Programme* (in Amharic).

92 ILO, *Socialism from the Grass Roots*, p. 213.

93 NLCCC, *14th-Round Programme*.

94 *Ibid.*

95 *Ibid.*

96 Andargatchew Tesfaye, 'Patterns and trends of crime in Ethiopia'.

97 See Mengistu Haile-Mariam, *Speech on the Fourth Anniversary of the Ethiopian Revolution*.

98 Andargatchew Tesfaye, 'Patterns and trends of crime'.

7 Rural transformation and the crisis of agricultural production

1 Population and Housing Census Commission, *Ethiopia 1984 Population and Housing Census Preliminary Report*.

2 Fecadu Gedamu *et al.*, *The Nomadic Areas of Ethiopia*.

3 Public Ownership of Rural Lands Proclamation, *NG*, 29 April 1975.

4 Peasant Associations Organization and Consolidation Proclamation, *NG*, 14 December 1975.

5 All-Ethiopia Peasant Association Establishment Proclamation, *NG*,

17 September 1977; Peasant Associations Consolidation Proclamation, *NG*, 24 May 1982.
6 Tegegn Teka and Tennassie Nichola, *Rural Poverty Alleviation*, p. 143.
7 *Ibid.*, p. 83.
8 *Ibid.*, p. 84.
9 Yeshitla Yehualawork, 'Agricultural credit and rural financial markets'.
10 Peasant Associations Consolidation Proclamation, *NG*, 24 May 1982.
11 Dessalegn Rahmato, *Agrarian Reform in Ethiopia*, pp. 84–92.
12 *EH*, 22 April 1982.
13 Alula Abate and Tesfaye Teklu, 'Land reform and peasant associations in Ethiopia'.
14 Dessalegn, *Agrarian Reform*, p. 90.
15 *Ibid.*, pp. 84–90.
16 Alula and Tesfaye, 'Land reform'.
17 Mengistu Woube, *Problems of Land Reform Implementation in Rural Ethiopia*, pp. 85–8, 140–1.
18 Dessalegn, *Agrarian Reform*, pp. 84–90.
19 Tegegn and Tennassie, *Rural Poverty Alleviation*, p. 84.
20 Dessalegn, *Agrarian Reform*, pp. 79–81.
21 Mengistu, *Problems of Land Reform*, p. 103.
22 Woldearegay Tessema, 'Marketing and distribution of industrial products in Ethiopia'.
23 Alula and Tesfaye, 'Land reform'.
24 Dessalegn, *Agrarian Reform*, pp. 92–5.
25 Mesfin Wolde-Mariam, 'Ethiopia's food security'.
26 SIDA, *The Predicament of the Peasants in Conservation-Based Development*.
27 J. W. Harbeson, review of A. Hoben, 'Land tenure among the Amhara of Ethiopia'.
28 For Tigray, see J. Firebrace and G. Smith, *The Hidden Revolution*, pp. 34–5; for Eritrea, see Jordon Gebre-Medhen, 'Nationalism, peasant politics and the emergence of a vanguard front in Eritrea'.
29 *EH*, 18 and 27 January 1977.
30 See J. Markakis, *Ethiopia: Anatomy of a Traditional Polity*, pp. 75ff.
31 See A. Hoben, *Land Tenure among the Amhara of Ethiopia*.
32 Dessalegn, *Agrarian Reform*, pp. 56–9 (percentages recalculated to exclude the category, 'others'); see also Mengistu, *Problems of Land Reform*, pp. 73–4, 136.
33 Mengistu, *Problems of Land Reform*, pp. 85–6.
34 See Dessalegn, 'Moral crusaders and incipient capitalists', p. 73; and also Ministry of State Farm Development, *The Ministry of State Farm Development*.
35 Dessalegn, 'Moral crusaders', p. 83.
36 Fassil Gebre-Kiros, 'Agricultural land fragmentation'; see also Dessalegn, *Agrarian Reform*, p. 31.
37 SIDA, *The Predicament of the Peasants*.
38 ILO, *Socialism from the Grass Roots*, pp. 4–5.
39 Public Ownership of Rural Lands Proclamation, *NG*, 29 April 1975, preamble.
40 *Ibid.*
41 See FAO, *Ethiopian Highlands Reclamation Study*, Executive Summary.
42 See A. Pankhurst, 'Social dimensions of famine in Ethiopia'.
43 F. Ponsi, 'Available demographic data and the level and patterns of population concentration and migration in Ethiopia'.

44 Dessalegn, 'Moral crusaders'.
45 Dessalegn, *Agrarian Reform*, pp. 41–4.
46 FAO, *Ethiopian Highlands Reclamation Study*, Social Survey, pp. 11–13.
47 From Ministry of Agriculture figures, cited in World Bank, *Ethiopia: Agriculture – A Strategy for Growth*.
48 Dessalegn, *Agrarian Reform*, pp. 61–2.
49 V. V. Sokolov *et al.*, *Considerations on the Economic Policy of Ethiopia for the Next Few Years*.
50 Mengistu Haile-Mariam, 'Report to the Sixth Plenum of the WPE Central Committee'.
51 M. Ottaway, 'Foreign economic assistance in the Horn'; J. M. Cohen and N. I. Isaksson, 'Smallholders vs. agricultural collectives'.
52 Ministry of Domestic Trade, *A Short Note on Current Grain Marketing and Price Policy*.
53 From unpublished AMC figures; see also ILO, *Socialism from the Grass Roots*, pp. 67ff.
54 Alemayehu Lirenso, 'Grain marketing in post-1974 Ethiopia'.
55 Mengistu, *Problems of Land Reform*, p. 106.
56 See report in *The Times* (London), 1 March 1985.
57 From unpublished AMC figures.
58 Calculated from AMC buying prices cited in Alemayehu, 'Grain marketing'; and from local market prices noted in Relief and Rehabilitation Commission, *Food Situation in Ethiopia, 1981–1985*.
59 Alemayehu, 'Grain marketing'.
60 RRC, *Food Situation*.
61 A. Saith, 'The distributional dimensions of revolutionary transition: Ethiopia'.
62 *Ibid.*, p. 162.
63 Mengistu, *Problems of Land Reform*, pp. 104–5.
64 Yeshitla Yehualawork, 'Agricultural credit'.
65 Tegegn Teka, *Producers Co-operatives and Rural Development in Ethiopia*.
66 Public Ownership of Rural Lands Proclamation, *NG*, 29 April 1975, art. 23.
67 In POMOA, *Basic Documents of the Ethiopian Revolution*.
68 See, for example, 'Towards the collectivization of agriculture', *EH*, 1 April 1981.
69 SIDA, *The Predicament of the Peasants*.
70 Tegegn, *Producers Co-operatives*; Tegegn and Tennassie, *Rural Poverty Alleviation*.
71 SIDA, *The Predicament of the Peasants*.
72 *EH*, 1 January 1986; see also Tegegn Teka, *Cooperatives and National Development: the Ethiopian Experience*.
73 Tegegn, *Cooperatives and National Development*; *EH*, 16 April 1985; Yeshitla Yehualawork, 'Agricultural credit'.
74 Tegegn, *Producers Cooperatives*.
75 Fassil Gebre-Kiros, *A Survey of Technological Information and Adoption Patterns in Welmera Woreda*.
76 J. M. Cohen and N. I. Isaksson, *Villagization in the Arsi Region of Ethiopia*, pp. 61–2.
77 Calculated from figures in National Bank of Ethiopia, *Annual Report 1983*; see also ILO, *Socialism from the Grass Roots*, p. 44.
78 Habtamu Wondimu, *Some Factors which Affect Peasant Motivation to Work in the Ethiopian Agricultural Producers' Cooperatives*.

79 *Ibid.*
80 ILO, *Socialism from the Grass Roots*, p. 228.
81 Tegegn, *Producers Cooperatives*.
82 B. Mulugetta and C. White, *Major Issues in Agrarian Transformation*.
83 ILO, *Socialism from the Grass Roots*, pp. 42, 47–9; Mengistu, *Problems of Land Reform*, p. 161.
84 A. K. Ghose, 'Transforming feudal agriculture: agrarian change in Ethiopia since 1974'.
85 Cohen and Isaksson, *Villagization*, pp. 5–6.
86 Tegegn, *Producers Cooperatives*.
87 Cohen and Isaksson, *Villagization*, pp. 6–7.
88 *Ibid.*
89 *EH*, 16 May 1985.
90 *EH*, 8 1985.
91 Ministry of Agriculture, *Villagization Guidelines*.
92 *EH*, 29 June 1986 (the reference to the '78th meeting' of the committee is evidently a misprint for '1978 (Ethiopian calendar) meeting'; see also *EH*, 2 December 1986 for the second meeting.
93 See *EH*, 29 September 1985; 1 and 30 November 1985; 1 and 29 December 1985; 4, 7 and 10 January 1986; 4 and 21 February 1986; 8 and 18 March 1986.
94 *EH*, 10 and 25 January 1987, 1 March 1987.
95 Mengistu Haile-Mariam, '1986 Revolution Day Speech'.
96 Mengistu Haile-Mariam, 'Address to the Inaugural Meeting of the National Shengo'.
97 See W. A. Shack, *The Gurage: a People of the Ensete Culture*.
98 See *EH*, 6 and 25 March 1987, 28 May 1987.
99 Cohen and Isaksson, *Villagization*; A. Roberts, *Report of Villagization*.
100 See *The Times* (London), 28 February 1986; 30 October 1986; *The Sunday Times* (London), 18 May 1986.
101 Official figures give far more houses constructed than ancillary buildings; see Mengistu Haile-Mariam, 'Report to the Sixth Plenum'; Cohen and Isaksson, *Villagization*, p. 21.
102 *EH*, 30 November 1985.
103 Yeraswork Admassie, 'Baseline socio–economic sample survey of the three highland Awrajas of Bale'.
104 Ministry of State Farm Development, *The Ministry of State Farm Development: its Role, Organization, Present and Future Activities*.
105 National Bank of Ethiopia, *Annual Report, 1984*; ONCCP, *Ten Years Perspective Plan 1984–85 – 1993–94*, p. 64; Solomon Bellete, 'An overview of Ethiopia's agricultural production strategies and policies'.
106 *EH*, 10 July 1980.
107 ILO, *Socialism from the Grass Roots*, p. 35.
108 Ministry of Domestic Trade, *Short Note*; ILO, *Socialism from the Grass Roots*, p. 80.
109 ILO, *Socialism from the Grass Roots*, pp. 37–9.
110 Tegegn and Tennassie, *Rural Poverty Alleviation*.
111 *Ibid.*
112 Kassahun Abebe, 'State farms in Shoa and Arsi administrative regions'.
113 Mengistu Haile-Mariam, *Central Report to the Second COPWE Congress*.
114 ILO, *Socialism from the Grass Roots*, pp. 42–4.

115 Dessalegn, 'Moral crusaders', pp. 83–4.
116 See *EH*, 10 October 1984.
117 ILO, *Socialism from the Grass Roots*, pp. 35, 38.
118 *Ibid.*, p. 35; Kassahun, 'State farms'.
119 *EH*, 23 November 1979; 2 February 1980; 13 and 22 November 1981; 3 January 1982.
120 *EH*, 9 November 1985.
121 Sokolov *et al.*, *Considerations on the Economic Policy*.
122 ECA, *Pricing Policy*.
123 ILO, *Socialism from the Grass Roots*, pp. 44, 144.
124 Ministry of Coffee and Tea Development, *Coffee Statistics Handbook*, table E1.
125 From figures supplied by the Ministry of Coffee and Tea Development.
126 ILO, *Socialism from the Grass Roots*, pp. 115–16.
127 Teshome Mulat, 'The share of coffee producers in the value of coffee exports'.
128 From figures supplied by the Ministry of Coffee and Tea Development.
129 *Ibid.*
130 ECA, *Pricing Policy*.
131 Coffee Trade Proclamation, *NG*, 27 June 1984.
132 *EH*, 14 October 1980.
133 UN Food and Agriculture Organization, *FAO Trade Yearbook*, 1971, 1972, 1975; Dessalegn, 'Moral crusaders'.
134 Dessalegn, 'Moral crusaders', p. 80; *EH*, 31 May 1979; *Ethiopia Profile*, vol. 1 no. 3, 1982.
135 *EH*, 12 June 1977, 20 September 1977.
136 *EH*, 15 February 1979.
137 *EH*, 7 and 10 October 1979.
138 *EH*, 19 July 1980, 31 August 1980, 8 October 1980, 16 and 25 November 1980.
139 *Ethiopia Profile*, vol. 1 no. 3, 1982.
140 *FAO Trade Yearbook*, 1975, 1978, 1980, 1982, 1984.
141 See P. Henze, 'Behind the Ethiopian Famine', *Encounter*, September 1986, p. 27.
142 See R. Pankhurst, *The History of Famine and Epidemics in Ethiopia*.
143 S. Maxwell, *Food Aid to Ethiopia*.
144 FAO, *Trade Yearbook*.
145 W. C. Robinson and F. Yamazaki, 'Agriculture, population and economic planning in Ethiopia'; other figures differ for the 1974–80 period, but show a similar trend.
146 See FAO, *Ethiopian Highlands Reclamation Study*.
147 Relief and Rehabilitation Commission, *The Challenges of Drought*, p. 15; this statement is sufficiently rebutted by information given in publications such as RRC, *1986 Food Supply Prospect (supplement)*.
148 *EH*, 10 February 1985.
149 RRC, *The Challenges of Drought*, p. 231.
150 Rainfall figures are regularly published in *Ethiopia Statistical Abstract*; for figures for Kombolcha and Mekelle, see World Bank, *Ethiopia: Agriculture*.
151 RRC, *Food Situation*.
152 *Ethiopia Statistical Abstract 1982*, p. 121.
153 Dejene Aredo, 'Foreign aid to Ethiopian agriculture'.
154 See *The Times* (London), 29 December 1986.

155 The word 'famine' was never used in official statements.
156 See, for example, G. Hancock, *Ethiopia: the Challenge of Hunger*, and P. Gill, *A Year in the Death of Africa*.
157 Figure supplied by the RRC.
158 RRC, *Introductory Statement by Comrade Dawit Wolde Giorgis*, 30 March 1984; *Review of Current Situation in Drought Affected Regions of Ethiopia*, 6 August 1984.
159 See Gill, *Death of Africa*, pp. 44–9.
160 I have searched *The Ethiopian Herald* for references, and there are none.
161 *EH*, 28 July 1984.
162 Gill, *Death of Africa*, p. 7; this has been confirmed to me by aid agency representatives in Addis Ababa.
163 Mengistu Haile-Mariam, 'Central Report', *Founding Congress of the Workers' Party of Ethiopia*.
164 ILO, *Socialism from the Grass Roots*, pp. 276–7.
165 Figures supplied by the RRC.
166 Mengistu Haile-Mariam, 'Report to the Sixth Plenum'.
167 FAO, *Ethiopian Highlands Reclamation Study*, executive summary, p. 21.
168 ILO, *Socialism from the Grass Roots*, pp. 68–9; see also K. Griffin and R. Hay, 'Problems of agricultural development in socialist Ethiopia'.
169 Figures supplied by the RRC.
170 See M. Colchester and V. Luling, *Ethiopia's Bitter Medicine*; *The Times* (London), 9 February 1985, 23 March 1986.
171 Colchester and Luling, *Ethiopia's Bitter Medicine*; *The Sunday Times* (London), 3 November 1985.
172 See *EH*, 3 November 1984.
173 Mengistu Haile-Mariam, 'Report to the Sixth Plenum'.
174 See Gill, *Death of Africa*, ch. 11.

8 The national question

1 A phrase coined by I. M. Lewis, in *Nationalism and Self-Determination in the Horn of Africa*, pp. 73–4.
2 See G. Salole, 'Who are the Shoans?'
3 See Pliny the Middle-Aged, 'The life and times of the Derg'.
4 Getachew Wolde-Mikael, 'The scope and limits of a student movement: the case of ESUNA in the early seventies'.
5 Tadesse Ayalew, *The Question of Nationalities in the Course of the Ethiopian Revolution (1974–84)*.
6 In POMOA, *Basic Documents of the Ethiopian Revolution*.
7 *EH*, 13, 19 and 29 April 1977.
8 See, for example, *EH*, 5 September 1979.
9 Institute for the Study of Ethiopian Nationalities, *Documents on the Establishment of the Institute for the Study of Ethiopian Nationalities*, p. 9.
10 Constitution of the PDRE, published in *EH*, 30 January 1987, art. 116.
11 *Ethiopia Statistical Abstract 1980*, pp. 20–2.
12 *Ethiopia 1984 Population and Housing Census Preliminary Report*, p. 15; on regional government, see J. M. Cohen and P. H. Koehn, *Ethiopian Provincial and Municipal Government*.
13 See D. Donham and W. James, *The Southern Marches of Imperial Ethiopia*, especially A. Triulzi, 'Nekempte and Addis Abeba'.

14 *EH*, 1 November 1977.
15 Lefort, *Ethiopia*, pp. 113–14.
16 These movements, throughout the Horn of Africa, have recently been examined in another volume of this series, J. Markakis, *National and Class Conflict in the Horn of Africa*, which I have been able to read in proof at a late stage in the preparation of this book. For Eritrea, see also H. Ehrlich, *The Struggle over Eritrea, 1962–1978*, and P. B. Henze, 'Eritrea: the endless war'; there is also a substantial polemical literature.
17 A fascinating account of this process appears in H. Erhlich, *Ethiopia and the Challenge of Independence*.
18 C. Clapham, *Haile-Selassie's Government*, p. 77.
19 Ehrlich, *Ethiopia and the Challenge of Independence*, ch. 7.
20 See C. Rosen, 'The Governor-General of Tigre province'.
21 For the transition to federation, see G. K. N. Trevaskis, *Eritrea: a Colony in Transition*; and for a biassed account which nonetheless contains much useful contemporary material, E. S. and R. K. P. Pankhurst, *Ethiopia and Eritrea*.
22 Published in POMOA, *Basic Documents*, pp. 148–57.
23 *EH*, 27 June 1979.
24 *EH*, 2 February 1982.
25 See *EH*, 26 January 1982.
26 See, for example, J. Firebrace and G. Smith, *The Hidden Revolution*; the Tigrean opposition is discussed in Markakis, *National and Class Conflict*, pp. 248–58, without, I feel, really tackling the problem raised here.
27 See Ehrlich, *The Struggle over Eritrea*.
28 See Firebrace and Smith, *The Hidden Revolution*, p. 24.
29 See TPLF Foreign Relations Bureau, *Tigray*, p. 4; the claim is faithfully repeated in Firebrace and Smith, *The Hidden Revolution*, pp. v, 18, and more surprisingly in Markakis, *National and Class Conflict*, p. 250; the area concerned, separated from Tigray by the impressive natural barrier of the Setit/Takazze river, has never been governed as part of Tigray at any period in the past, but has come under Gonder or Semien. The position of Wag is more complex; historically a separate province, it has links both with the Amharic-speaking areas to the south and with Tigray to the north, and many of its people are Tigrinya speaking; but it has never, to my knowledge, been administered as part of Tigray.
30 See *Adulis*, vol. 1 no. 11, May 1985; and *People's Voice*, special issue 'On our Differences with the EPLF', 1986.
31 Markakis, *National and Class Conflict*, p. 338.
32 *Ibid.*, p. 246.
33 Lefort, *Ethiopia*, p. 267.
34 See Firebrace and Smith, *The Hidden Revolution*, pp. 51–76 for Tigray; Jordon Gebre-Medhen, 'Nationalism, peasant politics and the emergence of a vanguard front in Eritrea', pp. 48–57, for Eritrea.
35 See Salole, 'Who are the Shoans?'; Levine, *Wax and Gold*, p. 47.
36 See 'Ethiopia's Forgotten Liberation Movement', *New African*, July 1985.
37 Markakis, *National and Class Conflict*, pp. 233–4.
38 See Kassim Shehim, 'Ethiopia, revolution, and the question of nationalities: the case of the Afar'; Dahilon Yassin, *The Rise and Fall of the Sultanate of Aussa*.
39 P. T. W. Baxter, 'Oromo perceptions of and responses to the revolution'.
40 *Ibid.*
41 Personal informants, Hararghe, March 1986.

42 See P. T. W. Baxter, 'Ethiopia's unacknowledged problem: the Oromo'.
43 H. Blackhurst, 'Ethnicity in Southern Ethiopia: the general and the particular'.
44 S. Pausewang, *Peasants, Land and Society: a Social History of Land Reform in Ethiopia*.
45 Clapham, *Haile-Selassie's Government*, p. 77.
46 U. Braukamper, 'Ethnic identity and social change among Oromo refugees in the Horn of Africa'.
47 *Ibid.*

9 The external politics of revolution

1 This is a theme which I have explored in C. Clapham, 'Ethiopia', in T. M. Shaw and O. Aluko, eds., *The Political Economy of African Foreign Policy*.
2 See H. G. Marcus, *Ethiopia, Great Britain, and the United States, 1941–1974*.
3 John H. Spencer, a foreign-policy adviser working in Ethiopia at that time, suggests that much of the credit for Ethiopia's post-war foreign policy should go to Makonnen and Aklilu Habte-Wold; see *Ethiopia at Bay*.
4 See for example T. J. Farer, *War Clouds on the Horn of Africa*; M. Ottaway, *Soviet and American Influence on the Horn of Africa*; Bereket Habte Selassie, *Conflict and Intervention in the Horn of Africa*. R. G. Patman, *Intervention and Disengagement in the Horn of Africa*, draws on the available Russian language sources.
5 See P. B. Henze, 'Arming the Horn 1960–1980'.
6 See D. Petterson, 'Ethiopia abandoned?'; and for an Ethiopian viewpoint, Negussay Ayele, 'The Horn of Africa'.
7 See Aleme Eshete, 'The Sino–Soviet conflict and the Horn, 1956–1976'.
8 Patman, *Intervention and Disengagement*, p. 222.
9 Pliny the Middle-Aged, 'The life and times of the Derg'.
10 Pliny the Middle-Aged, 'The PMAC: origins and structure, Part II'.
11 See Lefort, *Ethiopia*, p. 179; Patman, *Intervention and Disengagement*, p. 220.
12 *EH*, 5 February 1977.
13 See G. Galperin, *Ethiopia: Population, Resources, Economy*, pp. 17–18; Patman, *Intervention and Disengagement*, p. 193.
14 Galperin, *Ethiopia*, p. 163; Patman, *Intervention and Disengagement*, pp. 274–5.
15 Patman, *Intervention and Disengagement*, pp. 129ff.
16 Henze, 'Arming the Horn'.
17 See F. Halliday and M. Molyneux, 'The Soviet Union and the Ethiopian revolution'; while emphasising that the USSR did not formally support Somali claims on the Ogaden, the authors ignore the role of Soviet arms in achieving the same result.
18 Lefort, *Ethiopia*, p. 210; Bereket Habte-Selassie, *Conflict and Intervention*, p. 111; Patman, *Intervention and Disengagement*, pp. 231–2.
19 Lefort, *Ethiopia*, p. 208; Patman, *Intervention and Disengagement*, pp. 236–7.
20 *EH*, 7 May 1977.
21 See D. A. Korn, *Ethiopia, the United States and the Soviet Union*, dustjacket.
22 *EH*, 11 November 1980.
23 Korn, *Ethiopia*, pp. 66–70, 101.
24 Henze, 'Arming the Horn', p. 653.
25 Korn, *Ethiopia*, p. 93.

26 Halliday and Molyneux, 'The Soviet Union and the Ethiopian revolution', p. 180.
27 *Ethiopia Profile*, vol. 1 no. 1, 1982.
28 Korn, *Ethiopia*, p. 93.
29 See Sokolov, *Considerations on the Economic Policy of Ethiopia*.
30 See *EH*, 9 January 1980, for the statement.
31 See *Le Monde* (Paris), 26/27 January 1986; *The Guardian* (London), 26 January 1986.
32 *EH*, 17 January 1986.
33 *EH*, 25 June 1987.
34 Korn, *Ethiopia*, p. 97.
35 B. Lewytzkyj, ed., *Who's Who in the Soviet Union*.
36 See Korn, *Ethiopia*, ch. 3.
37 *Ibid.*, p. 100.
38 *EH*, 28 March 1985.
39 See *EH*, 1 March 1979.
40 *EH*, 26 November 1985.
41 *EH*, 15 May 1987.
42 Korn, *Ethiopia*, pp. 94–5.
43 *EH*, 9 June 1979, 9 November 1979; Korn, *Ethiopia*, p. 173, puts the total number at 20,000, but other estimates are lower.
44 US Embassy, Addis Ababa, *Presidential Determination on Ethiopia*.
45 See Korn, *Ethiopia*, ch. 7.

Bibliography

Published official sources

Ethiopia

Addis Ababa University, *Duties, Code of Conduct and Disciplinary Regulations of Academic Staff*, May 1985.

Central Statistical Office, *Ethiopia Statistical Abstract*, Addis Ababa, annual or biennial.

Civil Service Commission, *Organization of the Provisional Military Government of Socialist Ethiopia*, Addis Ababa, June 1978.

Constitutional Drafting Commission, 'Draft Constitution of the People's Democratic Republic of Ethiopia', *EH*, 7 June 1986.

'Revised Draft Constitution of the People's Democratic Republic of Ethiopia', *EH*, 30 January 1987.

'Explanatory Statement on the Draft Constitution as Revised and Enriched on the Basis of Popular Discussion and Comments', *EH*, 30 January 1987.

Ethiopian Revolution Information Center, *Ethiopia in Revolution*, Addis Ababa, July 1977.

Institute for the Study of Ethiopian Nationalities, *Documents on the Establishment of the Institute for the Study of Ethiopian Nationalities*, Addis Ababa, July 1984.

Mengistu Haile-Mariam, published speeches, in chronological order:

The National Revolutionary War in the North: Nationwide Address by Lt Col Mengistu Haile-Mariam on the Situation in the Administrative Region of Eritrea, Addis Ababa: Ministry of Information and National Guidance, 7 June 1978.

Speech on the Fourth Anniversary of the Ethiopian Revolution, Addis Ababa, 12 September 1978.

Towards Party Formation: Nationwide Address Delivered by Comrade Mengistu Haile-Mariam, Addis Ababa, 17 December 1979.

First COPWE Congress: Report Delivered by Comrade Mengistu Haile-Mariam, Addis Ababa, 16 June 1980.

Central Report to the Second COPWE Congress, Addis Ababa, January 1983.

Address on the Occasion of the Ninth Anniversary of the Ethiopian Revolution, Addis Ababa, 12 September 1983.

'Central Report delivered by Mengistu Haile Mariam', *Founding Congress of the Workers' Party of Ethiopia*, Addis Ababa, September 1984.

May Day Address, 1985, *EH*, 3 May 1985.

Revolution Day Speech, 1986, *EH*, 13 September 1986.

'Report to the Sixth Plenum of the WPE Central Committee', *Summary of World Broadcasts*, London: BCC, 23 March 1987.

'Address to the Inaugural Meeting of the National Shengo', *Summary of World Broadcasts*, London: BBC, 15 September 1987.

Meskerem: A Marxist–Leninist Ideological Journal, published by the Ideological Department of the Central Committee of COPWE, individual articles:

'History of the Struggle of the Ethiopian Working Class', vol. 1 no. 4, May 1981, pp. 20–39.

'The Role of the State and Cooperative Sectors in Socialist Economic Construction', vol. 1 no. 5, June 1981, pp. 26–40.

'United States Imperialism in Pre-Revolutionary Ethipia', vol. 2 no. 6, September 1981, pp. 42–771.

'The Ethiopian Revolution: Its Present Stage of Development', vol. 2 no. 7, December 1981, pp. 10–44.

'Opportunism under the Guise of Marxism', vol. 3 no. 10, September 1982, pp. 48–66.

'The Evolution of a Socialist Educational System in Ethiopia', vol. 3 no. 11, December 1982, pp. 59–87.

'Democracy and the Question of Nationalities in the Ethiopian Revolution', vol. 3 no. 11, December 1982, pp. 88–103.

'Economic Plan Preparation and Fulfilment in the Course of the Ethiopian Revolution', vol. 3 no. 14, June 1983, pp. 40–63.

Ministry of Agriculture, *The 1984 Annual Report of Producers' Cooperative Societies*, Addis Ababa, August 1984.

Ministry of Coffee and Tea Development, *Coffee Statistics Handbook 1961–62 to 1982–83*, Addis Ababa, September 1984.

Ministry of Education, *Education in Socialist Ethiopia: Origins – Reorientation – Strategy for Development*, Addis Ababa, 1984.

Ministry of Information, *Addis Zemen* (in Amharic), Addis Ababa, daily.

The Ethiopian Herald, Addis Ababa, daily.

Ministry of State Farm Development, *The Ministry of State Farm Development: its Role, Organization, Present and Future Activities*, Addis Ababa, 1984.

National Bank of Ethiopia, *Quarterly Bulletin*.

Annual Reports, 1980, 1981, 1982, 1983, 1984.

National Literacy Campaign Coordinating Committee, *Every Ethiopian will be Literate and will Remain Literate*, Addis Ababa, June 1984.

Ye14gnaw Zur Temeseret Timihrt Zemecha Program (Literacy Campaign 14th Round Programme), Addis Ababa, Meskerem 1978 EC (September 1985).

National Mapping Agency, *National Atlas of Ethiopia*, Preliminary Edition, Addis Ababa, 1981.

Negarit Gazeta (Official Gazette), individual enactments in chronological order, with volume and number:

Public Service Position Classification and Salary Scale Regulations, no. 2 of 1972, Legal Notice No. 419/1972, *NG* 31/15, 1 June 1972.

Special Courts Martial Establishment Proclamation, no. 7 of 1974, *NG* 34/7, 16 November 1974.

Special Penal Code Proclamation, no. 8 of 1974, *NG* 34/8, 16 November 1974.

Special Criminal Procedure Code Proclamation, no. 9 of 1974, *NG* 34/9, 16 November 1974.

Public Order and Safety Proclamation, no. 10 of 1974, *NG* 34/10, 16 November 1974.

Government Ownership and Control of the Means of Production Proclamation, no. 26 of 1975, *NG* 34/22, 11 March 1975.

Public Ownership of Rural Lands Proclamation, no. 31 of 1975, *NG* 34/26, 29 April 1975.

Government Ownership of Urban Lands and Extra Houses Proclamation, no. 47 of 1975, *NG* 34/41, 26 July 1975.

Declaration of State of Emergency Proclamation, no. 55 of 1975, *NG* 35/4, 30 September 1975.

Labour Proclamation, no. 64 of 1975, *NG* 35/11, 6 December 1975.

Peasant Associations Organization and Consolidation Proclamation, no. 71 of 1975, *NG* 35/15, 14 December 1975.

Urban Dwellers' Associations Consolidation and Municipalities Proclamation, no. 104 of 1976, *NG* 36/5, 9 October 1976.

Agricultural Marketing Corporation Establishment Proclamation, no. 105 of 1976, *NG* 36/7, 20 November 1976.

Provisional Office for Mass Organizational Affairs Organization and Operation Improvement Proclamation, no. 119 of 1977, *NG* 36/22, 14 July 1977.

All-Ethiopia Peasant Association Establishment Proclamation, no. 130 of 1977, *NG* 37/1, 17 September 1977.

National Revolutionary Development Campaign and Central Planning Supreme Council Establishment Proclamation, no. 156 of 1978, *NG* 38/4, 29 October 1978.

Commission for Organizing a Party of the Working People of Ethiopia Establishment Proclamation, no. 174 of 1979, *NG* 39/5, 18 December 1979.

Revolutionary Ethiopia Youth Association Establishment Proclamation, no. 187 of 1980, *NG* 39/15, 9 August 1980.

Revolutionary Ethiopia Women's Association Establishment Proclamation, no. 118 of 1980, *NG* 39/15, 9 August 1980.

1973 EC Budget Proclamation, no. 199 of 1980, *NG* 40/6, 24 November 1980.

Urban Dwellers' Associations and Urban Administration Proclamation, no. 206 of 1981, *NG* 40/15, 25 April 1981.

Revised Special Penal Code Proclamation, no. 214 of 1981, *NG* 41/2, 5 November 1981.

Special Court Establishment Proclamation, no. 215 of 1981, *NG* 41/2, 5 November 1981.

Working People's Control Committee Establishment Proclamation, no. 213 of 1981, *NG* 41/2, 5 November 1981.

1974 EC Budget Proclamation, no. 221 of 1982, *NG* 41/5, 22 February 1982.

Trade Unions Organization Proclamation, no. 222 of 1982, *NG* 41/6, 24 May 1982.

Peasant Associations Consolidation Proclamation, no. 223 of 1982, *NG* 41/6, 24 May 1982.

Joint Venture Establishment Proclamation, no. 235 of 1983, *NG* 42/6, 22 January 1983.

National Defence and Security Council Establishment Proclamation, no. 237 of 1983, *NG* 42/8, 30 March 1983.

National Military Service Proclamation, no. 238 of 1983, *NG* 42/9, 4 May 1983.

Establishment of the Military Commissariat and the Territorial People's Militia Proclamation, no. 239 of 1983, *NG* 42/10, 10 May 1983.

1975 EC Budget Proclamation, no. 240 of 1983, *NG* 42/11, 11 May 1983.

1976 EC Budget Proclamation, no. 253 of 1984, *NG* 43/5, 2 January 1984.

National Military Service Regulations, Legal Notice no. 82 of 1984, *NG* 43/6, 10 January 1984.

Medals, Orders and Prizes Proclamation, no. 257 of 1984, *NG* 43/9, 13 February 1984.

Office of the National Council for Central Planning Establishment Proclamation, no. 262 of 1984, *NG* 43/13, 7 June 1984.

Coffee Trade Proclamation, no. 263 of 1984, *NG* 43/14, 27 June 1984.

Special Contribution for Relief and Rehabilitation Proclamation, no. 272 of 1985, *NG* 44/6, 11 February 1985.

Constitution Drafting Commission Establishment Proclamation, no. 290 of 1986, *NG* 45/2, 14 February 1986.

Construction and Use of Urban Houses Proclamation, no. 291 of 1986, *NG* 45/3, 17 February 1986.

Office of the National Council for Central Planning, *Ten Years Perspective Plan 1984–85 – 1993–94*, Addis Ababa, August 1984, 350pp.

Population and Housing Census Commission, *Housing Census of Addis Ababa, August 1978*, Addis Ababa, January 1984.

Ethiopia 1984 Population and Housing Census Preliminary Report, Addis Ababa, September 1984.

Population and Housing Census of Ethiopia 1984: Analytical Report on Results for Addis Ababa, Addis Abba, January 1987.

Propaganda and Information Committee, *Ethiopia: Four Years of Revolutionary Progress*, Addis Ababa, September 1978.

Provisional Military Administrative Council, *Declaration on Economic Policy of Socialist Ethiopia*, Addis Ababa, 7 February 1975.

Support the Just Cause of the Ethiopian Peoples, Addis Ababa, nd (1977–78).

Provisional Office of Mass Organizational Affairs, *Basic Documents of the Ethiopian Revolution*, Addis Ababa, 1977.

Relief and Rehabilitation Commission, *Introductory Statement by Comrade Dawit Wolde Giorgis, Chief Commissioner*, Addis Ababa, 30 March 1984.

Review of Current Situation in Drought Affected Regions of Ethiopia (April–July), Addis Ababa, 6 August 1984.

The New Settlement Approach, Addis Ababa, September 1984.

Introductory Statement by Comrade Dewit Wolde Giorgis, Chief Commissioner, Addis Ababa, October 1984.

Address by Comrade Berhanu Bayih, Member of the Politbureau of the CC of WPE and Minister of Labour and Social Affairs, Chairman of the Aid Coordination Committee, Addis Ababa, December 1984.

Introductory Statement by Comrade Daiwit Wolde Giorgis, Chief Commissioner, Addis Ababa, December 1984.

Combatting the Effects of Cyclical Drought in Ethiopia, Addis Ababa, January 1985.

Progress Report on Activities of Relief and Rehabilitation Commission (December 1984–March 1985) by Comrade Dawit Wolde Giorgis, RRC Chief Commissioner, Addis Ababa, April 1985.

Fifth General Donors' Meeting, Opening Statement by Commissioner Dawit Wolde Giorgis, 8 October 1985, Addis Ababa, 1985.

Food Situation in Ethiopia, 1981–1985: Trend Analysis Report, Addis Ababa, October 1985.

1986 Food Supply Prospect (Supplement), Addis Ababa, November 1985.

Bibliography

The Challenges of Drought: Ethiopia's Decade of Struggle in Relief and Rehabilitation, Addis Ababa, 1985.

Statement at Extraordinary Donors' Meeting by Comrade Taye Gurmu, Deputy Commissioner, Addis Ababa, 23 January 1986.

1987 Food Supply Prospect, Addis Ababa, January 1987.

Teferi Banti, *Address by Brigadier General Teferi Bante on the Second Anniversary of the Revolution*, Addis Ababa, 12 September 1976.

Workers' Party of Ethiopia, *Declaration and Resolutions of the Founding Congress of the Workers Party of Ethiopia*, Addis Ababa, September 1984.

Rules of the Workers' Party of Ethiopia, Addis Ababa, September 1984.

WPE, Propaganda and Cultural Committee, *Ethiopia – A Decade of Revolutionary Transformation, 1974–1984*, Addis Ababa, 1984.

Opposition movements

Eritrean People's Liberation Front, *Adulis*, periodical.

Tigray People's Liberation Front, *People's Voice*, periodical.

TPLF Foreign Relations Bureau, *Tigray*, February 1982.

International organisations and United Nations agencies

Organisation for Economic Cooperation and Development (OECD):
Geographical Distribution of Financial Flows to Developing Countries (1971–77), Paris: OECD, 1978.

Geographical Distribution of Financial Flows to Developing Countries 1979–82, Paris: OCED, 1984.

Twenty-Five Years of Development Cooperation, Paris: OECD, 1985.

United Nations, Economic Commission for Africa, *Case Study on Pricing Policy in Ethiopia*, Addis Ababa, October 1983.

United Nations, Food and Agriculture Organization:
FAO Trade Yearbook, vol. 25, 1971 and later years.

Land Reform, Land Settlement and Cooperatives, no. 1/2, Rome, 1981.

Ethiopian Highlands Reclamation Study: Report on the Sociological Survey and Sociological Considerations in Preparing a Development Strategy, Addis Ababa, December 1983; executive summary, Rome 1985.

United Nations, International Labour Organisation, *Socialism from the Grass Roots: Accumulation, Employment and Equity in Ethiopia*, vol. 1 report 397 pp., vol. 2 Working Papers 141pp., Addis Ababa, September 1982.

Patterns of Industrialization and Impact on Employment and Incomes in African Countries: The Case of Ethiopia, Addis Ababa, 1983.

Briefing Workshop on the Ethiopian Economy, Addis Ababa, August 1982.

United Nations, UNDP/World Bank Energy Sector Assessment Program, *Ethiopia: Issues and Options in the Energy Sector*, Report no. 4741–ET, xviii + 170pp, November 1983.

World Bank, *World Development Report 1985*, New York: Oxford University Press, 1985.

Books, articles and published papers

Abegaz, H. Y., *The Organization of State Farms in Ethiopia after the Land Reform of 1974*, Saarbrucken: Verlag, 1982.

266

Abraham, W. I., and Seilu Abraha, 'Ethiopia's public sector: structure, policies and impact', *Ethiopian Journal of Development Research*, vol. 2 no. 1, April 1975, pp. 1–12.

Agyeman-Duah, B., 'The US and Ethiopia: the politics of military assistance', *Armed Forces and Society*, vol. 12 no. 2, 1986.

Alula Abate and Fassil G. Kiros, 'Agrarian reform, structural changes, and rural development in Ethiopia', in A. K. Ghose, ed., *Agrarian Reform in Contemporary Developing Countries*, London: Croom Helm, 1983.

Alula Abate and Tesfaye Teklu, 'Land reform and peasants associations in Ethiopia: case studies of two widely differing regions', *Northeast African Studies*, vol. 2 no. 2, 1980, pp. 1–51.

Amnesty, International, *Human Rights Violations in Ethiopia*, London, December 1977.

Report, London, annual.

Balsvik, R., *Haile Selassie's Students: The Rise of Social and Political Consciousness*, East Lansing: Michigan State University Press, 1985.

Baxter, P. T. W., 'Ethiopia's unacknowledged problem: the Oromo', *African Affairs*, vol. 77 no. 308, July 1978.

Bereket Habte Selassie, *Conflict and Intervention in the Horn of Africa*, New York: Monthly Review, 1980.

Blackhurst, H., 'Ethnicity in Southern Ethiopia: the general and the particular', *Africa*, vol. 50 no. 1, 1980, pp. 55–65.

Booth, R., *The Armed Forces of African States 1970*, Adelphi Paper no. 67, London: ISS, 1970.

Braukamper, U., 'Ethnic identity and social change among Oromo refugees in the Horn of Africa', *Northeast African Studies*, vol. 4 no. 3, 1982–83, pp. 1–15.

Chabal, P., *Amilcar Cabral: Revolutionary Leadership and People's War*, Cambridge University Press, 1983.

Chege, M., 'The revolution betrayed: Ethiopia, 1974–79', *Journal of Modern African Studies*, vol. 19 no. 3, 1979.

Clapham, C., *Haile-Selassie's Government*, London: Longman, 1969.

Third World Politics: An Introduction, London: Croom Helm, 1985.

'Ethiopia', in R. Lemarchand, ed., *African Kingships in Perspective*, London: Cass, 1977.

'Ethiopia', in T. M. Shaw and O. Aluko, eds., *The Political Economy of African Foreign Policy*, Aldershot: Gower, 1984.

'Ethiopia: the institutionalisation of a Marxist military regime', in C. Clapham and G. Philip, eds., *The Political Dilemmas of Military Regimes*, London: Croom Helm, 1985.

'Revolutionary socialist development in Ethiopia', *African Affairs*, vol. 86 no. 343, April 1987.

'The constitution of the People's Democratic Republic of Ethiopia', *Journal of Communist Studies*, vol. 3 no. 2, June 1987.

Cliffe, L., Davidson, B. and Bereket Habte Selassie, *Behind the War in Eritrea*, Nottingham: Spokesman, 1980.

Cohen, J. M. and P. H. Koehn, *Ethiopian Provincial and Municipal Government: Imperial Patterns and Post-Revolutionary Changes*, East Lansing: Michigan State University, 1980.

Cohen, J. M. and N. I. Isaksson, *Villagization in the Arsi Region of Ethiopia*, Uppsala: Swedish University of Agricultural Sciences, Rural Development Studies no. 19, February 1987.

Bibliography

Colchester, M. and Luling, V., eds., *Ethiopia's Bitter Medicine: Settling for Disaster*, London: Survival International, 1986.

Cole, E., *Ethiopia: Political Power and the Military*, Paris: BIDOI, 1985.

Crisp, J., 'The politics of repatriation: Ethiopian refugees in Djibouti, 1977–83', *Review of African Political Economy*, vol. 30, 1984.

Dessalegn Rahmato, *Agrarian Reform in Ethiopia*, Uppsala: Scandinavian Institute of African Studies, 1984.

'Moral crusaders and incipient capitalists: mechanized agriculture and its critics in Ethiopia', *Proceedings of the Third Annual Seminar of the Department of History*, Addis Ababa University, 1986.

Donham, D. and James, W., eds., *The Southern Marches of Imperial Ethiopia: Essays in History and Social Anthropology*, Cambridge University Press, 1986.

Ehrlich, H., *The Struggle over Eritrea, 1962–1978: War and Revolution in the Horn of Africa*, Stanford: Hoover, 1983.

Ethiopia and the Challenge of Independence, Boulder: Rienner, 1986.

Farer, T. J., *War Clouds on the Horn of Africa: the Widening Storm*, New York: Carnegie, 2nd edn, 1979.

Fassil Gebre-Kiros, *A Survey of Technological Information and Adoption Patterns in Welmera Woreda*, Addis Ababa: Ethiopian Science and Technology Commission, 1982.

'Agricultural land fragmentation: a problem of land distribution observed in some Ethiopian peasant associations', *Ethiopian Journal of Development Research*, vol. 4 no. 2, October 1980, pp. 1–12.

'An estimate of the proportion of the potential work-year allocated to socio–cultural observances in rural Ethiopia', *Ethiopian Journal of Development Research*, vol. 2 no. 2, October 1976, pp. 15–28.

'A critical evaluation of family planning prescriptions for rural Wollo and Tigre', *Ethiopian Journal of Development Research*, vol. 3 no. 1, April 1979, pp. 1–10.

Fecadu Gedamu, 'Urbanization, polyethnic group voluntary associations and national integration in Ethiopia', *Ethiopian Journal of Development Research*, vol. 1 no. 1, April 1974, pp. 71–80.

Fecadu Gedamu *et al.*, *The Nomadic Areas of Ethiopia, A Study Report Commissioned by the UNDP for the Relief and Rehabilitation Commission*, 5 volumes, Addis Ababa, September 1984. UNDP/RRC ETH/81/001.

Firebrace, J. and Smith, G., *The Hidden Revolution*, London: War on Want, 1982.

Galperin, G., *Ethiopia: Population, Resources, Economy*, Moscow: Progress, 1981.

Getachew Haile, 'The unity and territorial integrity of Ethiopia', *Journal of Modern African Studies*, vol. 24 no. 3, 1986.

Ghose, A. K., 'Transforming feudal agriculture: agrarian change in Ethiopia since 1974', *Journal of Development Studies*, vol. 22 no. 1, 1985, pp. 127–49.

Gill, P., *A Year in the Death of Africa: Politics, Bureaucracy and the Famine*, London: Paladin, 1986.

Griffin, K. and Hay, R., 'Problems of agricultural development in socialist Ethiopia: an overview and a suggested strategy', *Journal of Peasant Studies*, vol. 13 no. 1, 1985, pp. 37–66.

Habtamu Wondimu, *Some Factors which Affect Peasant Motivation to Work in the Ethiopian Agricultural Producers' Cooperatives*, Addis Ababa University, Institute of Development Research, research report no. 21, December 1983.

Hailu Semma, 'The politics of famine in Ethiopia', *Review of African Political Economy*, vol. 33, 1985.

Halliday, F. and Molyneux, M., *The Ethiopian Revolution*, London: Verso, 1981.

268

'The Soviet Union and the Ethiopian revolution', *Third World Affairs 1986*, London: Third World Foundation, 1986.

Hancock, Graham, *Ethiopia: The Challenge of Hunger*, London: Gollancz, 1985.

Harbeson, J. W., Review of Allen Hoben, 'Land tenure among the Amhara of Ethiopia', *Ethiopian Journal of Development Research*, vol. 2 no. 1, April 1975, pp. 55–9.

Henze, P. B., 'Arming the Horn 1960–1980: military expenditures, arms imports and military aid in Ethiopia, Kenya, Somalia and Sudan, with statistics on economic growth and government expenditures', in S. Rubenson, ed., *Proceedings of the Seventh International Conference of Ethiopian Studies*, Uppsala, 1984, pp. 637–56.

'Behind the Ethiopian famine', 3 parts, *Encounter*, 1986.

'Communism and Ethiopia', *Problems of Communism*, vol. 30, 1981.

'Eritrea: the endless war', *Washington Quarterly*, vol. 9 no. 2, 1986, pp. 23–36.

Russians and the Horn: Opportunism and the Long View, Marina del Rey, California: European American Institute for Security Research, 1983, 53pp.

Hoben, A., *Land Tenure among the Amhara of Ethiopia*, University of Chicago Press, 1973.

Houtart, F., 'Social aspects of the Eritrean revolution', *Race and Class*, vol. 22 no. 3, 1981.

Huntington, S. P., *Political Order in Changing Societies*, New Haven: Yale University Press, 1968.

Jackson, R. H. and Rosberg, C. G., *Personal Rule in Black Africa*, Berkeley: University of California Press, 1982.

Jordon Gebre-Medhen, 'Nationalism, peasant politics and the emergence of a vanguard front in Eritrea', *Review of African Political Economy*, no. 30, 1984, pp. 48–57.

Kassim, Shehim, 'Ethiopia, revolution and the question of nationalities: the case of the Afar', *Journal of Modern African Studies*, vol. 23 no. 2, 1985, pp. 331–48.

Keller, E. J., 'Revolutionary Ethiopia: ideology, capacity and the limits of state autonomy', *Journal of Commonwealth and Comparative Politics*, vol. 23 no. 1, 1985.

King, P., *An African Winter*, London: Penguin, 1986.

Koehn, E. and P., 'Edir as a vehicle for urban development in Addis Ababa', in H. G. Marcus, ed., *Proceedings of the First United States Conference on Ethiopian Studies, 1973*, East Lansing: Michigan State University Press, 1975.

Kokiev, A. and Vigand, V., 'National democratic revolution in Ethiopia', in J. Tubiana, ed., *Modern Ethiopia*, Rotterdam: Balkema, 1980.

Korn, D. A., *Ethiopia, the United States and the Soviet Union*, London: Croom Helm, 1986.

'Ethiopia: dilemma for the West', *The World Today*, January 1986.

Lefort, Rene, *Ethiopia: An Heretical Revolution?*, London: Zed Press, 1983.

Legum, C., *Ethiopia: the Fall of Haile Selassie's Empire*, London: Collings, 1975.

Legum, C. and Lee, B., *The Horn of Africa in Continuing Crisis*, New York: Africana, 1979.

Levine, D. N., *Wax and Gold*, University of Chicago Press, 1965.

'Ethiopia: identity, authority and realism', in L. W. Pye and S. Verba, *Political Culture and Political Development*, Princeton University Press, 1965.

Lewis, I. M., ed., *Nationalism and Self-Determination in the Horn of Africa*, London: Ithaca, 1983.

Lewytzkyj, B., ed., *Who's Who in the Soviet Union*, Munchen: K. G. Saur, 1984.

269

Lipsky, G. A., *Ethiopia: its People, its Society, its Culture*, New Haven: HRAF, 1962.

Luckham, R. and Dawit Bekele, 'Foreign powers and militarism in the Horn of Africa', *Review of African Political Economy*, vol. 30, 1984.

Marcus, H. G., *The Life and Times of Menelik II*, Oxford University Press, 1975.

Ethiopia, Great Britain and the United States, 1941–1974: the Politics of Empire, Berkeley: University of California Press, 1983.

Haile Sellassie I: The Formative Years, 1892–1936, Berkeley: University of California Press, 1987.

'The infrastructure of the Italo–Ethiopian crisis: Haile Sellassie, the Solomonic Empire and the world economy, 1916–1936', in R. L. Hess, ed., *Proceedings of the Fifth International Conference of Ethiopian Studies*, Chicago, 1979.

Markakis, J., *Ethiopia: Anatomy of a Traditional Polity*, Oxford University Press, 1974.

National and Class Conflict in the Horn of Africa, Cambridge University Press, 1987.

'Material and social aspects of national conflict in the Horn of Africa', *Civilisations*, vol. 32 no. 2 and vol. 33 no. 1, 1982–83.

Markakis, J. and Nega Ayele, *Class and Revolution in Ethiopia*, Nottingham: Spokesman, 1978.

Mengistu Woube, *Problems of Land Reform Implementation in Rural Ethiopia: A Case Study of Dejen and Wolmera Districts*, Uppsala: Uppsala Universitet Geografiska Regionstudier No. 16, 1986.

Moore, B., *Social Origins of Dictatorship and Democracy: Lord and Peasant in the Making of the Modern World*, London: Allen Lane, 1967.

Moreau, R. E., *The Bird Faunas of Africa and its Islands*, London: Academic Press, 1966.

Mosley, P., *Overseas Aid: Its Defence and Reform*, Brighton: Harvester, 1987.

Mulugetta, B. and C. White, *Major Issues in Agrarian Transformation: Report of a Regional Workshop on Agrarian Transformation in Centrally Planned Economies in Africa*, Arusha, Tanzania, October 1983. Rome: FAO, 1984.

Negussay Ayele, 'The Ethiopian revolution – seven years young', *Journal of African Marxists*, vol. 3, 1981, pp. 47–63.

'The Horn of Africa: revolutionary developments and Western relations', *Northeast African Studies*, vol. 2 no. 3, 1981.

'The Ethiopian revolution', *Ufahamu*, vol. 12 no. 3, 1983, pp. 36–66.

Ottaway, M., *Soviet and American Influence on the Horn of Africa*, New York: Praeger, 1982.

Ottaway, M. and D., *Ethiopia: Empire in Revolution*, New York: Africana, 1978.

Pankhurst, E. S. and R. K. P., *Ethiopia and Eritrea: the Last Ten Years of the Reunion Struggle*, Woodford: Lalibela, 1953.

Pankhurst, R. K. P., *The History of Famine and Epidemics in Ethiopia Prior to the Twentieth Century*, Addis Ababa: RRC, 1986.

Pausewang, S., *Peasants, Land and Society: A Social History of Land Reform in Ethiopia*, Munchen: Weltforum Verlag, Afrika-Studien 110, 1983.

Perham, M. F., *The Government of Ethiopia*, London: Faber, 2nd edn, 1969.

Petterson, D., 'Ethiopia abandoned? An American perspective', *International Affairs*, vol. 62 no. 4, 1986.

Pliny the Middle-Aged, 'The PMAC: origins and structure, Part II', *Northeast African Studies*, vol. 1 no. 1, 1979.

'The life and times of the Derg', *Northeast African Studies*, vol. 5 no. 3, 1983–84.

Ponsi, F., 'Available demographic data and the level and patterns of population concentration and migration in Ethiopia', *Ethiopian Journal of Development Research*, vol. 3 no. 1, April 1979.

Porter, B. D., *The USSR in Third World Conflicts*, Cambridge University Press, 1984.

Prouty, C., *Empress Taytu and Menilek II: Ethiopia 1883–1910*, Trenton, NJ: Red Sea Press, 1986.

Robinson, W. C. and F. Yamazaki, 'Agriculture, population and economic planning in Ethiopia, 1953–1980', *Journal of Developing Areas*, vol. 20 no. 3, 1986.

Rosen, C. B., 'The Governor-General of Tigre province: structure and antistructure', in H. G. Marcus, ed., *Proceedings of the First United States Conference on Ethiopian Studies, 1973*, East Lansing: Michigan State University Press, 1975.

Rubenson, S., *King of Kings Tewodros of Ethiopia*, Addis Ababa: Haile Sellassie I University, 1966.

Saith, A., 'The distributional dimensions of revolutionary transition: Ethiopia', *Journal of Development Studies*, vol. 22 no. 1, 1985.

Salole, G., 'Who are the Shoans?', *Horn of Africa*, vol. 3 no. 1, 1981.

Schwab, P., *Decision-Making in Ethiopia*, London: Hurst, 1972.

Ethiopia: Politics, Economics and Society, London: Pinter, 1985.

Scott, J. C., *The Moral Economy of the Peasant*, New Haven: Yale University Press, 1976.

Shack, W. A., *The Gurage: A People of the Ensete Culture*, Cambridge University Press, 1966.

The Central Ethiopians: Amhara, Tigrina and Related Peoples, London: IAI, 1974.

Sherman, R., *Eritrea: The Unfinished Revolution*, New York: Praeger, 1980.

Shiferaw Gurmu, 'An empirical analysis of recent price trends in Ethiopia', *Ethiopian Journal of Development Research*, vol. 4 no. 2, October 1980, pp. 13–39.

Skocpol, T., *States and Social Revolutions*, Cambridge University Press, 1979.

Spencer, J. H., *Ethiopia at Bay*, Algonac: Reference Publications, 1984.

Stahl, M., *Ethiopia: Political Contradictions in Agricultural Development*, Stockholm: Raben and Sjogren, 1974.

Steer, G., *Caesar in Abyssinia*, London: Hodder, 1936.

Tegegn Teka, *Cooperatives and National Development: The Ethiopian Experience*, Addis Ababa University, Institute of Development Research, Working Paper no. 18, August 1984.

Teshome Mulat, 'The share of coffee producers in the value of coffee exports', *Ethiopian Journal of Development Research*, vol. 3 no. 1, 1979, pp. 51–68.

Thompson, B., *Ethiopia: The Country That Cut Off its Head*, London: Robson Books, 1975.

Tocqueville, A. de, *The Ancien Regime and the French Revolution*, London: Fontana, 1966.

Treuner, P., Tadesse Kidane-Mariam and Teshome Mulat, eds., *Regional Planning and Development in Ethiopia*, vol. 1, Addis Ababa University and Universitat Stuttgart, 1985.

Trevaskis, G. K. N., *Eritrea: a Colony in Transition, 1941–1952*, Oxford University Press, 1960.

Walton, J., *Reluctant Rebels: Comparative Studies in Revolution and Underdevelopment*, New York: Columbia University Press, 1984.

Webb, B. and S., *Soviet Communism: A New Civilisation*, London: WEA, 1935.

271

Young, C., *Ideology and Development in Africa*, New Haven: Yale University Press, 1982.
Zewde Gabre Sellassie, *Yohannes IV of Ethiopia*, Oxford University Press, 1975.

Unpublished papers and theses

Ababe Teferi, 'Agrarian structures and politics in Ethiopia', National Seminar on Integrated Strategies in the Food Sector of Ethiopia, Harer, Alemaya University of Agriculture, December 1986.

Addis Ababa Master Plan Project Office, 'Space Utilization, Space Perception and their Trends: Report on the Survey Concerning the Needs of People in Addis Ababa', November 1984.

Alemayehu Lirenso, 'Grain marketing in post-1974 Ethiopia: problems and prospects', Eighth International Conference on Ethiopian Studies, Addis Ababa, November 1984.

Aleme Eshete, 'The Sino–Soviet conflict and the Horn, 1956–1976', Eighth International Conference on Ethiopian Studies, Addis Ababa, November 1984.

Andargatchew Tesfaye, 'Patterns and trends of crime in Ethiopia', Eighth International Conference on Ethiopian Studies, Addis Ababa, November 1984.

Asmerom Beyene, 'Regional development planning experience of Southern Ethiopia regional planning office', Second Regional Development Seminar, Debre Zeit, February 1987.

Baxter, P. T. W., 'Oromo perceptions of and responses to the revolution', unpublished paper, May 1985.

Cappiello, M. A., 'Draft report on the study of the building materials industry', unpublished paper, Addis Ababa, January 1984.

Cohen, J. M. and N. I. Isaksson, 'Smallholders vs. agricultural collectives: agricultural strategy debates in Ethiopia since the revolution', Washington, Smithsonian Institute, June 1987.

Dahilon Yassin, 'The rise and fall of the Sultanate of Aussa', Addis Ababa University, senior paper, October 1985.

Dejene Aredo, 'Foreign aid to Ethiopian agriculture', National Seminar on Integrated Strategies in the Food Sector of Ethiopia, Harer, Alemaya University of Agriculture, December 1986.

Ephrem Asebe, 'Analysis of employment and wage structures of members of the all Ethiopia trade union', unpublished paper, Addis Ababa, August 1984.

Ephrem Asebe and Ashenafi Belayneh, 'Analysis of employment and wage structure of employees administered under central personnel administration', unpublished paper, Addis Ababa, May 1984.

Eshetu Chole, 'The impact of industrial development on employment generation in Ethiopia', First National Symposium on Industrial Development in Ethiopia, Addis Ababa, August 1986.

Fassil Gebre-Kiros and Alemayehu Lirenso, 'Analysis of grain marketing and pricing policies in Ethiopia with particular reference to the staple teff', Addis Ababa University, Institute of Development Research, November 1985.

Gashaw Ashenafi, 'Local government and local self-administration in Ethiopia', Addis Ababa University, senior essay, October 1985.

Getachew Asfaw, 'Assessment of experiences of regional planning in the light of the office of regional planning for Northern Ethiopia', Second Regional Development Seminar, Debre Zeit, February 1987.

Getachew Wolde-Mikael, 'The scope and limits of a student movement: the case of

272

ESUNA in the early seventies', Eighth International Conference on Ethiopian Studies, Addis Ababa, 1984.

Gizachew Shiferaw, 'The choice and development of manufacturing technology in Ethiopia', First National Symposium on Industrial Development in Ethiopia, Addis Ababa, August 1986.

Hadgu Bariagaber and Asmerom Kidane, 'The dynamics of the Addis Ababa population with special reference to migration aspects of AAMPPO demographic and socio–economic sample survey', Addis Ababa, AAMPPO, April 1985.

Hailu Asefa, 'People's control committee of the USSR: lessons for Ethiopia', Addis Ababa University, senior essay, January 1985.

Hewett, R. M. G., 'Assessment of irrigation potential in the Ethiopian highlands', National Seminar on Integrated Strategies in the Food Sector of Ethiopia, Harer, Alemaya University of Agriculture, December 1986.

Jember Teferra, 'Case Study of the Health Component of Kebele 41 Kefetegna 3 Community Based Integrated Urban Development', Workshop on Community Health and the Urban Poor, Oxford, July 1985.

Kassahun Abebe, 'State farms in Shoa and Arsi administrative regions', unpublished paper, Addis Ababa, July 1984.

Leikun Berhanu, 'The management of industrial enterprises in Ethiopia', First National Symposium on Industrial Development in Ethiopia, Addis Ababa, August 1986.

Makonnen Abraham, 'Pricing policy for public manufacturing enterprises', First National Symposium on Industrial Development in Ethiopia, Addis Ababa, August 1986.

Makonnen Bishaw *et al.*, 'Special development needs in Addis Ababa', Addis Ababa University, School of Social Work, February 1980.

Maxwell, S., 'Food aid to Ethiopia: disincentive effects and commercial displacement', University of Sussex, Institute of Development Studies, April 1986.

Mekete Belachew, 'The need for regional educational planning within the context of integrated rural development: the case of Ethiopia', Second Regional Development Seminar, Debre Zeit, February 1987.

Melisachew Mesfin, 'Towards a strategy of industrial location policy: the case of Ethiopia', Second Regional Development Seminar, Debre Zeit, February 1987.

Mesfin Wolde-Mariam, 'Ethiopia's food security: problems and prospects', National Seminar on Integrated Strategies in the Food Sector of Ethiopia, Harer, Alemaya University of Agriculture, December 1986.

Ministry of Domestic Trade, 'A short note on current grain marketing and price policy', Addis Ababa, January 1986.

Ministry of Education, 'Results of the Ethiopian school leaving certificate examination 1985', Addis Ababa, 1985.

Ministry of Industry, Policy Study and Research Division, 'The evolution of manufacturing industry in Ethiopia', First National Symposium on Industrial Development in Ethiopia, Addis Ababa, August 1986.

Mulugeta W. Aregay, 'Analysis on the demand for food in the urban population of Ethiopia', National Seminar on Integrated Strategies in the Food Sector of Ethiopia, Harer, Alemaya University of Agriculture, December 1986.

Ottaway, M., 'State power consolidation in Ethiopia', University of California, December 1985.

'Foreign economic assistance in the Horn: does it affect Horn government policies?', Washington, Smithsonian Institute, June 1987.

Pankhurst, A., 'Social dimensions of famine in Ethiopia: exchange, migration and integration', Ninth International Conference of Ethiopian Studies, Moscow, 1986.

Patman, R. G., 'Intervention and disengagement in the Horn of Africa: the Soviet experience, 1970–1978', unpublished PhD thesis, University of Southampton, 1987.

Piussi, P., 'Report on forestry', unpublished paper, Addis Ababa, May 1984.

Roberts, A., 'Report on villagization in Oxfam America assisted projects in Hararghe province, Ethiopia', June 1986, cited from J. M. Cohen and N. I. Isaksson, *Villagization in the Arsi Region of Ethiopia.*

Sara Wolde-Mikael, 'The culture of poverty: a case study of two poor families in Addis Ababa', Addis Ababa University, senior essay, January 1986.

Sethi, M. K. 'Small-scale enterprises in socialist Ethiopia', Eighth International Conference on Ethiopian Studies, Addis Ababa, November 1984.

Shito Mersha, 'Urban development and housing planning in Ethiopia', Report on the Workshop on Urban Basic Services, Addis Ababa, Ministry of Urban Development and Housing, October 1983.

Sokolov, V. V. *et al.*, 'Considerations on the economic policy of Ethiopia for the next few years', unpublished memorandum, Addis Ababa, September 1985.

Solomon Bellete, 'An overview of Ethiopia's agricultural production strategies and policies', National Seminar on Integrated Strategies in the Food Sector of Ethiopia, Harer, Alemaya University of Agriculture, December 1986.

'The experience of RPO for north-eastern Ethiopia in regional development planning', Second Regional Development Seminar, Debre Zeit, February 1987.

Solomon Mulugeta, 'Meeting the housing shortage in Addis Ababa: the case of housing co-operatives', unpublished MA thesis, Addis Ababa University, 1985.

Solomon Rezene, 'Ethio–US relations since the 1950s', Addis Ababa University, senior essay, June 1986.

Swedish International Development Authority (SIDA), 'The predicament of peasants in conservation-based development', Stockholm, November 1986.

Tadesse Ayelaw, 'The question of nationalities in the course of the Ethiopian revolution (1974–1984), Addis Ababa University, senior essay, October 1985.

Tamiru Endale, 'Political organizations in post-1974 Ethiopia', Addis Ababa University, senior essay, February 1985.

Tegegn Teka, 'Producers co-operatives and rural development in Ethiopia', United Nations, Economic Commission for Africa, Regional Expert Consultation on the Role of Rural Co-operatives in the Productive Sectors in Africa, Addis Ababa, October 1985.

Tegegn Teka and Tennassie Nichola, 'Rural poverty alleviation: the case of Ethiopia', Rome, FAO, 1984.

Tesfaye Beza and Asefa Bekele, 'Servicing settlements', unpublished paper, Addis Ababa, January 1985.

Vigand, V., 'Problems of Ethiopia's socio–economic development: difficulties and prospects', Eighth International Conference on Ethiopian Studies, Addis Ababa, November 1984.

Woldearegay Tessema, 'Marketing and distribution of industrial products in Ethiopia', First National Symposium on Industrial Development in Ethiopia, Addis Ababa, August 1986.

Yeraswork Admassie, 'Baseline socio–economic sample survey of the three highland Awrajas of Bale', unpublished paper, Addis Ababa, October 1985.

Yeraswork Admassie and Solomon Gebre, 'Food-for-work in Ethiopia: a socio–

economic survey', Addis Ababa University, Institute of Development Research, 1985.

Yeshitla Yehualawork, 'Agricultural credit and rural financial markets', National Seminar on Integrated Strategies in the Food Sector of Ethiopia', Harer, Alemaya University of Agriculture, December 1986.

Zerihun Alem, 'The process of planning and its implementation in the state farm sector of Ethiopia', Addis Ababa University, unpublished MSc thesis, April 1982.

Index

Ababiya Abajobir, 202
Abdel Hafiz Yusuf, 72
Abdul Fatah Ismail, 231
Abdullahi Bedi, 202–3, 216
Abdullahi Yusuf, 203, 216
Abiyu Geleta, 202
Abyotawit Seded, *see* Seded
Addis Ababa, 15, 22, 26–7, 29–31, 34–8,
    42–3, 49–50, 55–6, 62, 67–8, 73, 77–8, 82,
    89–90, 95, 98, 102, 106, 108, 110, 111,
    112, 115–16, 124, 127, 129–32, 134–5,
    137, 140–5, 148–51, 154, 156, 168, 180,
    184–5, 191–2, 200–3, 205–6, 209, 215–16,
    222–4, 228, 230, 233, 235
Addis Alem, 58, 82
Addis Tedla, 71, 224
Aden, 226–7, 232
Aderes, 25, 54, 72
administrative regions, *see* regional
    administration
Adola, 121
Adwa, 19, 27
Afar, 25, 37, 104, 153, 187, 192, 199–201,
    211–12, 215–16, 218
Afar Liberation Front, 215
Afar National Liberation Movement
    (ANLM), 215
Afghanistan, 76, 231–2, 234
Agarfa peasants' centre, 97
agrarian involution, 166–7
Agricultural and Industrial Development
    Bank, 172
agricultural marketing, *see* marketing
Agricultural Marketing Corporation (AMC),
    216, 146, **168–71**, 173–4, 178, 180, 184
agriculture, 20–1, 29–31, 48, 72, 76, 81, 84,
    103–4, 106, 114–17, 120, 125–7, **157–94**,
    206, 213–14, 217, 223, 241–2
Ahadu Saboure, 202

Ahmed Gragn, 25
aid, foreign, 119, **121–3**, 166, 189, 191, 221,
    233, 235–8
    see also arms supply, famine relief
air force, 28, 38, 40, 109, 229
Akaki, 55, 136, 148
Aklilu Habte-Wold, 38
alcohol, 125, 148
Alemu Abebe, 67, 71, 83, 224
Ali Mirah, 215
Ali Mussa, 72, 74, 196, 204, 217
Ali Nasser Mohammed, 231
alienation, 33–5, 128, 151, 153–6, 179, 210,
    214, 218–19
    see also opposition
All Ethiopia Peasants' Association (AEPA),
    85, 87, 138, 157–9
All Ethiopia Trade Union (AETU), 55–6,
    67, 85, 87, **136–7**, 138
Aman Andom, 42–5, 52, 59, 80, 198, 204, 224
Amanuel Amde-Michael, 71–2, 83, 96, 105,
    197
Amhara people, 21, 23–4, 29–31, 37, 50, 55,
    57, 91, 158, 161, 163, 176, 195–6, 198–9,
    205, 213–14, 216–17
Amharic language, 14, 21, 23–4, 30, 72, 80,
    86, 94, 96, 136, 139, 151–4, 159, 196–7,
    200
Amin, I., 128
Amnesty International, 108
Andargatchew Massai, 207
Andreev, G., 232
Angola, 5, 8–9, 120, 239–40, 243
Anuak, 96
Arabs, Arabia, 59, 120, 186, 208, 214, 222,
    231
armed forces, 1, 8, 10, 14, 28, 34, 38–41, 51,
    54–5, 59, 62–3, 65, 69, 71–2, 76–8, 82,
    85–8, 92, 96–7, 101, 106, **109–23**, 147,

276

155, 196–8, 201, 217–19
Armenian SSR, 232
arms supply, 28–9, 60, 63, 121–2, 128, 220–31, 233, 236–7, 239–40
Arsi, 25–6, 30, 48, 59, 90–1, 103, 148, 158, 168, 170, 173, 175–80, 201, 217–19
Asela, 148
Ashagre Yigletu, 83, 224, 233–4
Asmara, 31, 38, 59, 111, 115, 129–31, 148, 168, 198, 206, 215, 221, 229
Asosa, 103
Assab, 77, 148, 200, 204, 215
Atnafu Abate, 45, 52, 59, 63, 70
autonomous regions, *see* regional autonomy
Awash, 30, 104, 165, 179, 181, 186–7, 215, 218–19
Awsa, 201, 204, 215
Axum, 20, 26, 60, 205

Bahr Dar, 148–9, 163
Bahru Tufa, 197
balance of payments, 120, 186
Balcha, Dej., 22
Bale, 26, 37, 47, 61, 80, 102–3, 148, 150, 156, 158, 173, 175, 178–9, 181, 192, 197, 203, 216–19
Barentu, 91, 110, 210
Batista, 5
Bebeka state farm, 179, 183
Berbera, 225
Berhane Deressa, 190
Berhane-Meskel Redda, 54
Berhanu Bayih, 70–1, 82, 96, 233
Berhanu Jembere, 191
Berlin, 234
Beshir Sheik Abdi, 204
Besse, A. & Co., 145
bigamy, 94
Bokassa, J. B., 128
Bolivia, 2
Boran, Borana, 197, 203, 215
bourgeoisie, 2, 7, 108, 116, 142
Brazil, 120
British, United Kingdom, 23, 27–8, 36, 86, 201, 205–6, 221–2, 229
broad masses, 56, 98, 134, 144
Bulgaria, 74, 83, 86, 224, 234
bureaucracy, 7–9, 14, 29, 31, 34, 50, 57, 86, 91–2, 102, 106, 117, 124, 128, 134, 139, 143, 148, 158, 191, 204, 212, 232
bureaucratic capitalism, 8, 98, 105

Calcutta, 144
campaigns, 124, 192
    see also literacy, Red Star, villagisation, zemecha

Canada, 154
capital, capitalism, 3, 19, 46, 104, 148, 150, 164, 172, 174, 180, 182, 234, 238
Caribbean, 3, 11, 235–6, 239
Carter, Pres., 61, 224, 226–7, 237
Castro, F., 8, 61, 69, 79, 99, 226
Catholicism, 93, 155–6
census (1984), 95, 129, 131, 142, 157
Central Planning Supreme Council (CPSC), 116, 169
chat, 120, **184–6**
Chercher, 216
China (PRC), 2, 4–6, 11, 16, 60, 99, 167, 224, 234
Christianity, 20–1, 26, 50, 94, 138, 175, 203, 205, 214, 216–17
    see also Catholicism, Mekane Yesus, Orthodox Church, religion
cities, *see* towns
class, 2–3, 7, 13, 30, 47–8, 50, 104, 158, 173, 198–9
coffee, 29–30, 103–4, 115, 119–21, 125–7, 163, 165, 179–80, **182–4**, 186–7, 206, 221, 237
collective farms, collectivisation, 2, 7, 76, 84, 98, 116, 167, 171–2
    see also cooperatives
colonialism, 4, 7, 14, 20, 24, 27, 101, 204, 206, 210–11, 221–2, 234
Combolcha textile mill, 123, 148, 234
Commission for Organising the Party of the Working People of Ethiopia (COPWE), 68–9, **70–7**, 78–9, 82–4, 89, 91, 93, 110, 133, 136, 172, 197
Communist Party of the Soviet Union (CPSU), 75, 99, 232
Confederation of Ethiopian Labour Unions (CELU), 35, 45, 54–5, 136
conscription, *see* military service
constitution (1955), 35, 108, 118
constitution (1987), 1, **93–6**, 108, 156, 200–1
cooperatives, agricultural producers', 7, 72, 84, 118, 126, 140, 150, 157, 164, 167–9, **171–9**, 180–1, 188, 193, 213
cooperatives, handicraft, 98, 149–50
cooperatives, housing, 143–4
cooperatives, service, 157, 166, 171–2
corruption, 41–2, 98–9, 113, 127, 132, 144, 146, 174, 184
cotton, 30, 179, 186
Council for Mutual Economic Assistance (CMEA), 120–1, 123, 228
countryside, 3–5, 10, 15–16, 35, 37, 40, 43, 49, 51, 58, 107, 115, 130, 140, 147, **157–94**, 242
coup d'état (1960), 33–4, 39, 44

coups, breakthrough, 41
crime, 129, 154–5
Crown Prince Asfa-Wossen, 37, 42
Cuba, 2–3, 5–6, 9, 11, 16, 61, 68–9, 86, 99, 120, 151, 221–2, 225, 234–6, 239–40
culture, *see* political culture
Czechoslovakia, 73, 148, 224, 234

Dahlac Islands, 121, 229
Danakil, *see* Afar
Daniel Tadesse, 55, 132
Dawit Wolde-Giorgis, 73, 190–1
Debele Dinsa, 89, 196–7, 204
Debre Zeit, 112, 132, 148
Demissie Bulto, 196
democratic centralism, 78, 93, 131, 133, 141, 201
Derg, 17, 39–40, 42–5, 49, 51–7, 59–60, 62–3, 66–7, 70, 72–3, 76–7, 79, 82–3, 85, 89, 92, 106–7, 110, 131, 137, 155, 196–200, 202–4, 208, 214, 217, 224–6, 233
Dessalegn Rahmato, 158–60, 163, 165–6
Dessie, 77
Desta Tadesse, 68
Dire Dawa, 129, 148, 157, 168, 235
distribution, *see* marketing, rationing
Djibouti, 27, 29, 31, 148, 186, 200, 206, 215, 221–2
Dmitriev, V., 232
drought, 181, 187, 190–1

Echaat, 54, 67–8
education, 27, 29, 33, 38, 49, 87–8, 117, 132, 149, **150–3**, 217, 221, 234–5
Egypt, 27, 41, 75, 204, 225
elections, kebelle, 55, 132–3, 158
elections, parliamentary, 36, 131
elections, shengo, 95–6
elites, 4–5, 7, 10, 29, 31, 37, 73, 87, 91, 128, 132, 151, 158, 243
Emaledih, 68–9, 74
Emalered, 54, 67
emperors, *see* imperial regime
employment, 123–4, 148–50, 183
Endale Tessema, 90
Endalkachew Makonnen, 38, 40
Engels, F., 63, 79, 96, 228
English language, 151–2
enset, 163, 176
Eritrea, Eritreans, 5, 14, 16, 20–1, 25–8, 3ı1, 34, 36, 39, 44–5, 47, 54–5, 58–60, 62, 71–3, 76–7, 89, 91–2, 96, 101–2, 109–12, 115–16, 129, 137, 150, 152–3, 155, 158, 160, 162, 165, 171, 176, 187, 189, 196–200, 202–3, **204–14**, 215–16, 218–19, 221–3, 226–7, 229–30, 236, 241–2

Eritrean Liberation Front (ELF), 36, 59, 208, 213
Eritrean People's Liberation Front (EPLF), 17, 59–60, 62, 91, 110–12, 150, 162, 198, 203, 208–9, 211–15, 227, 230, 236
Eshetu Aleme, 77
Ethiopia Peasants' Association (EPA), *see* AEPA
Ethiopia People's Democratic Movement (EPDM), 214
Ethiopia Trade Union (ETU), *see* AETU
Ethiopian Air Lines (EAL), 54–5, 229
Ethiopian Democratic Union (EDU), 58, 60, 62, 162, 185, 198, 203, 209
Ethiopian Domestic Distribution Corporation (EDDC), 145, 160
Ethiopian Highland Reclamation Study (EHRS), 165, 187, 213
Ethiopian People's Revolutionary Party (EPRP), 17, 52–7, 65, 67, 70, 107, 132–3, 198–9, 209, 214–15
Ethiopian School Leaving Certificate (ESLC), 149–50
ethnicity, *see* national question
European Community, 120, 123, 237–8
exploitation, 3–4, 13, 26, 30–1, 47–8, 182, 202, 214, 216–17

famine, 12, 17, 35, 37, 40, 78, 83, 116, 118–19, 125, 127, 130, 141, 146–7, 154–6, 165–70, 172, **186–94**, 206, 211, 220, 238–9, 241–2
famine relief, 91, 121–2, 187, **189–94**, 228, 237–8
Fassika Sidelil, 71, 83
fertiliser, 103, 166–7, 170–3, 178, 180, 183
feudalism, 13, 19, 22, 98, 106
Fikre Merid, 53
Fikre-Selassie Wogderes, 70–1, 82, 224
fisheries, 121
Fisseha Desta, 70–2, 82, 96, 197
Fomichenko, K., 232
foreign policy, 46, 51, 61, 84, 94, **220–40**
forests, afforestation, deforestation, 164, 177, 179, 183, 188
France, 1–2, 4,6, 10–11, 14, 16, 53, 79, 209, 222, 242

Galla, *see* Oromo
Gambela, 96, 161, 193
Gamu Gofa, 68, 83, 90, 126–7, 176, 204
Garamuleta, 175, 219
garrison socialism, 15–16
Gash-Setit, 91, 211
Gebre-Kristos Bale, 73
Gebreyes Wolde-Hana, 71, 112
Gedeo, 153

German Democratic Republic (GDR), 111, 120–1, 148, 151, 180, 191, 224, 134
Gewane, 200
Girma Habte-Gabriel, 90
Girma Kebede, 56
Godana Tuni, 197, 203
Gojjam, Gojjamis, 21, 37, 45, 47–8, 90–1, 96, 127, 148, 158, 162–3, 168–9, 172–3, 176, 185, 193–4, 200, 203, 214
gold, 121
Gonder, 21, 26, 30, 47, 58–9, 66, 73, 89, 91, 172, 176–7, 185, 193, 203–4, 211, 214, 216
Gorbachev, M., 229
Goshu Wolde, 71, 233, 238
grain, 30, 103–4, 121, 126–7, 145–7, 163, 168–70, 173, 179–81, 184, 187, 189, 238
guerilla warfare, 4, 17, 28, 43, 60, 207, 209, 216
    urban, 5, 55–6
    see also EPRP, terror
    rural, 5, 8, 57, 212
    see also ELF, EPLF, TPLF, WSLF, etc.
Guinea-Bissau, 9
Gurage, 22–4, 54, 86, 153, 176, 197

Habro, 219
Habsburg state, 26, 195
Hadiya, 153
Haile Fida, 53, 57, 66–7
Haile-Selassie, emperor, 12, 19–20, 22, 24, 27–33, 37–8, 40–3, 45, 52–3, 58–60, 71–2, 79–81, 136, 138, 201–2, 206–7, 210, 221–3, 232, 240
Haile-Yesus Aba-Hassen, 202
Hailu Yimenu, 71, 83, 105
Halliday, F. and Molyneux, M., 15
Handicrafts and Small Scale Industries Development Association (HASIDA), 149
Hararghe, 25–6, 29–30, 48, 57, 61, 73, 86, 90–2, 96, 102, 117, 127, 150, 158–9, 173, 175–7, 200–4, 216–19
Harar, 25, 30, 40, 54, 72, 112, 148, 155–6, 214, 216, 235
Hayder Abu Bakr, 231
health, 132, 135, 178, 191, 213
Heng Samrin, 8
heroes' centres, 112
Hickenlooper Amendment, 122
Holeta military academy, 71, 234
housing, 1, 50, 53, 55, 115, 124, 129–30, 132, 134, **141–5**, 177, 182
human rights, 61, 94, 108, 223
Humera, 30, 48, 58, 104, 106, 165, 179, 182, 184–5
Hungary, 234
Huntington, S. P., 5, 45

Hussein Ismail, 74

Ibnat camp, 89
ideology, 1, 6, 9–11, 15, 22, 41, 66, 71–2, 76, 81, 83–4, 90, 96–8, 144, 154, 212–13, 220, 224, 230, 232–4, 240–1
    see also Leninism, Marxism, Marxism-Leninism
idir, 35, 131
Illubabor, 26, 27, 47, 73, 89, 158, 173, 176, 193, 201–2, 217
imperial regime, 14, 19, 27–8, 31, **32–8**, 39, 41, 49–50, 55, 60, 65, 79, 101–4, 124, 128, 131, 138, 167, 189, 198, 201–2, 206–7, 216–17, 220–2, 240
Imru, Ras, 40
Imru Wonde, 203
India, 86, 228
industry, 114, 116–18, 125, 137, 148–50
institutionalisation, 7–9, 12, 23, 51, 57, 63, 235
intelligentsia, 3, 51–6, 65, 132
International Labour Organisation, 149
international relations, 2, 11, 60, 63, 94, 98, 190–1, 194, **220–40**
Iran, 2, 5–6, 11, 26–7, 31
Iraq, 11
iron ore, 235
irrigation, 181, 187
Islam, Moslems, 20, 25, 39, 50, 59, 72, 74, 85–6, 91–4, 96, 138–9, 152, 155–6, 175, 196, 202, 204–5, 207–8, 213–14, 216–17, 220–1, 231
Israel, 25
Issa clan, 202, 214–15
Italian-Ethiopian war (1896), 13, 19, 27, 29
Italian-Ethiopian war (1935–41), 19, 28–9, 201–2, 207, 221–2
Italy, Italians, 13, 31, 36, 85, 123, 148, 155, 194, 205–7, 210, 229, 238
Ityopya tikdem, 40, 42, 45, 199
Iyasu, Lij, 27

Jackson, R. and Rosberg, C., 80
Janssen, K., 194
Japan, 15, 26, 86, 119–20
Jijiga, 111, 235
Jimma, 77, 163, 201–2, 214

Kagnew base, 221, 223, 227
Kaffa, 23–4, 26, 29–30, 86, 89, 110, 150, 153, 158, 162–3, 165, 176, 179, 183, 193, 201–2, 217, 219
Kalitti, 55, 148
Kambatta, 23–4, 55, 86, 153, 197
Kampuchea, 2, 5–6, 8, 11, 234

Index

Kapital, Das, 97
Karamara, 111, 235
Kassa Gebre, 83, 105
Kassa Kebede, 105
Kassala, 58, 205
Kassaye Aregaw, 90
Kebede Bizunesh, 58
Kebede Tessema, 105
kebelles, 1, 10, 43, 51, 55–7, 63, 70, 86, 88,
    94–5, 98, 109–10, 113, 124, 129, **130–6**,
    139–47, 154–5, 158, 160
Kefelegn Yibsa, 98, 196
keftenya, 51, 110, 131–2, 135–6, 139, 145, 147
Kenya, 30, 45, 184, 222, 237
Kerensky, 4
Kereyu, 104, 187
Khirghiz SSR, 232
Khmer Rouge, 8
Kim Il Sung, 79
Kiros Alemayehu, 52, 70
Kismayu, 225
Kolubi, 156
Korea, North, 2, 79, 153–4, 235
Korean war, 221
Korn, D., 75, 78, 121, 224
Kotu Oromo, 216
kulaks, 7
Kunama, 153
Kuomintang, 4

Lalibela, 20, 205
land degradation, 165–6, 178, 187–8, 193,
    206, 213
land reform, 1, 5, 7, 15, 26, 43, 47–50, 58–60,
    62, 80, 105, 107, 114–15, 118, 126, 130,
    141, 144, 157–60, **161–8**, 177, 179, 187–8,
    193, 199, 203, 209, 212–13, 215–16, 242
language policy, 94, 152–3, 199–201
Latvian SSR, 232
leadership, 22, 32, 52, 63, 74, 79–81, 96–7,
    151, 159–60, 173, 209, 212, 230
League of Nations, 207
Lefort, R., 49, 53, 55, 213
Legesse Asfaw, 52, 67, 69, 71–2, 75, 82, 88,
    110, 112, 197, 224
legitimacy, 4, 14, 28, 41, 98, 102
Lema Gutema, 73
Lenin, V. I., 53, 63, 79, 96, 227–8
Leninism, 15, 77, 93, 96, 213, 242
Leninist party, 9–10, 53, 63, 66, 68, 75, 83, 90,
    97, 99, 112, 212, 225, 230–1, 234
Levine, D. N., 21
Libya, 41
literacy campaign, 51, 97, 135, 139, **150–3**,
    200, 213, 241
Lome Conventions, 120, 123

lumpenproletariat, 34, 51, 55–6, 16, 133,
    185, 192
Lutherans, *see* Mekane Yesus

Mahdists, 205
Maji and Goldiya, 201
Mao Tsetung, 8, 99, 224
Marehan, 197
Markakis, J., 15–16, 102
marketing, agricultural, 1, 48–9, 84, 104,
    126–7, 164, 167, **168–71**, 184, 186, 188
marketing, urban, 106, **125–7**, **145–7**
Marx, K., 14, 53, 63, 79, 96, 228
Marxism, 2, 6, 10, 12–13, 15–17, 26, 33, 58,
    60, 72, 76, 81, 98, 111, 198, 202, 212, 224
Marxism-Leninism, 1, 9, 213, 33, 52–3, 57, 60,
    63–4, 67–8, 70, 76–7, 81, 92–3, 96–7, 108,
    111, 136, 140, 155, 212–13, 222, 227, 230,
    236
Massawa, 20, 121, 206
Meison, 52–7, 62, 66–8, 70–1, 132–3, 136,
    198–200, 202–3, 215, 224
Mekane Yesus, 93, 155–6, 217–18
Melaku Tefera, 73, 89, 204
Melka Wakena hydroelectric project, 123,
    148, 234
Mengesha Seyoum, 47, 58, 60, 202–3, 209
Mengistu Haile-Mariam, 6, 12, 22, 24, 31,
    40–1, 44–5, 51–2, 56–7, 60–3, 65, 67–72,
    74–6, **79–83**, 89–90, 94, 97, 105, 109–13,
    116, 133, 144, 147, 171, 174–7, 181, 188,
    191, 193–4, 197, 199, 209, 224–35, 238–9
Menilek, emperor, 13, 19, 22, 27–31, 80
Merid Negussie, 71, 74, 112, 196
Merse Fatma, 211
Meskerem, 76, 136
Metcha Tulama, 216
Michael Asgedom, 198
Michael Imru, 40, 42
migration, 124, 129, 144–5, 147, 185, 206
military, *see* armed forces
military commissars, 90–1, 109–10
military service, 1, 63, 94, 100, **109–10**,
    112–13, 135, 154, 159–60, 194
militia, 1, 43, 50, 57, 59, 62, 109, 123
mining, minerals, 46, 103, 114, 119, 121, 137,
    235
Mitchell Cotts, 179
mobilisation, 4, 39, **41–64**, 107, 119, 205, 209,
    228
modernisation, 4, 26, 33, 35, 41, 98
Mogadishu, 37, 219
Mojo, 148–9
monarchy, 1, 4–5, 7–8, 11, 16, 26–8, 31, 57,
    114, 118, 195
Moscow, 61, 65, 71, 227, 229, 231–2, 234

Moslems, *see* Islam
Mozambique, 5, 5, 8–9, 120, 239, 243
Mugher cement works, 123, 144, 148, 233
multinational companies, 30, 103, 114, 119, 122
Mulugeta Hagos, 73, 89

Nakfa, 62, 110, 208–9
Nasser, G. A., 75
National Revolutionary Development Campaign (NDRC), 116, 118, 126, 148, 179, 185
national question, nationalities, 21, 23–6, 49, 54, 57, 64, 81, 93–4, 152–3, **195–219**, 225
nationalisation, 1, 6, 46–7, 50–1, 53, 107, 114–15, 118, 122, 126, 142, 148, 164, 179
nationalism, 4, 7, 10–11, 14, 19–20, 34, 42, 44, 46, 53, 57, 62, 195–6, 198, 200, 209–10, 216–18, 230, 232, 241
Nationalities Institute, 85, 93, 200
Nazret tractor plant, 123, 148, 233
neftenya, 41
Nega Tegegn, 58
Negede Gobeze, 68, 75, 231–2
Neghelle, 38
Nekempte, 163
Nesibu Taye, 71
Nicaragua, 2–3, 5–6, 239
Nigerian civil war, 194, 211
Nimairi, G., 15, 42, 56, 58, 75
Nkrumah, K., 222
nomads, *see* pastoralists
Nuer, 96

Office of the National Council for Central Planning (ONCCP), 82, 85, 116, 166, 169, 182
Ogaden, 34, 52, 111, 150, 155, 192, 198, 203, 206–7, 236
oil, 38, 120, 233
Olympic Games, 93, 228
Omo, 235
opposition, **204–19**
   see also alienation, individual movements
Organisation of African Unity (OAU), 32, 50, 110, 222, 228, 236, 239–40
Organisation of Petroleum Exporting Countries (OPEC), 38, 122
Oromo, 20, 23–6, 30, 50, 53–5, 59, 62, 68, 72, 82, 85, 87, 90–1, 93, 139, 152–3, 196, 109, 202–4, 206, 210, **214–19**
Oromo Liberation Front (OLF), 155, 175, 203, 216, 218–19
Orthodox Church, 25–6, 93, 96, 155–6, 205, 207, 217, 225

parliament, 35, 65
participation, 7, 15, 136, 159, 174, 218
parties, political, 36, 45–6, 51, 64, **65–100**
   see also Leninist party, WPE
pastoralists, 25, 104, 157, 187, 189, 192, 214–15, 217
Pawe resettlement, 160, 193–4
Peace Corps, 221
Peasant Agricultural Development Extension Programme (PADEP), 167, 171
peasants, peasantry, 2, 5–7, 16, 22, 31, 40, 43, 46–50, 58–9, 62, 73–4, 84–8, 93, 103, 106, 114–16, 118, 124–5, 128, 146, 157–74, 176–83, 185, 187–90, 193–4, 209–10, 212–13
peasants' associations, 1, 10, 47–8, 50–1, 63, 74, 84, 86–8, 95–6, 98, 109–10, 113–14, 117, 123, 126, 130–1, 137, 140–1, 155, **157–61**, 162–9, 172–3, 175–7, 182, 187, 194, 213
People's Democratic Republic of Ethiopia (PDRE), 76, 81, **92–6**, 108, 133, 137, 156, 200–1, 204, 243
People's Democratic Republic of Yemen (PDRY), *see* Yemen, South
Petros Gebre, 197
planning, 64, 76, 93, 104, **116–19**, 128, 144, 148, 230
   see also Ten Year Plan
police, 40, 85, 102, 113, 129, 131, 135, 154–5
Poland, 234
political culture, 10, 21, 23–4, 32, 39, 52, 63, 65, 96, 195, 210
political parties, *see* parties
population, 125, 129, 143, 150, 152–3, 157, 165–6, 176, 187–8, 193, 242
Portugal, 25, 221, 234, 240
praxis, 16
prices, consumer, 38, 115, 126, 144–7
prices, producer, 124, 126–7, 166–70, 179–80, 182, 187, 239
professions, 88, 137–8
Programme of the National Democratic Revolution (PNDR), 46, 53, 66, 81, 171, 199–200, 215, 225
proletarian internationalism, 98, **228–36**
proletariat, *see* workers
prostitution, 130, 140
Provisional Military Administrative Council (PMAC), 40, 45, 53, 57, 59, 71–4, 76, 79, 81–3, 92, 136, 224–5
   see also Derg
Provisional Office of Mass Organizational Affairs (POMOA), 53–4, 57, 66–9, 74, 91–2, 203, 216
Pyongyang, 235

rationing, 135, 145–7
Reagan, Pres., 237
Red Cross, 194
Red Sea, 20, 77, 121, 186, 200, 205, 211, 216, 229
Red Star campaign, 112, 208–9
red terror, *see* terror
Redd Barna, 135
refugees, 122, 177, 237
Regassa Jima, 196
regional administration, 28, 49, 76, **89–91**, 94, 102, 105, 197, **201–4**
regional autonomy, 44–6, 54, 60, 64, 81, 94–5, 198, 200–1, 204, 211
Relief and Rehabilitation Commission (RRC), 127, 188–93
religion, 25, 93, **155–6**, 176, 189, 195, 199, 214, 216, 218
    see also Christianity, Islam, individual churches
resettlement, 1, 75, 87, 93, 99, 109, 116, 127, 160–1, 165, 172, 190, **192–4**, 200, 212–13, 238
revolutions, **1–18**, 41–5, 50–1, 53, 59, 61, 63, 65, 107–8, 114, 116, 119, 123, 138–9, 145, 148, 150, 176, 179, 182–3, 191, 195–6, 205, 208–9, 216, 220, 223–8, 236, 239–43
Revolutionary Ethiopia Women's Association (REWA), 85–7, 91, 113, **138–40**, 160
Revolutionary Ethiopia Youth Association (REYA), 85–8, 91, 97, 113, 138, **140–1**, 182
rist, 158, 162
Romania, 234
rural, *see* countryside
Russia, *see* USSR

Sadat, 75
Saho, 153, 211
Saudi Arabia, 31, 237
scientific socialism, 66, 69, 225
Scott, J. C., 3
Seded, 67–70, 82, 198–9, 224
self-determination, 53–4, 57, 198–9, 222, 226
Senay Likie, 43, 54, 66–7
Seray, 210
Serto Ader, 76, 231
sesame, 30, 48, 104, 106, 179, **184–6**, 187
Seyoum, Ras, 202
Sheik Abajifar, 202
Sheik Hussein, 156
Sheik Jarra, 219
Sheneka state farm, 181
Shengo, National, 94–6, 134, 156, 204
Shewandagn Belete, 72, 83

Shimelis Alemu, 133
Shimelis Adugna, 71
Shimelis Mazengia, 71–2, 80, 83
Shoa, Shoans, 21, 26–30, 35, 47, 53, 68, 73, 80, 89–90, 102, 137, 150, 158, 161, 168–9, 176–7, 180, 185–6, 192–3, 196–7, 200–4, 206–7, 214, 216–19
Sidama, 153, 201
Sidamo, 22, 24, 26, 29, 38, 50, 61, 89–91, 121, 127, 158, 160, 163, 165, 176, 192, 197, 201–3, 215, 218
Simon Galore, 89
Sisay Habte, 52, 70, 224
Siyad Barre, 15, 60, 75, 197, 215, 227
Skocpol, T., 4, 7, 15
smuggling, 126–7, 186
socialist orientation, 225
Solomon Wada, 50, 203
Somali Abo Liberation Front (SALF), 218
Somali language, 152–3
Somali National Movement (SNM), 215
Somali people, 15, 24–5, 28, 37, 61, 72, 198–9, 202, 210, 214–15, 218–19, 221–2
Somali Republic, 15, 28, 37, 42, 45, 60–1, 68, 75, 101, 121, 153, 177, 186, 197, 199, 215, 222, 225–8, 236–7, 239–40
Somali Salvation Democratic Front (SSDF), 215
Somali–Ethiopian war (1977–78), 11–12, 57–8, 61–2, 92, 109, 111–13, 115, 118, 120, 175, 200, 203, 208, 214–16, 218, 220, 223, 230–1, 235, 239
Somoza, A., 5
South Africa, 110
Soviet Union, *see* USSR
Stalin, J. V., 6, 17, 99, 167
state, the, 7, 14–16, 20–1, 26–7, 41, 45–6, 74, 81, 84, 86, 92, **101–28**, 155, 161, 168, 170, 182, 190, 194, 205–6, 213, 217, 220–1, 240–3
state farms, 1, 7, 48, 84, 106–7, 114, 118, 126, 157, 160, 163–5, 168, 174, **179–82**, 183, 185, 188, 192, 215, 235
strikes, 35, 39, 42, 55, 108, 137
students, 26, 33–5, 38, 43, 45, 49–54, 56, 65–6, 69, 78, 99, 127, 150, 152, 198
Sudan, 15, 27, 42, 45, 56, 58, 62, 65, 75, 185, 190, 194, 205, 209, 211–13, 225, 237
Supreme Islamic Council, 93, 156

Tadesse Tamrat, 136
Tanzania, 175
Tatek camp, 62
taxation, 35, 37, 102–3, 106, **124–5**, 132, 161–2, 172, 196, 188
technology, 148–9, 181

Tefera Wolde-Semait, 74
Tefera Wonde, 72, 89, 203
Teferi Banti, 45, 52–4, 56, 61, 82, 224–5
teff, 146, 170, 184
Teka Tulu, 82, 196–7
teleology, 16–17
Ten Year Plan, **116–19**, 121, 125, 148, 172–3, 179, 193
terracing, 100, 164, 166, 188
terror, 6, 12, 17, 53, 55–7, 62–3, 66, 72, 89, 109, 118, 132, 136, 147, 154, 192, 224
Tesfaye Dinka, 71, 83
Tesfaye Gebre-Kidan, 71, 82
Tesfaye Habte-Mariam, 71, 197
Tesfaye Tadesse, 72
Tesfaye Wolde-Selassie, 83, 113
Tewodros, emperor, 14, 22, 27–8, 31
Tewodros Bekele, 67
Tigre language, 153
Tigray, Tigreans, 5, 20–1, 23, 25–9, 47, 54, 58–60, 62, 72–3, 82, 89, 92, 96, 104, 110, 137, 139, 150, 152–3, 158, 160, 162, 165, 171, 176, 184, 187, 189, 191, 193, 196–8, 202–3, **204–14**, 215–16, 218–19, 241
Tigray People's Liberation Front (TPLF), 26, 60, 62, 89, 162, 184, 203, 209–14, 236
Tigrinya language, 21, 86, 152–3, 204–5, 207, 211, 213
Tiruwork Wakoyo, 72
Tiyo, 211
Toqueville, A. de, 14
towns, 3–5, 10, 15, 35, 37–8, 40, 42, 48–9, **51–7**, 103, 107, 115, **129–56**, 165, 189, 242
trade, domestic, 115, 125–7, 160, 168–9
trade, international, 11, 20, 29, 106, 115–17, **119–21**, 128, 182–6, 220, 228, 233, 237
trade, terms of, 120
trade unions, 10, 34–5, 39, 51, 54–6, 74, 84, 86–8, 113, **136–7**
transport, 127, 129, 156
tribe, *see* national question
Trimberger, E. K., 15
Turkey, 15

Ugaz Hassen Hirsi, 202
unemployment, 130, 140, 147, 149, 151, 182
Union of Soviet Socialist Republics (USSR), 1–2, 4, 6, 8–9, 11, 14, 16–17, 28, 54, 60–1, 63–4, 67–70, 72, 74–9, 81–2, 86, 96, 98–9, 108, 110–12, 120–1, 123, 128, 147–8, 151–2, 154, 166, 182, 197, 201, 212–13, 220–40, 242
Unionist Party, 36, 207
United Kingdom, *see* Britain
United Nations, 31, 36, 144, 194, 207, 210, 228

UNECA, 50
UNICEF, 178
United States of America (USA), 2–3, 11, 28, 31, 52, 54, 60–1, 63, 119, 122–3, 151, 154, 207, 221–9, 237–9
university, 33–4, 38, 56, 66, 72, 93, 97, 99, 127, 133–4, 137, 141
urban dwellers' associations, *see* kebelles

vanguard parties, *see* Leninist parties
Vietnam, 2, 5–6, 8, 11, 16, 223
villagisation, 2, 51, 75, 80, 84, 87, 90, 93, 98–9, 116–18, 146, 154, 161, 167, 173, **174–9**, 214, 219, 238–9, 241

Wabe villages, 175
Wag, 201, 211
wages, 115, 124, 130, 145, 182, 185
Wako Guto, 37, 216, 218
water supplies, 142, 176, 178
Wazleague, 54, 66–7, 69–70, 72, 82, 198
Webbism, 17
Welega, 29, 53, 90–1, 110, 155, 158, 163, 173, 176, 181, 182–3, 200–2, 216–19, 235
Western Somali Liberation Front (WSLF), 214–15
Wolde-Giorgis Wolde-Yohannes, 32
Wollaita, 55, 152–3, 163, 203
Wollamo, 24, 31, 50, 86, 89
Wollo, 20–1, 26, 35, 37, 40, 47, 59, 92, 104, 133, 158, 161, 165, 170, 172, 176, 186, 189, 191–4, 196, 198, 200, 211, 214, 216–18
women, 10, 84, 87–8, 90–1, 93, 96, 129–30, 130–7, **138–40**, 152
see also REWA
Wondimu Abebe, 132
Wonji, 55
workers, working class, 2–3, 7, 10, 34, 48, 51, 55, 68, 73–4, 84–6, 88, 93, 128, 137, 185
Workers' Party of Ethiopia (WPE), 53–4, 67–8, 70–1, 74–6, **77–92**, 99, 105, 110, 113, 133, 136–9, 150–1, 172, 177, 190–1, 200, 203–4, 210, 224, 231–4
Working People's Control Committees, 99, 113
World Bank, 119, 167

Yayehirad Kitaw, 93
YeHebret Demtse, 68
Yekatit '66 Political School, 53, 57, 66–7, 72, 77, 85, 97, 230
Yemen, South (PDRY), 68, 76, 86, 111, 226, 231–2, 235
Yohannes, emperor, 27–8, 205–6

youth, 10, 129, 136, 138, 140–1
    see also REYA, students
Yugoslavia, 224
Yusuf Ahmed, 72

Zawditu, empress, 27, 138

Zeleke Beyene, 90
zemecha, 49–50, 54
Zewde Otoro, 202
Zimbabwe, 163